ROUTLEDGE LIBRARY EDITIONS:
SOCIAL THEORY

Volume 62

I0042392

THE SCOPE OF UNDERSTANDING
IN SOCIOLOGY

THE SCOPE OF UNDERSTANDING IN SOCIOLOGY

Towards a more radical reorientation in the social and humanistic sciences

WERNER PELZ

Routledge
Taylor & Francis Group
LONDON AND NEW YORK

First published in 1974

This edition first published in 2015
by Routledge
2 Park Square, Milton Park, Abingdon, Oxfordshire OX14 4RN

and by Routledge
711 Third Avenue, New York, NY 10017

Routledge is an imprint of the Taylor and Francis Group, an informa business

First issued in paperback 2015

British Library Cataloguing in Publication Data
A catalogue record for this book is available from the British Library

ISBN 978-0-415-72731-0 (Set)
eISBN 978-1-315-76997-4 (Set)
ISBN 978-1-138-79186-2 (hbk)(Volume 62)
ISBN 978-1-138-99808-7(pbk)(Volume 62)
ISBN 978-1-315-76248-7 (ebk)(Volume 62)

Publisher's Note
The publisher has gone to great lengths to ensure the quality of this reprint but points out that some imperfections in the original copies may be apparent.

Disclaimer
The publisher has made every effort to trace copyright holders and would welcome correspondence from those they have been unable to trace.

The scope of understanding in sociology

Towards a more radical reorientation in the social and humanistic sciences

Werner Pelz

Routledge & Kegan Paul

London and Boston

First published in 1974
by Routledge & Kegan Paul Ltd
Broadway House, 68–74 Carter Lane,
London EC4V 5EL and
9 Park Street,
Boston, Mass. 02108, USA
Set in Monotype Times New Roman
and printed in Great Britain by
Unwin Brothers Limited
The Gresham Press
Old Woking, Surrey
© Werner Pelz 1974

ISBN 0 7100 7854 4 (c)
ISBN 0 7100 8009 3 (p)
Library of Congress Catalog Card No. 74–77198

To Mary
for countless substantial contributions
and creative queries

Contents

Contents

Preface

We dare no longer ask with jesting Pilate, 'What is truth?' since we are not sure whether there is such a thing as truth, whether truth is a thing, whether truth *is*. Yet no society or group or person has so far managed to do without an explicit or implicit belief in some kind of truth. At one time the final truth as well as its guarantor was God, at another it was facts. Somewhere man's questioning had to come to rest, if provisionally and temporarily. For the Scholastic it could do so in the 'God is', for the scientist in the 'this is the case'. Today God does not function as guarantor, and in ever widening areas we are beginning to wonder whether we are altogether sure as to what constitutes a fact. In sociology in particular and in the social and humanistic disciplines in general 'facts' are becoming increasingly problematical constructs. Not only is there little agreement on how to establish facts, there is as little on the nature of facts. The question 'What is a sociological, psychological, historical or economic fact?' remains wide open for those who dare ask it at all. The social sciences have so far not answered but evaded it.

So I wish to ask once again: How does truth function in a society which no longer has a generally acknowledged Archimedean point in relation to which anything can be established as true or false? And what is the social truth-function within a society which generates sectional, interested, ideological Archimedean points – as, for example, in economics and industry, in technological science – which in turn need to be questioned? How does truth function when man tries to understand man, i.e. himself, when he begins to ask why society has found particular truth-functions or specific concepts of truth expedient?

I soon discovered not only the enormousness – almost enormity – of such a questioning, but also that it presupposes other questions of similar dimensions: What constitutes understanding in the social and humanistic sciences, in the *Geisteswissenschaften*? What is it we here wish to understand? When dare we say and how can we show that we have understood?

During the last few centuries the natural sciences evolved a method of understanding, a methodology for arriving at conveniently precise and definite constellations of knowledge, which proved startlingly successful – though by now the success itself is beginning to look problematical. At first economics, then psychology, sociology, historiography and philosophy, were tempted to adopt that methodology and adapt it to their respective purposes. Man wished to apply this purely manipulative, categorical apprehension of inanimate nature, which Kant called 'pure reason' and which at each step produces testable, i.e. verifiable or falsifiable, knowledge, to himself, to his own self. He was not sufficiently prepared for the dilemma that was bound to be encountered by the manipulator in his endeavours to manipulate himself.

So this essay investigates the character and function of knowledge and of understanding in the *Geisteswissenschaften*, especially in sociology and social philosophy, and with special reference to German sociological scholars who were more agitated by epistemological problems than their non-German colleagues. What do we understand by understanding in this area? When do we know we know? And what is knowledge here where the knower is both subject and object, where the knower and the known, the one who strives to understand and that which is to be understood, are inter-penetrating? Has the distinction the German tongue makes between *Kennen* and *Wissen* as between two disparate forms of knowing something to teach us?

I continue to ask whether the too uncritical acceptance of certain basic 'scientific' assumptions has not constrained and crippled the social sciences as much as it has undoubtedly established them as respectable; whether sociology – or psychology – can be or should wish to be exclusively a science, a science in the contemporary exclusive sense. I am pleading for more fully experiential and experimental uses and forms of understanding. I suggest that the *Geisteswissenschaften* have not only much to learn from each other, but from poets, prophets and artists, and from the wisdom of the more ordinary children of the world. I wonder whether and to what an extent scientific-manipulative conceptualizations have to be complemented by a kind of thinking I call, if only for the sake of convenience, contemplative. Finally I try to show that the constitutive insights of the 'founding fathers' of sociology – as of psychology and philosophy – have often been distorted and cramped by the scientific preconceptions they accepted and reactivated, and why.

This essay expresses my belief that the social and humanistic sciences at large, and sociology in as far as it could become their clearing-house, are in need of radical reorientation. This would involve a reappraisal of many scientistic or positivistic assumptions and presumptions, a questioning of much we take for axiomatic and self-evident. Such sociological reorientation may call for a more thorough acknowledgment of our subjectivity and inter-subjectivity as our actuality which constitutes objectivity as merely one of its many objectives. Hence it may suggest conversation rather than argument, dialogue rather than debate, mutual empathy and complementation rather than conjectures and refutations, as the appropriate intercourse between fellow searchers in quest of no-one yet quite knows what, between researchers who each and all are totally implicated in their research.

Of their very nature my reflections are inimical to strict logical presentation, since among much else they reflect on the scope of strict logic. However, I hope that the presentation cannot be shown to be illogical either. It is cumulative, intended to be suggestive rather than demonstrative, illustrative rather than argumentative. It is bound to appear and to be arbitrary in its selectiveness, since exhaustive treatment would have been impossible. The presentation is conversational in the sense that it is intended to involve the reader in a human intercourse rather than in a logical debate, is meant to hint at new possibilities of understanding rather than to fix, prove or demonstrate any particular method.

My bibliography, among other uses, represents my acknowledgment of and my gratitude to those who have helped me on my way. Yet only I may be held responsible for my deductions from their arguments, though I believe to have continued in the direction of their – sometimes merely implicit – intentions.

This essay is the result of four and more years of concentrated research and labour. It would have remained unwritten except for the most patient and generous help given to me by the Joseph Rowntree Charitable Trust.

Note 1   Wherever the reference to quotations in the text is to a book or article in German, the translation is my own.
Note 2   Throughout I shall avail myself of a distinction – introduced by some phenomenologists – between intention(ality) and intension(ality). I shall employ the former term as in conventional usage. The latter is to denote a purposeful directedness of which the underlying motives are mainly unconscious and which is therefore often misinterpreted by the 'intensioner'.

1 The problem poses itself

The problems implicit in any attempt to arrive at an understanding of that peculiar confluence of the individual and the social which, for our purposes here, we shall denote as 'social consciousness' are most complex and intricate. They also seem impermeable. In Marcel's usage they are 'mysteries' (Spiegelberg, 1964, p. 426). The observer is inevitably a part of them, is right inside them. Most of all at the moment when his attention is fixed on these problems, he finds himself at their very centre. For that reason the intellect can never quite get at them, cannot clearly comprehend or firmly grasp them, since it is part of that which it is trying to grasp. A kind of prestidigitation seems to be called for by the situation. The intellect must behave as if it were separable from the position and conditions of the observer, as if consciousness were detachable from the man whose *humanitas* it constitutes.

Such sleight of hand the Western mind has practised from its early beginnings. The primal division of labour, separating brain from brawn, shaped its peculiar character and encouraged it, for its own justification, to develop metaphysics and ontologies which ostensibly emancipated the mind from the body, also from the body politic and economic. Since then the intellect has pretended to the freedom of an enlightened tyrant unaware of its libidinal involvement in that over which it rules. Positivism or scientism is merely the latest feat of a prestidigitation which began with Plato or even with Thales. It creates the impression of a perfect extradition of the observing self from all its problems. There is no more mystery. The observation stands in splendid isolation – now of sovereignty, now of proud submission to the facts – over against the observed, even when the observed is a self or the observer's own self.

The juggling has proved most successful. It managed to edify and entertain the audience from the start, for both audience and per-

1

formers were, with few exceptions, on the tricksters' side. They were taken in because they wished and needed to be taken in. The habit of looking at one's embodied self, of trying to comprehend the community-carried self, my self, as if this could be done from outside any self, became inveterate. The growing individualism of the emerging bourgeois society far from breaking the habit entrenched it. The perfected abstractions of science radicalized metaphysical intentions to the point where the observer is not content with anything short of perfect control(ability) to be extended rigorously over the controlling self as well. This movement towards scientific autonomy and automation computerized knowledge long before computers were invented. It produced the vast superstructures of our civilization which are managed, by selves, as if the self mattered merely as a control unit. The machine is run by all for none (Weber, 1964, vol. 2, p. 900).

The questions are: How can we arrive at an understanding of this situation and of the chances and necessities which constituted it? Is it possible to reach an understanding not totally conditioned by the situation it tries to comprehend? Dare we hope for a kind of understanding which is not merely able more or less correctly or satisfactorily to register what is the case, but to transform the 'given' – though possibly in ways that cannot be predicted? Would not just such transforming understanding be merely another instance of that self-less, manipulating intellect of a detached observer? Or is there a form of knowing – Kennen – distinct from that which today claims sole, certainly sole effective, authority? (See below, ch. 3, B.) Which brings us to the question whether the Geisteswissenschaften, including sociology, have as yet begun to ask seriously what constitutes knowledge and understanding in their universe of discourse. Having taken over too uncritically the intentions and methods of the natural sciences, they neglected with too little justification, other kinds of understanding which philosophical, scientific and practical thinking has relegated to the sphere of the private.

Such questions, though severely disregarded by science, were kept alive by cranks, poets, idiosyncratic thinkers like Montaigne, Pascal, Kierkegaard; but also, if surreptitiously, by the never wholly exorcizable spirited and embodied self of even the most scientific observer. For reasons too complex to analyse here, German philosophers, social philosophers and sociologists, though as much impressed by scientistic assumptions as any, have continued to be agitated, beyond their Anglo-Saxon and French colleagues, by the problems of Verstehen implicit in any attempt at understanding which involves other understanding beings, persons, and therefore self-understanding.

Dilthey was among the first to raise the question of *Verstehen* self-consciously and in a vaguely sociological context. By nature a poet, he could not help seeing the individual, his experience, feeling, understanding, as constituting the basic human reality. To come to know the individual in his complexity and roundedness, within the intricate web of social inter-dependencies, was the task of *Verstehen*. It would inevitably include elements of sympathy, empathy, the endeavour to re-experience and reconstitute the life under scrutiny.[1] Dilthey was at his best when he permitted himself to approach his subjects in such a 'poetic' manner (Dilthey, 1919). But his philosophical and scientific assumptions gave him a bad conscience. He strove to justify his understanding before them and thus could not avoid submitting it to an alien, possibly a contradictory, discipline. Throughout his life he wrestled with the problem of how to reconcile the particular with the general. How could he refine the conceptual tools to the point where they would make the particular reveal its significance, its symbolic, i.e. general and transcendent, content in such a way that it became accessible to some process of verification? He believed that it was the sign of a poet's greatness, when he succeeded in penetrating an individual existence, until it revealed itself in itself as a universal symbol or signification. The poet fulfils his task by permitting life to interpret life without conceptualization. He permits the living context to reveal itself in its complex unity, its immanent significance (Dilthey, 1914, vol. 7, pp. 105–7). Yet for reasons explicable only within the context of contemporary scientific assumptions, Dilthey wanted to go beyond that. He wished to square the circle, to conceptualize the particular, to fit the irreducible into a generally acceptable system of scientifically established co-ordinates. Though at times he protested to the contrary, in practice he believed, if not as unambiguously as, for example, Durkheim, that science was or did more than poetry, was a more adequate pursuit of the human quest.

So psychology and not biography presented itself to Dilthey as the foundation of the *Geisteswissenschaften*, i.e. his concern for the individual merely made him choose psychology rather than sociology as the basic approach. Yet in either case the individual is, by definition, subsumed under the general. He is reduced to an instance or example, a case, to a datum yielding significant generalizations. The power and persuasiveness of conceptualization which a radical interest in the individual could have relativized is re-established (Dilthey, 1914, vols 1, 7, I/II). The pristine intention of metaphysics: to save man from the precariousness of his individual existence by subordinating it to unacknowledged societal interests parading as 'truth', this intention is reconstituted at the very heart of the *Geisteswissenschaften* by the man who believed his life's work to have been a struggle against metaphysics (Dilthey, 1914, vol. 2).

A closer reading of Marx might have modified Dilthey's ideologically distorted individualism and helped him to see the problematics involved in his psychological approach (as his altogether pre-Marxian approach over and again weakens his argument and blurs his insights). Unfortunately Marx himself was a victim of scientistic presumptions, his economism and sociologism as uncritical as Dilthey's psychologism. And his early work, where man, as this man, this woman, emerges for a moment most poignantly as the *telos* of history in all his vulnerability, only to be swamped again by inexorable intellectualizations, was not known to Dilthey.

Yet in spite of the many qualifications, Dilthey's work raised and kept alive the problem of social and individual consciousness within a sociologically relevant setting, though the mood, the *Stimmung*, of the age made him neglect its implications.

Meinecke, perhaps the most eminent Dilthey disciple, exemplifies some of the dangers of conceptualization met by the scholar who wishes to think or understand the individual. Conceptualization enables him, in his *Idee der Staatsräson*, to treat as individuals those very power complexes with their intensions, intentions and necessities, which inhibit or distort, often radically, most personal, i.e. individual, interests. He can exalt the necessities of power politics which override all personal desires, even those of the rulers, as *Staatsräson, raison d'état*, mainly because philosophers and scientists usually equated reason with necessity. Like the other German historists, Meinecke, in his battle against the Enlightenment understanding of reason and of history, merely substitutes a more complex conceptualization for a more simple one, not yet the individual for that which has been abstracted from him (Meinecke, 1963). So he does not become aware of the real contradictions between his understanding of the individual in *Die Idee der Staatsräson* and in *Die Entstehung des Historismus*.

In the latter he lets the poet speak, the *Dichter und Denker* (see below, ch. 3, B). For him indeed *individuum est ineffabile*, and Goethe speaks for all *Dichter und Denker* when he adds that 'from this I deduce a world'. So when the poet turns to the writing of history he naturally wishes 'to grasp the world as from the centre of man's soul'. For 'each condition, yes, each moment, is of infinite value, for it is the representative of all eternity'. 'What matters in life is life, not a result which life achieves.' Even when he adds, as counterbalance, 'only mankind as a whole is the true man, the individual is gay and happy when he has the courage to experience himself within that whole', the poet knows that what matters is the gaiety and happiness of the individual. Therefore Herder, as most poets, 'rebels against the royal highway of power. He gets wearied by the historical phenomenon of the state.' He rejects the 'frigid history' of *raison d'état* (Meinecke, 1959, pp. 390–527).

Meinecke does not seem to realize how radically the poet problematizes what the scholar is accustomed to accept as history. And he cannot realize this because by virtue of the scholar's habit he has already subordinated the poet to his thesis or argument. The poet's voice is used to illustrate an unpoetic intention. Yet, like Dilthey's, even in its distortions, Meinecke's work, sometimes against its author's convictions, illustrates the dilemma of the historian, the sociologist, the *Geisteswissenschaftler* in general, as we shall try to show.

Both Dilthey and Meinecke remained essentially historians of ideas. Franz Borkenau investigates the same changes in European thought patterns very much from the sociologist's point of view. In a brilliant and undeservedly neglected book, *Der Übergang vom feudalen zum bürgerlichen Weltbild*, he demonstrates how deeply the ideas of even the most original thinkers are conditioned by the contemporary societal reality – or by that which society takes for reality. By tracing philosophical development from the late Middle Ages and concentrating especially on the thoughts of Descartes and Pascal, he shows to what an extent even those ideas and systems of philosophy which seem far removed from the exigencies of the day and the immediate concerns of contemporary society, reflect and often merely formulate the generally accepted assumptions of the age.

Descartes's philosophical rationalism justifies and reinforces inexorable economic rationalization processes, and also serves them by encouraging the individual to adjust to them. Pascal's thoughts reflect, without as yet reflecting on, the actual split between societal rationalizations and compulsions on the one hand and the individual's aspirations on the other. He tries to escape from intolerable contradictions by means of a faith which, in turn, is infected by and mirrors the irrationality of societal rationalizations. Beyond this, so Borkenau suggests, Pascal experienced the contradictions as sickness or neurosis, as dis-ease. He thus came very close to raising the problem of social consciousness, of the individual in society, of the individual's awareness of society. His book ends where our questions begin. Perhaps it had to be so, because his approach, still exclusively intellectual and academic, precludes forms of understanding which may prove essential in this area.

For scholars like Tönnies or Durkheim the individual never became problematical. Both, however dissimilar in approach, had a nostalgic-utopian apprehension of society: once it had functioned as an organic whole within which the individual had his predestined

5

place and thereby his explanation. Durkheim explicitly, Tönnies by implication, look forward to a possible reintegration of society, a rejuvenation of its creative, cohesive powers – on a level of greater complexity – where the individual would once again become un-problematical. He would find his fulfilment in and be defined by his function in, for, and by the grace of, the whole which in turn would be the justification of his labours and his being. In the meantime the problematics of the individual merely reflect the societal confusion (cf. Durkheim, 1952. Also Durkheim, 1966, pp. 13, 35, 42, 45).

According to Durkheim, societal aspirations, pressures and necessities constitute and reconstitute our individuality as well as our capacities for apprehending it and society. Sociology, therefore, not merely complements epistemology, but supersedes it. For society, with its inherent possible and necessary differentiations, shapes the very categories of human understanding, of pure as well as practical reason (Durkheim, 1968, pp. 223, 264, 271; also 'Conclusion'). Durkheim does not ask what gives such shaping power to society, nor how society actually works, seeing that every experience, including that of society and its workings, is personal, individual. Thus he raises the problem of social consciousness, as of individual awareness, by and not in his work. For why does he work at all, if his understanding of society is totally constituted by society? Or does he understand society as a complex cybernetic mechanism in which the individual functions as automatic self-correction? This would simply by-pass the question why – or the fact that – human as against animal society took the enormous detour over individual awareness.

It is clear that Durkheim's sociology – as Tönnies's – was born of a passionate moral longing for the renewal of society, its awe-inspiring self-authentication. It seems hardly less clear that this concern influenced and encouraged contemporaries and successors at least as much as the not always equally obvious methods and collections of evidence. (Just as the power of Marx's influence may have had its source in the 'communistic mood' that inspired his work rather than in the detailed and at times disconcerting argumentation which was a result of that inspiration.) Is such a moral passion no more than the epiphenomenal twitch or signal of a social automatism? Or has it, at least in its turn, constitutive power? Durkheim, against the force of his own arguments, believed it had (Durkheim, 1966, 'Prefaces'; Durkheim, 1969, 'Preface to the First Edition'; Durkheim, 1952, 'Anomic Suicide').

Weber

Weber is better known in the West than his sociological compatriots.

He comes closest to its rationalistic, positivistic and empirical attitude. He ceaselessly elaborated more precise definitions, classifications, systematization, methods for the testing of objectivity. He moved mountains to isolate causes. He believed in the possibility, almost in the inevitability, of a methodology by means of which sociology would mature into a fully-fledged, value-free, objective science. Here we do not intend to analyse his ideas once again, we merely wish to ask whether and how he raised the problem of the individual *vis-à-vis* society: 1   By his overtly individualistic and voluntaristic approach. 2   By his understanding of objectivity, the separation of value-free science from value-soaked political and moral commitment. 3   By his titanism. 4   By his personality.

1   In contrast to Durkheim, Weber's starting point is the purposefully acting individual, though purpose is defined by the expectations and chances determined and allowed for by the close-knit interactions of persons and groups. His voluntaristic approach is not intended to prejudice any issue of primogeniture between person and group. Yet in emphatically anti-Hegelian fashion, Weber treats state, nation, society, church, etc., as abstractions and certainly not as things. In *Über einige Kategorien der verstehenden Soziologie* he outlines the process by which society is constituted through the interacting expectations of individuals, and in turn constitutes objectives and aspirations for the individual. Therefore sociology is not a dependency of psychology but an autonomous science. However, its relations to psychology are manifold and many-layered. For *Verstehen* is an operation which involves insights into the fluid motivations of individuals, ranging from the most purposeful, i.e. society-oriented, to the most irrational, i.e. private, instinctive, a-social. Therefore psychology and sociology start from opposite poles (Weber, 1968, esp. 102–7). Yet Weber also believes that it is beyond the competence of science to determine the rationality of ends. Science can merely establish the rationality of means used to attain a given end. Hence rationalization can and does proceed to absurd lengths in the service of possibly quite irrational ends, because these are societal objectives. There he stops and leaves wide open the question thus raised concerning the function and meaning of rationality and rationalization. Freud will tackle it having 'started from the opposite pole'.

2   In *Die 'Objektivität' sozialwissenschaftlicher Erkenntnis* Weber (1968) again by-passes the problem of epistemology, the question 'what can we know?', by reducing it to a question of value-freedom; as if the individual gained at least potential infallibility, if only he concentrated on value-uncontaminated analyses, using reason *sans* emotion. Such a belief pre-judges Dilthey's attempt to distinguish between the natural and the social sciences; or perhaps

7

it merely demonstrates that Dilthey's distinction was not a basic one. Weber knew what he was doing. Hence his enormous labours to show how *Verstehen* and causal understanding could be reconciled. Yet once more he merely raises the problem of how the individual can hope to understand society and his own position in and over against it, in order to shelve it. This is the bureaucratic way of dealing with problems. It is also the scientific and technological method. The progress of science depends on the elimination and not on the solution of problems, it proceeds via deproblematization. In the sphere of manipulative knowledge, of know-how, in technology, industry, administration, it is a most effective method. Weber's contribution to sociology would be unproblematical, if it were not for the doubt whether the social sciences are of the kind whose virtue consists in their effectiveness, remembering that effectiveness or efficiency is equivalent to manipulability. There is no doubt in physics, chemistry or biology, as to who is to do the manipulating. In sociology this problem is immediate and unshelvable. It is also self-perpetuating. It refuses to be eliminated. It subterraneously vitiates any research that does not face up to it by either turning it into an adjunct of one administration or another, or into insignificance. It blinds the researcher to the fact that in sociology, as in the *Geisteswissenschaften* in general, neutrality is cloaked ideology, implicit bias in favour of the *status quo*.

Moreover, the attempted elimination of the value problem, i.e. of the problem of social consciousness, of the individual *vis-à-vis* society, avenges itself in another way: to disconnect evaluation, emotive valuing, from scientific enquiry means to be compelled to manage without the exercise of judgment, of Kant's *Urteilskraft*. Now in the natural sciences mathematics and logic function as a kind of quasi-judgment. They formalize all arguments into tautology, into equations. Yet in both the natural sciences and in the *Geisteswissenschaften* the absence of judgment has led inevitably to illimitable proliferation. In the former, however, and because of their manipulative nature, even specialization has remained 'vectored' and, within an ever more narrowly chosen field, meaningful, purposeful. In the latter the proliferation has proved merely fissile. It is reducing sociology *inter alia* to meaninglessness in the sense of letting it become purely analytical, i.e. tautological, i.e. bureaucratic.

This development can be seen in Weber's own work, not to mention that of his successors. It takes, as usual, two different directions. First, in *Wirtschaft und Gesellschaft*, especially in the first two chapters, we find an overwhelming proliferation of definitions. Each could, and often does, delimit an independent field of research. The cross-references between any two or more of such fields may in turn constitute independent disciplines (Weber, 1964).

In his late *Vom inneren Beruf zur Wissenschaft,* science not just as a profession but a vocation, Weber surrenders to the impetus of an autonomous process in an act of a-religious self-immolation. Unless we are the prophet, which we are not, let us obey the summons of the day, *der Forderung des Tages,* which is that of an atomized science, technology, bureaucracy, self-perpetuating, self-authenticating, value-free. This we are told in tone of command. But can I accept a summons from something to which I have not first granted an ultimate authority, i.e. value? Second, in his *Religionssoziologie* the proliferation lies in the direction of an illimitable amassing of adequate and sufficient evidence to justify and validate the isolation of one particular cause in a manner in which such an isolation had to be established according to Weber's own arguments. Not only the fact that this enormous undertaking has remained a fragment suggests its inconcludability (see below, ch. 5).

Weber's dual asceticism, demanding acceptance of and committal to moral values in practical life as passionately as obedience to the demands of value-freedom in research, leaves the individual in double isolation: purely mechanically related to his fellow-researchers, he must give the best of his life to labours without passion – except the passion to be passionless. Utterly atomized in practical affairs, he must proclaim his moral and political convictions to other atoms, and on the market place where everything is priced according to the law of supply and demand; a truly heroic ideal which gives more than a touch of pathos or even tragedy to his two essays on 'Vocation'. This is schizophrenia as *telos*: the individual detached from society, detached in and from his thinking, committed to action which, though not unthinking, remains unthinkable. Weber seems to epitomize the final state of that bourgeois capitalism which he so unthinkably deplores: its splitting of the inexorable market mechanisms from any personal aspiration which that same mechanism reduces to private, merely tolerated, affairs. And here, of course, lies Weber's greatness: that his intensely personal, intellectual, devaluating objectifying struggle reflects the actualities of his age.

3   Obviously related to the above and its direct consequence is Weber's titanism. Like Nietzsche he is most German even in his efforts to break away from German predilections. He cannot escape the lure of Hegel – Fichte, Schelling, Marx – or should one rather say: he could not deny the fairly universal human longing for some kind of totalization to which Germans merely gave most intense and perverse expression. In one way or another each individual carries the world as a totality within himself. Whenever 'the world' is being spoken of, or anything as happening in or affecting the course of 'the world', this infinitely varied and shaded amalgam of subjective

conceptualizations, apprehensions, experiences and expectations, is both intimated and concealed by the word 'world' (cf. Husserl, 1950, vol. 1, pp. 57 ff; also Winch, 1958, pp. 15–18). The social world is structured by the interplay of all those subjective totalities which in turn are structured by this conglomerate. This is a Marcellian mystery.

Now the more conscious and consciously individuated a person becomes, the more he will experience his intellectual and instinctive endeavours at totalization as problematical, and will do so to the extent to which he will continue to strive for such a totalization. But once aware of the paradox, he cannot escape from it. He can resign himself to a kind of schizophrenia, as does the burgher to the split between public and private, the 'worker' to that between work and leisure, the scientist to that between research and life. Or he must try to do what Weber tried so desperately: *To hold together in a gigantic intellective effort that which all the time the same intellect increasingly fragments.* This explains the grandeur and pathos of *Wirtschaft und Gesellschaft*, the anguish of its breathless argumentation; but also the ending of the essays on 'Vocation' which are beyond pessimism and despair. They are titanic in their demand that man hold together what tears him apart, moral action and a-moral science, because the Messiah may come and must not find the faithful idle, though their incessant labours can neither hasten nor hinder his coming. Like Hegel and Marx, Weber is Atlas, but beyond them in endurance, for he has experienced the fragmentation which is our fate more deeply. And the fissure is located in the human heart and mind where what I value, love, appreciate, and what I can know must for ever stay apart (cf. Scheler, 1960, pp. 431ff).

4   In the light of subsequent developments and discoveries it seems of more than psychological interest to raise the question: 'Was Weber's thinking or, rather, was the quality or character of his thinking the result of his neurosis or psychosis which manifested itself in a long mental breakdown? Or was that breakdown the reaction of his being, of his emotive, embodied, hyper-sensitive nature, to his ruthless thinking?' (Cf. Horkheimer-Adorno, 1969, ch. 1, on rationality and tyranny; also Adorno, 1970, pp. 265–75.) It must be stressed emphatically that referring to this illness casts no more doubt or aspersions on his work and thinking as such, on its 'validity', than would a reference to pneumonia or a broken limb. Admittedly, the connection between thought and mental disorder seems closer than that between thought and physical illness. Which means that the question must be raised, and without prejudice.

We remember that one of the psychotic symptoms was an incapacity to read and write. Now we could immediately neutralize the question, deflect its impetus and evacuate it of meaning – value-judgment – on Weber's own prescription, by turning it into a question of causality on the one hand and of possible cure on the other. Thus we should have extricated ourselves from a whole complex of questions whose very function or *raison d'être* might have been to implicate us. We should have pre-judged the issue, as Weber would have wanted us to.

May we instead permit the question concerning this illness to question us? To let it involve rather than detach us? That this is no longer sociology can be asserted only by those who have pre-judged the issue raised by the question. It cannot be a question of causality, for causality only matters in the universe of discourse we have just stepped out of: the universe of – possible – manipulation. For example, for Weber's doctor, though perhaps even for him only because contemporary medicine reflects contemporary prejudices, the illness could have raised the question of causality. What we have to realize here is that questions of the kind we are asking or trying to ask now, remain questions. They also contain something that functions as in other contexts answers are designed to function, as long as they remain questions. So we ask: Is there a connection, an inter-dependence or interaction, between certain illnesses and certain kinds of and approaches to work and thought? Is there a relationship, and if so, of what character, between the temper, mood, *Stimmung*, of a peculiar physical and mental organization, and the *Stimmung* of and created by the work and thinking, bearing in mind that the originating temper or distemper may have been already the result of the person's encounter with the 'world' or society which his work is intended to reflect and to reflect on? Is it likely that there is no 'relevant' connection here? And what would we have to learn from such disconcerting disconnection? But if there were a connection, what light would the work throw on the illness, what darkness, if any, the illness over the work? What do illness and work together state about the person in whom they meet and who remains distinct from them although he is expressed through them? Maybe the interaction between illness and work is a reflection or expression or symptom, of the interaction of the individual and society. It may somehow mirror the tensions inherent in social consciousness which is the ever-precarious balance of tensions between individual and societal demands and aspirations. If our work reflects our state of health or disease, our putative health is in question, if Weber's work, undoubtedly of supreme importance and integrity, is an expression of dis-ease. What, anyway, is denoted by sickness and health, in how far dare we and must we apply such terms, if analogically, to society? (In this light cf. Durkheim, 1966, ch. 3.) And if Weber's life and work, like that of, for example, Pascal, could be said to reflect a societal malaise (Borkenau, 1934, on Pascal), is it a malaise of capitalism, of Western society in general, of contemporary Western society in particular, or a more universal social affliction? Again, these are questions to which there are no answers; except for those who come to know in the very process of such questioning something closer to what is usually experienced as 'answer' than what is commonly denoted by the word.

It would be interesting to trace the connections between Weber's psychosis and his puritanism of the intellect which enabled him to write the history of puritanical assumptions with such a deep understanding – and left him with a belief in predestination without belief in a God. It could prove illuminating to search for connections between both illness and work and his early upbringing. All this not to prove a Freudian point, but to test what might be discovered concerning the way in which individuals – mother and father, the positively most significant others – mediate the 'world', society with its achievements, compulsions and tensions, to their child. To see how the father's and the mother's worlds complement and distort each other, and shape and mis-shape the child in the process. Through such a focusing on a significant individual one might, as Sartre believed and practised, discover more about an age, in this case ours, than in any other way. Through such focusing, as, for example, Erikson, Laing, Oscar Lewis demonstrated, we might come to understand history and the structure and functioning of society in a way in which even the reading of the works of so great an historian and sociologist as Weber himself cannot make us understand. Once more we have come back to the problems concerning the individual in society and recognize that even Weber posed it by his life rather than by his writings (Erikson, 1965, 1972; Laing, 1964b, 1965, 1969; Lewis, 1964, 1968, 1970). Until now, only the poet, dramatist, novelist, has immersed himself in this problem. It can even be said about him that his staying power, possibly his quality as poet, is in direct proportion to his success in conveying the depth and breadth of the conflicts inherent in the human situation as constituted by the symbiosis of and the tensions between the self and society. (See below, ch. 2, Notes on literature. Cf. Mitzman (1970), especially pp. 148–80, 253–96. I only discovered this book after I had written mine.)

Freud

Freud's insights, so I believe, were and are epoch-making in the full sense of that word. There is as decisive a watershed between pre- and post-Freudian thinking, as there is one between pre- and post-Marxian thought (Habermas, 1969, pp. 341ff). The full extent and impact of Freud's insights have not yet been appreciated by either the psychological, sociological or philosophical disciplines. Nor has there as yet been a serious exploration – except by isolated individuals – as to what an extent they have opened these three disciplines to each other, point to their complementariness rather than clear-cut isolation. Freudian insights have been neglected even where apparently they have been given adequate airing. For, as we shall try to show presently, they raise their questions not on the psychological level, but on that of epistemology, ethics, politics, even religion, i.e. they raise them on the level of sociology. Moreover these insights pose their questions in the way in which e.g. Weber's illness rather than his arguments poses them. For that reason, much of the sporadic academic and more general intellectual acceptance of Freud's theories has often been a form of immunization against his insights. It has deflected rather than faced the questions by channelling them into academic argumentation. Unfortunately Freud himself set the precedent (Habermas, 1969, pp. 303–9).

Just because we assign extraordinary importance to Freud's works, especially in regard to sociology and the problem of understanding in sociology, of social consciousness, we must look at some peculiar difficulties they raise: 1 Freud as his own interpreter. 2 The character of Freud's originality. 3 Freud as an initiator.

1 Freud, not unlike some of the greater creative writers, was at times a most inadequate interpreter of his own insights. This was almost inevitable. His discoveries were not just another widening of our *geisteswissenschaftliche* perspective, but the beginning of a new way of looking at man and the human situation. Such seeing – *theorein*, theorizing before having theories – was bound to get into conflict with and strain beyond their resilience the old conceptual tools and machinery which, at one and the same time, it had to use and to put in question. The resulting tension existed first and foremost in the mind of Freud who, it must not be forgotten, was Weber's senior by eight years. That mind had been formed by the sophisticated rationalism of Vienna and Paris, by scientific, i.e. in those days almost mechanistic, assumptions and presumptions. The insights which were to question the very constitution of man's rationality more profoundly than ever before erupted in a mind complacently committed to Latin-Anglo-Saxon Enlightenment reasonableness. To the end Freud tried to contain his insights within and to confine them to that framework of rationality, by hook and by crook, at least in his published works. He had and expressed serious doubts concerning man's ability and desire to act reasonably. He never seriously doubted that peculiar rationality

13

which in the West has always been taken for reason *per se*. It remained the lodestar of all human endeavour. Freud's work throughout is haunted by the paradoxicality of this belief (for example, cf. Wollheim, 1971, with Rieff, 1960; Jones, 1964, with Habermas, 1969).

2   Originality, no matter how great, does not mean the discovery of something totally new. It consists in the confluence of previously disparate visions, interests, myths, areas of information, surmises. We have noted how Freud's rationalistic training made him constrain his insights. It may even be of sociological interest to ask whether, but for their rationalistic strait-jacketing, his discoveries would have turned him into a poet or prophet, i.e. into a completely uninfluential thinker. (A further question could be, whether such a constraint is still necessary today, or whether by now it has become lethal.) In the meantime other shaping influences enabled Freud to conceive and give birth to his insights. There is literature for which he retained a life-long, human, catholic interest. Not accidentally his basic 'complex' was called after a great literary hero. He loved Hamlet, Dostoevsky, Don Quixote. He was well acquainted with classic and romantic German literature. The strain of German romantic philosophy which, stirred by Kant and Fichte as well as by Rousseau, culminated in the will-philosophies of Schopenhauer and Nietzsche, was another influence.

Freud was obviously fascinated by religion. The conflicts this fascination set up in his rationalistic mind seem to have been furious. They made him lose his olympian detachment. Remembering his calm impartiality *vis-à-vis* the terrors of fascism, the acidity of his attacks on religion and the fact that he could not help returning to it in his last 'popular' essay prove its fascination. In the last analysis his discoveries raise religious questions or, rather, questions which up till now have been raised only by religion. And one of their more immediate sources can be detected in that Judaic, Talmudic, Hasidic tradition from which Freud never altogether dissociated himself (see Martin Buber, *Tales of the Hasidim*, 2 vols, Schocken, New York, 1968–9, especially the 'Introduction'). This tradition represents man's most intense attempt at casuistry in the best sense of this term: that there is no universal ideal, theory or law, which has not to be tested in and modified by the everyday life of the everyday person, by the individual, any individual, his background, circumstances, character, by all his contingencies. Just as vice versa there is no individual which is not related, however complexly, to the universal, the 'law of God'. For over two thousand years powerful and refined intellects had gone into the elaboration of the connection between the universal and the particular, idea and reality, individual and society, man and God. A thousand years of ghetto psychology which was also philosophy and religion burst into flower in psycho-analysis. (Sociology might profit from a comparison between Catholic spirituality, as it developed into modern scientific, manipulative psychology, generalizing in its intentions; and the Talmudic pariah tradition which always moved towards an understanding of the individual's predicament over against the general, an alien society.)

3   For me, and this must be stressed above all else, Freud's insights mark a beginning, not an end. They are seminal. We have not yet seen their flowering or fruition. Freud answers few questions. He proves nothing. His theories are questionable in both senses of the German *fragwürdig*: they have to be questioned; they are worth questioning, they might yield clues. They are mythological (see below, ch. 3, Prelude). On the other hand, his questions question our rationality – as, of course, his and their own. If he proves nothing, it is partly because his theories, or, rather, the insights underlying the theories, put in question the function and nature of proof. His theories are *fragwürdig* in that they make all theorizing *fragwürdig*, for better, for worse. And if they, like the theories of Marx, may be called mythological, it is because in them the power of all theorizing, as against its validity, is revealed as mythological. Naturally this raises problems beyond the stretching of academic arguments, because these are the expression of an alternative myth. The very tensions between Freud's insights and theories question, if not the validity, certainly the extent of the validity of academic argumentation. They suggest that our deference to the academic rationale may not be rational, that it may be the result of patriarchal, one-sided, tyrannous authority. Is it possible that the proof which concludes an argument beyond further contradiction functions as such to the extent to which it is the reflection and introjection of age-old patriarchal, regal, bureaucratic authority (Horkheimer-Adorno, 1969, pp. 20, 29, 92; Mitscherlich, 1969, pp. 81ff, 238ff)?

Not surprisingly, therefore, Freud's influence can be felt in art and literature, in common pursuits like the bringing up of children and the managing of one's personal, especially sexual, affairs, in advertising and propaganda, rather than in the departments of universities. Again for better and worse, the influence extends into areas where acceptance is not based on argument. But it also reaches into academic disciplines like anthropology, sociology, philosophy, mainly in as far as it is not dependent on and acknowledged by argumentation. Here we are not interested in the Freud of the psychology departments, if he exists at all, or of the psycho-analysts, but in his insights at work in people like Malinowski, Marcuse, Sartre, the Frankfurt School, Erikson, Laing, Rieff; and in writers like Mann, Musil, Joyce, Proust, Svevo, Bellow; in the

15

insights that often worked through Freud himself against his consent.

In the following I can barely hint at five aspects of Freud's thoughts, in as far as they have a direct bearing on our problem of the individual in society, his understanding of society, of himself in society. 1 His insights have made fluid the frontiers between body and psyche. 2 They have done the same to those between the individual and society. 3 They cut across old distinctions such as those between psychology and epistemology, philosophy and sociology, emotion and reason, religion and enlightenment. 4 They open up new possibilities of inter-subjective exploration – which already Freud himself partly closed again. 5 They have demonstrated new patterns of discovery in method and communication.

1 Body and psyche

It may well be that Freud's Hebrew ancestry asserted itself most powerfully in his brand of monism. Hebrew thought and Judaistic practice did not separate body and soul. The Greeks did. They absolutized a distinction into a divorce. European thought on the whole followed Greek inspiration. (Perhaps because it more neatly reflected the actual division of society.) Its monisms therefore tended to fall into either the soul or the body compartment reserved for either in the tidy mind: realism or nominalism, idealism or materialism, theism or naturalism. Or else it remained simply dualistic, as in St Augustine, St Thomas Aquinas, Descartes, Hume, Kant. Freud's monism is of an overarching or undermining kind. His only two notable forerunners happen to have been Hebrews as well: Spinoza and Marx. Descartes had salvaged the Graeco-Christian for modern philosophy and science. His doubts not merely left intact his belief in the ego, but also in the ego as distinct from everything, even its own body. The problems besetting what Ryle calls the ghost-in-the-machine-theories have therefore continued to haunt European thought, via such witty solutions as those of Leibniz, to such contemporary evasions as behaviourism, positivism, or Ryle's own attempt (Ryle, 1950). For each of these latter-day monisms, like their European precursors, implicitly accepted the division, before opting for one of the alternatives created by it. Within the dualistic conceptual framework the problems of inter-action between mind and body, man and nature, person and person, individual and society, freedom and determinism, are not so much posed as posited, created; they cannot be solved, because a solution would dissolve the frame. This may explain the accidie and acidity of the endless and by definition unresolvable arguments. Perhaps our very belief in argument as a highway to 'truth' rests on an unconscious acceptance of our being as an ultimate duality or schizophrenia.

Freud was not a philosopher. If his findings should eventually have the impact on philosophy they do not yet have, it might be because they cut across philosophical distinctions. Take the hoary problem: how do I become aware of another's mind, his thoughts and feelings? Through his gestures, his posture, his physiognomy, the sounds that proceed from his mouth, or in spite of them? How am I able to interpret the random messages my senses receive? Via introspective analogy – which merely pushes the question one rung further down towards the 'foul rag-and-bone shop of the heart' – or through direct spiritual contact or intuition? And how can I be sure any of these are not deceptive? And it is not to be forgotten that this problem lies rotting, if unperceived, underneath behaviouristic, scientistic assumptions. As long as our conceptual which is also our emotive thinking separates body from mind it creates either of two situations: (a) It leaves philosophical and ultimately all human discussions in the realm of duality, open or hidden, and so condemns them to fertility and futility, as pointed out just now. (b) Or it makes man reject the dualism and compels him to opt for either 'mind' or 'body', leaving a materialism or naturalism devoid of 'spirit', an idealism or intellectualism unrooted in individual bodiliness. (And it may be of sociological import that scientism can be defined as either materialism or idealism, indicating the ambivalence of this either/or of dualism.)

Freud's importance lies in his breaking of this deadlock, though he was doing it unawares and against his better knowledge. His explorations led him by their own inner rather than by any consciously imposed logic, to the discovery or rediscovery of the essential and essentially organic wholeness of man. The novelty of the discovery lay in what one may, perhaps more than playfully, call its Einsteinian elements. Freud understood the human reality as constituting itself in a kind of space-time continuum. In human life, as perhaps in all life, the past is never past. It is the continuing, fluid substratum or substance out of which the present with its demands for present responses is continuously constituted and 'gestalted'. He discovered how totally the past, our personal, familial, national and species history, not only refined but defined and confined our present and future. That is to say: he recovered the old Hebrew understanding of the psychic unity of body and mind, and of time as meaningful and directed, by discovering or positing a further unity, of past, present, future, of body-mind and time (cf. Heidegger, 1931, pp. 329ff, 381). (An analogy may and has been found in embryology which sees the foetus as embodying, i.e. condensing into spatial terms, the formal efforts of millions of years.)

17

Beyond Wordsworth's wildest surmise, Freud has shown the child to be father of the man – and since then others, like D. W. Winnicott, A. Freud, M. Klein, have taken his investigations ever closer to the womb. This view of the matter the cultured public has long since integrated into its intellectual armoury. And it has always been the social function of the intellect to domesticate disturbing insights and then use them for further domestication (cf. Weber, 1964, vol. 2, pp. 866–91). Freud's own rationalism, his suspicions of the id, his fears of the 'overflowing of the sewers', aided and abetted such an abuse, although, perhaps because, he was the first to have understood its functioning. He was not the first to appreciate the mendacity of this kind of domesticating process. From the days of the Buddha and Jeremiah, the cynics, via La Rochefoucauld to Schopenhauer and Nietzsche, there were those who had seen and felt it. Freud was the first to begin to perceive why and how the process functions as it does: it achieves and preserves 'order', the only kind of communal order we know and outside of which we suspect sheer disorder, by turning man's primal energies against themselves and himself, which means: by wasting them. Yet although Freud began to comprehend the whole extent of the ravages caused by this process in his very efforts to repair some of them, he still was enough of a child of the Enlightenment to prefer 'law and order' to whatever it is they seem to protect us from.[2] He could not yet raise the question in how far our fear of chaos is the result of our ordering repressions rather than their cause. (We recall his ideas about the goings on in the primeval horde and how close they are to those of Durkheim. Weber expresses the consensus of contemporary sociologists when he takes it for granted that civilization as symbol of any possible human order is based on the use of force and can be maintained only by force. The groups which today have chosen 'law and order' as their slogan suggest that the sociologist might profitably raise the question Freud did not.)

Notwithstanding all these necessary qualifications, Freud had learned and taught the West to take childhood more seriously than it had ever been taken before, even by Rousseau. He enabled us to understand how a man's experience, his very capacity for experiencing, is shaped by his early childhood. He began to appreciate to what an extent and to what depth our first few months and years make and unmake us. This is to say: they make us what we are also in the sense of preventing us from becoming what we could be, if only. . . . By showing how the whole of history is individuated as well as recreated through the contingencies of a person's upbringing, his earliest training and education, much of it pre-verbal, most of it pre-critical; and by suggesting how therapy can undo some of the damage caused by ignorance and misunderstanding, he gave a completely different meaning, power and 'reality' to that 'if only . . .'.

He also discovered, and some of his successors took his discoveries further, that the child's primal experience is one of 'undifferentiation' (Klein, 1959; Winnicott, 1958, 1965ab, 1969). The child does not experience himself and the mother, inner and outer, body and desire, imagination and reality, in separation or in any kind of priority. His experience is of total diffusedness, of diffused totality: now it is omnipotence, now utter helplessness, now total joy, now total despair, now all harmony, now world-shattering rage. All our adult feelings of impotence, despair, lostness, terror, our longing for power, joy, peace, even for rage, are rooted in and shaped by the experiences of that undifferentiated state. That is why they are so strong, so indifferent to reasons, so fertile in rationalizations; and also why they have such surprising and at times disconcerting subterranean links and can blend and change into each other.

Now if there really is such a close, causal, fateful not yet sufficiently explored connection between the child and the adult; if the adult is as much at the mercy of his childhood, as, because of this, his child finds himself at his mercy; if, in the language of the *Tao*, it is possible that the weak shapes the strong and that violence or force is a futile reaction to or defence against such 'creative' weakness which is merely the vulnerability of openness; what, if anything, has sociology to say on this matter from within a civilization based on force? (Cf. Lao Tzu, *Tao Te Ching*, Penguin, Harmondsworth, 1971, esp. XVII, XXVI, XLIII.) Furthermore what may and must social philosophy learn from the basic Freudian contentions that the primal human experience is one of 'totality and undifferentiation'? All the later, necessary processes of differentiation, discrimination, individuation, grow out of that primal knowledge. Their roots remain in it. It is their source, and this source is always present and active within us. There are no words for this state. Words themselves are part of the differentiation process. There is no inner or outer, no part or whole, no I or thou, in that state. Such words can barely hint at the condition they helped to undo. It may be that the mystical experience of ecstasy points to it (cf. Heidegger, 1931, pp. 123–30). That condition is logically and chronologically prior to thought. For thinking, like the words from which it is not separable, signals the break-up of the primal state which nevertheless continues to subsist in us, because my past is never only past. No judgment is implied on either the primal state or on the new consciousness which of necessity dissolves it. Yet a new understanding of their interdependence and interrelation as something not just of the past could raise anew all possible questions concerning the nature, function, validity and 'truth', of thought, understanding, communication, communion between I and thou, the individual and community.

For example, it is a well-attested fact that men, even heroes, in times of agony or near death often cry out for their mother, like babies, especially when the agony is protracted. Maybe persistent anguish is necessary to erode defences built up over a life-time. A man in an uncontrollable rage seems to regress into some kind of babyhood. His movements do not just become unco-ordinated. His abandonment to them expresses a belief, long since officially abrogated, in their utter effectiveness. A raging man tears to bits not only his enemies but the whole universe in such an ecstasy of abandon. We find reflections of this in myths, in figures like Ajax, Lear, in numberless films and TV serials, in the fascination of boxing and wrestling. And it may be that equally irrational and unconscious fears of the effectiveness of our rage force us to keep it bottled up, until special circumstances like war or riot permit us actually to effect what under ordinary conditions personal rage would not have effected.

When passionately in love, a man similarly regresses to a state of being where omnipotence and helplessness, ecstasy and the terror of impotence, are not so much balanced as one and the same. For at such times, the mind and the body, I and thou, are experienced as one and the same and yet are known, simultaneously, not to be the same, since we have eaten of the forbidden fruit. According to Freudian understanding, the behaviour of the wounded, the raging, the lover, does not express a rare and isolated synapsis. It reveals an underlying pattern which is always present, though we are able, under ordinary circumstances, to behave as if it were not. At times we are able to forget its existence altogether.

To return to the wounded hero *in extremis*: the cry for his mother is not wrung from him in spite of himself. It reveals his self. In this cry he returns to the self which he had been taught to deny and to feel ashamed of, to see as vulnerable and despicably weak, so that a whole hero had to be built round it to hide it from a world bustling with equally armoured and hidden selves. Let us listen, possibly with some of Oscar Lewis's creative empathy, to a young inhabitant of a slum in Mexico City (Lewis, 1970, p. 38):

The thing is, growing up in our environment here, we see the realities of life so close that we must learn to have a lot of self-control. Sometimes I had an intense desire to cry because of something my father said, but instead, because life, cynicism, had taught me to put on a mask, I laughed. For him I did not suffer, I felt nothing, I was a shameless cynic, I had no soul . . .

because of the mask I showed. But inside I felt every word he said.

I have learned to hide my fear, to show only courage, because from what I have observed a person is treated according to the impression he makes. That's why when I am really very afraid inside, outwardly I am calm. It has helped me, too, because I didn't suffer as much as some of my friends who trembled when they were grabbed by the police. If a guy shows weakness and has tears in his eyes, that's when the others pile on him. In my neighbourhood you are either a *picudo*, a tough guy, or a *pendejo*, a fool. Mexicans, and I think everyone in the world, admire the person 'with balls', as we say. . . . If someone shouts, you've got to shout louder. If any so-and-so comes to me and says, 'Fuck your mother', I answer, 'Fuck your mother a thousand times'. And if he gives one step forward and I take one step back, I lose prestige. But if I go forward, too, and pile on and make a fool out of him, then the others will treat me with respect. In a fight I would never give up and say, 'Enough', even though the other was killing me. I would try to go to my death smiling. That is what I mean by being '*macho*', manly.

And the father of that young man, remembering his father's hard experiences, had already said (1970, pp. 5–6):

Yes, at times we men want to be very strong and *macho*, but at bottom we aren't. When it is a question of morality or a family thing that touches the very fibres of the heart, it hurts and a man cries when he is alone. You must have noticed that many people drown themselves in drink and others grab a pistol and shoot themselves, because they cannot bear what they feel inside. They have no way to express themselves or anyone to tell their troubles to, so they grab a gun and that is all. They're finished! And at times those who believe themselves to be *machos* are really not so when they are alone with their conscience. They are only braggarts of the moment.

There can be few better and more poignant examples of social consciousness – and few to reveal more clearly that 'the sins of the fathers will be visited upon the children unto the third and fourth generation' and that this is a sociological and not a moral or religious statement. One seems to be listening to the universal, introjected morality of violence of five thousand years of civilization. The members of the first Assyrian military academy could have spoken like the young Mexican slum dweller, the young Spartan or Roman soldier, the recruit at Sandhurst or Key West. In the sphere of power politics politicians are still speaking with Manuel's voice, the voice of a man who grew up in the usual kind of slum produced by the only kind of civilization we as yet happen to know. He must learn to bear getting hurt by those who hurt him, because they are afraid of getting hurt, because they all had got hurt too badly as children. He must hurt those that are weak and cry, because they remind him of his own weakness and tears which he has been taught to fear by those who were afraid themselves, because. . . .

So we see: the strong man does not cry in spite of being a strong man. He becomes a strong man, because, for a variety of reasons and unreasons, he was not permitted to cry when he was a child. To put it most paradoxically: it may be that much heroism is a man's detour to his ultimate and primal anger and anguish, to the point where he is permitted to rage and cry without restraint. For the baby rage and grief are merely the two aspects of feeling hurt, feeling anguished beyond bearing. Later on we cry when we are not permitted to rage and rage when we are not permitted to cry. As we know, a man's raging is rarely caused by an occasion. Mostly it is the suppressed rage that seeks and, if need be, manufactures the occasion to find a justification for its open expression. For rage knows, if we no longer do, that in it, for a while, during its full flowering, we re-experience the ecstasy of omnipotence, of totality, which we long for, because we are not allowed to cry over its loss. Only our introjected standards of morality spoil the purity of the pleasure and adulterate it with elements of panic and of shame. Equally this may be the precariousness of our loving that through it we seek to reach the irretrievably lost wholeness, for which even this word is not an adequate expression, since 'wholeness' pre-supposes division, part, parting. And perhaps rage is so close to love, because it merely wishes to achieve violently what love could not.

It is essential to be wary here of any derogation or reductionism. We are *not* saying: 'The hero is merely an aged, perverse little child; the despairing lover is really only trying to get back to the womb; the revolutionary's fury is merely the inhibited baby's inchoate gesturing.' This would be a total misreading of the Freudian text – which however he himself already was at times guilty of.[3] We do not claim to have found answers, but that through a Freudian understanding we are able to question the character and necessity of our private and public virtues, our *humanitas*, its functions and structure, in a new way. For example, if it be true that our beginnings shape our ends, that our ends can never do more or better than explicate our beginnings – echoes of the acorn and the oak! – what implications has that for psychology, epistemology and sociology? How seriously are we to take our beginnings and in what way? Are they our 'reality', and what is reality anyway! Shall we have to rewrite history and therefore sociology along the lines pioneered by Erikson in *Childhood and Society* and *Young Man Luther*?

We try once more: the baby and young child slowly and inevitably outgrows his primal state. He outgrows it but does not leave it behind. As his past it remains active in every present and every determination of the future. Whether, for instance, he experienced 'totality' – we are using words for what by definition is prior to words – as predominantly threatening or comforting, will define the groundplan of his life. He learns to differentiate and distinguish, to focus, concentrate, co-ordinate his body movements. He begins to realize that the distinct and particular matters, and has to be grasped out of the indistinct background of totality. The breast becomes distinct from the mother, absence from presence, good mother from bad; later on body from body, self from self; still later inner from outer and later still fiction from fact. The latest is the hardest of all, since fact is no more than a peculiar fiction on which adult society has bestowed specific status and significance. (After all, fiction also is a fact.) The process must be painful: one discovers that all is not love, milk, joy which wills eternity. But the progress must also bring relief: one simultaneously discovers that despair, tornness, forsakenness, is not all, that time is not eternity, at least not altogether.

By this time the child has learned to speak. Education begins in earnest. What was distinguishable is now separated by language: I am not you, this is not that, here is not there, past is not present, what you say is not so and, above all – for this necessitates most further separations – mine is not thine. The law of contradiction closes in, imposing as law and against some incontrovertible experiences the exigencies of patriarchal authority and of private property. Thus there is the separation between right and wrong, good and bad. The one I must be and do, the other I must not. Yet the latter I often desire, the former I merely do, because I feel overwhelmingly compelled. Hence my ambivalent feelings towards right and wrong, good and evil, my ever-threatened belief that I am right-good against you or him or them. (This is of incontrovertible sociological import, for on this ambivalence of feeling are based the efforts of demagogues, educators, advertisers, of the entertainment industry and the popular – and not so popular – press.) The final separation is that between controller and controlled. This separates everything I see, hear, smell, touch, taste and feel, everything I know and am and which has to be controlled – why? – from that intangible, that 'nothing', as Sartre calls it, which I do not know, because it is the knower or merely the knowing which is to be in control.

It remains problematical whether this separation is characteristic of modern European society only or of civilization in general. Scientific thinking takes it *ad absurdum* but also makes it absurdly effective. Yet Eastern thinking seems to have striven for it with similar success if in a different manner. Horkheimer-Adorno (1969) make Hebrew monotheism responsible for the rule of 'nothing' over everything, of the invisible Yahweh over heaven and earth. Greek philosophy with its lust for abstractions can be cited, possibly with better justification. For the Yahweh of the prophets remained more immediately concerned with the full bodily being and doing of his subjects than the God of Plato and his successors. Be this as it may, the isolation of the intellect, its undisputed authority over that which it 'intellects', has reached critical proportions, certainly in the West. Freud's insights challenge us to question this state of affairs. For whatever else Freud's psyche – that mythological trinity of super-ego, ego and id – may represent and incorporate, it certainly marks a break with European philosophical preconceptions concerning the status of and the relationship between mind and body. Freud could by-pass these preconceptions so easily, because he spoke, or so he thought, as scientist, not as philosopher. However science is a direct offspring of religious and metaphysical thought-forms. It not only enshrines their preconceptions but made some of them axiomatic and unassailable. Freud's understanding of the psyche slipped, unnoticed by himself, through our universally accepted web of conceptualizations in which academicism is still totally enmeshed. This could explain why scientists have on the whole refused to acknowledge him as a scientist. From their point of view they are right. For science had absolutized the separation of mind from body, the control from that which is to be controlled – in whose interest? – of the observation from the observed, even where the observed is the observer's own body or psyche, or – final irony – mind. Science has virtually defined itself as this absolutization.

Freud understands the psyche as the complete inter-dependence of body and mind. The psyche is the sphere in which body and mind interact and inter-penetrate each other, and where they can be seen to do this. And this sphere is our being, our 'reality'. Once more language proves inadequate for what has to be said. It has been shaped by those preconceptions which the new insights could transcend, *aufheben*. Perhaps these insights can be expressed more directly in Hebrew or Hopi. They certainly call for articulation, need to find their own language. For language, our social and therefore personal habitat – according to Heidegger 'the house of being' – can keep us in ignorance of that part of our being for which it has as yet made no provisions. Hence Freud's insights sometimes strain terminologies beyond their limits. They compel him to mix topology, myth, anthropology, politics and literature, the abstract and the concrete. Beyond that he confounds matters by mixing all those loaned concepts and images with technical terms taken from medicine and neurology, and thus transposing the lot into some kind of mechanistic, positivistic science. This may explain Freud's own inability to follow his insights across the conceptual barriers. Its final if inevitable irony is that today psycho-analysis is a separate discipline.

How can it be conveyed, for example, that the id or the unconscious is neither a bodily nor a mental object, not something which one day, so even Freud hoped, could be expressed in neurological or even chemical terms? It is not an object at all, not a *Gegenstand*, something that stands over against me, for that presupposes the division of body and mind which the id denies. At times Freud calls it a system and uses the abbreviation ucs. – *ubw.* – for it. As a word it is a concept embedded in an idiosyncratic yet public universe of discourse. What does it refer to? What is the id? Now philosophy constitutes its own universe of discourse. All its references to something apparently outside this universe are in turn integrated into it. For science the relationship between its universes of discourse and the 'what' they refer to remains unproblematical by definition: it 'works' or it does not. Even dysfunction does not make the relationship problematical. It merely calls for change of method or hypothesis. Psycho-analysis is neither science nor philosophy, in spite of Freud's protestations. It is vitally and essentially interested in the 'what' it refers to, for this 'what' is a psyche which it does not and should not wish to manipulate, which it can only explore. Unlike the so-called *data* of science or philosophy which really are *facta* – *Tatsachen* or matters of action – the other psyche is a *datum*, it is given to the analyst, not constituted, not even reconstituted, by him. It remains the given over against all conceptualizations and reconstitutions in the analyst's mind. Psycho-analysis knows that its 'what', the other psyche with its id, has the power to shape and distort the very concepts by means of which it is to be explored and that the observer's id has a similar power over the observer's psyche while he is observing. This will say that the separation between observer and observed is *aufgehoben*. No longer is either of them just controller or controlled. Unfortunately the consequent fluidity of the situation in which the analyst found himself and in which he could have rejoiced, since *panta rei*, frightened Freud. So by means of his ego concept, as against the id and its eery ally the super-ego, he tried to establish a kind of *status quo ante*. Yet he remained open-minded enough to admit that even the ego was invaded, and not merely for its destruction, by forces which blur the outlines of authority, of 'law and order' (cf. Adorno, 1970, pp. 263–9).

Libido is another term which points towards a state of affairs where body and mind are fused even in the process of sorting each other out, where the observer is involved, interested, in that which he is observing (*inter-esse* means: to be with, in the middle of, to inter-be). Freud's understanding of sex, so close to that of libido, of full human *inter-esse*, has often been misunderstood, perhaps because sex, for Freud, is neither of the body nor of the mind, neither in the head nor in the genitals. It is the vectorized desire of the whole being, the wholly humanized being (cf. Marx, 1961E, pp. 100–1). Freud's sex or libido is precisely that force or fluid which makes body and mind function together in an infinite variety of ways, from the ascetic's discipline to the lovers' consummation, from parental repression to tyranny and mass destruction. It is the *inter-esse* or inter-essence of body and mind.

Our part-understanding and part-misunderstanding of libido have made the connections between violence and vital forms of sexual non-fulfilment an intellectual commonplace. It may be that Freud himself here confused the issue. In his later days he posited a death instinct to explain the persistence of the destructive tendencies in man. As if the persistent and increasing frustrations which our form of civilization has so far made inevitable, which Freud knew well enough, were not sufficient explanation. And, in a way, they are not. For the question remains: What compels men again and again to produce and reproduce conditions which frustrate him? Biological necessities and societal needs have not been established as in-controvertible answers. From our point of view it would be interesting to ask: Was Freud's belief in *thanatos* as the complement of *eros* an old man's gesture of resignation? Was his own approaching death insisting? Was the burden of hopefulness implied in the acceptance of erotic libido as the one and only driving force proving too heavy for a rational, sophisticated, slightly cynical and more than slightly pessimistic Viennese Jew? Was he panicked by the thought that the unreserved acknowledgment of what he called the libido would question civilization even more deeply than he had allowed? Perhaps it was easier to resign oneself to the growing wave of destruction that was rising in the heart of Europe, if one could understand it as inevitable.

Freud's earlier libidinal theories were too prophetic for such resignation. They would have continued – as Wilhelm Reich did – to probe the abysmal depths of non-fulfilment as the source of the aggressive tide. We recall the primal experience of undifferentiation and how it continues to underlie and to energize our inevitable unifying, totalizing, anthropomorphizing efforts. Positively it breaks through, if only occasionally, as religious, mystic, poetic vision, more often as 'falling in love'. Freud called it the oceanic feeling and insisted that he lacked it. I believe he experienced it in a peculiarly Jewish fashion: as an enormous drive towards final, rational unification which would not exclude the particular, the individual. The experience manifests itself in other absorbing passions, in orgiastic, communal Dionysian ecstasies for which most non-puritanical societies have made allowances. It gives to our passions their universalizing powers and urges which disregard all distinctions. It fills them with intimations of omnipotence.

Hence passion within our civilization is tragic and the theme of tragedy. At times of Dionysian abandon it can break through all conventional barriers and lets a whole community revel in limitless, regressive power. For as society becomes increasingly divided and specialized, it increasingly inhibits the universalizing energies, until they find outlet only in schizoid states or in schizophrenia, in the absolutization of fragmented and split-off areas of thinking or feeling. Until recently society has managed to cope with these individual psychotic states by means of what Rieff calls 'commitment therapies', Durkheim its creative powers: by the creation and maintenance of communal loyalties to family, tribe, state, institution or creed (Rieff, 1966; cf. Mitscherlich, 1969, Laing, 1964a,b, 1970b). Today these therapies no longer seem to be effective or, when used at all, manifest themselves as political, religious, racial fanaticism. For the first time in history man has to learn to cope with the psychic disturbance caused by the constraints of civilization on the personal level, since he can no longer, without fatal consequences, feed them back into the repressive mechanism.

Is a more rewarding task imaginable for sociology post-Auschwitz than the investigation of the roots of libidinal frustration and inhibition in the light of Freud's suggestions and insights? To ask whether his death instinct is a reasonable, necessary, desirable, hopeful hypothesis? Or whether his earlier understanding of libido points to a more adequate because more hopeful approach? And hopefulness, as I believe Bloch has proved to the point where the burden of disproof lies on his opponents, is a constitutive and essential ingredient of any investigation of human affairs as it is an integral part of the human condition and 'reality'. Its putative absence does not denote impartiality or objectivity. It simply changes the character of the investigation. It makes it a hopeless one. Our investigations might prove fruitful to the extent to which they do not aspire to be precise.

Freud was able to see the psyche as he did, because of his patient persistence and consistency. He merely saw what others had seen before him. But he accepted the logic of what he was seeing – unlike those who used logic to obscure what they had seen. *All experience is psychic*, reason, intellect, experience, knowledge, merely representatives of that psychic constituency. The experience of my body, its pain, weariness, pleasure, ecstasy, is as irreducibly psychic as that of my most abstract thoughts. My awareness of my body and all its manifestations is psychic. So is the interest in as well as the solving of intellectual problems. The distinction is not between body and psyche, but, within the psyche, between body-experience and thought-experiences, between two kinds of phantasy. My experience of others, their bodies, gestures, expressions, weightiness, smell, is as psychic and immediately significant, if in a different manner, as my understanding of their words and thoughts – though I may at times misinterpret it. My understanding of their thoughts and feelings, my trying to understand them for what they are and how they are 'meant', fitting them into my experiential patterns, is a psychic activity and experience (cf. Simmel, 1922, pp. 287–8). Nor is my experience of others separable from the more or less subtle, greater or smaller awareness of myself as embodied, as body among bodies, as somebody, as a man among men, as man before woman, as father, teacher, child. It may be that the barrenness of much academic discourse here is due to the forgetfulness of our psychic structure within which the insulation of the intellect and the separation of inner and outer is an arbitrary and, unless understood as such, a costly procedure. (Within this context one might wish to find out in how far the modern belief that we think with our brain is at least partially a superstition. I am not doubting the chemico-mechanico-electrical functioning of the brain as the central exchange of all sensory and motor impetuses. But as the telephone exchange does not conduct but transmits conversation, can we be sure, and why and how, that the brain functions in a totally different fashion in relation to the total web of intercourse and inter-penetration which is our psychic reality?) My abstract thoughts, as well as my thoughts and feelings concerning others and elicited by them, are inspired, tinged or warped by my body-functions as these are reflected or repressed in psychic awareness. My abstract thoughts can enhance, reduce or desperately impair my body-functions.

Furthermore we recall that Freud's psyche is not merely the fusion of mind and body, you and I, but of past and present. Even that is not put radically enough. Within the psychic totality and unity, we can distinguish between mind and body, past and present, you and me, only for reasons of convenience. The psychic unity is primary, all distinctions secondary. They are problematical, not it. My experience of myself and others is still also my babyhood experiencing, modified but never eradicated by later experiences and interpretations. And the baby is much more obviously related to the body and its needs, fears, desires and functions (cf. Klein, 1959; Erikson, 1965, pp. 66–91). These functionings in turn, as well as the baby's gesturings, are the expression, the embodiment of needs, fears, desires which, originally, as much produced this gesturing body as it in turn produces them. To claim priority for either body or desire is metaphysics, possibly bad metaphysics.

Clinical experiments, even by psychologists, seem to have established by now that a baby's passions, even the passion for learning, are utterly disproportionate to his size and to the actual capacity of the intellective part of his psyche. He experiences, knows, understands, much more than he can conceptualize and express, than he will ever be able to articulate adequately. If he is too sensitive, he might go mad with the effort of finding words for what he knows and what seems to require communication most urgently. More likely societal pressures will gradually manage to desensitize him, until his comprehension has shrunk to the conventions of grammar, vocabulary and logic (Horkheimer-Adorno, 1969, p. 274; cf. Simmel, 1911, pp. 296f). Nevertheless the growing child carries into adulthood disproportionate fears, hopes, loves and inarticulable longings and knowledge. These are always present. They are not only his, they are he. They can be denied, deflected, driven underground, and to that extent they may distort and cripple him. They will certainly, if only partially, become rationalized; and the fury of the rationalized drives will turn against those that escaped or resisted rationalization.

Yet these drives will never lose their subterranean power, almost amounting to omnipotence in subconscious phantasies, and in as far as they remain unexpressed, they will retain this quality of impotent omnipotence. Reason will remain extraneous to them, epiphenomenal, a will-o'-the-wisp. It may take its revenge, as in scientific or philosophical thought, and interpret its very dysfunction in turn as omnipotence, mistaking their phantasied powers for its own. (This constitutes the power of rationalization in the diverse senses of the term.) The divorce of the rational from its psychic reality or base gives to reason an appearance of freedom which is no more than free-wheeling and, like all free-wheeling, is bound to its own impetus. Rationalism interprets such bondage as authority, the authority of the juggernaut. *Vernunft*, which implies wisdom and understanding, remains the accomplice of rationalism, as long as it does not renounce pretensions of mastery and authority. But if it did, would it then become, as it fears, the servant of chaotic drives? Or is it possible that where the psyche is accepted in its totality a situation might gradually emerge in which terms like mastery and service are no longer applicable? Who can be certain that it is not our blind and isolated five-thousand-year-old rationality which makes us apprehend the relaxation of its rule as chaos? To think and act in the light of this possible belief requires hope. To deny or ignore

B*

this possibility in the name of science and objectivity expresses not impartiality but hopelessness (Bloch, 1970, Second Part).

Note   The power of our early experiences is both a danger and a hope. The danger is obvious and Freud himself pointed it out. Denied and deflected, as is almost invariably their fate in our society, the libidinal drives will inject their disproportionate passions, now turned to virulence, into whatever outlets society creates or permits. Worst of all, they will turn in upon themselves. Their internecine struggles will preserve 'law and order' by depleting and sickening the man whom 'law and order' are designed to protect. They will convince him that there is no health in him – and still less in 'them'.

Freud did not see with equal clarity the hopefulness inherent in the powers of early experiencing. Yet because of them there is hope in the possibility of understanding. Parents may be able to learn actually to make fewer disastrous mistakes or how to undo or balance those they have made. Thus the possibilities of a fuller humanity become embodied in a human, emotive situation in which idea and desire may yet learn to work together. There is also hope in this: that our early experience, if recognized and permitted to speak for itself, however fragmentarily, might act as an integrating force, a reconciler of desires and resources, a humanizer of public and personal endeavours. In the light of those early, constitutive experiences we may begin to ask again: How much of what we now work and fight for do we really want? How much does that for which we now are labouring stand in the way of what we desire?

Beyond this there is hope in the fact that all men pass through comparable experiences, that their very individuality is rooted in them. The everyday and everywhere constellation of mother-father-child-siblings should open up and keep open channels of communication and communion, as we learn to acknowledge it as our source. It is possible that only repressed libido becomes virulent and creates barriers and barricades. Where its flow is not too badly impeded, men may come to recognize their interdependence as underlying and nourishing rather than as contradicting their differentiation (Auerbach, 1957, last chapter). For underneath all distinctions and separations between mind and body, I and thou, mine and thine, fact and fiction, lies the early experience of totality which relativizes them all. This is revealed in times of crisis. It often makes times of crisis ecstatic. Can we reach ecstasy without crisis?

2   *The individual and society*

Just as psycho-analysis points to possibilities of understanding human nature as a body-mind continuum, so it can transform some problems and obviate others concerning the individual's relations to and within society. We already saw how our primal experience of undifferentiation includes the other – mother, father, brother, sister – and begins to distinguish the other as other, before the I becomes aware of itself as self. We noticed that certain problems of human interrelation arise only once we have separated body and mind. When and how do bodies interact? How minds? How can minds know whether or when or how or why bodies interact? How is the mind's ruling translated into motor response? How can I know you know I know? (Laing, 1970a). There is a comic pathos about the millennia-old debate between men who at times seem to have been able to relate to each other outside their debate.

However, bodies cannot interact or interrelate. They can only impinge upon each other with greater or lesser force. Such force can be apprehended and measured only by minds. Even in sexual intercourse or in a wrestling match the interaction is not between bodies but between persons. Can one speak of the interaction of minds? It seems a frigid affair. And of course, the problems as to how an embodied mind can get in touch with another embodied mind proliferate endlessly. Such problems disappear, though others may arise, when we take our departure from the psyche, the *nous-soma* sphere, in which all our experiences are unified at least as experiences.[4] The psyche knows reality primarily as totality. All differentiation is a slow process of discrimination, of getting acquainted with particular things and persons, with persons and things in their particularity. It is also a continuous fissuring of totality. It leaves the psyche with a more or less manageable fragmentation in which neither inner nor outer, neither body nor mind, neither I nor thou, have any but the most arbitrary priority. Is my self-awareness a reflection of my awareness of my mother as a self? Do I become aware of my mother as a self only when separation, helplessness, desolation, have made me experience my isolation as my selfhood? These are hen-or-egg questions. They start from preconceptions which our attempted understanding of psychic actuality has *aufgehoben* – at least for the time being and for the sake of further questioning.

The psyche is the meeting point of the individual and society. It is not a place where I and you meet, it is the actuality constituted by such meetings. The psyche is the mediator between the individual and society in both directions via operations summed up as 'projection' and 'introjection'. These can be understood as functioning in a rather mechanical manner, as Freud himself was sometimes tempted to understand them. That is the scientific way of looking at the evidence, i.e. one that has pre-judged the issue. It contradicts Freud's own insights which grew out of encounters between persons

31

(Habermas, 1969, pp. 277–80, 319, 330). Aspects of a multitude of such encounters were condensed into the auxiliary concepts of introjection and projection. These stood as ciphers for two immensely complicated and individuated processes of receiving and handing on the most complex and interdependent achievements of civilization and, beyond that, of our humanity, at least to the degree to which we have come to know it up to date. To interpret such processes as mechanistic is a high-handed procedure, certainly not warranted by the evidence. Not only is the evidence not yet sufficient, it can never be sufficient, for the observer here is essentially as much part as judge of the evidence. His understanding is as totally an interplay of introjection and projection as that of his subjects and subsists in a dynamic inter-relation and inter-penetration with them. To put it crudely, the conversation with them is the judgment over his understanding of them and of himself, not his intellect the judge over the conversation. The intercourse, not the intellect detached from it, constitutes understanding.

3 Cutting across old distinctions

Dilthey had tried, over and again, to trace the philosophical development which led from metaphysics to epistemology. In German there are two words for the latter: *Erkenntnistheorie* and *Erkenntniskritik*. The first is circumscribed by Kant's question: 'What can I know?' The second by the further question: 'How can I know I know? How can I be sure?' In all his effort to lay scientific foundations for the *Geisteswissenschaften*, Dilthey never forgot those questions altogether. Simmel remained preoccupied with epistemological questions. They never proved particularly fruitful for his sociology. The same can be said about Scheler and Tröltsch. Weber, we saw, cut the Gordian knot. He ruthlessly shelved *erkenntniskritische* doubts in the name of science. The justification of such a procedure depends on the acceptance of the *Geisteswissenschaften* as analogous to the natural sciences. For in them, as Husserl asserts, dogmatism is not only justified but necessary. Weber's attitude reflects the summons of the day. For the successes of the natural sciences, which seem to demonstrate just how well one can get on without epistemology, have driven it not only out of the laboratories, but out of the philosophy departments – except as an historical study. Only now it is becoming increasingly obvious to us that the self-regulating acceleration of science-technology-industry is causing intolerable and imponderable strains and stresses in the individual psyche, to the extent that it has become measurable in terms of lost working hours and the percentage of hospital beds. Success, efficiency, the 'it works', no longer inevitably serves as an ultimate criterion, at least not for all. The question as to what could or should take its place raises itself, practically and epistemologically, by psychic disturbances, the loss of 'objectivity', i.e. of the feasibility of commitment therapies, by the breakdown in interpersonal relations, by a general disorientation prevailing throughout society (Habermas, 1967, 1969). *Erkenntnis-kritische* questions are being raised now, because an increasing number of thinking people experience their situation within the society which scientific-technical successes have created as intolerable.

It is significant that Freud made his contribution to epistemology as a doctor who was confronted by its problems in the *Gestalt* of the patient whom society seemed to have sickened. As a thinker he remained a positivist (Habermas, 1969, pp. 271f). As doctor his understanding of the psyche transformed the epistemological problem. He saw the total interdependence of knowledge and interest in quite a new way (Habermas, 1969, p. 352; also ch. 12, *passim*). His understanding of interest is far wider than that of, for example, Pareto or of the economists; wider than Weber's, for it includes the author's and scholar's interest in his work, the author's and his subjects' unconscious as well as conscious interests. Especially *vis-à-vis* the economists it should be stressed that the particularly powerful unconscious interests are rarely, if ever, economical, for to the child money was meaningless. What Freud understood as interest is closer to Schopenhauer and Nietzsche's 'will'. Yet in his never-ending attempts to understand and define it, he is less burdened by preconceptions than either. (There are subterranean links between his and Marx's apprehension of interest. As neither of them was aware of the full implications of his understanding, it might prove hard to trace the connections, but possibly worth while.)

Freud's view of the psyche enables us, though it did not yet enable him, to go beyond many of the old questions concerning priority and authority: What is cause and what is effect? What rules and overrules what in the psyche? These reflect the authoritarian status structure of patriarchal society. His view points, beyond his own hopes and fears, to non-patriarchal, non-authoritarian individual and communal possibilities (cf. Mitscherlich, 1969). In a similar way the interdependence of reason and interest must be understood psychically, organically. Reason is not the tool of interest. That was implied by Fichte's omnipotent 'I', by Hegel's *List*, cunning. It was proclaimed despondently by Schopenhauer, exultingly by Nietzsche. Nor, on the other hand, is interest inspired by reason. That belief made strange bed-fellows of the Scholastics, Descartes, Voltaire and the economists. Nor are interest and reason tied together like Goya's despairing couple, as Kant saw it from the Prussian, puritan pinnacle of a not yet fully experienced schizophrenia. Interest and reason –

and once again language fails us, because it encapsulates pre-Freudian preconceptions – are inter-penetrating. Reason is always interested. Interest is always reasonable, no matter how fine or how gross personal and communal distortions of either reason or interest may be. They even have these distortions in common. Reasonable interest is merely the active, discernible aspect of our psyche, our being, which in turn is rooted in and symbiotically contained by its *Umwelt*, its surrounding world.

Such an approach to reason and reality transposes the *erkenntnis-kritischen* problems for all kinds of reasons. Here we are interested in one: *Erkenntniskritik* of the modern kind came into being as a consequence of the deification of reason in the form of rationalism and rationalization. It was the successor of the theodicy. As the latter was intended to justify the ways of God to man, so epistemology was to justify the often equally inscrutable ways of reason and rationalization. Only when reason has taken the place of divinity and of faith, of totem and taboo, when, like God, it becomes both the final paradigm and the final arbiter, does it require and produce the kind of vindication epistemology supplies. (In the intellect the law of supply and demand not only obtains, but reveals that the twain are as interdependent as reason and interest.) Reason now must buttress its authority in a twofold manner: it must prove that it knows what it knows. It must show that what it knows it knows certainly. It is obvious that metaphysical and religious longings have taken shelter here. The irony of the situation is this: reason is judge, prosecutor, counsel for the defence, plaintiff, defendant, jury and whatever audience has been admitted to the court. It is hard to see before whom it needs to be vindicated.

Perhaps epistemology is also a mirroring of a peculiar societal state of affairs. A new ruling or managing class without traditional authority has just begun to usurp that authority as a consequence of the success of its rationalism and its rationalizations. The new class is not yet secure and powerful enough, either politically or psycho-logically and morally, to be able to do without attempts at self-vindication. Yet it can no longer defend its position along traditional lines, having overthrown that tradition. So it must try to justify itself and its authority in terms of that power which gained authority for it and constitutes its authority: rationalism and rationalization. It had to prove that its authority was rational. Moreover it had to establish its authority as ultimate, partly because the authority it had just transplanted had claimed ultimacy, partly because it so recently had proved it not be ultimate. It had to demonstrate that its rational authority was established beyond reasonable doubt. So the new class's methods of argumentation reflected the method which had gained it the power the arguments were to justify as just: rationalization for rationalization's sake. Or, as it was to be put more briefly: nothing succeeds like success.

As capitalism became consolidated in the very psyche of Western man, epistemology gave way to positivism: success for the sake of success, in order to succeed. Positivism or scientism, although in its *naiveté* it goes back to well before Kant or even Hume, to Locke, Hobbes, Descartes, Bacon, is nevertheless a post-epistemological phenomenon. It ossified the proof which epistemology had been intending to supply without actually doing it. Epistemology was rationalism's court-poet, court-jester and public relations officer. Positivism became its executioner, prison and asylum manager.

Now in the psyche, as in the light of Freud's insights we have come to understand it, rationality does not rule. Its interests, are not supreme nor are they the same as those of the psyche as a whole. When reason pretends to such supremacy it becomes rationalization. In the psyche rationality is part or aspect of the whole. It pervades all psychic manifestations and is pervaded by all of them. It is the rhythm without which there is no music and which apart from the music is nothing. It is form, not matter. And matter, as the individual, is what matters, yet cannot matter apart from reason. Such reason needs no vindication. It does not claim to know, certainly not to know certainly. It tries, again and again, to understand. It moves, yet is not supremely interested in watching its own movements. It suspects that such watching would merely be another form of movement and, besides, it is interested in everything except itself. In a utopian perspective we might come to see how such an understanding of reason, *Erkenntnis*, could point towards that genuine interdependence and interpenetration in the individual and in society, of the individual and society, which the feudal theologians had once thought to have established (cf. Borkenau, 1934).

4   *Inter-subjective exploration*

The enthronement of reason reflected, rather unreflectingly, the growing rationalization of society, its totalization. Rationalization meant and means manipulation, power, extension of the power of manipulation, ultimately even over the manipulator himself. It was a peculiar twist of the rationalization progress that its successes charmed the manipulators into the belief that all would be well, if only men, including themselves, could simply become part of that which was so successfully manipulated.

Rationalization means above all efficient manipulation, more manipulative manipulation, more manipulable rationality, more rational manipulation. It was the task of reason to preside over this circle. *Erkenntniskritik* represents the period of reason's qualms, its internal if belated struggles of conscience. Positivism marks reason's acquiescence masked as victory (cf. Heidegger, 1954, *Die Frage nach der Technik*). In his *Theorie und Praxis* (1967) Habermas analyses the dangers of this situation (for example, pp. 22, 30, 246–51). In *Erkenntnis und Interesse* (1969) he shows how Freud's understanding points towards an exit, though the master himself did not make for it (chs 10–12). All Freud's theories – except for his more ambitious but also more playful excursions into anthropology and religion – grew out of, and are meant to define, describe and explicate, experiences gained in personal encounters. True, these were en-counters between doctor and patient, though of a peculiar kind. But Freud consciously and conscientiously, and in spite of many backslidings, tried to keep any elements of manipulation out of them. Admittedly he did so, because he regretfully believed he could not yet do better. He was enough of a positivist to hope for the time when drugs, i.e. manipulation, would do the trick and would do it better. Nevertheless, in the meantime he did not approach the psyche of the patient which is the patient, as the surgeon would approach his body, the psychologist or psychiatrist his mind or brain (cf. Laing, 1968, pp. 13–35). He met the analysand, even if more than half-way.

It was of the very essence of the meeting that the analyst remained Socratic, midwifely. He was wholly involved in this encounter, as one who had everything to learn from it and in it; though all his wisdom, knowledge, experience, sympathy, gained from previous encounters, were to be at the analysand's disposal. They were not to be imposed upon him. On the contrary, Freud discovered how explanation, interpretation, rationalization, would merely drive further underground that which they intended to bring into the open, how they would be used as a further defence. So the analyst's experience was simply to be 'there', available, to be used by the analysand or not, as, when and how he saw fit. It was to be deployed in such a way that, far from hampering the analysand's inner or outer movements, it created extra space for him, extra human, meaningful space. The analyst would not and could not do anything for the analysand. Or one could say: his being there was his doing, as long as it was not obstructed by any doing. Through the analyst's being and being there with the other, an opportunity was created for the analysand – and, of course, for the analyst – to discover whatever could and had to be discovered, uncovered, because it was there, but was there in a depleting instead of an invigorating fashion. Only when the analysand had grasped the opportunity could the analyst's former experiences serve as interpretations. Yet even then it had to be left to the former to decide whether or not to accept them. No 'good' was done by any amount of proof that the analyst's interpretation was 'true', for in this situation proof is revealed as compulsion and violation. The analyst in turn will let himself be guided by the analysand's responses and discoveries. He will not do this as father, teacher, expert, who may, out of the security of his superior knowledge, yield temporarily to childish ignorance and perversity. For he recognizes that the analysand's discoveries, always unique in one aspect or another, are the source of his own; as he acknowledges that his accumulated experiences as analyst reflect the discoveries of the analysed to the extent to which he had been able to listen to them without preconceptions.

In the analysis situation we see reason at work, and that which is at work in it is reason. It is a reason trained by positivistic discipline, but imbued with qualities, and open to suggestions, intimations, influences, which one has long since been taught to think of as contrary to reason, as irrational. We see non-manipulative reason at work in an intentional healing process, i.e. in a purposeful situation. The purpose is healing, making whole, or at least a little less unwholesome. At times it seems to have been achieved, and in such a case the analyst as well as the analysand has profited. (Now healing is proof or better than proof, at least for the sufferer, though even this our rationalistic and economic thought-forms make us forget.) We see reason at work beyond rationalization and manipulation, beyond the possibility of or the need for proof or ultimate verification – which can only be understood as death by mortals. It is at work between subject and subject, as against its exercise by a subject on an object. We cannot say with certainty, 'it works'. It cannot be proved that it heals. But it hints at possibilities of healing and thus raises questions concerning our present state of wholeness which science as yet and by definition has excluded from its universe of discourse. (Cf. 'We feel that, even when all possible scientific questions have been answered, our life problems have not yet been touched.' Wittgenstein, *Tractatus*, 1961 edn., 6, 52.)

Finally, the kind of reason we see at work in the analysis situation is, of course, no more nor less than a refinement and sharpening of the reason which is at work in our living, loving, believing. This reason has been so persistently neglected and scorned by logic and science that we dare no longer exercise it beyond those private areas where, as a matter of fact, we are also forgetting how to use it. In analysis it is both exercised and refined in the process, which even raises the hope that its healing qualities may filter back into the ordinary day-by-day thinking and thinking together, living and living together, where it had belonged once, yet had never been fully appreciated, before it was almost totally forgotten (cf. M. Buber, *I and Thou, Between Man and Man*).

5 *Patterns of discovery*

Human 'reality' is communication, communion, intercoursing. Once again words prove inadequate. For us 'communication' means bringing together, linking, bridging, what is fundamentally separate. The word – like most words – has taken into itself certain long-standing preconceptions which trigger off their own associations. The general constraints of civilization broke many older ties and imposed new ones. But the most peculiar and stringent demands of bourgeois capitalism have created such a fossilized atomization that today it is almost impossible to imagine that the prevailing state of individual isolation and privatization is not the fundamental human condition (cf. Borkenau, 1934, on Pascal). It is even harder to imagine what another state of humanness could be. One has to go far back into the past or far from European civilization to get glimpses of different possibilities which are not just variations on the same theme. And none of those possibilities could ever again become ours.

Now according to Freudian preconceptions as understood by, for example, Marcuse, such a going-back is precisely what psycho-analysis enables us to do. It helps us remember, recollect, relive, the past which lies beyond or before the total constraints of civilization. Like Freud, Marcuse believes the ontogenetic and the phylogenetic to be analogous, that 'our' as well as 'my' past has its roots in the undifferentiated (Marcuse, 1969, p. 34). *Therefore: communication or communion does not so much establish as re-establish, try to re-establish, a primal at-one-ment between I and Thou, I and it. Its motive and emotive power lies in this: it takes us closer to, rather than further from, our primal experience which is our primal 'reality' or, rather, that unutterable meta-reality against which we measure, whether we know it or not, the 'realness' of any 'reality'.*

Now if there be any substance to such contentions, if they reflect, no matter how inadequately as yet, the structure of our experiencing, however thoroughly that has been repressed or warped by the summonses of the day, then much of our thinking may have to be re-thought. New thought-forms, new ways of thinking, a new quality of thoughtfulness – Heidegger calls it *Besinnung* or re-orientation – may be needed to do justice to the changed situation which a new understanding of our psychic reality is bound to con-stitute. Our thinking is one of the aspects of our inter-subjectivity, our mutual inter-penetration – the early Greek theologians' des-cription of the relationship within the Holy Trinity. As such it will have to become unreservedly dialectical and dialogic. This not only in the Hegel-Marxian sense or that of Adorno's negative dialectics; but in the sense which is given to it in the analytical situation. Within such inter-penetration, intercoursing, there can be no certainties, only ever-shifting and changing patterns of mutuality, of understanding and misunderstanding – which two are inseparable – of clarity and confusion. The better part of thinking will be in listening, in making room for the other in such a way that he/she in his/her totality – in his need to talk and be talked to, with his thoughts and his discrepancies between thoughts and being, in his truth and distortion – may be contained by me as I would wish to be contained by him or her. Thus the psycho-analytical practice, the fountainhead of all its theories and insights, could become exemplary not only for ordinary human conversation and intercourse, but for all research, certainly within the social sciences, the *Geisteswissenschaften*.

Post-Freudian contributions

Habermas discusses Freud's ideas, their sociological and epistemological significance, within the context of his unbroken preoccupation with interrelated problems raised by society, especially by our late, almost post-bourgeois, capitalist society. In Marxian terms one might say they are problems raised by the peculiar form of our division of labour. They centre round the tensions between private and public, theory and practice, reason and interest (Habermas, 1965, 1967, 1969). Within this context he understands the Freudian approach as a possible resolution, not, of course, of the conflict itself, but of some fundamental difficulties created by our misunderstanding of it. Some of these difficulties, so Habermas argues, were created by the man who helped us to understand the nature of societal conflicts more deeply than ever before. Marx had not been able to explain satisfactorily the genesis of those conflicts. This was achieved by Freud, precisely because he started from the structure of the psyche as a paradigm not only of individual but of communal experience, because he broke through the body-mind and therefore through the individual-society division. He understood the conflict, any conflict, as the expression of a failure in communication, a distortion of all communication. And this was the consequence, on the personal and communal level, of the break between reason and that which it reasons about or with, as also of the break between the ego and the id, which the constraints of civilization have brought about (1969, pp. 277–80, 341–2, 335–6; also 262–9). This enabled Freud to understand institutions as analogous to neuroses, as misdirected defensive organizations, as arbitrary and premature fossilizations, as inadequate responses to 'reality' – which, as we said before, is communication and communion.

Marcuse, in *Eros and Civilization*, embarked on a depth exploration of Freudian insights in their social, political and economical implications. As a Hegelian Marxist who cannot help thinking in terms of 'mankind', 'history', 'civilization', 'revolution', he cannot easily be accused of psychologism. His work is therefore another instance of the suggestiveness of Freudian ideas. In him too we find that confluence of Marxian interpretations of society with Freudian interpretations of the psyche, and are helped to appreciate how they complement and interpret each other. While psycho-analysis can elucidate societal distortions which Marxism cannot, Marxism can illuminate the depth to which even psycho-analysis – and analyst – is conditioned by the very distortions it has helped to uncover and to understand. Once more we have reached a point where it becomes clear that the conversation between the individual and society, between psychology and sociology, may and must continue.

Marcuse is most suggestive in what he says about remembering. He uses the word for that particular and usually repressed form of remembering which psycho-analysis has made available. This takes us into very early childhood, back to the time before civilizatory constraints became introjected, before they became total. For Marcuse as for Freud re-membering, *er-innern*, means more than 'having memories of'. It has a Hegelian as well as Freudian fulness. It is a reconstitution here of the 'reality' which lies before, underlies and underpins all that which we have been constrained to accept as the only 'reality'. Such re-membering radically questions our understanding of reality. Here it is Hegel and Freud who illuminate each other and possibly us. We can see the analytical act of remembering in its cosmic implications. We can see Hegel's universal spirit as being rooted in the individual psyche, yet in such a way that the psyche explains the spirit as much as the spirit the psyche (cf. Laing, 1965, 1970b).

Adorno is the most complex and at times almost perversely complicated thinker of the Frankfurt School (Lichtheim, 1971, 'Adorno'). It is as if he really tried to do in and with his writing what I should love to be able to do and what Lévi-Strauss wished to do, because he believed it would enable him to demonstrate the validity of his myth analysis, namely, to put everything in three dimensions. Words, if it were possible, would be written on transparent screens. These would be hung behind each other, in as many layers as required, a multiple palimpsest with none of the underlying script erased. Words and sentences would not only follow each other. One could see through them and their interstices to other words and sentences. All these super-imposed statements would cross-interpret each other, supplement and contradict each other at one and the same time. Such is Adorno's method, certainly his intention. In his mind German philosophy and world literature, Marx and Freud, music and sociology, are at work together purposefully and, at times, purposefully at cross-purposes. In interpreting each other they are modifying each other. And all the time these diverse approaches in their interplay are shown up in all their contradictoriness to emphasize that no thinking, no conceptualization, can do justice to the particular, the individual; and that nevertheless we have to pass through that contradictoriness in order to arrive at the individual, since he has been buried under millennia of conceptualizations (1962, 1970).

With Horkheimer, Adorno is aware of how easily concepts can be used like magic, how negative therefore any dialectics has to be to prevent new conceptualizations from taking the place of the old, i.e. he carries Freud's practice into philosophizing and sociologizing, he understands human understanding to subsist in the intercourse of and with ideas, not in the fixing of one idea rather than another as 'truth'.

Mannheim, as the representative of the sociology of knowledge, was much attacked by Frankfurters and Marxists for his relativism – and for Germans the problems of relativism have remained serious. These attacks are not altogether justified. Mannheim had made a very valiant attempt to say something about the nature of truth in his *Ideology and Utopia*, especially in as far as it functions in society and thus presents a problem for sociology which cannot be expressed easily in a terminology designed to enshrine dissimilar assumptions about truth. His understanding of truth as fluid, as relational and not necessarily and for that reason relativistic, as neither fixed nor even dialectical in the academic sense, his contention that fluidity may be our 'truth', brings him also into the vicinity of Freudian insights, though he got there by a very different route.

It would be interesting to ask, it would require a Weber to attempt an answer, why Anglo-Saxons since Bacon, Hobbes and Locke never seem to have been seriously troubled by the problems of epistemology, though they are the problems of the individual in society, of social consciousness. They certainly were not troubled to the extent of their German colleagues, not even to that of Durkheim or Sartre, for example. Maybe British ambitions, imperial successes and activities, left them with little time and less inclination for other than administrative questions, questions of how best to manage a given situation which had to be managed because it was an imposition. As the situation seemed most satisfactory – Archbishop Tillotson of the late eighteenth century actually believed that the kingdom of God had come – there was no need to think about it or its causes and justifications. One only seeks causes and justifications for something one feels troubled about. The many who would not have found the situation quite so satisfactory had not yet been given a chance to make their thoughts known.

Thus the sciences, technology, most of all the social sciences, became quite naturally a part of the general managing and organizing. The far-reaching personal liberties of the few to whom the articulate belonged, or wished to belong, obviated epistemological and societal problems. Everyone did as he pleased within generally acceptable and fairly flexible conventions, within which even eccentrics could be accommodated and potential rebels could be treated like eccentrics. Some kind of mechanism, either of masked force, as in Hobbes, or of reciprocal automatic adjustment, as in Locke and, later on, in Bentham and Mill, would multiply individual strife into social harmony (cf. Habermas, 1965, pp. 117–25). Within the wealthy, sheltered ruling class, held together by an iron though barely openly-acknowledged purpose, such doctrine seemed to apply, and was reinforced by the successful few who managed to gain entry into it. One does not easily remember the violation of others on which the smooth functioning of the mechanism depended. By the time the situation of that ruling class had changed fundamentally, the habits of thought it had engendered had become ingrained. They proved as serviceable to the new, more fully democratic bureaucracy, as to the old.

W. James, G. H. Mead, C. S. Peirce etc., who each in his own way was led into the neighbourhood of our problems, always by-passed them. That precisely seemed to be the virtue of their pragmatism. It so obviously seemed to solve all sorts of problems by ignoring them, that there seemed to be no reason to bother. In this pragmatism clearly reflected the political and economic temper of the day with its motto, 'Let us get on with it', and with no-one to worry over the status of that 'it'. Thus the mythological, rugged individual of American society was imperceptibly but completely integrated into the most democratic-communal pursuit of *pragmata* (see Scheler, 1960, ch. '*Arbeit und Erkenntnis*'). Pragmatism was a virile form of utilitarianism and deaf to questions like Lessing's 'What is the use of use?'. One was simply and inevitably and thankfully part of a vast machinery for the production of utilities for the production of utilities for the. . . .

In *Mind, Self and Society*, Mead should have taken us to the very heart of our questioning. He does nothing of the kind. He shows sensitively and imaginatively how far a behaviouristic approach can be taken profitably. He makes no exorbitant claims for it, perhaps because his belief in it was too unshaken. Theoretically he leaves our questions open (Mead, 1967, pp. 268–9). Practically he ignores them, until they are forgotten. In a universe of symbolic interaction everything is immanent. This is pantheism without *theos*. Even the purposefulness of pragmatism has been left behind by now, its apparently pointing beyond itself without actually doing so. Now all things are what they are what they are. Bureaucracy is fully established and need only run itself. It needs no justification. It justifies. We are fully on the way to the consumer society where we shall learn to don and doff roles according to the summons of the day, for even work and academic and scientific work has become a purely consuming affair. The epistemological problem, the problem of social consciousness, has been dissolved into problems for advertisers, entertainers and, at times, demagogues.

In this chapter I have attempted to pose the problem once more.

2   Philosophical background

For most sociologists and social philosophers, we have seen, the
problems posed by the individual in and *vis-à-vis* society remained
peripheral. Only Freud's labours directly illuminated the area
where the organic relations between the individual and society are
constituted, where consciousness is socialized, where society becomes
conscious of itself, where social consciousness actually functions. It
was therefore important to stress that the others nevertheless posed
the problem through their activities and their existence as scholars,
as individuals who conducted their researches in an obvious attempt,
not necessarily admitted openly, to contribute to the self-understanding of society, if only academic society, which had shaped them
and their capacity and their tools of understanding. In this sense
any scientific work, but most of all that of the *Geisteswissenschaftler*,
raises questions of epistemology, even of metaphysics.

Many German sociological and socio-philosophical thinkers of
stature were aware, often oppressively so, of the philosophical
conundrums raised by their labours. They did not comprehend
these problems as aspects of the intricate and complex tensions
between man's individual and social reality (yet cf. Lukács, 1963,
1964). Nor had those philosophers done this who, from Plato to
Husserl, represent the academic canon and into whose controversies
German sociologists felt themselves drawn willy-nilly. Perhaps
because *individuum est ineffabile* philosophy has extradited him.
Montaigne, Pascal, Schopenhauer, Kierkegaard, Nietzsche and the
young Marx, who were seriously concerned with just those tensions
between personal and public destinies, were and are, perhaps for
those very reasons, kept out of any strictly philosophical syllabus.

Here I am trying to focus the problems centred in the one as one
among many, in the many as constituted of ones. I believe them
to be of crucial importance in any context and therefore *a fortiori*

for sociological thinking. I believe that some German thinkers were moving towards an appreciation of these questions. In the following I shall try to extricate some of the insights relevant in our context from their comprehensive involvement in age-old controversies. These always go back to Hegel and Kant, often via Leibniz and Descartes, the Scholastics, the Stoics, to Aristotle and Plato. But since those insights cannot be extricated too neatly, we must indicate how the carriers of the great tradition figured in German sociological controversies. For at least in Germany the mantle of the philosopher who had wondered concerning the nature and destiny of man and society had fallen on the shoulders of the sociologist by the end of the nineteenth century.[1]

For Dilthey history was the ultimate. The historian was a philosopher, *the* philosopher. His task was the uncovering and interpreting of the unique development and growth of mankind, and to distinguish clearly between uncovering and interpreting. All other *Geisteswissenschaften* were the auxiliaries of history. Its culmination, never quite attainable, was *Universalgeschichte* (Dilthey, 1914, vol. 1, pp. 26–39). Within this context the individual is both irreducible and yet explicable solely in terms of his historical situation. The historian does the explaining, biography is his basic pursuit. This has to be carried out under the auspices of a descriptive psychology which has already subsumed the individual under formal generalizations, i.e. the individual's irreducibility is affirmed against a background of scientific notation which ignores him as individual. This is ideology reflecting the social reality: the market mechanism within which rules a necessity which needs 'individual initiative' for its smoother functioning.[2] In other words, Dilthey mirrors the ideological individualism of his age which reserves for the individual the kind of respect Kant reserved for the thing-in-itself – which in his Practical Reason is the self – while seeking to explain all its visible and tangible functions and manifestations in mechanistic generalizations. Within Kant's philosophy *Innerlichkeit*, inwardness, is total.

Dilthey considered all metaphysical explanations as mistaken. They abstract from the particular and its motions and constitute a sphere of universals and of fixity as 'reality'. From Plato to the Scholastics philosophers were unable to understand the creative part played by the mind in any act of *Erkenntnis*. He criticizes Hegel, whose dynamic view of history he appreciates, for ultimately constructing or acknowledging a similarly absolute *topos* over against the actualities of human, individual events weaving themselves into history. Now it is illuminating to see how Dilthey's Kantian approach, which Kant himself had elaborated to accommodate the Newtonian conception of the universe, vitiates his own understanding of the individual and the particular. For in it the central Platonic concern has survived and by-passed *Erkenntnis-kritik*: namely some form of separation between the unchanging and the ephemeral, the ideal and the real, the control and the controlled. (And this Popper had understood as reflecting Plato's desire for a fixed society with a fixed division of rulers and ruled.)

Dilthey longed for a *Geisteswissenschaft* worthy to be the successor of metaphysics (Dilthey, 1914, vol. 2). He saw its development as analogous to that of the natural sciences, though he protested that such an approach must not become a new metaphysics. He had not yet realized that the scientific method has already internalized all the necessary metaphysical intentions. It functions within a universe of discourse where function is beyond question – as God never was – and which has been identified surreptitiously with *the* universe. With Heidegger one might say: metaphysics outwitted its critics. Via their critique it found in the sciences, its avowed enemies, its home and fulfilment. It now rules the social reality as metaphysics had ruled only in the imagination of the philosophers (Heidegger, 1954, ch. 3 '*Uberwindung der Metaphysik*'). For metaphysics is the expression of the belief that concepts have power and reality, that the controller and the controlled have separable identities, that reality is management. This belief could survive its critique, because neither Dilthey nor any of the critics really faced the problem of individuality, of the particular and contingent, as experienced by a being whose contingency is death.

Since Plato the idea has prevailed that mind rules and must overrule matter, that mind matters more than matter. Since Aristotle the individuating principle had been found in matter, in that which matters least. This idea has remained alive, if implicit, through Descartes and Kant – in spite of ideological protestations to the contrary – to Hegel and Whitehead; also, if less obviously so, in the tradition that runs from Bacon via Hobbes, Locke, Hume, to Russell. So instead of taking seriously the fact that for the individual contingency spells anguish or death, these were treated as mere contingencies by the philosopher – except, perhaps, on his deathbed. Goethe once said that for him 'the accidental was the most loath-some aspect of history' (Meinecke, 1959, p. 511). In him this went hand in hand with an abhorrence of tragedy, an incapacity to face the tragedy implicit in some of his works. Here the poet gives away a secret which may well have been the chief motive power behind science-technology and academic disciplines: the endeavour to eradicate the accidental, *Zufall*, i.e. death; to circumvent death, because it cannot be controlled. Hence it is of more than academic and certainly of sociological interest to ponder Heidegger's claim that we must learn to live and think as mortals (Heidegger, 1954, pp. 159ff; 1931, pp. 254–66).

Dilthey's desire to establish the *Geisteswissenschaften* as science betrayed them to the metaphysics he was combating. Nevertheless his creative contribution, which was also that of historism at its best, pointed towards a better appreciation of the individual, of the contingent, even though it bore reluctant witness to the strength of a two-thousand-five-hundred-year-old monolithic tradition which it could not shake off so easily. (Empiricism has not even tried.) Meinecke's work was such a pointer. Having mistaken and glorified *raison d'état*, that mechanical interplay of mechanized impersonal forces, for a nation's individuality, he did grope in his essay on historism for a new understanding of the individual in history (Meinecke, 1963, 1959).

Weber's severe separation of a value-free science from moral, existential commitment to value-judgments, mirrors the Kantian distinction between 'pure' and 'practical' reason all over again. This in turn had reflected the Lutheran and Calvinist dualism of reason and faith which Weber understood so well. Luther and Calvin had reflected the dualism of St Augustine whose main labour had been the baptizing of Platonism. And that Platonic, Christian, Stoic dualism reflected the reality of the Roman Empire which had been all-powerful and in which everyone was totally impotent.

Simmel's rationalism is more easy-going. Although also rooted in Kant, it points back to Descartes, the father of modern rationalism. Cartesian as against Calvinist dualism is of a more complacent kind, almost monistic in that reason is well-nigh omnipotent in its sphere outside which it acknowledges nothing. (This is Heidegger's 'nothing' which Sartre turned upside down by calling reason the nothing.) Descartes's rationality absorbed into itself and activated once again the whole realm of Platonic ideas. It is the Aristotelian god who makes all things move towards himself. It is the mirror of the scholastic Christian God whom it indeed enlists, not as illuminator but as guarantor of its own illumination. Reason constitutes reality. All matter, including the philosopher's own body, even his soul situated in the pituitary gland, has to obey reason. Everything is only in as far as it obeys reason. (It was not Hegel who first believed this.) Only what is clear and distinct and functions smoothly is rational. The rule of reason equals rationality. The end of rationality is further rationalization.

There can be little doubt that such a doctrine reflected rather than created the growing bourgeois capitalist mentality and necessity. Its incisive and persuasive concision, however, its apparent simplicity and obviousness, its apodeicticity, contributed much to the further shaping of that mentality, of which the academic spirit is as direct an expression as technology and industry. Everywhere the aim is

47

rationality for rationality's sake or for the sake of further rationalization, and rationalization as perfection. The degree of perfection
corresponds to the degree of rationalization. Academic debate is
still rooted in these rather tautologous assumptions. Simmel's two
main works, *Soziologie* (1922) and *Die Philosophie des Geldes* (1907),
still illustrate the implicit belief that what the mind has solved to
its own satisfaction has been solved. (Compare the economist's
belief in, for example, the balance of payments as a gauge of social
reality.)

Descartes's omnipotent rationality was at the same time tame and
submissive. Reason, the absolute ruler, is at the mercy of that over
which it rules, its facts. Yet, being reason, it surmounts this dilemma
with ease. One cannot change the world and one's circumstances,
Descartes admits, but need not. Reason is perfectly able so to adjust
itself to circumstances, and do the same for the philosopher's
body-soul, that it will find happiness even in spite of them and the
philosopher through it. Here Descartes is betraying the secret of
Western – possibly of all – philosophy: it is the functioning of
reason in such a fashion that matters, the individual lump of matter
or flesh, the actual individual, cannot interfere with its smooth
progress.[3]

Now something peculiar and, for my purpose, significant has
taken place in Descartes's mind: the *ego* of his *cogito* seemed for a
moment to carry the whole weight of the existence of the universe.
Because I am, everything is. Because I cannot doubt my self without
affirming it even in the act of doubting, my world is. Descartes
experienced this proof as an overwhelming enlightenment. It
obviously was a mystic experience, similar to that expressed by
Angelus Silesius: 'I know that without me God cannot live a wink;/
when I cease he with me to nothingness must shrink.' This experience
could have taken Descartes beyond the confines of scholasticism
and metaphysics, had he been able to trust his experience as a most
individual one. Together with Montaigne, he might have started off
Western thinkers on a road of new self-discovery. There is no doubt
that his experience was genuine, overwhelming and personal. There
is none either that his training in philosophy – which is not the love
of wisdom but of rationalization – was bound to make him misinterpret it. For what is philosophy, if not the possibility of escape
from any serious doubts raised for the philosopher by his individuality?

So *qua* philosopher Descartes put the emphasis neither on the
ego nor the *sum* which expressed the matter or substance of his
experience, but on the *cogito*, its formal and intellective aspects. He
knew as well as anybody that 'I am, therefore I think.' The inversion
was merely to function as a philosophical proof of the reality of the

sum: even when I doubt my very being, when I think I am not, my doubt cannot help confirming my being. As a philosopher, a scholastically trained one, he was taken in and carried away by his own argument. He mistook the proving for that which it was meant to prove, the concept for what it was meant to grasp, the means for the end. Reality was in the thinking. Not, 'because I am, the world is', but, 'because I think, the world is as I think it.' A fairly straight line runs from here to Kant's *Vernunft*, Hegel's *Geist*, Husserl's phenomenological reduction, to science in all its shapes. A similar line seems to run backward through Aquinas to Aristotle and Plato.

Scholasticism reflected a highly structured society. In it both the administration and those it administers, both the intellect and that which it intellects, are subsumed under and united in 'being'. Hence to see clearly means to have an adequate image in one's mind of something that is out there. To understand properly means to have a clear representation of reality in one's intellect. God himself guarantees the correspondence – as he still did for Descartes, if for different purposes. For being has its source in God who, above all, is. But God, as against all other beings, not merely is, but his being is his existence. He exists necessarily. His being is never just potential, but always actual, actualizing, creating. His existence is essential, beyond contingency. All other beings depend on him for a peculiar quality of their being: existence. The essence of all things is grounded in God's will and reason. God wills it to be. His will being rational, God cannot will it not to be. The essence of all things is beyond contingency. The particular individual existence is neither necessary nor essential. It is contingent, expendable, most of all when his existence does not correspond to his essence, when he or she or it is not what he/she/it should be, what he/she/it is in the mind of God, i.e. does not live up to the ruler's expectations.

This ontology is clearly a projection of the feudal, hierarchic society. The structure matters, not the person. The person signifies merely as an upholder and defender of the whole. The only individual whose existence as an individual seemed necessary, was the emperor or the pope. In him the authority of the governors and the right of the governed are reconciled, at least formally. His existence, not just his essence, guarantees the essential structure precisely to the extent to which the individual's existence and status are really at his mercy and in his gift. In his existence subsists all social truth in that he is the final court of appeal – and truth is judgment, vindication or condemnation. This medieval ontology was also of a utopian character. Although it reflected society as it was, it made it appear as it could or should be. In as far as it was not conscious of this utopianizing, ontology became and remained ideology.

Medieval ontology in turn had grown out of Stoicism (Dilthey, 1914, vol. 2, *passim*). That had been the metaphysics of the Roman Empire after it had been shaped by the Athenians. Aristotle's own universalizing efforts reflected the failed Greek, the almost successful Macedonian ambitions. Plato's Utopia is the ultimate in conservative vision. It reveals the fears and hopes of any privileged, articulate, managing minority whose conserving tendencies are rooted in the simple desire to continue managing. Thus the *Republic* by its very shape which is designed to mask its intentions demonstrates the relationship between metaphysics and ideology (Popper, 1942, vol. 1).

Now some German scholars, including Borkenau, saw the transition from feudalism to bourgeois capitalism as a vast societal upheaval, an almost total reversal of values. Borkenau in particular believed that the philosophies accompanying that change underwent an equally thorough transformation. Yet it seems to me that Descartes, timid and conservative by nature, was a continuator as much as an innovator. His enormous doubts could not seriously impair his conservative assumptions, but merely enabled him to formulate new rationalizations. *Qua* philosopher he could not help wanting to do what philosophers had done since Plato: to categorize, define, fix; to clarify, generalize, order; to conserve, take out of the flux as much as possible, if must be the flux itself. He cannot escape being a conservative, utopian ideologist, if at times against his own intentions. Do philosophers wish to preserve and fix, because their predecessors had done this? Or do they turn to philosophy, because, being timid, they wish to preserve and fix things once and for all? To fix in thought what others fix by force? Is it arguable that Cartesianism is not a radically new departure, nor the philosophizing of Locke, Hume, Kant, Hegel, of positivists and linguists? That we are still waiting for a new beginning? Then, accepting the view of Marx, Borkenau, Scheler, *inter alia*, on the interdependence of philosophy and society, the implication would be that the societal change was not radical either.

We note once more that from Plato to the Scholastics the problem of our individuality and mortality and, therefore, of the interrelations of the individual with society and the tensions between them were never seriously raised in philosophy. Whenever the individual did appear above the horizon, he was treated as an instance of the problematics concerning the particular and the universal, matter and form, essence and existence. Or he was made the butt of exhortations, of generalized morals. The philosopher thought as if his thinking could be aseptically severed from his vegetative, imitative, willing and desiring being on the one hand and from the peculiar singularity of his society-shaped idiosyncrasies on the other. Philosophy became the exclusive preserve of such thinking. (Right up to Peirce's and Popper's expectations of an objective, communal, scientific tribalism washed of all mere subjectivity.) It remained thoroughly esoteric and clannish. No wonder then that the individuating principle continued to be found in matter which, as we saw, matters least to the philosopher and obtrudes upon his considerations mainly as a nuisance and which can always be managed by force. All this in spite of or because of the philosopher's own personal vicissitudes.

Has philosophy been an escape from individuality from the beginning? Does it reflect the structures of society so persistently, because these are a similar escape, another form of commitment therapy? Does this explain why literature has often been a more powerful protest against society in the name of the individual? It is possible that philosophy, as against the outbursts of the poets, contributed to our belief that the individual of the past did not experience the pains of individuation as we do. He certainly did not become a central philosophical concern. Did this situation change fundamentally with the advent of the man whose *dubito* abolished a world before his *cogito* restored it?

Indeed much has changed in philosophy as in politico-economic 'reality'. Reason is no longer the discoverer of hidden harmonies between different aspects of creation. It no longer mediates between a man and the ultimate by means of finely differentiated balances and counter-balances, as church and city and guild had done in order to hide from him the nature or merely the claims of his individuality. These he had experienced only at moments of passion, crisis or accident, and such moments reason had always treated with contempt. Gradually his individuality was divested of those layers of protective covering. He stood as naked and helpless before the Calvinistic God, as before the Renaissance prince or the mercantilistic monarch. The transition from a *Nahrung* or subsistence to an *Erwerb* or acquisition economy exposed him to a market mechanism as inexorable and incomprehensible as Calvin's predestination (Sombart, 1927; esp. pp. 31, 188, 200, 211, 220). Man has to prove himself before this inexorableness, and such proof can never be complete or conclusive. He can at best succeed in order to try again. So he experiences his individuality, whether in success or failure, mainly as anguish, striving without end, as motion without goal, emotion without consummation, as irreducible irrationality. He must escape from this at almost any cost. The irrational has to be rationalized, i.e. placed into a context within which it can be shown to function. Then the anguish can be explained as guilt, failure, inadequacy, weakness. It can be overcome or repressed by strict discipline, which means by de-individuation. Motion and mechanism, energy

51

and impetus, are exalted into ends in themselves. Means like profit, measurement, accountancy, production, are libidinized, so that the self may put itself at their service, a means to a means.

A further rationalization of functioning for functioning's sake is quantification. By its aid all functioning can be measured by a gauge which is perpetually generated by the process itself. In this newly constituted universe the individual functions as producer and consumer – with neither production nor consumption regulated in reference to his needs – as buyer and seller, as ledger clerk and reader of gauges. To the extent to which he learns to function smoothly and not to ask questions, 'theirs not to reason why', he is rid of his anguish, or should be.

Descartes's philosophy reflects, without reflecting on, this process of by-passed individuality, of rationality for the sake of rationalization, of rationalization as constitutive of reality. He finds in mathematics – and this makes him rather than Bacon the father of modern thinking – the new language, untainted by emotion, sheer gauge, implying no meaning beyond the measure. Today mathematics, as physics and chemistry, as statistics and accountancy and technology, constitutes, defines and confines reality. Science, including sociology, can only be scientific, real, realistic, in as far as it can be expressed mathematically. Descartes with his Gallic love of clarity went further than, and is therefore closer to us than, any of his greater or smaller successors. He is the true father of science, of positivism, even of pragmatism (Borkenau, 1934, pp. 353–71). And all this he is, not because he abolished but because he transposed metaphysics. He showed that 'it worked'. He thus put it beyond criticism, for he achieved the proof at the time which began to take it for granted that whatever 'works' is its own justification. In comparison Locke's and Hume's sensationalism was an anachronism. It merely proved what after Descartes no longer needed proving: that apart from our reason, as defined by philosophy, there is neither rhyme nor reason in the universe. Kant's enormous effort to rehabilitate reason after Hume's onslaught essentially did little more than repeat, with German thoroughness and opacity, what Descartes had been saying concisely.

Descartes had subordinated the individual to his rationality. Not that *I* think matters, but that I *think*. Hume had totally and quite unnecessarily dissolved the individual into the flux of – whose? – sensations, as if Descartes had not already shown that it is not the flux that matters, but the control reason exercises over it. Kant, having first subordinated individuality to *Vernunft*, like Descartes but with Prussian severity, then tried to retrieve it. By that time however he had become so fascinated by the Cartesian-Newtonian rationality that his moral law was little more than its pale analogy, yet as radically an imposition. Obedience to it alone gave freedom to the individual, yet in the sense which Descartes would have approved that it liberated him from his individuality, its motives, emotions, decisions, claims and mortality. Furthermore it only made him 'free' within the total 'givenness' of reality which he could not hope to affect. In Hegel's vast perspective the individuals are reduced to episodic, anecdotal significance. For Schopenhauer the individual was a mistake which should, and with effort and erudition could, be rectified. Nietzsche as poet was well on the way to a rediscovery of the individual in all his irrationality and irrepressibility. As the compulsive, positivistic rationalist, he lost his tracks again.

Phenomenology occupies a peculiar position within this context. Husserl's originating insight which expressed itself unfortunately and prophetically in the motto, *'Zurück zu den Sachen'*, back to the matter under consideration, could have signified a new departure for philosophy. It might among other *Sachen* have retrieved the individual whose individuality, under certain circumstances, presents itself as a phenomenon. It did not. Husserl immediately and persistently deflected phenomenology into a subjective rationalism which added little to that of Descartes and subtracted little from Kant. Merleau-Ponty's exploration of intensionality right into the structure and function of perception was bound to take him along the same road. For as soon as we focus 'Reason' or 'perception', i.e. treat as fundamental phenomenon not the individual but any or all of his functions, the individual is forgotten. This may be justified within strictly circumscribed areas of, for example, psychology. Whether or not it is justified in philosophy and, above all, in social philosophy, is precisely the point at issue here. Sartre wrestles with the problems of the individual in society and has to take refuge in novels and plays in order to be able to explore the tensions of the individual, as they reflect those of the group and of the self as member of a group. He advocates an approach to history and sociology through the individual (Sartre, 1964). But between his Hegelian Marxism, the drive towards *totalization* which leads him into giddying abstractions, and an ever more detailed psychologizing which represents an abstracting in the opposite direction, the individual gets lost again – both in his novels and in his philosophy (cf. Spiegelberg, 1964, pp. 465–6).

Only Heidegger really begins to accept individuality and mortality as the inescapable starting point of a human philosophy. In *Sein und Zeit* (1931) already, but even more so in his later essays, the problem of the particular, of the *Ding* and the individual, the problem of *Sein* and of *Dasein* in time, remains central. If the language is difficult at times, though in German never nearly as opaque as in translation, it may be due to the fact that the last two-thousand-five-hundred years of European philosophy have not yet shaped the conceptual instruments or 'feelers' for the kind of approach Heidegger is pioneering. Philosophy may well have shaped conceptual tools which are positively inappropriate for the apprehension of that which constitutes our humanity. Thus if a man wishes to speak philosophically about man he is left without a generally acceptable linguistic currency. Philosophy is still 'on the way to language'. Unfortunately it does not realize that it has not arrived yet. Everything Heidegger's thinking is concerned with has still 'to find the proper words', *will zur Sprache gebracht werden*. In the meantime we shall have to listen to the poets – those who were *Dichter* as well as *Denker* – as he himself did increasingly in his later years. For as philosopher he felt that up till now only the poet had been concerned with questions of *Dasein* which should have been but never were those of philosophy.

Note Heidegger's style is not particularly difficult or obscure. Compared with Kant or Hegel he writes lucidly and simply, if at times a little pompously. At times he seems to be playing about with language in an etymologically inexcusable fashion. This presents almost insuperable difficulties for the translator. For the German reader it presents none. Most Germans love serious punning and I, being one of them, often find it illuminating providing it is not taken for anything else. When handled with discretion and poetic sensitivity such punning can get closer to the wisdom contained in the language which is often greater than that of its present user.

We return to our contention: European philosophy is essentially a unity. It had many vicissitudes. It was carried from Greece to Rome, from there all over Europe and later on into America. It fluctuated, often violently, between realism and nominalism, rationalism and empiricism, idealism and naturalism. Yet these oscillations, their episodic, almost rhythmic movements, suggest the underlying unity of concern: to forge the most adequate conceptual tools for the intellectual comprehension and mastery of reality as a whole, and to preserve them from any emotive or idiosyncratic corruption or abuse. European philosophy was designed to circumvent the individual, both by treating him merely as an instant or part of a whole, and by silencing his every possible protest by defining it as unphilosophical and irrational. We must not be misled here by the apparent modesty of, for example, linguistic philosophy. It seems to claim so little for itself, because it believes science to have or be that perfect tool for the apprehension of reality which linguistics merely has to keep polished.[4] The unity of European philosophy is reflected in the unity of academic syllabuses. These define a fairly hermetically sealed universe of discourse, spacious enough to contain everything except the philosophers themselves. Again we ask, was and is this at least one of the philosophers' intentions: to create a realm in which contingency holds no sway?

Two facts strengthen such a suspicion: first, from the Eleatics to Husserl the philosophic quest has been for certainty, for fixity, precision, the incontrovertible – none of them attributes of life. Second, there were those who experienced the mystery of their individuality, its anguish as well as its parabolic character, with unwonted intensity. For that reason they were unable or unwilling to conceptualize it. When they projected their experience into legendary or fictitious characters, they were respectfully defined as poets, i.e. as those who by definition were not philosophers. When they reflected directly on the mystery of their self and, most of all, its contingencies and mortality, like Montaigne, Pascal, Kierkegaard, they were equally firmly, though for less definite reasons, excluded from academic philosophy.

In nuce, European philosophy is united in its endeavour to protect the individual from his individuality. It tries to achieve this – in contrast to the rather different methods of Eastern philosophy and religion – by the elaboration of a conceptual tool kit for the mastering of everything except the self and by channelling all passions into arguments concerning its refinement and use. As man gets better at using the kit and, because of this, is gaining an increasing measure of control over his surroundings, he becomes fascinated by the tools and forgets his individuality in his tinkering, except for moments of irrational obtrusion which he learns to treat as irrelevant (cf. J. Conrad, *The Heart of Darkness*).

I believe that the unitary, almost monomaniacal philosophical effort of Europe reflects a similar unitary societal endeavour and intention. This single-minded civilizatory endeavour underlies and cuts across the various stages of historical development discerned by Marx, Hegel, Comte, Spencer, not to mention Dilthey, Meinecke, Sombart, etc. I do not wish to contest the inevitably limited validity of any of the developmental views within their context. It would be ludicrous to deny that significant changes have taken place since the founding of Ur and, especially in Europe, since the Middle Ages. But I wish to suggest that as straight a line runs from Athens, Sparta, Rome, even from the Egyptian, Babylonian and Persian bureaucracies to our contemporary society, as runs from Thales to Husserl (cf. Weber, 1964, pp. 672–4, 866–73, 890–900).

For the sake of convenience, I put my suggestion in Hegelian terms: I see man's development from his uncertain beginnings to the late Neolithic age as his *thesis*. In that period the area of his humanity was staked out. Everything that opened up the possibilities for his growing into his humanity, for his life to become fully human, the potential created by the comparative freedom from need, had been accomplished. Language, tools, cereals, domesticated animals, family, village and tribal structures, had been introduced and elaborated. How varied the possibilities were even at that stage, has been studied in great and often surprising detail by anthropologists among the survivals that reached or almost reached into the present (cf. Lévi-Strauss, 1967).

In Egypt or Ur or in some other place as yet undiscovered under sea or sand started the *antithetical* movement which is still in fullest swing. Man set himself against himself, divided himself from himself and from his self; he subordinated himself to himself, separated the control from the controlled, mind from body, power from that over which it was to be exercised. He detached reason from that which was to be rationalized. His libido which lived, and still lives, if subterraneanously, in the embodied imagination, in the imagined possibilities of the psyche, was channelled into realizing, securing and preserving the actual which, in the shape of the Pyramids or of the hydrogen bomb, for example, strained the limits of phantasy. Within the actual which is no more than one particular ossified possibility, the possible survived, as a kind of temptation, in the imagination which we no longer take for reality but for a fringe benefit of the power state. Only power is real, for it alone can make real: armies, empires, super-markets, moon-rockets, i.e. the gadgets and organizations necessary to achieve, preserve and justify power. What is left outside the 'real and solely necessary' remains disembodied, mere phantasy, spare-time occupation (cf. Horkheimer-Adorno, 1969, '*Kulturindustrie*').

Of course I am weighting the argument emotionally. It has been weighted for too long on the other side with emphatic rationality which is a form of emotion. It has been maintained, for instance, that scarcity was the mother of civilization. Because the earth did not naturally yield sufficient sustenance for all, man had to organize and master it and himself. He had to accept the constraints and discontents of civilization in order to survive. Many saw this as man's permanent situation, Freud among them. Marx thought that via the capitalist antithesis man would arrive at the communist synthesis, a state of affairs beyond the need of such constraints. Today there are those who think that the belief in original scarcity is largely erroneous, based on the facts of poverty which civilization only too often produces. Anthropological evidence suggests that originally civilization was the result of plenty. Not only capitalism but civilization altogether is based on surplus, on surplus value (Mumford, 1967, ch. 8). It is therefore not necessary to assume that civilization, and in the shape in which we know it, was or is inevitable and necessary.

By now, however, it has indeed produced a situation which makes any return to the past impossible and any movement forward – except that of its own acceleration – exceedingly difficult to conceive. Yet what is difficult is not impossible and, anyway, it remains doubtful whether new conceptions are likely to point in any but the inevitable direction. We need something more than and different from conceptions and concepts, for it is possible that a failure to find an *Aufhebung* of our form of civilization, a *synthesis* of the pre- and post-Neolithic positing of our humanity, may herald mankind's total failure. Civilization, I am trying to argue, is not necessarily mankind's necessary attempt to control, organize, order, manipulate, his surroundings and his own being. Millions of species have survived without such an achievement. The earth does not seem inevitably inimical to what it brings forth. 'Nature' has produced man as it produced so many other forms of life. For no-one knows what reasons or whether for any reasons man went beyond them and it. He did not adapt, as the biologist understands the term. Perhaps he could not. He survived to reach the stage where he in turn could adapt nature to his needs, produced his own nature and natural surroundings. For a long period he lived in a state of symbiosis with that nature. (Until almost today Eskimoes and Bushmen, for example, found such life possible under nature's most stringent conditions.) Finally this brought him to the point where he took – wanted to, had to, merely happened to take – a further step.

Since symbiosis had enabled him to take that step, had given him the necessary surplus and surplus energy, the new possibilities of control and mastery could not have suggested themselves primarily as control of nature or as the necessity of such control. Societal, hierarchic organizations, sacred and profane, the use and joy of power over others, must have been his archetypal experience of power. At that far distant stage too, the social experience will have been primal and primary. Gradually it and its rationalizations will have been read back into nature. Only then in turn would the new understanding and experience of nature be used to justify the social structure. The fear that uncontrolled nature would devour us, or that our own uncontrolled nature would make us devour each other, may be the projection of fear engendered by societally introjected controls, i.e. it is possible that it was not the fear which produced the controls, but that the control, with its assumptions and presumptions of necessity and mastery, produced and produces the fear. We recall Freud's understanding of neurosis and Weber's of puritanism. Also the fact that literature from the days of Gilgamesh explored qualities of life, aspects of our emotive, passionate humanity, very different from and often at odds with the kind of humanity assumed by the makers and writers of history, by philosophers, sociologists and economists.[5]

I suggest that the longing for control, which is expressed quite indifferently and interchangeably as desire to control and to be controlled, is the longing to escape from the contingencies of our individuality. For controls – government, conventions, creeds, laboratories – create necessary patterns, structures, functions, to which a man's individuality may, even must, be subordinated. In putting himself at their disposal, his individuality, so he feels, is *aufgehoben*, transcended, even *gut aufgehoben*, in the best of hands. Whether civilization creates the new experience of power as control, or whether it merely refines, reorganizes and energizes ancient tribal structures of totem and taboo, is beyond our scope. But two points must be stressed here: 1 The extent, 2 the nature of the civilizatory discontent.

1 Freud, far from going too far in his description of it and of its mechanisms of repression, did not go far enough. The depth-explorer of the psyche shied away from his own discoveries and their consequences. As a civilized man he could not appreciate the full extent of the repression. Furthermore he was afraid of the repressed and ultimately believed that it needed repression. He therefore was ready to work towards the weakening of the super-ego only in order to strengthen the ego, the agent of perfectly rational control. He could not admit yet that even the ego is a structure of controls, a conceptual frame, a balance of powers, a kind of enlightenment super-ego. Thus his understanding of the ego already by-passed and pre-judged the real problems of individuality (Adorno, 1970, pp. 269–70; Mitscherlich, 1969, pp. 48–9, 81, 121, 283ff).

For concepts as well as any other form of control are anti-individual safeguards. And balance of power, possibly an appropriate aim in the game of politics based on the assumption that power is reality, in the psyche merely means waste of power. It means the use of psychic energy for the curtailment of psychic energy. It turns man's strength against himself (cf. Nietzsche, *Genealogy of Morals*, 1924). Here Freud, like so many before and since, seems to have fallen into the trap laid by Plato's *Republic*, where the ordered soul is compared to the ordered *polis*. Yet does the psyche need or engender that Platonic order? Is this not already introjected violation, introjected class-structure and conflict? And could we possibly learn more about the psyche by looking more closely not at the *Republic* but at the vicissitudes and the end of the Greek *poleis* and of the various empires since? Could we learn more about the state, if, bearing in mind the psychic analogy, we would ask whether 'balance of power' is a very useful concept even in politics, whether it is not merely a label affixed to a muddle we feel unable to resolve (cf. Marcuse, 1969, last chapter)?

2 At least some of the problems relating to the individual in society and to social consciousness seem to be coterminous with civilization itself. Marxists may have made bourgeois capitalism responsible for damage done by civilization as such. Yet their faith in as yet unrealized possibilities, which may often have made them look for the causes of frustration too near home, is to be taken seriously. It enabled them to look steadily at society as it is in the light of what it could or should become, to see any society as one possibility among others, as a stage of development, not as a terminus (Bloch, 1970, pp. 257–88). In other words, the fact that man 'has always been like this' does not mean he will always have to be. Marxians and Marxists remained open to the possible, to Bloch's hope-principle – though the latter are inclined to fossilize one particular possibility in turn. For this reason theirs is still the most sustained attempt at a philosophical approach to man and his history which does not by definition exclude the individual. This may sound odd in view of the fact that much Marxist writing, including that of the master, sounds particularly a-human in an Hegelian fashion. Yet when humanity does break through, as in the *1844 Manuscripts* and the many documentary passages in *Das Kapital*; in Lukács when he writes on *Minna von Barnhelm*, on Kleist, Keller, Goethe or Tolstoy; in Bloch when he turns to *Don Quixote, Faust*, to 'music as utopia', the real, full, individual man, enmeshed in the fatefulness of his contingency and of his social conditioning, but also in the destiny of his hopefulness, is permitted to make his appearance in a context from which he is usually excluded.

Adorno appreciated this. If he nevertheless accuses Marx of still being so tied to Enlightenment philosophy, *Vernunftsphilosophie*, that he cannot treat contingency with due earnestness, he demonstrates that the truly post-Freudian philosophy which would try to embrace the whole man has not yet appeared. Can it appear before a new society has come into being? A scoiety that would encourage man not to be afraid of his individuality? Is the philosopher or sociologist imaginable who would dare to face up to the full implications of our as yet quite unexplored individuality and contingency within the framework of a society still almost exclusively geared to their denial or domestication? Could Marx and Engels have survived their investigations of workers' and child-labourers' living conditions, unless thousands of years of philosophical conditioning had protected them from a too immediate contact and concern? Could Horkheimer and Adorno have gone on living after Belsen and Auschwitz, had not their intellectualizing as much protected them as it enabled them to see through many layers of that protectiveness? In spite of all this it must be asked whether

59

society is likely to change, unless man learns to think differently of himself and his *Dasein*.

Notes on literature

We have arrived at the point where the poet seems to be picking up the cudgels dropped by the philosopher. The poet has always been concerned with the individual as individual, with the problems and the mysteries of his singularity, with the fatefulness and *Zufälligkeit* or incidentality of his whence and whither. Since the creation of Gilgamesh the poet, whether consciously or subconsciously, has been aware of the individual not merely or even mainly as the playground of private accidental passions, but as the battlefield on which the person and his society are locked in mortal combat (cf. *The Epic of Gilgamesh*, Penguin, Harmondsworth, 1966). The poet knew, and it was this knowledge which made him a poet – dramatist, novelist – that all social conflicts are generated in and carried out in the individual psyche, that psychic conflicts mirror the tensions between the person and the community – to the extent to which the latter has not yet been a community – between a person's understanding of his own and of society's aspirations.

It is no accident that many of the great works of literature are known by an individual's name: *Odysseus, Prometheus, Oedipus, Antigone, Aeneas, Beowulf, Tristan, Njal, Don Quixote, Hamlet, Faust, Anna Karenina.* (It may be ominous that Kafka's three epics not only do not carry a human name, but that their respective heroes progressively lose their names.) For millions of mortals, even today, any or each of those names conjures up a glimpse of a particular and yet universal human condition, far more meaningful and precise than that evoked by any historical, philosophical or sociological work. And the more fully the individuality of the hero unfolds itself in all its singularity and idiosyncrasies, the more completely he seems submerged in all the trappings of his historical and ethnic uniqueness (Lear, Don Quixote, Taras Bulba, for example), the more immediately we recognize him and our self in him. Our relationship to him subsists in our shared individuality, in our shared self through its contrasting individualities. It is as if the self which is most properly expressed through our unique individuality and its otherness from all other individuals, is also that which we have in common with all other selves.

The individual as the embodiment of social consciousness is inevitably the central concern of literature. As individual he constitutes its subject matter underneath all its protean changes. Literature is 'good', has a chance to live, in as far as it succeeds in expressing individual immediacy, of the most particular and personal kind – as character in epic, drama, novel, as most subjective experience and reflection in lyric poetry. Only the poet's very own passions when recollected in tranquillity turn verse into poetry. Literature is 'bad' to the extent to which it has recourse to generalities, to specification instead of individuation, to clichés. Yet even bad literature cannot help trying to do what the good achieves. It apes and initiates. It recollects all kinds of passions, except the writer's own. It often has all the ingredients that seem to be required and the cook has all the imaginable skill. Yet the result is tasteless and proves the Hasidic saying that everything can be imitated except the truth.

However, just because of its distortions, its capacity to find and depict the 'truth' in accordance with some contemporary ideal, bad literature often much more immediately reflects society's unreflective self-understanding with its distortions and will reveal it and them clearly to a later generation, though it will hide them from its contemporaries. For it will inevitably hide the real conflicts, as society is hiding them from itself. Good literature will bring them into the open, just as inexorably, because it reveals the individual whose reality in our or any society is conflict. Bad literature is often popular or popular literature bad, since it expresses the individual's fashionable preference for escape. It reiterates and reinforces societal conventions. And conventions function as escape from individuality. Good literature, at least at the time of its inception, is usually appreciated only by the few. But while popular writings pass away on the shifting escapist fashions, the good speaks ever more clearly. It embodies our human solidarity for successive generations precisely because of its radical individualism. It continues to point towards our never quite achieved *humanitas*, precisely because it refused to compromise with that which society, public opinion, political and economical realists, philosophers and sociologists took for granted. (It is of sociological interest that structures and conventions designed to solidify our ephemerality pass like fashion, while the ephemeral experiences they are meant to preserve remain alive.)

It might come as a shock to a newcomer to our planet that the ingenuities of our division of labour have gone to the extreme of not only compartmentalizing our thinking into sociology, philosophy, literature, but to insulate each form from the other. There is such a thing as the sociology of literature. It is analogous to rewriting poetry in prose. Only a few neo- or near-Marxists seem to have turned towards literature as social philosophers. Lukács is at his best in the appreciation of the writers he loves. His essays on Lessing, Kleist, Balzac, Gorki, Keller, illuminate the whole texture of our communal reality, its frustrations and aspirations, its problems

C*

and possibilities, as his other works rarely do. Bloch's literary samples of his hope-principle constitute rather than illustrate his thesis, make one realize where it has its roots. They elaborate that principle more clearly and fully than his philosophizing. For his attempts to carry that hope-principle into philosophy, two-thousand-five-hundred years overdue, meant trying to carry the individual there. Hope is inseparable from the individual and his contingencies. To integrate the hoping individual into Western philosophy as it is, is impossible. Such an attempt would reconstitute it. And part of such a reconstitution would be its reconciliation with literature, the at-one-ment of philosophy and poetry, of *Dichter* and *Denker*, and of both with sociology.[6] Is it not possible, and if possible essential, for the sociologist to develop quite a new capacity for listening to what the poet as well as the psychologist and psycho-analyst wish to say, sometimes wish to but cannot yet quite say, sometimes say in a way that conceals rather than reveals what they wish to say? Could it be or become the sociologist's particular task to learn to comprehend and to interpret the mysteries which the poet incarnates and which underlie the conceptualizings of the academics? (Cf. Wilson, 1960; also his *Triple Thinkers, Axel's Castle, The Shock of Recognition*; also L. Trilling, *The Liberal Imagination.*)

The poet, we said, discovers our common humanity to the degree to which he is able to allow his hero's individuality to find its fullest development in response to and always in conflict with his surroundings. The manner of his achievement changes, often radically, from generation to generation. Compare Kyd's *Spanish Tragedy* with *Hamlet*, Aeschylus with Euripides, Elizabeth Bennett with Jane Eyre, Faust with the Prinz von Homburg, Lord Jim with Stephen Dedalus, Zola and Proust, Fontane and Kafka, Pushkin and Gogol. Certain literary changes seem to measure social develop-ments with something approaching precision, for instance the societal changes reflected by Stendhal, Balzac, Flaubert, Zola, Proust; those from Pushkin to Gorki, from Lessing to Kafka. The works of these men describe, define, explicate, a certain historical movement more precisely and fully than any comparable history or sociology. It is only our peculiar European philosophical training which, having taught us to take conceptualizations for understanding, makes us mistake the historian's abstractions for explanations, while it leaves us intellectually at sea among the concrete evocations by drama and novel.

Not only the hero's individuality and his problems change from age to age. The function of literature changes, more slowly but equally radically. One of those changes Nietzsche traced: from the orgiastic Dionysian goat-play or horse-play, in which each citizen was involved in a role contradicting that imposed upon him by his citizenship, to the austere tragedy which he watches respectfully from his seat (Nietzsche, 1970). A similar change can be detected among the Hebrews: from Amos, Hosea, Isaiah, Jeremiah, who declaimed their poetry as a direct social and political challenge, to the age of Nehemiah when their written-down remains were read out ritualistically in the course of a 'service'.

These changes may represent the primal transformation which constituted literature as literature, as something taken out of the ordinary daily context, out of 'real life'. Such a process must have occurred everywhere in the course of progressing civilization. It not only reflects the division of labour and the increasing need to stem orgiastic protests; it also shows when and how and why soul became separated from body, holy from profane, real from ideal. (This separation is different from the distinction which, according to Durkheim, the primitive already made between sacred and profane.) From then on even to this day we call 'real' what is left over when the 'ideal' has been evacuated, for example, into a sanctuary or a theatre. This has the apparently paradoxical consequence of externalizing and internalizing man's basic conflicts at one stroke. On the one hand they were being dealt with out there, on stage or altar, to which access was barred except to initiates. On the other hand, those stage characters, those holy books, conveyed and therefore reactivated intense and heightened individual experience. This gave them their power. They reminded the listener of the power of his own experience. Yet at the same time they kept him in his seat, at a distance from his experience. They alienated his experience and lived it for him. They made him powerless at the moment of confronting him with his power, which is not that of politics. Furthermore by keeping each individual in his own seat, they left each alone with his now totally internalized and split, i.e. private, experience. In this way the civilizatory division of labour cuts first and foremost through our individual being, our existence as individuals. For what we experience, and in total separation, as the external and the internal, as private and public, are two separated halves of our existence, our *Dasein*.

Because of this it remains the utopian function of literature to hold the 'other', the 'unreal' and 'power-less' aspect of life before our eyes with all the possible persuasiveness of 'reality'.

None of the later changes in the function of literature were of comparable magnitude. Many were significant and could be explored with profit, by sociologists among others. For example, the almost ritualistic, numinous tribal function of the Athenian stage when Aeschylus wrote for it, was barely recognizable in the democratic, intellectual use to which Euripides put it. By the time drama had turned into an entertainment for the Roman unemployed, the separation of the ideal from the real was complete. Christian literature, following the example of the Old and New Testaments haltingly and with little success, once more tried to bridge the gap between real and ideal, at least to the extent to which Aeschylus's dramas had still done this. The Renaissance reopened the gap which medieval attempts had plastered over mainly by conceptual means. Real and ideal, private and public, theory and practice, poetry and politics, were finally divorced. Self and 'reality' pull in opposite directions. This the individual experiences as a kind of schizophrenia. Was Hamlet the first example, or Don Quixote, the fool who tried to put the two together again? With Kafka's quixotic K of *The Castle* modern anonymous man finds himself on the impossible quest of looking for reality within the phantasy that parades as total and exclusive reality (Bloch, 1970, pp. 1230ff).

The printing press made it possible to put the extremes of agony and ecstasy between the same two covers and multiply them million-fold. With a book on his lap, the secluded reader seems to have bridged the outside and the within. It only seems. He has simply given up any effort at reconciliation and at-one-ment. He has become the gourmand and gourmet of the battles he no longer fights although they are his own. This is privatization. After the victory of the novel, the stage, in as far as it survived at all, under-went a further change. It became a novel looked at through a window, a projected novel. Whatever tensions there still had existed in the Globe between stage and stalls had ceased. The tragedy became a play – a *Schauspiel* or show – a sophisticated game. To go to the theatre became a 'social occasion', a euphemism for something which is neither an occasion nor of social significance. For a moment or two it looked as if the stage might become an ally in real social struggles. Ibsen and Shaw, later on Brecht, carried the controversies of their day into their plays. Even they could merely demonstrate that in a schizoid society such a road to integra-tion is blocked. Today we 'enjoy' Ibsen, and Brecht came into his own only when the struggles his plays portrayed had ended and we could 'enjoy' him as well. Chekhov's plays alone among moderns achieve a reality beyond dispute. Perhaps their power resides in the fact that he managed to carry the split itself and its tensions, the schizoid experience, into the plays.

Apart from him the stage came into its own once more in opera. Music, from Mozart to Schönberg, achieved what the word no longer could: it individualized the universal and universalized the personal and most intimate. It was able to give concreteness to and to embody the many-layered interactions within the psyche and between persons, as these reflect the tensions of social consciousness, by means of counterpoint, harmony, the *leitmotif*, of rhythm, variation, modulation. Mozart's *Figaro*, Beethoven's *Fidelio*, Wagner's *Ring* and Schönberg's *Moses and Aaron*, are profoundly revolutionary, or could be. The social structure they intended to dissolve proved solid enough to confine the revolution to the stage. Then the gramophone privatized music as well.

Today we are surrounded by paperbacks, television sets, radiograms and tape-recorders; boxed into separate houses or flats. All the great battles on behalf of and between the two separated halves of the psyche, the conquests and defeats, joys and despairs, come to us at the turning of a knob, pre-packaged, until we experience ourselves as no more than a package. The endless conflicts of the individual as a social being, of society as mediated in and through and by and for individuals, now take place in almost total privacy and isolation. They are conducted under conditions which make victory and defeat equally insignificant – as entertainment.[7] Is all this of no concern to the sociologist and social philosopher?

The reprojection of the novel on to the stage produced the cinema. There seems little doubt that the best films of this century are more interesting – sociologically, psychologically, philosophically, even aesthetically – than the contemporary theatrical productions of old or new plays. The paradox inherent in our understanding of the external and the internal comes to a climax in the film. At its most popular and common it manages to externalize everything. It is undiluted entertainment – i.e. it suspends us between the reality of past and future by means of an *Ersatz*, unreal, unrelated present. At its best, the film is able to let the external express the internal with a power, immediacy and intimacy impossible for the stage. In this way it demonstrates, if chiefly by implication, that the external subsists as the expression of the internal, that it is significant only in as far as it is such an expression, because it is the explication of man's divided soul. (This had been the message of Expressionism and Surrealism.) The film is able to achieve this kind of externalization with a new intensity, because it can juxtapose the close-up of an eye with a galactic panorama, past and present, dream and reality, one and many, with startling immediacy. It does take the juxtapositions of 'I' and 'all' through the whole gamut of possibilities, to its logical conclusions and *ad absurdum*. It thus dialectically yet quite untheoretically reaches the point where the 'I' dare realize its separation from the 'all' as a division within itself.

Television privatizes the cinema. It internalizes – in the schizoid understanding of the term – all public concerns which are also personal concerns still further. Under the appearance of bringing them into every house, TV permits them to fizzle out in millions of privatized minds in whom the distinction between fact and fiction has become blurred. This in turn may lead, and may at times already have led, to a situation where a new attempt to arrive at an understanding as to what constitutes human reality may have to be made; just because the arbitrary separation of fact from fiction that was accomplished between the seventeenth and twentieth centuries seems to be *aufgehoben*, can be *aufgehoben* – as is done in the best documentary programmes.

Notes on music

If reality is a social or psycho-social construction, what aspect of it does music, a most social function, constitute? Why do slaves sing? Why congregations and the crowds at the cup final? What does it mean that music can transform anguish into something we experience as joy or beauty and which we can share and experience communally? Religion, magic, ritual, have often gone together with music. Love, from the beginning, expressed itself in music, song, dance. Death and burial were often surrounded by music, Bach's *St Matthew Passion*, a series of solemn dances, merely a deep sophistication of that connection between death and music. Can anything be gleaned from the fact that at the time when religion lost its hold over Western imagination and became a sphere of expert controversy it was internalized in music? For there seems little doubt that, from Palestrina or before to the latest pop festival, music has absorbed into itself most of those experiences that would once have been called religious. Is this a further step on the road to privatization, or is there a kind of dialectical hope premissible that through this inevitable process music might preserve and reactivate what religion had already privatized by ritualization? Could it point to a new and more comprehensive experience and understanding of our individuality in society as not being private?

In music as much as in literature the universal finds expression through the individual. Only faithfulness to his most individual genius, to the genius of his singularity, enables a composer to express something of our common humanity. Only thorough exploration and embodiment of what seems exclusively his own expresses what is universal in the human experience. The *Mass in B minor* is indubitably Bach, *Don Giovanni* and *The Magic Flute* inimitably Mozart. The last quartets are idiosyncratically Beethoven. No-one but Schubert could possibly have written his late string quintet. And because of this each work speaks immediately of and to our condition, to what was and is and could be (Bloch, 1970, ch. 51).

Music transcends the spoken word not only in the obvious sense of breaking through language barriers. It reveals an infinitely complex and infinitesimally graded emotive and intellectual realm, as yet quite beyond words, which is both intimately personal and quite public, communal. Music is utopia. It not only points towards intimations of reconciliation between conflict and harmony. It already is such a reconciliation and as such must be reflecting some psychic reality. It holds transcendental sound patterns as hope and light into the anti-utopia of death. It proclaims against all possible fears that we need not be bored in utopia, for the possibilities of differentiation within each ordinary everyday joy or sorrow, as well as the strange interrelations between these two sides of all experience, are limitless. 'Few understand what a throne of passion each single musical movement is; and few know that passion itself is music's throne. . . . Thousands have intercourse with music and yet do not have its revelation.' Thus Beethoven, who knew as well as Shakespeare – and better than any social philosopher as yet – that passion is the shaper, preserver and breaker of social consciousness and social reality. Therefore going to the opera or to a concert may, as a matter of fact, be little more than a 'social occasion' for many. Really listening to music is, if only potentially and utopianly, a revolutionary, orgiastic act, a reaffirmation of another possible reality. (Who, for instance, will ever be able to determine how much or how little the marvellously humane and witty portrayal of a social conflict with all its personal implications and its transcendental musical resolution in *Figaro* has contributed to the fact that this particular kind of conflict no longer exists?)

A peculiar quality of affirmation is inherent in music. In the hands of a master it cannot help conveying 'truth': true passion, sentiment, experience, joy, grief. As, for example, in *Cosi fan Tutte*, it inevitably raises unreal feelings into their potential reality, judges the unreality by measuring it against the full possible realization. It can, as in the Pizarro aria in *Fidelio*, convey the energy of the villain's emotions, not really their wickedness which is revealed rather by the words set against the music. Music is highest morality in that it does not know evil. It knows all passions from ecstasy to despair. It knows the reality of the human situation well enough to portray it on all levels and express in its very structure the inevitability of conflict. Yet it can never avoid being already a kind of victory, the light that shines into the darkness and which the darkness cannot overcome – except, of course, by silencing it. Music knows evil, distortion, intrigue, violation, merely as something that offends its very nature. When it seriously tries to delineate 'evil', it manages only by turning and offending against itself, violating and negating itself. It intrinsically craves for or is reconciliation. If this intrinsic musical craving and being reflects, as we believe it does, a universal human longing and psychic reality, then 'evil' is revealed as distortion, as misdirected passion, not as a passion or reality in its own right.[8]

Does music represent a corroboration of the contentions of the post-Freudians who believe, a little like some medieval theologians, that evil is a bending of our nature, not inherent in that nature itself? That it is the result of not inevitable pressures, conditions, misunderstanding? Is man fundamentally as good as his music? Does it show or illuminate or point to his 'true' nature, or is it the subtlest ideological obfuscation of his reality?

3 Diverse approaches to the problem of understanding

Prelude: myth, a tentative and provisional definition

For convenience's sake, I shall use the word 'myth' to denote a rather complex intellectual-emotive pattern or structure, a web of explications designed to catch no less than the whole of reality or reality as a whole, which nevertheless can be and often is expressed in comparatively simple terms and images. Hesiod's *Theogony* and medieval Catholic doctrine are elaborate examples. The Hebrew's *'sh'ma* – 'Hear, O Israel, the Lord your God is one' – and the modern belief in facts, objectivity, efficiency, are simple ones. These latter myths can be expressed in a few words. They inhere in certain assumptions, so universally shared and taken for granted, that they are often no longer recognized as myth.

In regard to myth the question of truth or falsehood cannot be raised, except ideologically in the context of a conflict between differing myths expressing and generating divergent interests. For a myth is precisely that which 'in the beginning' constitutes a universe, a universe of discourse. Only within such does the question of truth become meaningful and urgent. (It should be noted in passing that no 'universe' can ever be more than a universe of discourse.) A myth can be almost totally imaginary or imaginative, just as it may appear as totally factual or historical. It can never be totally unreasonable, since it is the shared product of many minds and has its own rationality at least to the extent to which it remains distinguishable from the babblings of an idiot (cf. Durkheim, 1968; Lévi-Strauss, 1966). A myth can be almost completely rational and logical, yet never quite so, for reason itself has its roots in the a-rational – as, for example, Leibniz, Hume and Kant believed, as against Descartes, Voltaire and Bentham. Total rationality can be approximated only inside a mythical system or a system constituted by mythical assumption.

Myth is that which is taken for granted by a group, a society, a whole epoch. It constitutes any possible rationality. And the kind of rationality it constitutes is in turn claimed for the myth itself, and whenever self-reflection has reached the point where it deems such justification desirable. Myth is the peculiar form in which a society or sometimes an individual – Plato and Kafka – sums up a generally felt need for coherence, an *ultima ratio*. It is interesting to note that in Western society *ratio* was and is understood primarily as reckoning, as fine weighing, measuring, discriminating, equating, as 'final reckoning' – as in book-keeping. Therefore, to judge other myths in the light of our peculiar rationality, could not mean more than a confirmation and affirmation of our myth.

Myths can be profusely pictorial, as in Hinduism. They can be historico-philosophical, as Hebrew prophecy and Marxism. They can represent a mixture of staunch enlightenment, rationalism and uneasy eclectic imagery, like Freudianism. They can have the austerity of a Mondrian painting which fairly adequately represents the contemporary Western myth, its compulsive tendency to reduce reality to a system of co-ordinates, in which everything can be explained precisely in terms of a definite *locus* within a system designed to give everything a definite *locus*. Tautology becomes explanation which is satisfactory to the extent to which it is tautologous, certain. Or, to put it differently, a thing or matter or individual is explained when it/he has been identified. Tautology and identity as myth reflect the bureaucratic-technological structure of society in sociology as well as in other sciences.[1]

We also believe that ultimate reduction is explanation. We therefore should not be startled when the binary computer answers all possible questions and seems able to explain everything. We forget that it merely expresses the ultimate of our mythical determination not to admit other, non-reductive, non-tautological, explanation. It is a fact that the reductive myth 'works', that it almost 'works wonders' at least in certain spheres. But then myths have always 'worked in a mysterious way their wonders to perform'. They ceased to be myths when they no longer worked or were no longer felt to work, which in terms of social reality is the same thing (Merton, 1968, p. 20n, quoting W. I. Thomas). What are called myths nowadays are fossils.

In regard to the contemporary myth we may have to ask: Are there spheres in which it does not or cannot work at all? 'We feel that when all possible scientific questions have been answered, the problems of our life have not even been touched', says Wittgenstein. The individual as the bearer of social consciousness, society as the inter-penetration of individuals, may not be reducible, may not fit into the scientific myth. Can sociology be a reductive science? Does individuality require at least a complementary myth? Is individuality a myth? Only a myth?

We must now turn to a more detailed discussion of the different ways in which scholars have tried to cope with the problems of understanding, both in sociology in particular and in the *Geisteswissenschaften* in general, which are raised by any attempt to comprehend the individual in society. In as far as the *Geisteswissenschaften* are concerned with these problems they remain a sociological concern.

A Positivism and scientism

Today positivism is pervasive. It is the only really respectable creed, attitude, myth. As mood and method it is taken for granted. It simply is the one factual, trustworthy, desirable, the only scientific approach to all matters, at a time when all matters clamour for the scientific approach. Positivism first and foremost intends to look-at-things-as-they-are, not as they ought to be or could be. It is interested in facts, and in theories in as far as they order facts, are verifiable by facts and make the apprehension of further facts possible. Positivism wishes to 'let facts speak for themselves', and recognizes no discourse as scientific, even as rational, beyond the language of facts, beyond that which can be factually verified. It would have us remain silent on matters that cannot be discussed thus 'rationally'. The positivist would avoid subjectivity and particularity in the observer and the observed, as the puritan had been determined to avoid the devil and all his works – and Weber has pointed out the connection (Weber, 1967aE). However, as we have already argued, facts are neither as simple and obvious, nor as immediately 'there' and 'given', as positivism presumes (Popper, 1969, pp. 54, 181, 294; also 167–73).

Facts are constituted by theories, by human *theorein*, gazing, focusing, by being looked at with intention and interest. (Shades of Berkeley!) Whatever there be outside my looking and not yet looked at, it is not a fact. It cannot be more – or less – than that 'whatever' which my attention alone 'facts' (Mead, 1967; Gehlen, 1970a). And what are those things to-be-looked-at-as-they-are? Are they not what they are, because we are looking in a peculiar way? And how do we distinguish this kind of looking from any other? It is certain that Galileo, when he started to experiment with marbles on an inclined plane and with pendulums, did not look at any of these objects as any man before him and many men since actually looked at things and thought they were looking-at-them-as-they-are. His looking was a feat of immense intellectual abstraction. It left of things-as-they-are no more than a few vectors to which even the finest pencil lines are but a crude approximation.

This leaves us with the question of what things 'really are', what constitutes their reality, their thingness, their factuality. For instance, what are the facts concerning a young woman? Her beauty and attractiveness to her lover? Her vital statistics? Her character, conditioning, inheritance? Her talents, her stupidities, her knowledge, her ignorance? Her biography, physiology, anatomy, biology, chemistry, physics? And even if one could hold together in a Laplacean totality all those possible facts concerning her, or concerning anything, how could one be sure that this looking-at-her/ it-as-she/it-is is doing justice to her or to it or to one's looking? Who can prove that the positivist is actually looking-at-things-as-they-are? Is it not easier to demonstrate that his looking is of the kind that sees only what it wants to see and is interested in anything only in as far as it corresponds to his intentions? In brief: the belief in looking-at-things-as-they-are (LATATA) assumes, even presumes, too much (Habermas, 1969, pp. 91–108). At the same time it implies a total conditioning by and dependence on things as they are presumed to be. The *status quo* is accepted, quite a-historically, as an absolute. Yet not to permit oneself to ask why things are as they are, prohibits the questions why one should wish to LATATA.

Thus positivism implies a crude form of materialism, even though it be masked as pragmatism, actionism or symbolic interactionism. It implies a Lockean understanding of the human mind. As against that, most German philosophers since Kant or even Leibniz, and most social philosophers between Dilthey and Habermas, have argued that *Erkenntnis*, the act of comprehension or apprehension, yea, already the act of perception, has constitutive power or character. Our thinking and knowing, our conceptualizing and theorizing, determine facts and things. They argue that our thinking is not determined by facts but by social consciousness, by the weight and authority it grants to facts. Consequently *the belief that I can and must* LATATA, *that things-as-they-are determine my thinking, amounts to this tautology: That I am determined to be determined by my determination.* It has not established the truth of determinism or the necessity of LATATA (cf. Pareto, 1935, para. 13, 150–8), though it may have established a useful method of manipulation.

In discussing positivism one is in danger of wishing to be either as positivistic as possible or particularly unpositivistic. Should one pay homage to it by tracing its origins, demonstrating how it was caused by *a b c* rather than by *d e f*? Or, on the contrary, by reducing it to *an . . . is only . . .*? What is to be proved? Should one want to prove anything? Is it possible to do justice to both our contention and positivism by recalling that either is a form of social consciousness? Positivism – like any -ism – is a specific group-determined and determining attitude of particular individuals who, as is not infrequently the case, wish to claim objectivity, i.e. a kind of absoluteness, for their understanding. As one way of looking, positivism has proved immensely fertile. As the one and only way it refutes itself and the humanity of the investigator and his subject. As a myth, positivism is neither right nor wrong. It is. It cannot be refuted. As an exclusive myth it is highly dangerous. Perhaps it can be *aufgehoben*.

Positivism emerged triumphantly as the end-product of a long historical transformation. Gradually the feudal order disintegrated, economic interest changed from *Nahrung* to *Erwerb*, from making things to making profit. The difference between things is qualitative, a matter of taste and skill. That between profits is quantitative, a matter of exact measurement. And it cannot be stressed enough that 'quantity' is one specific 'quality', an acquired taste. Gradually profit became a thing-in-itself, even *the* thing-in-itself of which all things, now commodities, were the phenomena. It became the primary quality in relation to which all other were secondary (Scheler, 1960, pp. 92ff, 124ff, 221ff). Double-entry book-keeping enabled man to separate profit completely from all the processes, processers and products that produced it, to measure it exactly and to establish it as the measure *per se*. Once profit had been established as *telos* or myth, total rationalization became desirable, hence possible. As it was controlled by and directed towards profit which is measured exclusively in figures – which share with profit the quality of total abstractness – rationalization became mathematization. This in turn fascinated the technologist and scientist like Galileo. His LATATA was in fact a looking at things in terms of profit, in terms abstracted from all their sensuous, enjoyable qualities, from their reality and particularity. He abstracted from things their quantifiable properties or qualities – *Eigenschaften* – analogous to the way in which profit had been thus abstracted.

Via Descartes and Newton, precise accountancy was introduced into the natural sciences, nature made accountable to man in terms of his interests, and proved there as profitable as in economics. Was the success of mathematics in the sciences as surprising as it seemed at first? If mathematics is fundamentally the compressed language of accountability in terms of profit, was it astonishing that it should prove profitable, i.e. successful where success is measured in terms of profit, of success? Mathematics made science successful by turning our approach to nature into an undertaking in which understanding itself is measured in terms of success, profitability, manipulability, rationalization, in terms extraneous to itself.

73

Positivism is rationalization for rationalization's sake. It constitutes a self-contained argumentation of great power – comparable to that of the Roman legionary organization or of early enthusiastic Mohammedanism, most of all comparable to the power released by nuclear fusion which was the result of the most highly organized argumentation ever. Positivism thus reflects more than the intentions of bourgeois capitalism. It reflects, in a new *Gestalt*, civilization's oldest belief in power, the belief that power is proof.

Are the dialecticians, from Hegel to Adorno, wrong to see positivism as tyranny, as the arbitrary rule of a rootless and therefore insatiable rationality? Rationality for its own sake is reason's cannibalism. It is power for power's sake, hence totally irrational. The young Hegel hated it as positive religion, as an imposition frustrating all organic growth. Marx understood it as the ideological weapon of the ruling bourgeoisie, the absolutizing of the means which had brought it to power, and a moratorium on all questions concerning its claims. Adorno sees positivism as the papering over of the dichotomy between the individual and society, as the finalization of man's ideological, rationalistic imprisonment in sheer externality and generality. Hence schizophrenia is the only truth today. For in our situation the subject, the individual, has become a myth outside the myth. Happiness is found in being able to divest oneself of one's individuality. 'For when today, at the end of the process which totalized negative, i.e. rationalistic, domination, the thrall which holds human subjects imprisoned has itself become total, then all talk of human subjectivity has become sheer ideology.' (Adorno, 1970, p. 275.)

I wish to illustrate my contentions by excerpts from *Der Positivistenstreit*. This book reports the proceedings of a sociological congress in which positivists and dialecticians discussed their disagreements. The central discussion was between Adorno and Popper.

Positivism, Adorno says, is based on the assumption that 'contents of the conscious or unconscious mind which form a statistical universe function without further ado as keys' (p. 85). Questions of method overshadow those of content. 'Method, not the dignity of the subject, determines the selection' (p. 86). This, as we saw, merely reflects an epochal process. Quantity having taken the place of quality, only what can be measured matters. Gradually methods of measurement absorbed into themselves the creative, libidinal intensities that had formerly gone into the creation of qualitative differences in the making of things. 'Exchange-value, a mere concept as compared with use-value, governs human needs. . . . Appearance supersedes reality.' Once profit, measurable success, success as measurable, has become the ultimate criterion in society, 'statistical universes' have indeed key-function. Method usurps the dignity its subjects have lost. This is no more than bureaucratic functioning in science as in a society where today everyone is governed, not by anybody but by autarchic methods and methodology. The atomistic approach of positivistic science is 'the mirror of the Medusa of an atomized society'. Yet such an approach which merely reflects 'demands to be reflected on'. 'Otherwise empirical social science mistakes the epiphenomenon for the matter itself.'

Classifications, insulation, specializations, are pre-formed by society. At one time they, like classical economics, may have functioned purposefully, not only as weapons in the class struggle, but as means of overcoming old and newly-made poverty. Today they reflect those self-perpetuating processes which automatically recreate purposes no longer ours. 'It is therefore all the more urgent to transcend isolated researches, since mass-media so totally pre-form consciousness itself that it is no longer aware of the fact.' (p. 88.) 'Neglect of the dialectics between the particular and the general leads to ideological distortion. Unless theory remains transparent to the whole and its complexities, it cannot subsequently blow light into crude facts.' (p. 18.) 'The antagonistic character of society is central. It is juggled away by mere generalization.' (p. 91.) 'This would be science: to become aware of the truth and falsehood of that which the investigated phenomenon insists on being.' (p. 97.) 'The data of sociology, its facts, are not something ultimate but something conditioned. Sociology is therefore not permitted to mistake its knowledge for reality – its *Erkenntnisgrund* for its *Realgrund*.' All this, as Adorno appreciates, is open to the accusation of subjective idealism, of trying to smuggle the Kantian thing-in-itself back into methods of thinking which by their success have demonstrated the obsolescence of such a makeshift. Furthermore, his contentions can certainly be construed as ideological in turn, as pre-judiced. No assertions implying essential criticism of existing society can hope to escape such imputations. But it may be urged that by their very existence the contentions demonstrate at least the possibility that the *status quo* itself is an embodiment of *prae-judicare*. 'Average opinion is no approximative gauge of truth but of social appearance. This is true of those whom sociology considers its *ens realissimum*: the interrogated. If here critique is suppressed and only facts are reproduced, such reproduction is simultaneously falsification of facts into ideology.'

It is difficult to deny the arguability of this, especially at a time when increasing specialization is counter-balanced by increasing and increasingly complex interactions of politics and economics – interested pursuits – with science and technology – disinterested or, rather, differently interested pursuits. Today the interdependence of all social and sociological thinking can be seen clearly. For instance:

where the money is there is the major research. And not only economic, but political, military and prestige considerations determine where the money is going; that it does not go into the combating of rheumatism, bronchitis, cancer or ecological deterioration, to the extent to which it goes into researches that promise industrial or military applications, i.e. profit and power. It is possible that the continued academic insistence on specialization and specific responsibility expresses as much as anything else the fear of having it otherwise. 'Comte's hope that sociology would be able to guide society was naive. Now one no longer dare think of the whole, because one despairs of being able to change it.' (p. 142.)

Popper represents a rather refined kind of scientism. He states his argument in twenty-seven theses:

1 We know quite a lot. 2 Our ignorance is boundless. For that reason, though Popper believes in the existence of truth, our efforts can be no more than approximations. 3 It is the task of epistemology to interpret the tension between knowing and not knowing, for 4 the ever-shifting boundaries between them constitute its problem. (This assigns to epistemology not merely a restricted but a pre-judiced task, as if we knew the nature of knowledge, hence where it is and where not.) 5 The social as well as the other sciences are dependent both on the interest generated by their problems and on honesty of attack. 6 The main thesis: The scientific method is essentially not verification, but a progressive formulation of hypotheses which can be falsified. It proceeds by conjectures and refutations. It is a creative process, an adventurous exploration, in which the power of a hypothesis is in inverse proportion to its probability. It seeks corroboration, not certainty. 7 For that reason only a false naturalism in either the social or the natural sciences can believe that the tension between knowledge and ignorance can ever be eliminated. Like Kant, Popper believes that facts do not speak for themselves, but are created by and speak to our interest (Popper, 1969, pp. 189, 94, 48, 58, 47–8). 8 The relationship between sociology and anthropology has been reversed. The sociologist has become the 'observer of the totems and taboos of white natives'. 9 This reversal denotes the victory of a pseudo-naturalistic method. 10 A Pyrrhic victory, illustrated by an anecdote: an anthropologist had remained silent throughout a conference. His belated comment: he was not interested in the contents of the arguments but in the observable behaviour of the disputants. 11 It is quite mistaken to believe that the objectivity of science depends on the objectivity of individual scientists. 12 It lies exclusively in the critical tradition and therefore depends partly on social conditions. 13 This point is missed by the sociologist of knowledge who explains non-objectivity from an illusory scientific

vantage point. 14 Value-freedom pertains to the tradition, not to the individual scientist. (At this point the divergence from Adorno becomes marked. Here the functioning of tradition and society is understood and accepted, as by Peirce and the pragmatists, in a manner which corresponds exactly to what Adorno calls the juggling out of sight of the conflicts between the individual and society. The automatic harmonization which the process imposes inevitably, since it was elaborated for just that purpose, is taken for its justification.) 16–18 Popper deals with logic as organon and exercise of rational criticism. 19 Theory is a rational explication open to criticism. 20 Falsifiable claims to the truth in conjunction with logical structures of explication constitute an approximation to the truth and its explanatory power (*sic*). 21 There is no pure observing science, only a more or less critical theorizing. (Again the individual is subordinated to the automatism of an absolutized intention. Cf. Adorno (1970), p. 133): 'Refutation is fruitful only as immanent criticism. Seen from outside everything and nothing is refutable. One needs to be especially sceptical about the discussion game itself. It shows a trust in organized science as a final court of truth against which sociology should make itself impermeable.' It may be worth adding that the freedom Popper wishes to secure for the researching individual is analogous to that granted to the citizen by a bureaucratic economy.) 22–24 These deal with the relationship between psychology and sociology and insist on the latter's autonomy. The argument illustrates the border conflicts that are bound to continue, but only as border conflicts while the interest of specialists defines the spheres. 25 Economics is exemplary for the social sciences. It demonstrates that behaviour patterns are independent of psychological motivation. (What Popper does not seem to see is that economics can do this, because it concentrates exclusively and by definition on behaviour patterns detachable from psychological motivation. For example, I can make valid statements concerning rush hour behaviour precisely to the degree to which I abstract from any individual need or purpose.) Economics points to a new, general sociological approach: situation logic. Everything becomes explicable within the context of a given situation and the inherent logic of its demands. 'I in the place of Charlemagne would have done what he did.' (Popper does not explain how a situation with its peculiar logic can be detached from and delimited over against others. But then positivism has never experienced difficulties in connection with definitions and abstractions. The very word 'situation logic' denotes its perfect congruence with what I have called the myth of the system of co-ordinates: the particular, the individual, is explained by being placed, framed. He is identified with his position in a 'statistical universe'. That is to say, not his psychological motivation is eliminated, merely the wish to take it into account.) 26–27   It is admitted that an over-simplified situation logic is false, but argued that the method as criticizable approximation to truth is preferable to psychology. (Obviously, for the individual has been exorcised from the start. The method itself is already an over-simplification. Popper has arrived at a position not easily distinguishable in its essentials from behaviourist pragmatism or symbolic interactionism, Gehlen's actionism.)

It has been the ambiguity of Popper's falsification thesis that everything and nothing can be established in such a universe of counter-criticism. Yet it is inevitable that in it the predilections of the age will predominate. For instance Popper's own deprecation of psycho-analysis as non-falsifiable, of existentialism as a malaise, reflects an intellectualism impatient of what Adorno calls the antagonism of the general and the particular; an intellectualism which in turn reflects a belief in economic necessity and efficiency as criteria of truth (see for example Popper, 1969, pp. 34ff; 1942, vol. 2, pp. 214ff).

In his reply Adorno tried to show that sociology even as a science cannot adopt the scientific method as adequate. 'There are social theorems, insights into mechanisms at work behind the societal façade, which so fundamentally and for societal reason contradict the appearances that they simply cannot be adequately criticized by these.' (p. 132.) Adorno's final contention is as unacceptable to any form of positivism – except as metaphysics – as it seems inevitable to anyone who finds positivism 'metaphysical' and oppressive. 'Only for him who can think of society as different from what it is will it become a problem. Only through what society is not can it reveal itself for what it is.' (Cf. Heidegger's understanding of the *Nichts* as a constitutive aspect of reality, cf. 1967, '*Was ist Metaphysik?*') Comte, the arch-positivist, still wanted to bridle the newly-unleashed social forces. He still understood the antagonisms of society which his followers later evacuated of meaning. Finally 'positivism internalizes the compulsions of a totally societized – *vergesellschaftlichte* – society so that it could function perfectly. It is the puritanism of *Erkenntnis*.' (pp. 56–8.)

This last sentence evokes Weber who had most forcefully insisted on the connection between Puritanism, capitalism and bureaucracy, and whose life and thinking had been an embodiment of that hated and fascinating puritanism as one of *Erkenntnis* – not altogether unlike Nietzsche's. It led him to protestations, immediately disavowed, and to tragic resignation. For Weber, the positivist, was great enough to appreciate the implications of positivism, this intellectual complement to total bureaucracy (Weber, 1920, pp. 203–4):

The idea that modern professionalism bears an ascetic imprint is not new. The exclusive concentration on specialization which demands the renunciation of any Faustian wholeness of our humanity, is today the condition of any worthwhile human action. Which is to say that today 'deed' and 'renunciation' irrevocably condition one another. This ascetic groundswell of bourgeois life-style – in as far as it at least wishes to be a style and not stylelessness – Goethe had already wanted to point out to us from the height of his wisdom in *Wanderjahre* and in the ending he gave to Faust's life. For him this *Erkenntnis* signified a resigned adieu to an age of full and beautiful humanity. . . . The Puritan had willed to be a professional, we have to be. . . . Like a flimsy cloak that could be doffed at any moment, so the care for external goods was to lie on the shoulders of the saints. Fate let this cloak turn into a shell, hard as steel. Because ascetism undertook to transform the world and to get to work in it, external goods gained increasing and finally inescapable power over man. . . . Today the spirit has escaped from the shell. Victorious capitalism, since it has come to rest on mechanical foundations, no longer requires its presence. Even the rose-tinted mood of the Enlightenment, asceticism's laughing heiress, seems to be fading into nothing. And like the ghost of some former religious meaning of faith the idea of professional duty haunts our life. . . . No-one knows as yet who will inhabit that shell in the future; whether at the end of this uncanny development there will be new prophets or a mighty renaissance of old thoughts and ideals; or, if neither, a mechanized ossification frilled with a kind of contorted self-importance. For the 'ultimate man' of such a cultural development the words could indeed come true: 'Specialists without spirit, Epicureans without heart: This nothing imagines to have ascended to a stage of humanity never before attained' . . . But here we intrude upon a sphere of value judgments and judgments of faith with which this purely historical representation shall not be burdened.

No anti-positivist could have thought of a more powerful epitaph, written at the time when positivism was entering its maturity. Yet Weber continued to obey its summons of the day, the summons of a spiritless capitalism, and urged others to do likewise.

B The natural versus the social sciences

We begin by looking at a few German words which present peculiar difficulties of translation. This might enable us to formulate more clearly our critique of the attempts to distinguish between the natural and the social sciences.

Erkenntnis, Wissen, Kennen

How can one render *Erkenntnis* in English? Knowledge is often used. It can also mean perception, cognition, sometimes reason. None of these terms is adequate. To put it crudely, knowledge, even reason, is what I have. *Erkenntnis* is what I do. Yet as against 'reasoning', *Erkenntnis* signifies that my active apprehension is of something existing in its own right and beyond my apprehending.

Erkenntnis comes from *Kennen* which is quite distinct from *Wissen*. *Wissen* is both 'to know' and 'knowledge'. *Kennen* is to be acquainted with. I know this, that and the other, know how to do this, manage that – *ich weiss*. *Ich kenne* means I am acquainted with this person, an animal, a flower, a picture, a thing. I cannot *wissen* them. Even my subject: physics, sociology, bookkeeping, even aspects of it, I *kenne*. I merely can and sometimes must *wissen* how certain concepts, propositions or rules of procedure work within an agreed universe of discourse or activity. I may and must *wissen* how to run a certain machine or, up to a point, organization. *Kennen* denotes something personal, subjective, unfinished and unfinishable, involving me, interesting me. It is less certain than *Wissen* or, rather, as against *Wissen*, has really nothing to do with certainty.

Wissen is certain or *gewiss*, yes, or no, binary. For example, I must *wissen* with *Gewissheit* when, as an engineer I permit an overhauled plane to take off. *Wissen* gives manipulative power. It is tool-like, utilitarian, at the service of a purpose outside itself. It is a matter of skill, cunning, intrigue, precision. As such *Wissen* has no respect for anybody or anything. It is formal and intellective. It deals in propositions. It is not even concerned with facts which can only be *gekannt* as they are interest-shaped, but with statements concerning facts, with that which 'facts' the facts. It is general, repeatable, verifiable. It is the emotive complement to logic, mathematics – and to magic. Or, rather, these are the elucidation of its peculiar interests. Thus to say that only *Gewissheit* constitutes *Wissen* is both a tautology and the proper definition of *Wissen*. It is concerned only with itself not with that which it *weiss*. It is turned towards something outside itself only in as far as in my hands it becomes a tool, a concept, a *Begriff*, by means of which I want to grasp, not to *kennen* it.

Kennen recognizes the other in his or her or its otherness, as in his/her/its 'givenness' totally distinct from the *Kennen*. *Kennen* remains standing over against things, matters, persons, trying to appreciate them in all their complexities and the infinitesimal gradations of their shading. That is why it involves a personal *Stellungsnahme* or attitude. I have to take up a particular position *vis-à-vis* whatever is. Whatever I affirm, confirm or deny concerning that which stands over against me and which therefore I can begin to *kennen*, has the character of a *Bekenntnis*, a confession of faith, of an *Anerkenntnis* or acknowledgment. This is so in face of any *Gegenstand* or object, much more so in face of a *Gegenspieler*, one not just standing but playing over against me. Perhaps because I am afraid that he is playing against me and feel compelled to play against him, I am not satisfied with *Kennen*, cannot enjoy it, and wish to *wissen* all sorts of things about him. Such *Wissen* gives me a feeling of or real power over him.

Kennen implies judgment, discrimination, taste, wisdom, sympathy, empathy, patience, openness, deference. It is close to love. Only what I love I desire to *kennen*, and it may be that whatever I come to *kennen* more fully I cannot help loving. Only what I *weiss* or think I *weiss* about you can often make me fear and hate you. *Kennen* brings me close and closer to the other, at times enters the other, as the lover the beloved, as 'Adam knew Eve'. *Kennen* does not disdain analysis but is suspicious of it. Any *Zergliederung* or dismemberment brings me face to face with other entities which in turn can be *zergliedert*. Such *Kenntnis* does not necessarily aid a better *Kenntnis* of the whole. What I may come to *wissen* about the functioning of the parts can at times help me to help you – for example, as a surgeon – it cannot help me to *kennen* you better. Above all *Kennen* is concerned with re-membering.

Kennen is close to the senses, to tasting, savouring, feeling, seeing, smelling. It comes to rest in and has its reward in that which or him whom it comes to *kennen*. It is a kind of contemplation (see below, ch. 6). It is an end in itself, the end in itself, as any lover of anyone or anything *weiss*. The love-object is not used, except for a greater love. *Wissen* is concerned with handling, managing, manipulating. It inevitably and by right – for it is *Gewissheit* – presses towards the point beyond which it cannot go, at least not yet. It is brought to a halt not by respect for anything but by some inherent limitation. The only context in which *Wissen* has been applied rigorously in a human situation as *Wissen* is war and that perpetual state of war which economics, for its own purposes, defines and assumes as the natural human condition. Hence it is not surprising that science has often originated in and then perpetuated conflict situations, that it has always been immensely stimulated by them. In conflict we treat others as things which must be manipulated, lest they manipulate us, if need be to the point of elimination. (We need not *kennen* our enemy as a self. We wish to *wissen* all about him – and if nothing else, war propaganda could have taught us to be suspicious of what we think we know.)

Erkenntnis has always retained memories of the richer meaning of *kennen*. It is therefore neither knowledge nor reason. It is the act of making something available to reason, of bringing something to the notice of reason, so that it might become acquainted with it. There could be a refreshing shyness and humility in *Erkenntnis*, had not the philosophers first neutered it and then made it brazen. Even so, it cannot altogether shed its religious, its intensely personal, almost erotic connotations or associations.

In spite of all this, in Germany as elsewhere the scientific spirit asserted itself so powerfully that the wisdom of language was ignored completely. In grammar the distinction between *Wissen* and *Kennen* is clear and definite. I cannot substitute one word for the other. What I *kenne* I cannot *wissen*. What I *weiss* and can be certain of does not, as such, help me to become better acquainted with that about which I *weiss* so much. Yet what had been impossible idiomatically became intellectually respectable, as gradually *Naturphilosophie* became the grammatically monstrous *Naturwissenschaft*. If anything, nature of which I am a part and aspect is something I cannot hope to *wissen*, can at best hope to get a little better acquainted with as I become better acquainted with myself. Yet the *Wissen* I could acquire concerning the functioning of certain aspects within 'nature' which I cannot comprehend, was presumed to give me *Wissen* of nature. The logic of language would have suggested *Naturkennerschaft* (connoisseurship of nature), or *Naturbekanntschaft* (acquaintanceship with nature). *A fortiori* this logic should have produced *Geistesbekanntschaft*, for if there is one thing even beyond nature which, by its very nature, we cannot *wissen*, as it is that which *weiss*, it is *Geist*, *l'esprit*, mind-spirit or spirit-mind, for there is no English equivalent for *Geist*.

Nevertheless the monstrous *Natur- und Geistes-wissenschaft* became legal tender and drove out all other currencies in accordance with Gresham's law. Language was bent not to accommodate new experience but to distort and falsify it. For language is wise when it forbids me to claim that I *weiss* nature or *Geist* or you or myself or my dog, my garden, my academic research. On the other hand, of course, language remained true to its nature. In its distortion it reflected a distorted social reality. Most markedly since the Renaissance, but in a way already since Plato and Thales, Western man had desired to *wissen* what he could merely *kennen*, because he wished to manage and manipulate rather than appreciate and experience. (One may begin to appreciate Heidegger's belief that language is more philosophical than the philosophers. Had they followed its differentiation they might have avoided some fundamental confusions. It could be interesting to investigate the distinctions made by other languages and why English was left with one word. Perhaps the rise of Puritanism and capitalism made the libidinal drive to know contract into our narrow, rationalistic understanding of it, because 'carnal knowledge' was frowned upon. The means – rationalization etc. – became libidinized, because the 'ends' were no longer to be desired.)

Begreifen and Begriff

Kennen is concerned with the particular: fact, thing, constellation, structure, person. It cannot know and be sure. It can merely try to *begreifen* (touch, grope for, feel all over, comprehend) its object-subject. It cannot *greifen* or *ergreifen* (grasp, apprehend) or, rather, when it does this it ceases to *kennen* and to *begreifen*. *Begreifen* is never accomplished. It is exploratory, but also interested, purposeful or guileful, like a lover's caress. It must and wants to try again and again. It can then make for itself and its use a *Begriff*, a concept, of what it is trying to *begreifen*. I must not mistake that *Begriff* for my *Begreifen*. The latter is as concrete as it is tentative, my most real and personal emotive-intellectual activity and experiencing. The former is merely a provisional mental construct to aid me in the never ended process of *Begreifen*, and to signpost the process, possibly progress, for me and for others.[2] When I take the *Begriff* for more than this I am on the way to the Platonic idea and to that schizophrenia from which the wisdom of language would preserve me. The German *Begreifen* retains the association of tentativeness; both *Begreifen* and *Begriff* that of referring to something outside the self and with which it has to get in touch. Moreover, even the *Begriff*, as language would insist if we but listened, does not penetrate matter, its subject matter, the particular or individual. It builds up an image in the memory – it *erinnert* or re-members – possibly analogous to that which the continuous touching and tracing by a blind man constitutes in his mind. The *Begriff* certainly does not get at the heart of the matter. Hegel might have saved himself and us a lot of trouble, if he had listened more attentively to the associations of *Begreifen*. His sleight of hand consisted in the simplest of all tricks: he identified the *Begriff* not only with *Begreifen*, but with that which is to be *begriffen* by our *Begreifen*. And although man can never have more than a *Begriff* of that, or perhaps because of this, Hegel's trick worked. And his success revealed what had always been done by philosophers, including positivists, possibly because they always wanted more than they could get.

Vernunft and Verstand

We cast just a glance at these two terms. Here the German makes a distinction for which there is no proper English equivalent. These two words can be and have been translated quite indifferently as reason, mind, sense, understanding, discernment, judgment. Nor do any of the distinctions we might detect between the English synonyms reflect those between *Vernunft* and *Verstand*. I must hasten to add that here idiomatic usage is confused. It is incomparably less definite in distinguishing than in regard to *Kennen* and *Wissen*. We are dealing with a philosophical distinction. Goethe says: '*Vernunft* in its tendency towards the divine, deals exclusively with that which is growing and alive; *Verstand* with that which is finished and ossified.' *Vernunft* comes from *Vernehmen*, meaning to perceive, mainly through the ear, to take into oneself, to 'take to heart'. The underlying connotation of listening to someone may point to a religious provenance – in the sense in which religion has its provenance in the experience of the other as mystery. *Vernunft* never quite lost that connotation. It is a sublime faculty, concerned with the perception of ultimates even when, as in the case of Kant, with the ultimate limits of its own capacity. *Vernunft* has become an opaque mixture of passivity and aggression – compare the roles Kant assigns to the pure and practical *Vernunft* respectively and Hegel's understanding of it as the struggle of the Spirit towards self-realization. Now it is all ear, full of trepidation concerning its ability to perform the simplest operations. Now it is the stern lawgiver whom to obey against all claims of the world and the senses is perfect freedom. In Hegel it becomes omnivorous. In Schopenhauer and Nietzsche it is humiliated. Marx tried to give to it a clear-sighted modesty and pride *vis-à-vis* that which is other than itself and does not lose its independence just because *Vernunft* can perceive it by means of *Begreifen* and *Begriff*. *Erkennen* is the activity of *Vernunft*.

Verstand functions on a lower level altogether. It comes from *Verstehen*, meaning to stand in the place of, put oneself in the place of. The English 'understanding', though the obvious translation is really as close to *Vernunft* as to *Verstand*. (Which precisely opens up our problem of understanding in the *Geisteswissenschaften*.) It has preserved associations of 'standing under', submitting oneself to, at least in the sense of being open to. Unfortunately just here Dilthey and Weber in their use of *Verstehen* have complicated and confused matters, not only for us but for themselves. Idiomatically they were justified: I *verstehe* you as well as it or that 'it is so' and 'how to do it'. Dilthey had tried to give to the word its full meaning of 'to understand'. Yet it remained his problem to the end, how to demonstrate that, how and in how far one had understood, or could, as interpreter, put oneself into the place of another. No demonstration proved satisfactory. It could not. It will always remain problematical what is to be proved here, what would constitute a proof; and any proving will remain part of the *Verstehen* which the proof is to establish as *Verstehen*.

Proof would not have been required, if Dilthey had not wished to *verstehen* but to *vernehmen*. One cannot prove that one has *vernommen* or perceived, heard, experienced. Any question as to whether or not one has heard correctly, can be answered – and never finally – only by listening again and by once more trying to convey to others what one has heard, in such a way that they would want to listen. This was what Dilthey really wanted to do, and his readers or listeners with him. His *Verstehen* was closer to *Vernunft* than to *Verstand*. Yet the unthinking use of a word, the abuse of it, reflecting a complex of socio-philosophical preconceptions, avenged itself and distorted his efforts, disoriented his quest. That the misuse seemed and seems quite justified idiomatically may point to societal implications. It also illustrates how anything that is taken for granted, and perhaps most of all language, not merely reflects but reinforces the distortions of the *status quo*. (This implies a fundamental critique of linguistic philosophy.)

It was easy and natural for Weber to pick up Dilthey's *Verstehen* without being any longer troubled by its problematics. For him *Verstehen* is manipulative, it is a function of the *Verstand*, i.e. of the faculty of manipulative rationality. As a German he could not altogether fail to *vernehmen* the overtones of sympathy and appreciation still ringing in *Verstehen*. Yet these served no other function now than the paradoxical one of hiding from him and others the fact that they no longer mattered. On the contrary, his striving for objectivity was designed to neutralize and, if possible, to eliminate those overtones. From the point of view of contemporary sociology, Weber merely burdened himself with an unnecessary word. He does not really want to *verstehen* but to *wissen*. (Causality and objectivity constitute areas of *Wissen*.) This is precisely what every scientist by definition, and if it must be in the teeth of reality or the evidence, wishes to do.

Aufheben, Erinnern, Tatsache

Aufheben and *Aufhebung*, great words since Hegel, have these connotations: to pick up, to lift, raise. This implies two further actions: to make something cease to be on one level, to eliminate it there; to bring it into being on another level, a higher one, in a different context, and to preserve it there in its new *Sinnzusammenhang* (meaningful context), in and as a new reality. So the word has gathered into itself the meaning of all kinds of 'bringing to an end' – a law, a siege – so that something new can now be achieved or attempted. It has kept its full meaning of: to keep, preserve, treasure. It denotes the full act of eliminating something in order to preserve it in a new context which it will change and by which it is being changed. As there simply is no English equivalent, I shall sometimes have to use the German words.

Erinnern is a specific form of *Aufhebung* in all its three connotations. It lifts something out of one context, a partially external, contingent, ephemeral one, that now has passed and is no longer, into another context, an inner, controlled, personal and no longer quite so ephemeral one. The something *erinnert*, for whatever reasons, has ceased to exist in its original 'place', and is taken up to be preserved through the present for the future, but in a different 'place'. Now to re-member has similar associations. Something that has somehow gone to pieces is reconstituted into a new totality, an inner one. But while the stress of the English lies on the act of re-constitution, the German stresses the transposition into the inner world, into pure subjectivity. It is useful to recall that both the English and German language insist that re-membering, *Erinnern*, is something we do, not something that happens to us. It is a creative activity. And this again is significant in relation to the fact – *Tatsache* – that all *Kennen* and *Wissen*, all forms of knowledge, are a form of re-membering, a kind of *Aufhebung*.

Tatsache is the result of a constituting and creative activity, of a particular, continuous and, on the whole, social re-membering or *Erinnern* (cf. Nietzsche, 1924, *Genealogie der Moral*, part 2, paras 1–3). *Tatsache*, as a form of *Erinnern*, is an even more specific kind of *Aufhebung*. The English 'fact' already could tell us much. A *factum* is not primarily 'something that is there'. That as such cannot be a fact. There is too much of it. A fact is something we have made, constituted, 'put there'. It is as much a 'thing' as any manufactured object. It is likely that in primitive society tools were the first and only facts. These gradually created an increasing number of further facts, artifacts, possibilities, interests. (It is interesting that for the late-comer Marx tools again were the only 'real facts': the means of production producing facts. And we remember Durkheim's treatment of social structures and functions as 'things', as facts.)

A fact, like a thing or a word, is constituted by its context, which in turn is a vectorized social need, purpose, interest. There is no fact that does not serve a purpose within our general factuality, *Wirklichkeit*, and *Wirklichkeit* is that which has been wrought, accomplished. Outside that factuality which is the result of our act-uality there are no facts. Beyond it lies the sheer otherness. We call it *un-wirklich*, un-factual, un-real. For 'real' comes from *res*, thing or matter, is a *factum*. Yet we are not permitted to think of the *Unwirkliche* as non-being, though we are right to think of it as no-thing. We cannot say it is not, simply because we have no word or thought for it, but must remember that only word and intention create facts.

The German *Tatsache* emphasizes the connotation of fact. It literally means a thing or matter constituted by a deed, an action-thing, a matter of deed. Now *Sache* in itself denotes not merely a thing, matter, cause, but, as *res* in *res publica*, a public affair, concern, even action. *Das ist meine Sache* means 'This is something I have to do something about'. So the emphasis on deed in *Tatsache* is particularly strong. Again we re-member and *erinnern* that the vast web of scientific-technological, of economical and political actuality or factuality is – merely – a fact. Through it we are impressed by our expressions. 'Nothing succeeds like success.' Such a state of autosuggestion on a cosmic scale can be dangerous, just because our factuality is only one possibility among many. It may therefore be important to add to Vico's contention that 'we can understand only what we have made': we can unmake, de-fact, *aufheben*, what we have made. Language once again proves wiser than our intellect and could help us to 'realize' possibilities of 'reality' beyond factuality. As Heidegger puts it, Man's *Sein* or *Dasein*, the 'truth', i.e. the unveiling, uncovering, revealing of his being, is possibility (Heidegger, 1967, p. 148; 1954, pp. 173ff; 1931, pp. 143–4).

Dichten and Denken

In German *Denken* (to think) is closely related to *Dichten* for which there is no English equivalent, though 'thought' corresponds etymologically to *Dichten* as 'thinking' to *Denken*. *Dichten* has remained a distinct term in German. It is more than the activity of composing a poem; more than the imagining of something that is not, or the 'poetic' delineation of something that is but not so. A poet is *Dichter* as much in his essays or his philosophical writings, as in his lyrics, epics or dramas. Great writers are often called *Dichter* and *Denker*, and note the order of priority. This has deep roots in German thought. Perhaps because it was Luther's translation of the Bible, truly the work of a *Dichter* and *Denker*, which more than anything else consolidated the German language. It may explain why the German Enlightenment since the days of Lessing was so much less purely intellectual than the French and English variety. (It is worth comparing *Nathan der Weise* or *Minna von Barnhelm* with *Candide*. Lukács, 1964, pp. 21–38.)

Schopenhauer and Nietzsche, both in their work and in its

influence among artists and writers rather than among academic philosophers, demonstrate the persistence of the *Dichter-Denker*. Nietzsche himself was torn by a violent love-hate between the two in his breast; and so in our days were men like Benjamin, Adorno, Bloch, Heidegger, Lukács. On the other side we have the *Denker-Dichter* like Rilke, George, Kafka, Mann and Musil. This synoptic view of *Dichten* and *Denken* explains Goethe's rearguard action against Newton – also why it was bound to fail – and Adorno's *Negative Dialektik*. It explains the *Positivistenstreit*, the polemics between positivists and dialecticians and the efforts of the former to prove the scienticity of their thinking. This *Dichten-Denken* is expressed by the word *Besinnung*. (Cf. Heidegger, 1954, '*Wissenschaft und Besinnung*'.)

Sinnen and Besinnung

These words are quite frequently and idiomatically used with little awareness of their distinct expressiveness which, however, they never shed completely. *Sinnen* means meditating, reflecting, speculating, wondering, musing. It also preserves an association of going back to, giving oneself to, listening to one's senses. *Besinnung* is the result of *Sinnen*: recollection, reorientation. It is thinking not exclusively about the matter under scrutiny as about its *Sinn*, meaning, significance, reality. It involves the thinker in his relation and attitude to that which he is thinking about. In *Besinnung* the *Sinnende* asks himself where he stands, where he is, where he is going; but also who he is as a thinking-sensuous being in relation to his thinking. *Besinnung* is a brooding over something like a hen that something may come to life, may break out of its shell, reveal itself and its *Sinn*. It is 'making sense' and yet not quite. For it does not so much try to make as to find sense, to let sense show itself. Is it possible that English, because of its preoccupation with 'making sense', has no word for *Besinnung*? Has it ever had one and lost it? Perhaps Puritans and capitalists had no time for *Besinnung*, as they had evacuated all *Sinn* into the invisible and inscrutable God and were left with a demythologized, a *sinnlose*, senseless, world in which sense had to be made (Borkenau, 1934, pp. 91–5).

Erscheinung

This means appearance. The word is important in connection with phenomenology which is concerned with *Erscheinungen*. Now *Schein* and *Scheinen* not only mean appearance and to appear, even false appearance. They also mean shining and to shine. *Der Schein trügt* does not just say that appearances are deceptive. For *Schein*, because it shines and glitters, reveals and deceives. It denotes something both better and worse, more and less, than appearance. We can *erkennen* anything only because it shines, because it illuminates something or is illuminated by something, makes us see something. But precisely because we are dependent in our looking on the thing's *Scheinen*, we can never be sure we are not being deceived. Therefore, and the *Geisteswissenschaftler* should prick up his ears, if we are after certainty and definiteness in our thinking, we shall continue to be troubled by *Schein*, by 'mere' appearance, by the perpetual possibilities of deception. We shall for ever try to reach the point where we may say we are beyond all *Schein* – i.e. in darkness – and from where we shall be able to manage all *Erscheinungen* according to our intentions, since we no longer enjoy the *Schein*. If, like Heidegger, we believe that the search for certainty is the fundamental mistake which constituted and perpetuates metaphysics, we are reasonably free to rejoice in whatever shines, because all *Schein* reveals something – as every artist and every woman knows. It may even reveal the illusoriness of intentions which make us afraid of *Schein* as of something that might deceive.

In as far as we are not afraid of deception, believing it to be revelation as well – we recall the psycho-analytical process – appearances cannot deceive, for we shall not be trying to fix and fossilize their motions or moments. We shall be satisfied with *Erscheinungen* as those *Lichtungen*, the clearances in the forest from where light is cast over the surroundings. The difference between Husserl and Heidegger can be traced to the different mood, *Stimmung*, *Schein* and *Erscheinung* had for either. For Sartre *Schein* and *Lichtung* had become the *néant*. He remained the badly hurt child who could not rejoice in *Erscheinungen* (Sartre, 1969b).

Stimmung

We have said that a difference in mood might account for a so much more substantial-looking difference between important thinkers. This leads directly to a word Heidegger uses specifically: *Stimmung* or mood (1932, pp. 134ff). The words are equivalent, up to a point. Beyond that the differences become marked. This becomes clearer when we look at the cognates of *Stimmung* which show that German evaluates it differently, that it takes mood more seriously. It accepts the fact, or as fact, that reality is coloured by my mood, that there is no reality not thus coloured. The mood may be personal, it may be that of a whole age. *Stimmung bestimmt*, it determines something. When anything *stimmt*, it is in accord with something else or with everything else, as my experience of reality is in accord with my *Stimmung*. *Stimmung* also has the association of 'being in tune with, attuned to' something, the universe, for example. For *Stimmen* is to tune, to tune an instrument until it *stimmt*, until it is correct and able to convey *Stimmung*. No hard-headed British empiricist or French rationalist would ever have dreamed of assigning such constitutive importance to mood or *humeur*. The German answer could be that both empiricism and rationalism are *Stimmungen*, i.e. they could not have been conceived, unless they gave to some men a feeling of satisfaction, the experience of *es stimmt*. (Does the truth of a poem reside in its capacity to convey *Stimmung*, so that one feels and knows *es stimmt*? What does that signify, even sociologically?)

Entschliessen

This means to decide, determine, resolve. Beyond that, in German it contains overtones of to unlock. Again the equivalence of English and German is fair. Yet while de-termine fixes the end so one can move towards it, *entschliessen* could stress a new openness to one does not know yet what. Resolve and resolution could be given such overtones. *Entschliessen* is close to *Erschliessen* (to uncover, make available, open up).

These *Besinnungen* are not to be mistaken for amateur etymology. They were a *Sinnen* over some words in the hope that they might yield illumination; also a *Sinnen* over the difficulties of expressing the thought of one language in another. Different languages have grown out of different experiences. They also define and delimit the capacities for further experiencing (cf. Whorf, 1967, pp. 57–64, 233–70).

We return to the question of how to distinguish the social from the natural sciences, of what constitutes a scientific approach in the *Geisteswissenschaften*. We started by pointing out how scholars, especially German social philosophers, often created peculiar difficulties for themselves and others by disregarding the wisdom of language. Was this inevitable?

This much is certain: *Wissen* and civilization are intricately interwoven, perhaps synonymous. Both express a peculiar and exclusive respect for power. It is obviously the highest court of appeal. The forcefulness of an army or of an argument establishes facts, justice and truth. The irresistible and irrefutable is real. In some ways our thinking is so deeply conditioned by these civilized assumptions that we find it hard to escape from the power of their cogency. 'In the impartiality of scientific language, the powerless has lost all power to express itself.' (Horkheimer-Adorno, 1969, p. 29. Cf. Weber, 1964, pp. 536, 562.) Weber took it for granted that power was the ultimate social reality to which the merely ideal had to be sacrificed in case of conflict. He would naturally subordinate his most burning concerns for social justice to the demands of power-politics. A nation had to be strong in order to be just (1964, pp. 672–4). Pareto and Durkheim were equally persuaded. Older sociologists and philosophers had not yet begun to question the assumption underlying the belief in power. As far as politicians are concerned, two World Wars and a few dozen minor genocides have not radically shaken those assumptions: that power establishes order and peace. (Today power is often exercised economically rather than militarily. The consequences are similar.) Even non-politicians find it difficult, when thinking philosophically, scientifically or historically, to remember that their actual human experiences and relations are not expressed through or based on the exercise of power, that they are merely distorted or destroyed by the use of force – as only too often happens among people conditioned to think in terms of power and possessions. (Most of literature, from the beginning of the *Iliad* to the death of Anna Karenina and beyond, bears witness to this fact. And so does the peculiar character of the power or non-power literature exerts. We will not take it seriously, we cannot let it go. As a whole it is a protest against our civilized assumptions as radical as that of the Hebrew prophets, though often more tactfully or timidly expressed.)

Plato already wanted above all else to *wissen*. Was he the first to ignore the admonition of language and to confuse *epistamai* and *gignosko*? As poet he understood the difference. *Phaedrus* and the *Symposion*, his use of myth, the moments when his dialogues really are dialogues, show him as true philosopher, lover of wisdom, *Dichter* and *Denker*. Later philosophers discarded precisely this aspect. They could do it easily, for Plato himself had set the precedent. Largely for political reasons he became fascinated by the power of logic, the conclusive and compelling nature of its processes, overriding all mere personal predilections, the fixity of its conclusions. Plato could not yet realize that the syllogism merely transferred conviction from premise to conclusion, that the conclusion no more than exposed the premise, that the conclusiveness added nothing to the truth or untruth of the fact, conviction or belief, implicit in the premise. But he illustrated from the beginning that, and how, logic serves ideological interests. As Pareto insisted, the capacity of logic to give to the emotive experience of confirmation the character of revelation has preserved its fascination through the ages. For *the syllogism is an engine especially designed to transport conviction to the place where it is most needed at a particular moment.*

Plato had barely begun to explore the possibilities of logic, before he employed it not only in the construction of his realm of ideas but in the building of his Republic. It seems to me that what happened there was crucial for all later European thinking and unthinkingness, both philosophical and scientific. It conditioned Western thought more deeply than even Popper claimed, for it conditioned Popper's thought as well – and, of course, mine. Logic is the perfect methodology of *Wissen*, the lubrication of all *Wissensprozesse*. It promotes the most effective and frictionless transition of all possible kinds of *Wissen*, each of which, in its proper sphere, may represent a justified, because well tested, conviction or skill, or a tautology. One could also say that logic is the functioning of all *Wissen*, the directive for the proper use of the instruments of manipulation.

This logic Plato, immediately and with utter lack of inhibition, began to put to work in the sphere of *Kennen* and *Erkenntnis*, as if such a heart transplant presented no problems whatsoever. He transferred the method of manipulation from the field where it applied to one where it does not. His *Republic* and *Laws* suggest it was done intentionally and that it reflected the civilized intention. *Wissen* is grasping. It conceptualizes and systematizes. Concepts and systems are ordered by logic. *Kennen, Erkennen*, does not grasp. It looks, listens, *be-greift*, touches, tastes, smells. It lives in leaving the subject-object inviolate (Heidegger, 1954, pp. 150ff; 1967, pp. 148ff). In the act of grasping it ceases to be *Erkenntnis*. What I have grasped I no longer *kenne*. *Ich weiss es*. It exists for me now only as a point or function in a field of co-ordinates – just as the prospective citizens of Plato's *Republic*, the actual citizens of contemporary bureaucracies. Plato took the fatal step of subordinating *Kennen* to *Wissen*. He did it, because he was afraid of that which could merely be *gekannt*, recognized, acknowledged, respected, and which might hit back one day; which could not be *gewusst*, predicted, managed, organized, contained, defined and confined. Plato's supremacy in European thought may be due to the fact that he symptomatizes the civilized fear of life, of unpredictability and fluidity. He gave voice to the fear of the violator, to be violated in turn, unless the *status quo* can be fixed for ever. Since philosophers have always been civilized men and usually on the side of the violators, they have followed in his footsteps. And so have the scientists who do not wish to be one whit the less civilized. So *Wissen* and *Kennen* have been confused to the point where we believe to *kennen* only when we feel sure we *wissen*.

Now *Wissen* and *Kennen*, though denoting two radically different approaches and attitudes, are not easily separable in regard to any given subject-object. I should never want more than to *kennen* you. Unless the acquaintance contains its own reward, I might as well turn elsewhere. But I can *wissen* a lot about you and there is a fluid but real interaction between these two kinds of knowledge. For example, you, my friend, may survive, because I, your doctor, *weiss* what is wrong with you. I love you because I *kenne* you, not on account of what I happen to *wissen* about you. Yet such *Wissen* can influence, enhance or destroy my love. The artist must *wissen* how to do what he wishes to do. His accomplished work he can only *kennen*. This may explain why the artist is an artist in as far as he manages to express more than he *weiss* (cf. A. Ehrenzweig, *The Hidden Order of Art*, London, 1967). What are the implications of these contentions for science in general and for the social sciences in particular? If it is possible that *Wissen* can become destructive of *Erkenntnis*, how can we safeguard the latter and use the former in its service?

Wissen, as related to skill, *techne*, is instrumental. It is directed towards an end in which it is *aufgehoben* – as, for example, Rembrandt's in his late self-portraits. This is so even when, as in modern science, it appears as if the end of *Wissen* is further *Wissen*. *Kennen* is an end in itself. It is inter-subjective, personal, essentially non-objective, having no objective beyond itself, no ulterior motives. Moreover, the Rembrandt I *kenne* is not the one you *kennst*. Here is nothing to prove – taste is not a matter for argument – but possibly much to talk about; for in talking one often reaches further *Erkenntnis*. (*Kennen* as the end in itself is acknowledged by the rational mysticism of Aristotle for whom man's *telos* is the *Erkenntnis* of God; more emotionally by Paul, 'then I shall *erkennen*, even as I am *erkannt*'. It is recognized by Hindu, Tantric, Jewish erotic mysticism as that of which the bond between man and woman, their carnal knowledge of each other, is the symbol.)

Even today it would be admitted that when I am using my acquaintances for the furthering of my purpose, I either do not or do not wish to *kennen* them. I simply wish to use what I *weiss* about them for my ends – which, as we have seen, usually are not ends. The marriage of convenience is the most obvious example. Because I *weiss* what I want of her, I need not *kennen* her. Unfortunately bourgeois marriage in general, as the Christian *Geschlechtsbetrieb*, the sex-organization within a repressive sexual morality, has always had the character of a marriage of convenience. No wonder sociology, equally deeply conditioned by the libidinization of the means, has forgotten the distinction between *kennen* and *wissen*. It seems to hold no special interest for it.

I now turn to a late *Besinnung* of Heidegger, not because it demonstrates anything, but because it will help me to clarify a point I here wish to make. In his talk '*Bauen, Wohnen, Denken*' (1954) he reflects on the connotation of the first two words. Once again neither has an adequate equivalent in English. *Bauen* does not merely mean to build, though in contemporary German usage it means little more than that when used without prefix or not in conjunction with other words. But in *Gartenbau, Ackerbau* (horticulture and agriculture), in *Anbauen, Bebauen, Erbauen*, the older, more comprehensive sense of cultivating, nurturing, letting grow, is still fully alive. For example, *Erbauen* means both to erect and to edify. *Erbaulich* is what is both edifying and enjoyable. For while edifying suggests the imposition of moral structure on psyche or community, *erbaulich* suggests the nurturing of whatever there is ready to be brought forth. Hence it is enjoyable. *Wohnen* means to inhabit, to live in, to be at home. *Wohnung* is not just my flat but the home in which I am at home. English has no verb to correspond to the noun 'home' – except for birds. *Gewohnheit* means custom, habit, is that in which I *wohne*, in which my living has its *Wohnung*. (In English there is the connection between habit and to inhabit, yet the latter has lost most 'homely' associations.) Originally, so Heidegger maintains, there was only one word, *wuon*, for both *Bauen* and *Wohnen*. For a hunting and/or farming community this was natural. Man lives among and on that which gives him life and lets him grow and which, for that very reason, he grows, lets come to life and nurtures. He is at home in his nurturing and what nurtures him is his home.

The separation of *Bauen* and *Wohnen* may reflect the advance of civilization. One now can *bauen* beyond the needs of *Wohnen*: palaces, for instance. On the other hand man can be reduced to a *Wohnen* far below his capacity for *Bauen*, far below his needs, and perhaps because he has to build palaces. Anyway, he now simply happens to live in what he or others happen to have built. So *Bauen* becomes *techne*, to erect, construct. It no longer serves the bliss and needs of *Wohnen*. It can soar. It can follow its own laws, free of the *Gewohnheiten* of communal life. On the contrary, it imposes its demands, its impersonal necessities, on the needs of *Wohnen*. *Wohnung* becomes the place where a man recuperates from today's *Bauen* to be fit for more tomorrow. Or it becomes a place of ostentation. Heidegger reflects on the obvious which a thousand cities shout to the sky: that we shall not know how to *bauen*, until we have rediscovered how we want to *wohnen*. In the meantime we are building so hectically that we have no time to find out what we want.

A *Bauen* that expresses a *Wohnen* cannot be an imposition. Perhaps it cannot be imposing. It does not construct. It nurtures, lets grow, lets be. Science has become exclusively concerned with *Bauen*. In this preoccupation with itself it has moved so far from the requirements of *Wohnen* that Wittgenstein could say it no longer touched upon the problems of living. Two things are becoming clearer now, though we may still be far from being able to formulate satisfactorily even the questions they raise: 1 The problematics of the natural and the social sciences is not altogether different, since the sciences themselves as expression of our *Bauen* and *Wohnen* are interacting. 2 The question whether it is desirable for sociology to be or become a science remains open.

1 It is only too well known that since the days of Comte and Spencer, then again since those of Dilthey, Weber, Durkheim, Freud, the social sciences have tried to appropriate the methods that had proved so effective in physics and chemistry. These in turn had reflected the equally successful economic methods that had been developed since the end of the Middle Ages, and in which everything worked for the best except for most of the people, i.e. both economics and the natural sciences express the same societal intention: profit. For success, like profit, means increase, measurable increase, and presupposes the – possibly infantile – belief that 'more' equals 'better'. All sciences are united in this concentration on the measurable, quantifiable advance – where to? – on the elaboration of theories which make increasing areas accessible to interpretations pre-determined and pre-formed by the theories.

Once again the instrumental character of science emerges, its tool-like functioning. Like the stone-mason, the carpenter, the couturier, the scientist is equally ruthless in the elimination of whatever is not required for his purpose, in the imposing of his purpose on the material. His concentration has the edge of a chisel, the point of a pin, the divisiveness of a pair of scissors, the insistence of a drill. Hence refined technology advances scientific possibilities, scientific progress makes for greater technical precision and creates new technical possibilities which in turn advance science etc. Both scientific and technological achievement is proportionate to the degree of precision with which either can define purpose and method. It matters little whether a rocket or a bridge is being built, a star spiral or the position of an electron investigated.

Of the social sciences only economics has a comparable precision. It managed this by means of a similarly ruthless elimination and audacity of abstraction. Any remnant of mere humanity, man's individuality, willing, desiring, hoping, fearing, even his irrational desire to keep alive, his communal cravings and cravings for communion, all this was discounted totally. Of all possible communal interactions one aspect of one particular interaction and its attendant interest was isolated and all further attention exclusively concentrated upon it. This was economic interest, interest in profit, now treated as interest *per se*, i.e. an interest hermetically sealed off from the multitudinous interests engendered by living and

95

loving and believing. Attention was focused on precisely that form of individual and social directedness and their interplay which epitomized the capitalist development: insulation and apotheosis of profit as the measurable entity, the *ens realissimum*. Thus economics was able to treat its subject matter as physics and chemistry treated theirs.

The universe of interest which the economist defined and explicated is as far removed from actual human relationships and motivations, as the Galileian-Newtonian-Einsteinian constructs from the world of everyday things. It is as meaningful or meaningless to say that economics represents the social reality, as to insist that a girl or a chair is 'really' a vortex of infra-atomic tensions. Yet this capacity for near total conceptualization which gives to economics the appearance of cohesion exactly proportionate to its concentration on appearances is the envy of sociology and sociologists, even of philosophy. (We are reminded of the quarrel between the instructors of the *Bourgeois Gentilhomme*.) Maybe economics was able to do what it did, because it reached maturity before capitalism had begun to develop the rudiments of a conscience, to be disturbed by its inner contradictions. This meant that no epistemological question had as yet raised its head (Habermas, 1969, p. 64). Sociology and psychology of the modern kind are the result of that disturbance. This does not prevent them from striving for a precision only appearances attain – sometimes, and under stringent conceptual constraint – nor from forgetting that they came into being as an attempt to break through appearances to that which they were intended to hide. (In this connection one is tempted to ask: How would Marx's thoughts have developed, if he had taken his early sociological and philosophical insights more seriously, and had understood better not only the function but the pretensions of economics 'as a science'? If, in other words, his battles had been fought over something less impermeable than surplus value.)

We are now approaching the central problem science poses today, that of scientism. If science is an instrument of understanding, it must be at the service of something for the sake of which it is being employed. *Wohnen* and nothing else gives significance to *Bauen*. Now science came into being at a time when man still felt very much at home in the world. He may have fought, and at times virulently, against all kinds of religious, moral, metaphysical and political doctrines. His conviction of a structured universe was yet unshaken. In a way that conviction, like all others a *Stimmung*, was the basis of science. Descartes remained a believer. He needed the creator God to guarantee the reality of his intellectual concepts. Newton remained a mystic. Leibniz wrote a *Theodicy*. Voltaire could still say that if there were no God, he would have to be invented. Kant did invent him for the sake of a private morality which could expect no reward at all in a market-controlled world. Even Machiavellianism and Hobbesism believe, if parasitically, in a well-structured if appalling psychic reality. By the time two or three generations of founding fathers were trying to define and delimit sociology, they, as most of their fellow men, still had implicit faith in moral imperatives – as valid at least for others – and in the impregnable structure of the mind, *Vernunft*.

The scientism from Comte to Durkheim, from Spencer to Peirce, from Marx to Weber, was still soaked in moralism. Even Weber's passionate insistence on a value-free science was fuelled and victualled by a belief in honour, integrity, the readiness for sacrifice. Until the end of the First World War, in which workers and intellectuals, even sociologists, fought enthusiastically on either side, science had, as a matter of fact, been at the service of a peculiar ethos, of a class or class structure, of a diffuse, fairly general and penetrating socio-political attitude. It was the handmaid of a bourgeois ideal and ideology and in that role, for better or worse, produced the present situation. The bourgeois ethos has not survived the wars of the twentieth century, certainly not unimpaired. The mixture of optimism, humanism and scientific technology went bad. World-strategic, geo-political necessities, military and economic, both hastened and expressed the emancipation of science and technology, the subordination of all other considerations to theirs. The invention of the computer became inevitable.

Hence the real problematics of a value-free science has arisen only today. Only now the implications of building for building's sake are beginning to become explicit. The impetus of autonomous science-technology overrules all non-scientific interests. Automation rules in a fissiparous society, both in the proliferating specializations and in the purely economical, mechanical attempts at reintegration. As the only scientific among the social sciences, economics and its considerations or interests rule supreme, and yet do not rule. For the tragic irony of the situation lies in this: from the beginning the scientific method had reflected the unearthing processes of the newly-evolving capitalism with its libidinization of the means. For centuries both capitalism and science had been able to live on the millennia-old investments in religion, morals, conventions. By now the capital has been reinvested, to the last penny, in the process itself which can feed only on itself. Today for the first time Western man is totally homeless and his desperate free-wheeling presents ecological problems of unimaginable proportions.

2   Therefore the question whether and in how far sociology can be or become a science remains wide open, in spite of almost unanimous protests to the contrary. According to Husserl, each science

qua science is absolved from phenomenological and epistemological doubts concerning its subject matter. According to Heidegger it cannot, for those very reasons, approach it at all (Husserl, 1950, p. 52; Heidegger, 1954, pp. 45–70, 133–4; cf. Adorno, 1970, pp. 38–41, 142). *Besinnung* becomes imperative. A place has to be found where 'reflection of' may become 'reflecting on'; where questions of truth, order, reality, being, may be asked, even though there be no answer yet or ever. Otherwise reason will rationalize itself out of existence. What is needed therefore is either an exception, i.e. a science not absolved from epistemological doubts, or a discipline which cannot and will not be a science in the strict sense of that term. It seems to me that psychology as well as sociology and both with the aid of philosophy could qualify for such a discipline. For they are dealing directly with the problems of the individual in society. Yet how can they begin to come to *kennen* their interrelation when they are actually split by the social reality?

Horkheimer and Adorno say (1969, pp. 20–33): 'The self who has learned about order and subordination through its subjugation of the world, soon identifies truth altogether with such ordering thought – *disponierendem Denken* – though truth cannot subsist except in definite distinction from it. By its taboo on mimetic magic, the self has taboo'd that knowledge which alone meets its object.' 'One no longer attempts to achieve a kind of ecology within or symbiosis with nature by means of adaptation. Nature is to be ruled by work. Only the work of art still has affinity to magic.' Increasing mathematization leads to 'the subjugation of everything to logical formalism at the price of reason's obedient submission to the immediate *status quo*'. Because the self, when treated as wholly reasonable, does violence to itself, and because it in this way assumes a task which only an impossible completion or totalization could justify, the Enlightenment was not simply a liberation. It also was 'mythic dread become absolute'. Its positivism – in the contemporary as well as in Hegel's use – could not permit anything 'to remain outside itself. That outside is the real source of all dread' and the self remains outside (cf. Borkenau, 1934, on Descartes).

Already Kant had taken the dichotomies of Descartes to the point where all science stood on one side and the isolated individual in his solipsistic freedom on the other. It may be that this philosophy expressed the bourgeois reality with its purely ideological balance between an omnipotent and deceptively scrutable market economy, and an impotent, sometimes comfortable, always precarious privacy. No wonder that neither Comte nor Durkheim, neither Spencer nor Peirce, practical men of science, citizens of capitalist democracies, with little penchant for inwardness, could take the individual very seriously or the tensions between him and society, between him and the scholars' abstractions. Even for Weber who so much more consciously makes the individual his starting point, he is essentially no more than a fictitious cluster of choices, chances, actions, purposes, an 'ideal type'. Only outside an omnipresent and omniscient scientific web does he subsist as an individual, in the midst of deeper than Heideggerian nothingness, as one of whom enormous decisions and commitments are demanded which cannot possibly have their desired effect. Still less wonder then that most contemporary sociologists have simply forgotten the individual as a possible subject for sociology. Even where, as for example in Sartre, he seems to be at the centre of the sociological concern, he is not really there at all. For Sartre is altogether a Kantian, and the bleakest of all. His concepts of choice and freedom and of consequent determinism are the demythologized categorical imperative of the bourgeois *déraciné*. His individual is a focal concept, a final abstraction (Sartre, 1948, 1964).

Scientism has become a habit not easily broken, an addiction. Outside it is the nothing, including the self, haunted by all the exorcized superstitions and abortive efforts of the past which it has proved to be nothing. The sociologist is likely to resist any attempt to drag him out of his magic circle into that nothingness. Hence Adorno's and Horkheimer's growing pessimism in regard to the feasibility of any action, since all activity within the charmed circle is at best futile, possibly aggravating. Yet there seems to be no possibility of leaving the circle, except as crank or prophet. So all one can do at present is to try to understand as deeply and fully as possible 'what is the case'. Here as often, and always against his intention, Adorno meets Heidegger who maintains that scientism is the culmination of millennia of metaphysical thinking which all along had been an imposition, the subordination of *Dasein* to thinking, of life to concept. This thinking has produced the sciences whose methodology both constitutes their subject matter and, at the same time, stands impermeable between them and it. (For each science its *Unumgängliche*, that without which it would not be, is also its *Unzugängliche*, that to which it has no access.) Nature is no longer visible or tangible to the natural scientist except as a conceptualization which has predetermined, prejudged and precluded any possible encounter. Equally the historian *qua* historian cannot decide whether his understanding and use of history illuminates or blocks his *Kennen* or *Erkenntnis* of that which it seeks to understand and interpret. Is sociology any more than the expression of the sociologist's longing to avoid any direct encounter with his subject-matter which is first and foremost himself?

Habermas tries to mediate between science and a dialectical sociology: in *Theorie und Praxis* (1967) between positivism and dialectics, between knowledge and wisdom; in *Erkenntnis und Interesse* (1969) between the social sciences as they could be reconstituted by a better Freudian understanding and the natural sciences. He believes that the scientists could become the bearers of a new understanding mediated for them by dialectical sociology. He argues well, yet his intense intellectual efforts, even while they persuade on the intellectual level, also seem to confirm Heidegger's assertion that a bridge between science on the one hand and wisdom or thinking on the other is neither feasible nor desirable. On its own ground the scientific method is irrefutable or, rather, impregnable, precisely because it is self-correcting. In as far as it claims to cover the whole ground of rational understanding, that outside its definitions there is only irrationality, it should not be argued with, for such a contention is unscientific and irrational by its own standards. Unfortunately just these irrational presumptions which function on an emotive level buttress the scientistic pretensions. Beyond that science derives its power not from rational arguments – these often prove quite impotent – but from social and economic circumstances and processes. In turn it solidifies them. The attempt to break this circle by argument is bound to prove a failure because: (a) The power of an argument does not lie in the argument itself. After all the logical paraphernalia has been discarded, one is left with certain assumptions beyond argument and in these resides whatever power there be. These assumptions need to be challenged. (b) The belief in the power of argumentation has already surrendered to the position which the dialectical sociologist wishes to question. (c) All arguments are inconclusive and inconcludable, lose themselves in infinity or infinitesimality, unless conducted in a mutually acceptable myth.

Today nothing can directly challenge the hegemony of science or of scientism, as nothing can directly brake the progress of technological-economical rationalization. (Except material exhaustion or disaster.) The progress may be inexorable, and blessed that sociologist alone who together with other scientists resigns himself to the summons of the day, Weber's *Forderung des Tages* (cf. 'Science as Vocation', conclusion, in Weber, 1958E). Blessed he who, like Camus, manages to extract masochistic pleasure from such Sisyphean labours. Apart from that there is only the way of *Besinnung* which is first of all a retreat. Arguments that this is useless and ineffective have no validity here, where first and foremost 'use', 'effectiveness' and 'power' are being put in question.

Besinnung does not judge, still less condemn. It suspects all solutions and too much clarity. It is ready to listen to all kinds of voices, from Einstein to the Hindu *guru*, from Freud to Reich, to exoteric and esoteric religions, to advertisements and astrology and the claims made for extra-sensory perception. Above all *Besinnung* will listen to the poet and artist, will wish to compare art with life, desire with reality, the ideal with the actual, and all this without pre-judice. With Goethe it would say: 'Nothing human is alien to me.' With Keats it aspires to Shakespeare's 'negative capability' of bearing and containing contradicions rooted in experience without premature efforts at solutions. *Besinnung* does not wish to prove, merely to understand. It may have to rediscover or to discover for the first time levels of emotive wisdom, of experiential understanding, without which life is a protracted suicide by sedatives and stimulants. For the intellect cannot help seeing life diagrammatically and one cannot love diagrams and cannot live without love. That is why man now loves the means: science, money, success, sex, i.e. the treadmill. Will sociologists, social psychologists and philosophers have the courage to take the suicidal step into *Besinnung*, as possibly a life-enhancing step in a suicidal age where only schizophrenia is truth? Will they be able to separate the necessary scientific chores – for no-one is denying the various uses of science, not even for sociology – from that kind of sociological thinking which might one day make even the chores appear significant?

C Value, value-freedom and objectivity

I have often been tempted to ask questions like: What would the Buddha feel about the various Buddhist sects? What would Jesus have made of early medieval and contemporary Christianity? What would Descartes be thinking, if he thought today? Would he still be able to deduce with such assurance that he *was* merely because he thought he might not be, at a time when computers can do much of his kind of thinking better and without doubts? What would Kant care to write post-Auschwitz? Would Hegel wish to revise his understanding of history and the spirit in the light of those gas ovens? Would Marx be a Marxist and Freud a Freudian? Would any of the above have been happy to join in the academic researches on and discussions of their work?

Of course these are silly questions, yet they raise, if in a crude fashion, the central problem of hermeneutics. Obviously we have to try to understand a man's work in the context of his age, its problems, controversies, presuppositions, predispositions. We believe we can arrive at a proper appreciation of his individual contribution only by taking into account the many influences that shaped him and his thoughts, how these latter in turn modified the influences, went beyond them and became influential themselves, i.e. as a matter of course, in any study of a thinker or a man of action of the past, we take the intricate confluence of individuality and social conditioning for granted. We can never evaluate to what an extent even the most original response or insight of a Descartes, Kant, Freud remained conditioned by the thinker's personal and social history and background. The individual cannot be wholly explained in terms of his background, nor can he totally transcend it. Which is to say that the social reality resides exclusively neither in him nor in society but in the tension between them.

Nevertheless a further difficulty of interpretation remains which the above nonsense questions tried to spotlight. (Nonsense questions are necessary, because that which we call sense is extremely limited.) How can I, living after the great, appreciate just that quality and aspect of their thinking which helped to create the climate of mine? The climate which at their time did not exist. Or to put it the other way round, how can I avoid fixing and devitalizing their thought and emptying it of essential quality and power, if my interpretation does not include or at least imply the problem of what and how would they have thought in my situation, which has been partly created by their thinking? How, in other words, would they have gone on thinking? That is why an undialectical, academic, undialoguic approach is disqualified by its very nature from doing justice to the insights of those through whom social consciousness became transformed. They – as any thinker of significance – can only be misinterpreted, as long as they are our *Gegenstand* and not our *Gegenspieler*, object rather than protagonist or antagonist. This is what dialecticians have meant since Hegel, it is not what they often practised. The desire, even compulsion, to argue has still proved stronger than the readiness to listen, especially to the contemporary implication of thinkers of the past. Yet 'the business of argumentation never attains the way of a thinker. It is part of that petty-foggery which the public requires for its entertainment' (Heidegger, 1954, p. 121).

Quite a multitude of problems raise their heads here, concerning the use and abuse of quotations, reconstructions, condensations, within the general business of interpretation. In how far can a quotation do justice to the work out of whose context it has been torn? How changed is it, inevitably and essentially, by its new context, by the inevitably biassed, never complete understanding of the interpreter, conditioned by his time, history, sensitivity? How much had intervening interpretation already added and lost? Yet equally searching are the questions: Can condensation, reconstruction, detailed analysis, do greater justice? Are these not likely to reflect even more markedly the changed mental, emotive, conceptual climate and, of course, changed interests? In how far does the Hasidic saying that 'everything can be imitated, except the truth' apply to the interpreter? And in what way? More subtly, is it possible that precisely a too detailed account, a too logical, chronological, careful treatment, does less than justice especially to an original thinker? (For example, cf. Lukács, *Der junge Hegel*; Dilthey, *Schleiermacher*.) For, as with Marx and Freud, the very originality of their thinking which proved to be its moving power was often at odds with the elaborated, rationalized systems into which they felt constrained to fit it. Anyway, how can the interpreter circumvent the fact that his commentary is likely to be duller than the text?

The physical sciences have managed to design in their field and for their specific purposes, a method which keeps discussion alive from generation to generation. It can absorb into itself each particular contribution, if at the price of anonymity. The contribution remains alive, an organic part of the whole, until it is expelled in a kind of metabolic process. Dilthey stresses the promising, universalizing aspects of this methodology, Weber its Moloch-like qualities. It may not be as deplorable as Merton thinks that sociology has not yet devised such a method which would 'obviate the need to read the classics' (Merton, 1968, pp. 30–8). It is deplorable that it, like psychology or philosophy, is as yet merely reading its classics. It has not yet begun to explore possibilities of mutuality and dialogue through which, analogous to the scientific method but not in imitation of it, the conversation, not argument, between the living and the dead, is kept alive, so that the originality of a thinker may retain some of its pristine originating power and impact.

We can now face Weber's central concern: the constitution of sociology as an objective, causal, value-free science (Weber, 1968, pp. 186–262). We shall look at 1 objectivity and 2 value-freedom.

1   Why should objectivity be the objective of a sociology which Weber himself bases squarely on the subject, the individual? States, parties, churches, he treats as abstractions denoting interactions and cross-expectations of individuals of varying degrees of certitude. Yet we soon notice that what was then and is today of scientific interest in the individual is anything except his individuality. This idiosyncratic instance of *Dasein*, of unique and merely contingent thereness, is of no particular interest to those whose idiosyncrasy consists in wanting to abstract mere generalities from it. That such a procedure 'works' is undeniable. It reflects a civilization and society in which smooth working, an end in itself, depends precisely on such an abstraction from individuality. Armies, factories, offices, parties, churches, function efficiently to the extent to which they succeed in subordinating or suppressing the individual's individuality. Within the interrelated processes of rationalization which constitute society, sociology as science – perhaps it should be called sociometry – can play a part which may or may not be useful. If it did no more than this, it would simply reinforce the *status quo*. Its findings would

be ideological, in the last analysis propaganda – which equals objectivity in an objective, object-directed society.

I have tried to show why and how the desire for a show of objectivity vitiated Dilthey's more perceptive insights and his principles of hermeneutics. He intended to *wissen* where only *Kennen* is possible, wanted to know rather than converse. Similar positivistic tendencies and intentions had marred Freud's insights and methods. Weber as well failed to break through certain scientific preconceptions and prejudices, just at the point where his approach, as Freud was to demonstrate, had made such a break-through possible and imperative. It was his endeavour to distinguish clearly between sociology and psychology and to justify the autonomy of the former which was to continue the depletion of both (Weber, 1968, pp. 102–9). An unsociological psychology remains as insubstantial as an unpsychological sociology. Unfortunately the discipline of social psychology does not represent the dialectics of individual and society, but merely subsumes both under a separate generalization.

Man can begin to understand man only in conversation. In arguments he merely comes to understand logic. The understanding is inevitably mutual and double-edged: in conversation I come to *kennen* the other *and* myself. In as far as sociology is concerned with the understanding of men by men, it has to become conversation, it has to discover Habermas's *machtentleertes Bereich*, a realm from which the pretensions of power, and that includes those of arguments, have been evacuated (Habermas, 1967, pp. 220–32). It was Weber's personal tragedy and proved tragic for the development of sociology that he knew this and that the ascetic demands for and of an 'objective science' made him suppress such knowledge as irrelevant.

Especially here then we must distinguish Weber's formulations and their powerful influence from what they 'meant', intended, within his situation which was, of course, similar to that of other social thinkers of his time. Like Durkheim, Pareto, Simmel, Freud, he grew up amidst the open and implied politico-economical controversies sparked off by rapid industrialization, Marxian interpretations and counter-interpretations, by conflicting nationalisms. The air was full of emotional assertions and affirmations, of ideological rationalizations. Within that context objectivity assumed a utopian quality. It seemed to represent not just a viable counter-ideology but the anti-ideology *par excellence*. It promised to take discussions out of the hothouse of inflamed passions – which were to explode in 1914 – into the cool study of the unbiased scholar who first and foremost simply wished to clarify what the arguments were really about. Such an attitude assumed what the scientist, especially the social scientist, in the course of his studies will discover to be a mistake: that human passions and social stresses yield to rational arguments and stop outside the study door. Before the First World War this was understandable, not so easily afterwards. Yet it has prevailed and as scientific positivism has become entrenched in the midst of overwhelming evidence against it. Rationalism has become rationalization in the Freudian sense. Unable to shape or change the irrational objectives of society, the scientist accepts them as the Calvinist accepted predestination. He thus both justifies the *status quo* and creates for himself within it an enclave of total rationalization. In this way his objectivity is not very different from that of the demagogue or the advertiser.

Weber himself was torn by doubts. As politician he counselled stoicism and heroism in the teeth of almost certain defeat. As scientist he called for resignation and sacrifice in deference to a method which could not keep its promise. (Would he have found it agonizing to break an oath of loyalty under Hitler?) Yet in his earlier battles for objectivity he had given expression to a passionate, subjective conviction. Had it proved justified, it might have helped towards the creation of a saner and more peaceful society. Had the War proved, at least to Weber himself, that his conviction was not justified? Half a century earlier, Marx had contended that only a much deeper, more subterranean, more contradictory and dialectical understanding could hope to contribute to the possible transformation of social and private passions which not only will resist rational argument but use it for their own purposes. And at the very time when Weber fought his battles, most of all with himself, Freud's explorations began to point in a direction where one day passions and their arguments, as well as man's need of arguments and battles, may be understood and *aufgehoben*.

2 I believe that the power of Weber's arguments for objectivity was derived from their subjectivity, from his own and from that diffuse inter-subjective conviction of the age which saw in objectivity a persuasive rationalization of academic escapism and ideological acquiescence. The subjective convictions and intentions of the protagonists determined the power of the arguments, their interested disinterestedness constituted their value. (For example, Schopenhauer, the *rentier*, experienced all life-movement 'out there' as threatening will, jeopardizing his capital. Hegel, the professor, understood the same force as spirit. It has appointed him and paid him.) At that moment in time, it was deemed supremely valuable to establish a value-free sociological method. Weber appreciated this fact but hardly the width of its implications.

To speak of value-free physics is either tautological or nonsensical. Of course physics does not moralize. But the actual pursuit of physics by physicists expresses personal and social, emotive and economic interests, value-judgment, if only the judgment that I think it more profitable or enjoyable to be a physicist than a street sweeper. Moreover, money attracts research, and is meant to. Yet it is allocated according to quite non-scientific considerations. Who decides, and why, that it is more rational to spend money on defence pretending to be able to protect me from possible enemy attacks, than on cancer research while cancer might kill me as painfully and with greater likelihood? A value-free, objective pursuit of sociology is dependent on someone, somewhere, considering such to be valuable. This someone or, more likely, something most probably not only has money but wishes to keep it. He/it, and for the most bureaucratic-democratic reasons imaginable, will be interested in the preservation of the *status quo*. He/it has learned by now that objective, value-free research is most conducive to such preservation. In brief, we may have got our values wrong, but we cannot move one step without them. In as far as 'I' have no values, I am simply at the service of the values of those who pay me.

Weber argued in favour of a value-free sociology in a society torn by conflicting social, national and economic interests. Such interests are inevitably expressed as values and experienced as such. He believed in the possibility and virtue of a value-free approach – and this I wish to stress – precisely because he still believed in values. It takes little penetration to perceive beneath the scientific armour a heart and mind utterly dedicated to very definite ideals and a secret yet none the less powerful belief in their truth. Thus Weber could advocate a value-free science, only because he had as yet none of our corrosive doubts concerning all values, because he still saw a value-free science at the service of values. For that reason we do not do justice to his intentions, unless we keep alive, at least by implication, the question as to what he would be saying today, long after the ice-age he predicted has come, but also in the more hopeful light of Freudian discoveries to which his sensitivity would not have remained deaf (cf. Dahrendorf, 1962, ch. 2).

Here particularly, and for future reference, we must counter an only too likely accusation: that of historism and of psychologism, especially of the analytical kind. Popper formulated it persuasively and mockingly (1942, vol. 2, pp. 214ff; 1969, pp. 34ff). Now it must be admitted that both historism and psycho-analysis can be and have been used as a kind of academic gamesmanship: I am the knower whose knowledge relativizes yours and everyone else's, for you and they know not and cannot know what they are doing. From my vantage point I can perceive the errors into which you not only must fall inevitably, but which as inevitably you will not be able to perceive as errors. Needless to say that such a pretence at wisdom refutes itself. But if we take the thoughts of the historists from

Herder via Goethe, Hegel, Marx, to Dilthey and Meinecke; and those of the psychologists from Humboldt via Schopenhauer, Nietzsche to Freud and Laing; and then take them beyond the point their originators had reached but in the direction of their intentions, the situation may become transformed.

The genuine historist and psycho-analyst, far from wishing to relativize the position of the other to buttress his own, will want to use his new and tentative insights to understand better, and make the other understand better, both the other and himself in all the particularity and mutual conditionedness of their respective and yet shared *Erkenntnis*. Through such an acceptance of all understanding as conditional, partial, in need of complementation, new possibilities of inter-subjectivity may become open to experimentation. A further understanding of the self and of the other would become possible. Historism and analysis subsist in an atmosphere where falsifiability is not a criterion. If they take their discoveries and contentions seriously they cannot help wishing to divest themselves of all dogmatism, most of all of doctrinaire implications and innuendoes. On the one hand they could help to achieve the very tolerance Popper advocates. On the other they would not absolve that tolerance from the necessity of further committal. My conversation with you is part of such a committal, for you and for me. That it why it must not deteriorate into debate or argument. (We recall the double meaning of 'argument'.) For we are not ultimately committed to logic or method, science or facts, but to the dialogical human reality, to the dialogue itself, to each other. Historism and analysis could make us understand the conversation itself as our 'truth', namely our reality. In it I am committed as much to you as to my convictions, which excludes easy-going indifference as much as the desire to 'make a point'.

We once again can apprehend the qualitative difference between the natural sciences and what could be the *Geisteswissenschaften*. In the former, by mutual agreement and definition, I fulfil my commitment to the other through argument – as I do in a game by obeying its rules. He and I have already consented that in a certain area which does not immediately touch our life interests, such a condition should prevail. Here Popper is right, also his insistence that none of such universes of discourse is beyond revision. Though even here he is mistaken in his belief that any, except strictly tautologous or immanent, 'truth' is approximated by continued discussion. For the scientific or critical method, however successful and justified in its sphere, does not solve but raise the question of 'truth'. In the social sciences where all those who are conversing as well as the subjects/objects of their conversation are part and parcel of an overarching attempt at mutual understanding, at communion as much as at mere communication, no understanding which does not involve the individual as individual can be adequate. There is no *Erkenntnis* which does not imply involvement.

And what does such understanding-which-involves-the-individual mean, if not the readiness to listen to the other as to myself, as I would wish him to listen to me and to himself? It means a move towards an acceptance of the other's *Erkenntnis* in that depth where my acceptance and conviction of my own *Erkenntnis* has its roots, where I take it as self-evident. As Liebrucks says (1963, pp. 90–1):

> As the single one as speaker is related to the language, the single word to the whole of language, namely that in its individuality it is harnessed to it or tensed towards it, so the single one is in tension with the society in which he lives and knows himself to be. The single one is such only within a whole. The whole is merely a wholeness made up of single ones. Philosophy which conceives its thinking as derived from its language, has to fight against the insulation of these abstractions from each other – single one, whole – as bad metaphysics of the perceiving consciousness. On the *Aufhebung* of these abstractions into a relation of mutual tension depends nothing less than the salvation of the new science which calls itself sociology and which seems to have given up this tension already in its name.

Therefore (Adorno, 1962, p. 85):

> Nothing is more inappropriate for the intellectual who intends to practice what was formerly called philosophy than wishing to be proved right in discussion, one almost would like to say in his demonstration. This desire itself, right into its most subtle forms of logical reflection, is an expression of that spirit of self-preservation the dissolution of which constitutes the concern of philosophy.

In sum, value-free science serves non-scientific values. In as far as science increasingly absorbs all rationality, understands its own as the whole of rationality, it increasingly serves purely irrational, namely impersonal, interests, no matter how successfully these can mask themselves as scientific. For the natural scientist this situation is problematical enough – for example, in questions of ecology which involve intricate economical, political and personal decisions. Popper's contention that only science and not the individual scientist need be objective and value-free, evades rather than solves the problems surrounding objectivity and value-freedom themselves. For the sociologist, psychologist, philosopher, even the economist, the contemporary situation represents *the* problem. As essentially dialogue, as endeavour to understand without wishing to be proved right, as an exploration of the tensions within social consciousness which does not wish to dissolve them conceptually, sociology as against sociometry could spell commitment to the situation. What Dilthey and Weber call value-judgments are as much and as directly tools for the appreciation and managing of any given situation, for comprehending and circumscribing reality, as positivist assertions. On the contrary, positivist assertions are merely a limited and limiting example of value-judgments. They are the result of a particular way of thinking, willing, desiring, i.e. of valuing. Value judgments cannot be detached from even the selection and constitution of facts or from the formulation of theorems. According to Weber's own definition, rationality is equivalent to the most effective attainment of one's purpose, interest, the realization of one's values. Has the sociologist no purpose?

The fact that in the context of the sociological discussion 'value' almost always goes together with 'judgment' throws light on one aspect of our problem which further complicates the situation. As Adorno pointed out, the word value had its original home in economics (cf. Simmel, 1907, pp. 32, 67–8, 73, 80, 98). It was almost synonymous with price. With the advance of positivism and the expansion of economic automatism – reflected in the change from mercantilistic to classical economics – a peculiar confluence occurred. Everything was not only found to have its price, but price became the essence of everything, even of a painting, for example. The value of anything was its price and its price its value. Now such a contention is legitimate in economics. One could say it is the constitutive axiom of economics: *Economics be that approach to all human interaction and interdependence, and exclusively that, which treats, and only in as far as it can treat, all questions of value as questions of price.*

Gradually, as economic preconceptions usurped the place of reality, value which was not at the same time price had to take refuge in religion, poetry and the ideologies of 'human relationships'. On the other hand, the movement of economics to its present prominence gave to value at least some of its present connotation. By gradually transforming all use value into exchange value, all things became comparable and exchangeable, and equally all persons as producers or consumers of things. Value, like profit, became abstracted from things and persons and their particularities, their peculiar relations to personal need and desire, and was subsequently tagged on to them like a price label. Value = price = comparability = exchangeability. Even the incomparable, the original work of art which once symbolized the creative character of all activity, certainly for the young Marx, is now 'valued', because its price compares favourably with that of a copy. Certainly most individual, unpredictable, incomparable eventualities were generalized into things, utilities, commodities, by means of price tickets, as, for instance, enjoyment which has become entertainment and at so much per hour. Value as price became universalized to the degree to which the market mechanism came to constitute reality. It is now both the measure of everything and that which alone can be measured by itself: a means towards a means becomes an end.

Therefore the attitude towards value calls for discrimination and judgment. I judge the value and by means of the value I judge. This is circular thinking, reflecting the circularity of economic, rationalizing thought, of economic interests which fathered our value concept. Value-price makes all things comparable by making distinctions precise. The rationality resides in the precision, for the distinction itself may be as irrational as can be. Judgments concerning values are the result of arguments which, like public auctions, establish the value of everything by approximation. If such an understanding of value is then carried into philosophy, sociology, politics, the confusion need not be imagined for it actually prevails. Weber carried the concept of value-judgment into the sphere of existential, personal decision where it least belongs.

The confusion was due to the fact that 'value' had retained some of its older associations which still have a rather ghostly life in usages like: 'I value my freedom above . . .', 'this is invaluable' – as also in 'my dear' which does not yet mean 'my costly one', 'my treasure or *mein Schatz*'. Here value denotes precisely that which has no price, because it is incomparable, unique, has merely 'sentimental value'. It is totally personal, individual, creating and expressing, calling forth and answering, my needs and desires. Such value can also be inter-personal, inter-subjective, and is then close to *Kennen, Erkennen, Anerkennen, Bekennen*, while *Wissen* indeed knows and has its price. Or again, my highest value is what I love most. My value is my love. And it is interesting to note that 'my love' means both that which I feel and she who evokes the feeling, both sentiment and object. I can love money, yet never quite. The man who has made money, unless a psychopathic miser, proceeds to spend it on someone, if largely on himself never exclusively so. Ultimately I love and value a self, even if mainly my self. Even myself I cannot love without, however distortedly, valuing others. Literature has always known that the loss of one's love, to another, to death, to one's false self, is the only real tragedy. All newspaper reporters and producers of documentaries know it. They call it 'personal interest' and use it to bring home what would otherwise remain impersonal events like earthquakes or wars.

110

To pursue this would take us too far. Here my intention was to retrieve a meaning of 'value' which cannot be linked easily with judgment and may bring us back to our main contention: that because value is personal and incomparable it cannot be argued or fought over. It cannot be established like price. We must not carry back into this experience of value methods elucidated to aid us in areas from which this kind of value has been excluded. The former is quite a different expression of social consciousness. It defines and expresses with immediacy the tensions inherent in the situation of the individual in society. Since I furthermore believe that desires, interests and all kinds of love, shape our means as well as our ends, I believe that sociology does express values and that it therefore has to develop modes of intercommunication beyond arguments which do not touch upon but evade 'value'. A work of art is powerful and impressive to the extent to which we cannot or do not wish to argue with it.

The belief that values can be judged or that they in turn judge, has led to a great proliferation of academic arguments. For instance Dilthey, Popper, Lukács, Adorno, each in his own way and at times against each other, tried to argue as to what constitutes rationality and who, therefore, may or may not be called rational (cf. esp. Lukács, 1960; Popper, 1942; Adorno, 1969a). Now diverse rationalities express diverse values, as diverse values shape diverse rationalities. They cannot be defined, delimited, they are an aspect of man as de-finer. Positivism or scientism, as a peculiar rationality expresses and gives substance to peculiar values. It cannot be argued with as such. It need not be listened to in turn when it begins to argue against different forms of *Erkenntnis*.

D Dialectics and negative dialectics

Dialecticians do not argue the desirability of the dialectical method. They do not claim that it is better or more true than positivism, Platonic or Aristotelian essentialism, Cartesian rationalism, Kantian idealism. Their claim is both bigger and less arguable. Hegel and Marx, if in different fashion, assert that all human developments, of *Erkenntnis*, of the capacity for new perceptions and experience, are the result of extreme contradictions. The advancement not only of life, of living standards, of sensuous discrimination, but also of knowledge and learning, depends on the a-rational confrontation of rationally irreconcilable rationalizations. As Adorno says (1962, p. 107):

> Restraints and retractions are not means for the representation
> of dialectics. Dialectics moves through extremes and drives

thought through its furthest consequences into sudden change
rather than qualifies it. The caution which forbids it to dare
too much with one leap forward is usually an agent of
societal control and therefore of stupefaction (*Verdummung*).

The movement even of reason is unreasonable. For as the Eleatic
school already had proved, movement is irrational, i.e. life is. Or
should it rather be said that dialectics is an attempt to supersede,
aufheben, a rationality which since before the days of Plato had been
unable or unwilling to understand movement, change, growth,
individuality, fluidity, as of the very essence of reality, of phenomena? Dialectics challenges the metaphysical efforts to prestidigitate
eternal, unshifting, clearly defined idealities or methods out of a
shiftless, ephemeral, contradictory actuality or phenomenality, in
order to subordinate the latter to the former. Metaphysical thinking,
so the dialecticians maintain, has been an imposition from Thales
to contemporary scientism. And the more man succeeded in imposing on nature his categories of pure reason, which are also his
interest, his often misdirected and misinterpreted interests, the more
he, as part of nature, became himself subordinated to and fixed by
his own thinking. 'The more self-assuredly the I rises above all
reality, the more it imperceptibly becomes an object itself and
ironically countermands its constitutive role.' (Adorno, 1970,
p. 176; cf. Horkheimer-Adorno, 1969, ch. 1.)

Hegel had begun to appreciate what Marx made the very basis
of his *Erkenntnis*: that non-dialectical, metaphysical thinking is
always at least partly an ideological obfuscation or rationalization
(cf. Hegel, 1952, part IV, A). The 'rule' of reason, intellect, the idea,
of rationalization, reflects the power-structured constitution of a
labour-divided society, in which the ruling class, the 'workers of the
head', claim to govern by reason, while in fact their reasons which
are rational only in that they reflect the ruling interests are imposed by force. All rationality contains an element of compulsion,
though this can be exercised more or less crudely. It is, for instance,
not accidental that all modern justifications of war are based on
arguments of *raison d'état*, that militarists claim to be rationalists,
that pacifism is discounted as sentimental, unreasonable. From the
Star Chamber and its equivalents to the research laboratory reason
rules.

Non-dialectical philosophy, science, social science, methodology,
involves the thinker in a concatenation of impositions in which his
own self as thinker and as more than thinker is a link. Undialectical
thinking merely reflects the *status quo* and absolutizes it, instead of
reflecting on it and fluidizing it. Where reason wishes to rule, its
enslavement, paradoxically, is a foregone conclusion. For reason

from the start bows to its own necessities which cannot help mirroring those of its own circumstances, since it takes those for reality. Moreover reason is an instrument of life. When it ceases to be employed in the service of life it finds itself at the service of nothing. As against all this dialectics wishes to insist that between the knower and the known or the to-be-known, between *Erkenntnis* and its *Gegenstand*, exists a relation of mutuality beyond that admitted, on the one side, by the realists and their successors, the empiricists and positivists, on the other, by the rationalists, even by Kant and Fichte. This interdependence of knower and known presents itself as first, an epistemological problem; second, as problems of social conditioning; third, as a question of interest. These problems in turn are interdependent and cannot be kept apart in separate academic compartments. Here I can no more than glance in their direction.

1 *Epistemological*

Dialectical thinking insists that no thought, concept, idea, method, system, can grasp, comprehend fully and do justice to anything, any matter. All these are generalizations and abstractions from the inconceivable particular and individual, as well as impositions on it (cf. Husserl, 1950, pp. 134ff; also 100–1; cf. Heidegger, 1954, '*Das Ding*'). This, says Adorno (1970, p. 137), 'was the *proton pseudos* of idealism since Fichte' – why not since Plato? – 'that in the movement of abstraction one gets rid of that from which one is abstracting.' On the other hand the Lockean to positivist belief that thinking is a kind of representation and imaging in the mind – brain? – of something that is and is so outside it, remains unreflecting, a realist or naturalist metaphysic. It is an undialectical contradiction, for without reflection there is no theory, and without theory, as the dialecticians are not alone in arguing, there are no facts (cf. for example, Popper, 1969, pp. 114ff). That is to say, without theories – the word after all comes from *theorein* – there would be nothing that could be represented in or imaged by the mind.

Yet the appearance of paradox remains: 'Subjectivity, thinking itself, has not got its explanation in itself, but in something factual, above all in some societal factuality', of which language, for example, is a basic ingredient. 'But on the other hand, objectivity of *Erkenntnis* does not exist apart from thinking, subjectivity' (Adorno 1970, p. 137 continued). (Cf. Durkheim, 1968, 'Conclusion', for undialectical contrast.) Adorno says (1970, p. 142):

Such paradoxicality springs from the Cartesian norm: Explanation has to deduce that which is subsequent, at least logically subsequent, from that which precedes what has to be explained. If this norm were binding the dialectical position would be a simple contradiction. If not, however, the dialectical position cannot be explicated by calling in a hierarchical scheme of order, some form of pre-established harmony. Otherwise the explanatory attempt would presuppose the explanation it first has to find. It would assume that an ultimate lack of contradictoriness, i.e. of a subjective principle of thought, of rationalistic expediency, were inherent in the object, in that which is to be thought. In a way dialectical logic is more positivistic than the positivism which anathematizes it. Even in thinking it respects that which is being thought, the object-subject, even where this refuses to obey the rules of thought. The object under scrutiny is permitted to make its impact on the rules of thought, it is not bent into harmony with them. Thinking need not be satisfied with its own validity or legitimacy – *Gesetzmässigkeit*. It is able to think against itself, without surrendering itself. If a definition of dialectics were possible, this could be suggested as one.

2. *Social consciousness, social conditioning, the general and the particular*

The dialectical problematics concerning the relations between the individual and society is obviously intimately related to its epistemological questioning. There already dialectics demonstrated the ambivalence of the concept which generalizes by definition and with intention to grasp, not to *verstehen*, the particular. It asserts that already in relation to his subject-matter the individual gets caught in his own coils, unless he continuously lets the matter have its own say – which, as we have seen, is not the same as 'letting facts speak for themselves'. Adorno (1970, p. 172) says:

> The circle of identifying thinking which ultimately merely identifies itself was drawn by a kind of thinking which tolerates nothing outside itself. Its imprisonment is its own work. Such a totalitarian and therefore particular kind of rationality had been historically dictated by that which appeared threatening in nature. This is its limitation. Identifying thought, the equalizing of everything unequal, perpetuates in its dread our bondage to nature. Unreflecting reason is blinded to the point of madness in the face of anything that eludes its rule. In the meantime reason is sick. It were reason to cure oneself of it. Even the theory of alienation, ferment of dialectics, confuses the longing to approach the heteronomous and, in that respect,

irrational world, the longing 'to be at home anywhere', as Novalis put it, with the archaic barbarism which makes it impossible for the longing subject to love that which is different. It confuses the longing with a mania for incorporation and persecution. Were the alien no longer proscribed, alienation could hardly exist.

Sociology is concerned with social phenomena, i.e. with the individual, the most particular among all particulars, in his interaction and interrelation with society, i.e. with a multitude of particularities and constellations of particularities. Furthermore a sociologist is himself an individual, partially a direct and indirect product of the society he is investigating, always in a complex web of immediate and not so immediate interrelations with his subject-matter. How can he avoid violating both his subject and himself, unless his approach is one of encounter, confrontation, conversation, participation, committal? The difficulty here consists in this: that we have not as yet been able to focus the interrelations, the interpenetration, of the parts and the whole, the individual and society, because since Plato we have been taught to think the parts and the whole in separation. Only subsequently and synthetically are they brought together somehow, by diverse thinkers in diverse manners. Yet neither the single one has priority nor the whole; neither the collection of abstract single ones, private men, nor those abstract wholes like nation and state. (We recall the Freudian contention concerning the undifferentiated as our primal reality.) 'For what makes the whole a totality is not the whole but the parts.' Yet 'since the days of the Assyrians the whole has been used to permit the killing to go on.'

Liebrucks says (1963, p. 98):

On the other hand, the whole as conceptualized in antiquity was in truth one that had the parts not in but outside itself. Today, for the modern single one the whole is completely outside himself. . . . The misfortune of Eastern and Western politics today lies in this: that affairs have progressed along the lines of this logic. . . . What is needful is practice in dialectical thinking which tells us that the political relationship between whole and parts is still sub-human.

'Whole and part *scheinen* in(to) each other', i.e. they appear to be in each other, appear as being in each other, but also are shining into each other. Also (ibid. p. 96; cf. Heidegger, 1931, pp. 38–57):

Their independent existence over against each other is *Schein*, mere appearance. The *Scheinen* in(to) each other is the truth of

115

being. 'Each in its independence is altogether relative to the other.' (Hegel, *Logik*.) In the substantial independence of and relativity in regard to each other lies the contradiction. This contradiction routs all politics which stick to either of the apparently substantial independencies.

Dialectics sees its task as a new way of understanding the whole as more and less than, as different from, the sum of its parts; the individual as more and less than, as different from, merely a part of the whole. Such an understanding may, for the time being, remain unattainable. For the contradiction between the general and the particular, which is expressed also in this: that the single one is less as well as more than his general *Bestimmung* (definition and destiny), 'has its content in the fact that individuality does not exist yet, that where it establishes itself, it is bad' (Adorno, 1970, p. 152; cf. Simmel, 1922, pp. 21–30). If dialectics envisages the possibility of an approximation to the 'truth', it is the 'truth' which is the whole as well as the wholeness of the parts. 'For truth is that totality of subjective capacity and objective possibility for which we have no word yet, perhaps because it does not yet exist' (Liebrucks, 1963, p. 101).

Of that truth-which-is-the-whole, my apprehension, acceptance, protest, critique, my conversation concerning it with you, are parts, yet never merely parts (ibid, p. 107):

> For the individual is individual as social being. . . . The social being is such only as . . . individual. In this lies the necessary unity of psychology and sociology which is still called philosophy. Does such a philosophy remain a blown up 'concept', a bad hope? Hope is a good thing as an undefined condition, an openness of the way. As certain, hope is as inferior as the Greeks knew it to be. . . . Dialectics is not only placeless because it lives on the sea, even in the air, of language. It never lands. Only at the cost of such homelessness does it speak the truth concerning the condition prevailing, for example, in our Europe.

I would like to end by asking again in how far Freudian insights give greater concreteness to such contentions and are in turn illuminated by them.

3 Interest

Freud says (*Gesammelte Werke*, vol. 14, p. 380; quoted by Habermas, 1969, p. 352):[3]

> It has been tried to devalue scientific endeavour radically by saying that it, being bound to the conditions of our organiza-

tion, cannot supply any but subjective results, while the real nature of things outside us remains impenetrable for it. Here certain aspects are being neglected which are decisive for our understanding of scientific work, namely that our organization, i.e. our psychic apparatus, has developed precisely in the endeavour to reconnoitre the outer world and thus must have embodied a certain purposiveness in its structure. It is forgotten that our psychic apparatus itself is part and parcel of that world which we are to explore and that this makes such an exploration admissible. It is forgotten that the task of science is fully circumscribed, if we confine it to the demonstration of how the world is bound to appear to us in consequence of the peculiarity of our organization; that the final results of science, just because of the manner of their acquisition, are not merely conditioned by our organization, but also by that which has effected this organization. And finally it is forgotten that the problem concerning the constitution of the world apart from our perceiving psychic apparatus is an empty abstraction. No, our science is no illusion.

Here it is most tangible that Freud is trying to express a Hebrew apprehension of reality in Greek, Platonic terms. Habermas does not understand this, but realizes all the more clearly how close such an argument comes to positivism. He shows how Nietzsche was taken by a similar train of thought into the no-man's-land where positivism, really appreciated as positivism, precariously balances a radical nihilism. For Nietzsche reason is nothing except interest, a scratching of sustenance from insignificant soil. Truth thrones austere beyond such efforts of the will-to-live and would destroy the knower (Habermas, 1969, pp. 353–64).

Habermas argues that the emancipation of reason from its positivistic entanglement, from its pre-epistemological attitude, demands the recognition of the dialectical interrelation of reason and interest. As long as this remains unrecognized, both reasoning and communication would suffer distortions, because they would have to deny and conceal, i.e. to rationalize, their interest. They have to idealize it and thus turn themselves into ideology. Habermas believed that Freud's discoveries, when detached from Freud's own causal-scientific interpretations, have opened up new possibilities of dialectical understanding. By consciously accepting interest as that which guides perception, conceptualization, cognition, this interest in turn can be criticized. Arguments would no longer reflect it cryptically. They could include reflection on it. *Arguments can become conversation to the extent to which it is realized that nothing except interest, hidden interest, is interested in masking its intentions as argumentation.* Only hidden interest feels compelled to prove. One might even take Habermas's contention a step further and say that it may be true that Freudian insights into neuroses, and their reflections in institutions as partially blocked and therefore distorted communication, can explain societal conflicts and their genesis better than even Marx who understood the conflicts so much better. But, as Marx saw more clearly than Freud, it was precisely the unrecognized and unacknowledged interests which underlie and cause the blockages and distortions in communication. It must however be emphasized that Marx's understanding of these interests as almost exclusively economic or economically based seems too narrow in the light of Freud's discoveries concerning the complexities of psychic interests and their interaction with social ones. This seems to prove once again the need of conversation between Marxists and Freudians, between sociology and psycho-analysis (cf. the work of Sartre, Laing, Fromm, Reich).

Habermas says (1969, p. 330):

> While we in our technical dispositions and because of our knowledge of causal connections let nature work for us, the analytical insight meets the causality of the unconscious as such. Therapy does not consist in the employment of recognized causal connections, as it does in the more narrowly causal somatic medicine; rather its effectiveness depends on the *Aufhebung* of the causal connections.

That is to say that in the psyche 'causality' is quite actually experienced as tyranny. No matter whether or not we agree with Habermas's Diltheyan definition of natural science and its distinction from the social ones; what he describes as the aim of the analyst in the psycho-analytical situation could, and perhaps should, apply to all human conversing. In that way alone can it take place in the authority-free sphere in which he himself wants it to be conducted. As Habermas says (in Horkheimer, 1963, p. 501):

> If, of necessity, experiences conditioned by a situation enter into the very axioms of even a mathematical sociology; if the interests which guide *Erkennen* can merely be formalized and not suspended, then they have to be brought under control, must be criticized and legitimized as objective interests within the whole societal context. [Control may be the wrong word here where we may wish to escape from 'controlling' altogether.] Reflections on such interests compels one into dialectical thinking, even if dialectics were nothing else except the attempt to understand the analysis at each moment as part of the social process that is being analyzed and, at the same time, as the

possible critical self-awareness of it. That means to renounce the assumption of a merely accidental and external relation between the analytical instruments and the data to be analyzed, which may be held concerning technical dispositions over objects and objectified processes. Only in this way can the social sciences get rid of the illusion, so full of practical consequences, that scientific control of the social sphere would make possible a similar emancipation from natural compulsions in history and with similar methods of scientifically produced technical powers of disposition, as has already been actually accomplished in regard to nature.

Already Adorno had claimed that rational argument still contains too much of that compulsion, even physical compulsion, by means of which the rationality, the *raison d'être* of a ruling class, was and is maintained. For that reason philosophy can begin only where the struggle for self-preservation and self-assertion has ceased (1962, p. 85). Which may mean that philosophy, sociology, psychology, even economics, could come into their own only when they no longer saw their interest almost exclusively in the establishment of 'truth', factuality, validity, i.e. in their scientism; but when they would begin to explore the extent to which their interests coincided with each other and with those of the artist and writer. The latter's interests may seem so far removed from those of science, mainly because science, social interest, would have it so; because society has already misjudged or pre-judged its own interests or at least the extent of its best interests.

It is the artist's interest to express and communicate with all possible precision and clarity—even when, as in Kafka's case, it is the clarity of opacity – an actuality which is not arguable, which is experienced as 'true' in as far as it is not arguable. This truth, as was shown above, is universal in as far as it is totally individual and subjective. It does not exclude other truths, does not argue or contend. It might contribute a little to the exclusion of falsehood or falseness, in that it might refine the capacity for discrimination, for smelling out the ungenuine. It reveals truth as unreservedly dialectical or dialogic, as intercourse and in this the expression of an ultimate interest which is sometimes called love, also humility. Is it altogether unphilosophical and unsociological to remember that man's, even the sociologist's, ultimate interest is 'love' – for example, the love of wisdom? And that such memory may have repercussion in scientific researches, if the scientist, as man, heeds it and thus becomes truly scientific? Liebrucks says (1963, p. 100; cf. Bloch, 1970, vol. 3 *passim*):

Art is always the movement from the universal to the particular to the single one; the movement from the single one to the particular, to the universal; i.e. the movement which is that of the Hegelian *Begriff*. This *Begriff* is the love which unreservedly betrays the universal to the particular-special. Hegelian logic lives in this movement. . . . Each single work of art means the whole, wills the whole, and thus means and wills what it is, namely the dialectical whole, this movement in which the details are already the whole; which cannot very well be affirmed about our society. Art is in this way the accusation of our age, evocation out of the midst of confusion, in the face of enormity.

What then is sociology's interest, in this intricately interwoven *double-entendre* of 'interest' and 'love'? What is sociology's 'love'? What does the sociologist believe to be the interest of and in the interest of his subjects which are both his subject-matter and the *Aufhebung* of all subjects as mere matter? How can he best explore, explicate, express, communicate, depict those interests of his subjects in his own and in their best interest? What approach to such an undertaking, what attitude of mind and – dare we say – soul, what preconceptions and assumptions, methods and tools, will the sociologist think to be in the interest of sociology? And may this in any substantial way differ too markedly from the interests of its subjects?

Three corollaries

1   A sociology which is ready to understand at least part of its task in the light of the dialectical challenge could accommodate many conflicting approaches; not, one hopes, as a musuem, but as being in itself the kind of Academy Plato had envisaged in his more poetic moments. As yet it has not existed, but need not, for that reason alone and of necessity, remain non-existent. In it there would be no position to attack or defend, no exclusive truth to be established or demolished. Sociology could be a wide open field for all kinds of explorations, possibilities of discovery and experimentation. No-one would have to pretend to others or to himself that his peculiar, limited, conditioned, idiosyncratic position was the inevitable consequence of facts and figures and logical stringency. One would be much less hampered in fully dialectical explorations of the kind Adorno thought desirable, namely to follow any thought to its extreme conclusions and implications. One would be able to accept, if provisionally, whatever impresses itself as beyond argument, i.e. speaks to our whole emotive-intelligent being. One would learn from Weber *and* Scheler, Popper *and* Adorno, Dilthey *and* Lukács, Bloch *and* Heidegger, Lévi-Strauss *and* Sartre. For each has

120

built his arguments around some *Erkenntnis* or another which is unarguable, illuminating, blurred only by arguments, their own and those of others. The sociologist might then become what original thinkers have, as a matter of fact, always been, though their incorporation in the academic syllabus, and the subtle modifications of their thoughts' implications which this involves, have usually hidden this fact: *Dichter* as well as *Denker* (see below, ch. 5). He will not let these two argue but converse in his breast and in his head. Montaigne, Pascal, Herder, Goethe, Herzen, will be his exemplars as much as or more than Galileo, Descartes, Newton; Hegel rather than Comte, Marx rather than Spencer, Freud rather than Watson. Even today and as sociologist he might wish to ask in how far academic procedure, as now defined and accepted, is a socially, psychologically and economically conditioned falsification of the actual human thought-processes, i.e. in how far academe serves hidden social interests rather than those of thinking itself. Finally he might ask whether perhaps academic disciplines were instituted and elaborated to hide the possibility that some scholars are not original thinkers and whether that is sufficient justification for their continuance.

2 (a) Interest originally denoted 'being among or in the midst of', being in the middle of something, so that one was, wished to or had to be 'interested', could not help taking notice purposefully. Common usage still implies a watered-down understanding of the original meaning. (b) Interest also has the narrowed down connotation, at least in most Western languages, of something that is to my advantage, conducive to my advancement as against being merely enjoyable, something that is profitable. I may be interested in many things which it would not be in my interest to pursue. (c) From there, in English, French, Italian etc., but not in German, it acquired its technical, financial meaning. It became measurable, down to the fraction of a penny, what my 'interest' was. Within the all-embracing market mechanism of modern society, it became everyone's interest (b) to forego all interests (a) for the sake of interest (c). Economists use 'interest' exclusively in the sense of (b) and (c) and in such a way that the former approximates the latter ever more closely. Such a procedure might have appeared suspect even to economists, had they ever been troubled by epistemological and psychological scruples. Keynes was, but perhaps not enough (1964, ch. 12, V, 4–5). Was even Marx, in spite of his Hegelian training, misled here? Was he reflecting without adequate *Besinnung* the facts of totalized capitalism in which indeed all interests have shrivelled into the connotation (b) → (c)? It is comprehensible but disturbing that sociologists, in as far as they do consider interest, look at it with the eye of the economist. Weber did so. He would

not understand value-ethics as the expression of an interest. For Pareto only interest as economical interest approaches the rationality of the scientific method itself. Today rationality and rationalization mean the production of higher 'interest' rates. Is it really in our interest that everything should be measured in terms of such interest?

3 It is not the intention of this essay to denigrate the scientific method, not even within the confines of sociology. Within its own definitions, which it sometimes tends to forget, it has revealed formerly unthought-of possibilities of thinking and widened our horizons. How to make it fruitful in the context of sociological – or *geisteswissenschaftliche* – intentions which of necessity are wider than those of science, remains an open and urgent question. Not even the suggestion of an answer can be attempted here beyond saying that it may have something to do with the embodiment, i.e. the acknowledgment as well as institutionalization, of the distinction between *Kennen* and *Wissen*.

E   History, dialectics of the individual and society

The word 'history' in its common and academic usage defines and circumscribes, as well as masks and evades, a cluster of problems of daunting complexity. They have to be glanced at, because German sociology has almost invariably been historical in its approach and believed, as I still do, that sociological considerations cannot be divorced from historical ones. German *Geisteswissenchaftler*, certainly during the nineteenth century, grew up in an atmosphere in which historism, not as method, creed or dogma, but as an all-pervasive attitude and sensibility, was the constitutive element. No-one, apart from the old Hebrews, has ever viewed reality, especially social reality, so exclusively and totally as historical. This is not to say that Germans were more interested in history than others. The Florentines and Venetians, Montesquieu, Hume and Gibbon, had not only preceded them, but each in his own way and concerning his own country had a more glorious and imperial story to tell. Perhaps for that reason, and more or less consciously, they had modelled their style, method and scope on those of the Roman imperial writers and the political historians of Athens.

The chequered progress of the German 'Holy Roman Empire' was not easily amenable to straightforward glorification or the tragic treatment. By the time Germans became historians with heart and soul, it had split into the precarious Austro-Hungarian conglo-meration and the splinter states and statelets of Germany proper, just when these began to be troubled by the growing power of Prussia. Hence they experienced history in a different way, less complacently, more individually and inwardly, interlaced with Utopian longings, and inevitably interpreted it in the light of that experience. The consequences were twofold.

First, in France and Britain, if for obvious reasons not in Italy, the pursuit of history remained a clearly defined, particular interest and discipline in public and academic estimation. It needed no justification. It did not seriously influence other 'departments', possibly because it seemed so evidently self-contained. Even in literature – and very much unlike in Germany – the historical novel and the costume play developed into distinct genres.[4] Both Comte and Spencer use a fairly crude and purely provisional historical scaffolding for their sociological ideas. In de Tocqueville the nostalgic historical memory functions, as in Comte, though with reversed intentions, as a grid for the present. In the early pages of *The Elementary Forms of the Religious Life*, Durkheim can sovereignly wave aside the most daunting complex of historical problems (1968, pp. 1–8). Neither Sartre nor Lévi-Strauss, in spite of their obscure argument on the subject, has any use for history in the sense in which the Germans cannot help using it (Lévi-Strauss, 1966, ch. 9). Each in his own way views history as a kind of obstacle race towards an understanding of humanity in its present perfection.

The German historical pursuit, perhaps because of its greater inwardness, its concern with *geistige*, transpolitical growth and development, which may have been a form of escapism from a miserable political reality, deeply permeated all the *Geisteswissenschaften*. (Croce's philosophical historism has its roots in a similar political situation.) In Germany everything from science to literature was seen in its historical, almost theological, perspective, for historism, even Marx's dialectical variety, always retained an element of *Heilsgeschichte* (redemptive history). As literature until the days of Lessing and philosophy up to Kant and Hegel, even to Nietzsche, had to fight for its emancipation from theology or implied theological assumptions, so first the natural sciences and later on the humanities had to fight for their emancipation from history. (Marx still understood the natural sciences as an aspect of social history, an historical expression of social intention. See 1968, pp. 245–6.) The extra-sociological battles of the First World War achieved this emancipation for sociology *inter alia*, for better, for worse. For reasons far from clear the Second World War confirmed the emancipation. Yet even today some German sociologists cannot escape from historical perspectives and methods in their arguments (cf. Dilthey, 1919, 'Gotthold Ephraim Lessing').

The second consequence of the peculiar nature of the German preoccupation with history can be illustrated from Meinecke's *Entstehung des Historismus*. Montesquieu, Voltaire, Gibbon, Hume, so he contends, were rationalistic in their approach. They implicitly and sometimes explicitly believed in canons of reasonableness against which all past events, the passions and reasons which produced them, could be measured and judged. They could do this – and here I am going beyond Meinecke – because they experienced their age and the position their country had achieved as a consummation of both history and reason, and thus could look at past developments from an Olympian vantage point. The comfortableness of their circumstances and that of their immediate surroundings suggested arrival. It made it easy for them to accept a peculiar Enlightenment cluster of abstractions, generalizations, preconceptions and prejudices, which made them blind to any contradictory evidence, i.e. they could generalize so happily, because they experienced their situation as consummation. They could understand their situation in this way, because their generalizations enabled them to cover over anything which might make them wish to question their convictions.

The German historian had no such vantage point. The political situation of his country was not a happy one. His personal position *vis-à-vis* the petty, conflicting powers was one of impotence, experienced as all the more painful, because it was helpless before pettiness.[5] His age and society did not present themselves as culmination – not until the brief idealistic moment in the history of Prussia which produced Hegel's apotheosis (Meinecke, 1962, ch. 8). The German historian could only hope or despair and would inevitably carry his emotive attitude into his studies. He could not generalize happily. So as he investigated other historical epochs, he was able to preserve towards them the openness he was compelled to preserve towards his own, unless he was a diehard or a pessimist. He looked at history with different eyes and thus saw a different history. He found different evidence, because different assumptions were self-evident to him. For him history was not so much a progress as a progression, even a procession, of unique individual flowerings, each with its own pattern of growth and decay, with its peculiar odour and flavour, each 'equally close to God', as Ranke put it. Moreover the rationalism of the German historian was different from and far less self-confident than that of his Anglo-French colleagues. Therefore Herder as well as Vico, again the Italian and the German, could show a much greater interest in and appreciation of the 'passions' as being not merely creative or destructive, but as having their own reasons and rationality, as being the ground of all rationality. (Hume as philosopher knew this, as historian admitted it, but only in the sense that having brought forth reason, passions could be dismissed. Pascal knew that the heart had its own reasons, but would not let them interfere with his *Thoughts*.)

From Herder to Meinecke, historism is the endeavour to understand and savour each historical manifestation in its individuality, to understand its unique position in and its equally unique contribution to the intricate web of political, social, cultural, religious, psychological interdependence. However this individualism was of a severely communal kind. Epochs and groups and nations were seen as individuals, the concrete individuals only in as far as they represented the 'consciousness of the age'. This meant that in its own fashion German historism could get away from abstraction as little as its more rationalistic and generalizing counterpart in the West. It explains why, even within that historism, Hegelianism could scale heights of abstraction beyond those of French and British historiographers. Nevertheless, like many such uncertain beginnings, the insistence of historism on the uniqueness of the historical progression and of each individual's position in and relation to it, was to point towards a new understanding of individuality and its interpenetration with society which by now Freudian insights could help us to explore. This insistence also tells us why German sociology finds it so hard to sever its ties with history.

In France and Britain, history is rational in this double sense: historiography proceeds from a well-established position of rationality. And it concentrates on those forces in history which moved society towards the establishment of that rationality. The further generalizations and rationalizations which were to constitute sociology could be detached easily from such history and historiography. One might see Anglo-French history as the forerunner of sociology, its preformation. Hence there are few problems here for the sociologist. His German colleague, on the other hand, had to justify his attempts to derive generalizations from the unique. The relation between history and sociology presented urgent problems. Was sociology the auxiliary of history or vice versa? Did one investigate the general in order to arrive at a better understanding of the particular or vice versa? i.e. Did one want to *wissen* in order the better to *kennen*? Or was the study of the indubitably particular, the historical process as a whole or each of its aspects, merely to provide cannon fodder for valid generalizations? Did one try to *kennen* in order to *wissen*? (Cf. Croce's unreserved historism which nevertheless remained in the realm of abstraction, 1966, 'History as the History of Liberty'.)

Having said all this I have barely scratched the surface of the problem. I have merely tried to justify raising it at all. The following five queries can do no more than focus one of the problems of history in as far as it is related to our question concerning the possibility of understanding in sociology.

E*

1 *October 21, 1805, The Day of Trafalgar*

This is the title of a book, merely an entertaining book of no pretensions. It copiously documents all kinds of events that took place, hour by hour, between New York and Moscow, while Britain defeated France, Nelson Napoleon, on the day when England expected every man to do his duty. Two navies closed in upon each other. Finally one rather than the other retired, for reasons that were certainly not clear till afterwards. During those hours, even that part of society which represented England most self-confidently, which *was* England in that whatever were to be the gains of Trafalgar would accrue to it, was lunching, flirting, wining, pursuing its interests. The French nobility was doing likewise. In one place a man was condemned to death, in another a boy to exile, etc., *ad infinitum.* However much is added, there remain undocumented as many events of life-and-death significance for the participants, as one cares to choose; unrecorded a few million minor agonies and ecstasies in the two countries alone whose fate was said to have hung so totally in the balance when Nelson died, knowing he had done his duty. This was history, while making love with Lady Hamilton had merely been the pursuit of private and reprehensible pleasures. Compared with the world-wide myriad events of immediate import to the actors, what significant difference would it have made in concrete terms, if the British instead of the French had retired? A few more dead on one side rather than the other, i.e. a few more desolate women in Britain rather than in France. Some people who were now to become richer would have remained merely as wealthy as they had been before. Some money would have flowed into other pockets. Ultimately some boundaries – visible only on maps – would have been redrawn differently and men in differently-coloured uniforms would have paraded along different streets. All other differences would have been much like what the actual results of the victory actually were: abstract, imaginary, not changing everyday, ordinary, universal life-and-death human actuality, but merely slightly rearranging incidences.

Or am I biased? Did the victory 'make all the difference' (cf. Robert Southey, 'After Blenheim', *Golden Treasury*, no. 216)? Did it save England and Europe? Or would a French victory have 'made all the difference'? Would it have hastened the unification of Europe which British insularity helped to prevent? And would that have saved or merely more rapidly bureaucratized Europe? Would it have spared Europe two great and many smaller wars, or would it have embroiled a united and even more ambitious Europe in even greater wars? Or do all such wars bear witness to an underlying drive or malaise which no unification 'from above' could contain?

126

Such a variety of possible questions demonstrates the arbitrariness of both the selection and the emphasis of the historiographer, of any possible evaluation of cause or result.

And there are more: did the battle matter, or rather the political conditioning which made it inevitable? Or the social conditions that brought about the political situation? Or the psychology of human interrelations which brought about and perpetuated the social conditions as much as it was shaped by them? Or those meta-psychological factualities of which the psychological relations are the inexorable or not so inexorable expression? Already the *Book of Kings* poses the question: was it historically more significant that King Ahab strengthened Israel's military, diplomatic and economic position, than that he took away a man's vineyard and his life? Is Nelson's victory at Trafalgar more significant historically than his love or lust for Lady Hamilton? And if so, why? And is the fact that we cannot help thinking of Trafalgar as of greater historic importance than Nelson's love affair, contributory to the inevitability of a never-ending series of further 'Trafalgars'? Or does this fact merely express the inevitability? What are we to make of Weber's attempts to establish canons of historical causality in the light of these questions (cf. Parsons, 1968, pp. 610–11)?

2 Marx's utopia of post-history

Gibbon had called history little more than the register of the crimes, follies and misfortunes of mankind. Yet he obviously relished the registering. Perhaps he hoped, like Thucydides, Livy, Montesquieu, that it would deter and instruct the future. Most serious historians had written with such hope in mind. Marx's own historical accounts have that intention. They are beginning, moreover, to probe layers which before him had never been of interest to historians. Yet even he was compelled by the logic of an age-old discipline into abstractions which cannot do justice to the actuality of the conflicting individual interests, no matter how thoroughly both the interests and the understanding of reality have been shaped by society and its obfuscating abstractions. (Cf. *The Eighteenth of Brumaire of Louis Bonaparte* with Ranke's *Wallenstein* on the one hand and with Lewis's *Pedro Martinez* on the other.) Was Marx conscious of this? Did *Das Kapital*, with its comparatively simple prophetic intentions, grow to such monstrous proportions because in it he tried to reconcile the irreconcilable: an understanding of the individual with the demands of a discipline whose essence was an abstracting method designed to avoid direct confrontation with the individual, his sufferings, joy, fears and hopes, in order to make the intolerable tolerable? That may have been his reason for piling up statistics to document the appalling labour and living conditions by one official report after another. Marx had come to understand that history and historiography could be and was being used as an ideological smoke screen to conceal painful facts concerning irreconcilable interests from those whose interest would have lain in a more complete comprehension of the situation – but also from those whose interest it was to stabilize the *status quo*. Was he beginning to suspect that the very character of historiography contributes to the perpetuation of a situation for which it also has to be the ideological apology?

For instance, had history been written as the Hebrew prophets tried and partly managed to write it, had the great epics and tragedies and novels been taken for what they really were, namely a kind of history, possibly closer to *Geschehen* (what actually happened) than historiography, could that have changed the course of European history? At least of historiography? Could this then have contributed to a change in sensibility out of which a changed attitude to life and society is born which might have resulted in different kinds of action and reaction? Or should history, like any self-respecting science, drop all pretensions to edify and content itself with registering and filing, with inevitably being *post-festum* and *post-holocaust*? Which would merely raise new questions concerning the 'reality and significance' of human events, i.e. which of them are to be registered, described and how and why, which of them are to be given priority and in what order (see para. 1, above)?

For instance, to describe adequately one battle in terms of the individual reality of its participants would produce a work of unmanageable proportions, more bulky than anyone's go at *Weltgeschichte* yet, a *War and Peace* multiplied by the number of direct and indirect combatants. It would not be enough to describe the expectations, feelings of terror and triumph and the various agonies. (And anyway, how does one describe how a man dies slowly, because his stomach has been shot through? How does one compare his agony with that of another?) A biography of each of the protagonists would have to be attempted, to show and make us re-experience why they came or had to come and what they felt about this battle in particular and about the war in general and about the society that had sent them to war, what, for example, 'my country' meant to each. A parental biography would have to be added, for many societal compulsions and convictions are mediated by mother and father. Each man's attitude to life and society is shaped by the way in which his father and mother complemented each other, related to each other, interpreted themselves and the world to the child, which in turn would depend on their social standing and on the way in which their parents related. . . . No wonder no historian has as yet attempted to write history, that the history of the historiographer is a most peculiar artifact which, unlike art, conceals rather than reveals the human actuality it is ostensibly recording.

Marx's early attitude to this kind of history, which may have remained his by implication for the rest of his life, is clear: It will come to an end when man has become fully human in a society which permits him to give full expression to his humanity. For 'the *Bildung* (education and 'gestalting') of the five senses is the labour of the whole of universal history until today.' In that sense 'history itself is an actual part of natural history, of nature's becoming man.' Marx sees history as our often anguished movement towards our humanity, a detour to it (1968, pp. 239–40):

> Private property is only the sensuous expression of the fact that
> man becomes objectified and moreover and at the same time
> an alien and inhuman object to himself. That which is to
> manifest his life conceals it, that which is to make it real makes
> it unreal, turns it into an alien reality. Thus the positive
> *Aufhebung* of private property, i.e. the sensuous appropriation
> of our humanity and human life, of the objectified man and his
> human works for and through man, is not to be understood
> exclusively in the sense of enjoyment, of possession, of having.
> Man appropriates his complete being as total man completely,
> each of his human relations to the world, as seeing, hearing,
> smelling, tasting, feeling, thinking, looking at, experiencing and
> willing, acting, loving, in brief, all organs of his individuality,
> as well as those which in their form are directly communal
> organs. . . . Their conduct towards the object is the activity or
> activation of the human actuality. This is therefore as many-
> sided as the definitions and activities of humanity themselves;
> human activity and human suffering, understood humanely,
> are forms of man's self-enjoyment.

Therefore (ibid., p. 238):

> Above all it must be avoided to look at society once again as an
> abstraction over against the individual. The individual is the social
> being. The expression of his life . . . is an expression and
> confirmation of social life. In man his individual life and the
> life of the species are not different.

And finally (ibid., pp. 234–5; cf. Marx, 1961E, pp. 100ff):

> In his relationship to woman . . . is sensuously revealed . . . in
> how far humanity has become man's nature or nature has
> become man's humanity. Man's relation to woman is the most
> natural relation between human beings. In it is manifested

in how far the natural conduct of man is human or in how far humanity has become his natural being. . . . This relationship declares to what extent man's need has become human need, to what extent he is a social being in his most individual existence.

I have not tried to smooth out the awkwardnesses of Marx's style in my translation. They too reflect the fact that he is wrestling with a mode of historical understanding for which the Western intellect is not yet ready. Yet even so these quotations point far beyond any conventional, even conventionally Marxist, understanding of history. They go beyond Kierkegaard, as Sartre pointed out (1964). They point towards Freud and Heidegger. They illuminate those later insights and are in turn individualized and embodied by them.[6]

3   *Heidegger's Man, Schicksal and Geschick*

Too much injustice has been done to Heidegger already by friend and foe. Translation has often proved the greatest of all. I do not wish to add to this by another attempt to sum up his complex thinking which, as he himself knew best, has not yet become thought (cf. Nietzsche, *Beyond Good and Evil*, concluding aphorism). Here I merely wish to use some of Heidegger's insights, without any intention of committing him to the use I make of them, in as far as they seem useful to me for focusing another aspect of the problematics of history.

Heidegger understands man's *Dasein*, his existence, actuality, individuality, as his mortality. This has been taken for pessimism or nihilism, especially since the *Nichts* or *nihil* features decisively in his thinking. In his late *Vorträge und Aufsätze*, where he calls death the border of life, he adds: 'A border is not something where something else comes to an end, but from where something is defined and constituted' (1954, p. 151; cf. pp. 155, 177, 196). Mortality is the urgency of human individuality, just as the *Nichts* constitutes both the precarious reality and the real precariousness of everyone who lives on air, has to draw breath to live. It is this urgency, my mortality, the fact that my *Dasein* as against its idea or concept or essence is surrounded and constituted by that which I experience as *Nichts, Nichten, Vernichten* (nothingness, turning into nothing, annihilation), which makes of all historiography as so far practised and understood *Gerede* (chatter). For it leaves me out and most of all when it seems to be talking about me. It is *Gerede* in that, like most talking, it is divorced from the actuality of that which, or him whom, it is talking about (1931, pp. 167–70; also 170–80; cf. Adorno, 1970, pp. 142–3).

130

History talks about the *man*, the impersonal, indeterminate and indefinite 'one' of 'one knows', 'one couldn't care less'. It is neither one nor many nor anyone, it is no-one. Yet he/it is the no-one or *Nichts* in which your and my individual *Dasein* has actually got lost. That is why history chatters and cannot help chattering about him/it and not about you and me. Yet because history chatters about *man*, the *Man* maintains its position as that in which you and I are merely lost, lost sight of.

My mortality is my reality, my *Dasein*. It, and at present apparently only it, can prevent my ever totally forgetting that I cannot be completely fitted into any *Man* – in Rieff's words, that no commitment therapy can be completely satisfactory for me. My mortality constitutes my *Dasein* as historical (1931, p. 381; also pp. 314–15). It makes of me, as mortal, the subject of history. For there is no *Dasein*, no human actuality, outside that of the mortal I. Yet it is obvious that this 'I' has not yet risen above history's horizon. History's concern with battles, the growth and decay of empires, with economic movements, cultural developments, merely blinds the historian, who is an individual, to the fact that he himself has up till now got as little into his history, as Hegel, according to Kierkegaard, had managed to get into his perfect system. History is interested in *man* in all kinds of ways, even in the manner of his death and his dying-for. It has not yet been able or willing to focus mortality as that essential individual historicalness of which all dying-for has been an evasion, an escape into the *Man*. So far the individual appears in history only anecdotally. He is history's aside, its footnote.

Intimately connected with this is the historian's unproblematical view of time. The movement as of past through present into future is assumed. So is the intellective counter-movement, as falling or flowing of present into past or future. The historian can take time for granted in this way, because as a mortal individual who does, as a matter of fact, only very partially experience time in such a fashion, and possibly only in as far as he has already fallen into the *Man*, he has not yet entered his history. Even his practice as a historian is an evasion of his historicalness. Freud's insights have shown how deeply, totally, and yet individually, a person is 'gestalted' by his history: his personal history, that of his group, that of mankind as mediated by his group and refracted in his personal experience. Heidegger insists that a man is as personally and completely shaped by his particular understanding and acknowledgment of his mortality. Freud suggested that a man has a better chance to discover his self, his freedom, being, independence, scope, the better and more fully he comes to understand his history. Heidegger suggests that a more total recognition of his mortality which is his individuality and historicalness, his precarious *Dasein*, his *Dasein* as precarious, contingent, might give him a better chance to achieve his *Dasein*, to become himself.

A self, however, whose *Dasein* is so peculiarly constituted by his beginning and his end and by the complex interaction between past and future, a self who is his history and is a self in as far as he achieves the history he is, does not experience time as the abstraction as which it figures in history writing. Heidegger, I am convinced, intends to be descriptive rather than explanatory when he speaks of past, present and future, as the three ecstasies, *ex-stases*, of time, and leaves the word to its ambivalence (1931, p. 329). It is no use having a clear concept of something that is not clear. By means of his formulation, I merely wish to pose the question: In how far is the past ever past? In how far can it be my or our past, unless as past it is present? In how far is the future more than an abstraction, except as explication of the past and directedness of the present? And is not the present a total abstraction – an Eleatic one – as long as it is not understood as that *ex-stasis* of time which is explicable solely in terms of the other two, as these are explicable solely in terms of it?[7]

Heidegger's view of the individual and his *Sein und Zeit* leads him to a further distinction which also makes historiography problematical, that between *Geschick* and *Schicksal* which are only inadequately translated as fate and destiny (ibid. pp. 384–95). *Geschick* is the sum total of everything that happens-to-be and happens-to-be-so, the conglomeration and condensation of all the individual refusals 'to be', the ossification of all escapes from *Dasein* into *man*, including that of historiography. *Geschick* embodies the *Man*, its temptations and compulsions, the fact of our lostness in it. To put it crudely, just as Freud could see public institutions as analogous to private neuroses, so a Heideggerian might view them as public ramifications of individual refusals of individuality, as mistaken projections – *Entwürfe* – of those who dared not face the care – *Sorge* – of their *Geworfensein*, their being thrown, ejected-from-the-womb, their individuality (ibid. pp. 296–315).

Schicksal, on the other hand, is the individual's possibility, his acknowledgment of his situation as his possibility, within the reality of *Geschick*, as something he must care about and care for. For *Geschick*, the sum total of everything that happens-to-be-so, does not represent or constitute the individual's situation, but rather the temptation and possibility of its denial. *Geschick* denotes the circumstances, the *Man*, the conditions by which *man* is totally conditioned – and I as well, in as far as I am lost in the *Man*. My situation however, which remains mine as long as I am not totally *man*, is open, but open only to the degree to which I am not *man*.

(From here we might appreciate the importance for the *Geistes-wissenschaften* of Heidegger's distinction between *Seiendes* and *Sein*. The former denotes what happens-to-be-so. The latter queries whether what-happens-to-be *is* what it pretends to be, is all that possibly could be.)

The mere possibility of such an understanding of man once again makes history writing radically problematical. It poses the question, how can we ever be or make sure that any historiography will not block our possible understanding of history as our possibility rather than aid it? Unless we learn to give quite a different weight to the *ex-stases* of time? Does not history writing by its very nature fix the past as past, and is it not therefore bound to remain what our present historical writing is in its very essence, the denial of the possible? It is the academic discipline of history which has conditioned us to think of the question 'what would have happened if . . .?' as illegitimate.

4 *Literature and art*

Literature has always been – naturally among other things – a loud protest against historiography and history. As tragedy and comedy, satire, idyll, epic, lyrics, ballad, as novel and autobiography, it convicts historiography of unreality. It does this powerfully, because of its immediate appeal to our sensibilities which are not exclusively conditioned by our rationalizing faculties. We can salvage our belief in the authenticity of historiography only by denying this quality of reality to literature in the face of our outraged sensibilities.

Men have cried with Gilgamesh over the lost friend, over the loss of friendship as an ultimate loss. They have cried over and with Andromache, as she and her baby take leave of Hector. But they know – *wissen* – or think they know that seeking out dragons is a necessity beyond ultimate loss, that war is inevitable, even if it is fought over the love of a woman not unlike Andromache. One loves Antigone, but *weiss* how right Cleon is, for what would happen to society, if men and women were permitted to express their love freely? Gradually both author and reader become overwhelmed by the substantiality of Don Quixote, by the authenticity, the fulness and hopefulness of his maddened humanity which makes what is commonly taken for reality look like the charade it is. Don Quixote is both the most tragic and the most comic figure; he is the only one who took literature seriously, more seriously even than his creator (cf. Bloch, 1970, vol. 3, pp. 1216–38; esp. p. 1230). Goethe experienced and expressed the tragedy of Gretchen from the heart. As minister he countersigned the death sentence of the infanticide.

As a man afraid of tragedy he says: 'I prefer to commit an injustice to the toleration of disorder' (Meinecke, 1959, p. 561). While actually listening to the *Rheingold* we feel the whole weight of the folly that wants power rather than love. We experience a little of the consternation that rent the universe when Alberich demonstrated for the first time that love could be bought by the powerful, or at least the tokens which the powerful will take for love, as he mistakes power for that which it is meant to reveal. The final curtain restores us to 'reality' where only possessions are real and love only in as far as it can be possessed. For a moment Rembrandt's *Jewish Bride* convinces us of the reality and centrality of human tenderness and desire. Soon the exigencies of life, business, education, career, take over. The memory of the *Jewish Bride* becomes nostalgic, i.e. it reminds us of a past that never was. Or it becomes ideological, i.e. it helps us to pretend that the present is what it is not; while the present might become what it is not, if we did not pretend. For we also know that the picture speaks the truth.

In literature and art man confronts himself with his hidden and yet clearly identifiable identity and actuality: with his possibilities. The power of art resides in its capacity to compel us into this confrontation and identification with our individuality and its possibilities as our actuality. But this actuality, being our mortality, is so precarious, that we cannot bear it except as fiction. Only that which we are not, that which happens to be because we do not want to be what we are, is actual, real, non-fiction, history: activity for activity's sake and for the sake of forgetfulness, our objectifying efforts which produce ideologies to die for; also science, historiography, above all economics, industry and commerce, the means to an end we have lost sight of. Art confronts man with an image of himself, his self, he cannot yet deny. Therefore he fictionalizes it and turns to historiography which, rather than art, is the fictionalizing of history, to make art bearable. Which is the neurotic escape: art, or that which we seem to *wissen* about reality? Or both? Are we waiting for a third manifestation beyond fact and fiction, an *Aufhebung* of both, seeing that either is an aspect of our split social actuality?

Art is about me and you and the demands of the I-you situation which cannot be neglected, not even in inter-stellar space. Art has remained external to history – and sociology! – in spite of historical novels and plays, in spite of histories of literature. It has remained a protest against history, a contradiction of what we call its study. Such it will remain as long as Antigone and Othello, Minna and Faust, Hamlet and Don Quixote, remain alive, yet continue to live as fiction. Till then literature will query all history and historiography – and, of course, all sociology, even the sociology of literature.

5 *Freud's practical use of history*

History now becomes case-history. Though a German equivalent is neither idiomatic nor technical usage, the term spotlights the gain and loss.

It is not new to call the story of one life, in either fact or fiction, history. There are the histories of Alexander and Napoleon and *The History of Mr Polly*. Yet the Freudian case-history is different in kind. The former is the account of actions, of purposeful inter-action of the hero and his age. Whether he attacks or defends any or all of its particular forces, creeds, institutions, conventions, whether he wins or loses, ascends a throne or ends in a dungeon, reforms his order or is burned at the stake, he is actor, even when he is a victim. His suffering is the consequence of his action. His life has or is history to the extent to which he is not merely a victim. Mere victims, i.e. the great majority of mankind, had as yet no history; possibly because history is one of man's attempts to cover up the extent to which he is merely victim. This covering up is done both by those who need and by those who are victims.

In psycho-analysis history is unveiled as that which a man suffers and suffered, that which made a 'case' of him. Perhaps he is a case, because or partly because we have so far concentrated on those aspects of history and turned that into historiography which makes victims of the vast majority of people and finally even of the victim-izers (cf. Marcuse, 1969, ch. 8). In analysis man's victimhood, his victimization, is put into the centre of 'historical' investigation. That is his history. He is object, not actor, and is this inevitably, at least in our society. That is his trouble. For history is mediated to him, made his history, through mother or father or their substitutes, at a time when they are experienced as overwhelming presences and when the tradition which they embody rather than profess cannot be critically weighed. This is to say that analysis helps us to under-stand history as something we suffer, not only in the sense that it makes us suffer, but also in the sense that it can only be suffered, has to be borne, makes us willing to suffer. The whole civilizatory structure, its functions, justifications, conventions, the ossified violations and mutilations man has inflicted on himself in his fear of his self, the demands for sacrifice, the colossal institutionalized misinterpretations of his actual drives and desires, all this is imposed on us, stamps and 'gestalts' us, long before we act or think, choose or escape. It sets the pattern of our reactions as well as of our actions, of our conformity as well as of our rebellion. Or rather, from the beginning it twists all our actions into reactions. We hardly ever act, we react and most of all when, as in politics or industry, we think we are acting (Mitscherlich, 1969, pp. 9, 48–9, 54, 81, 121).

135

Above all it determines the form of our suffering.

That is why, and this implication Freud was not yet willing or able to consider, liberation, in as far as it could become our possibility, would have to be liberation from what we understand as history. It would have to be liberation not only, as Freud wished, from the super-ego, but from the ego which is equally history-made, i.e. from the ego as we know it.

Adorno says (1970, p. 267; cf. pp. 264–9, 271–2, 287).

> The uncritical rule of reason, of the ego over the id, is identical
> with that repressive principle which psycho-analysis has shifted
> into the unconscious realm, because its critique becomes silent
> before the reality principle of the ego. The separation of the
> super-ego from the ego which constitutes its topology is dubious;
> genetically both can be reduced to the injection of the father-
> image. That is why analytical theories of the super-ego weaken
> so rapidly, however boldly they set out. They would have to
> be applied to the pampered ego.

Such a liberation from the historically constituted ego would also be a liberation *for* history, but for a different kind of history altogether: my history. Anything short of that is 'adjustment' which could be defined as: denial of the possible, acceptance of what-is-so as inevitable, learning to tolerate the intolerable (Marcuse, 1969, 'Epilogue').

Again comparisons with Marx and Heidegger obtrude. The former understood history as much more radically dependent on underlying, meta-historical forces and stresses than had ever been admitted before, outside theology. He had understood liberation as from history. He had thought it possible as the result of growing consciousness of and insight into the underlying, i.e. unconscious processes which imposed themselves as historical necessity, while they remained in the dark. Heidegger has helped us to suspect all historiography as an imposition of the *Man*. Liberation, as he saw it, lies in the acknowledgment of my individuality in its full historicalness as mortal, the acceptance of my contingent *Dasein* as possibility, as *Schicksal* over against *Geschick*. Psycho-analysis, like Marx, believes that the grip of compulsion or of so-called necessity can be loosed only by a growing awareness of its nature, complexity, history. But it goes beyond Marx in its insistence that this progress in awareness is more than an advance in intellectual understanding, moral commitment and political action. It involves a *nesis* – re-membering, *Erinnern* – almost religious in character, a descent into Hades or the mother's womb, a retrieving, reliving, reconstituting of the past. It involves the re-experiencing of the terror, pain, anguish, and the consequent dread, rage, hatred, by means of which human history as condensed into my parents' being, into their loves and fears, is made my history.

Freud's patients and their parents may have belonged almost exclusively to the Austrian middle class, indeed a most peculiar manifestation of humanity. But just as the novel reveals the universal through the individual, so a peculiar member of a particular society, looked at steadily, with sympathy and penetration, can reveal our shared humanity as much as any man. Anyway, where would Freud have found patients not equally peculiar? And what generalization could ever hope to *aufheben* the insights gained by looking at peculiar individuals?

From Heidegger psycho-analysis could learn to take its understanding of history and historicalness, its commitment to the individual and his intimate history, its *geistige* implications, more seriously. For it is still reacting to that specific historical distortion of religion and of the *Geistige* which prevailed in Freud's days and especially in Austria. Without the rediscovery of such an extra-psychological dimension, the liberation offered by analysis is likely to degenerate into adjustment.

I am turning to the term 'case' in case-history. It epitomizes both the lack of that extra-psychological dimension and the inner contradictions of analysis – so similar to those experienced by Dilthey (Habermas, 1969, compare ch. 11 with chs 7–8). A case is an abstraction from and therefore a denial of the individual and his historicalness as seen by analysis. 'Case' is an instance of. . . . As soon as the analyst looks at me as a case, even his case, he has already subordinated my individuality to some kind of non-individual non-historical generalization. He is trying to distinguish between me and my distorting history, as if my past were past. He implicitly assumes a concept of health and normality – though he may explicitly deny it – which cannot help being conditioned by the very society and its history which has victimized me – and him. Unwittingly he has turned into a psycho-synthesist, a man who knows how to repair a psyche as a surgeon knows how to repair a body; though Freud himself had called psycho-synthesis a 'thoughtless phrase', since the health of an individual psyche cannot be synthesized, can only be given a chance to constitute itself; though Freud had maintained that the fixing of a border between the normal and abnormal was not feasible (ibid. pp. 286, 333).

The term 'case' meaning *Fall* enshrines Freud positivism, the Enlightenment belief that history could be *aufgehoben* via a less painful process than that of unreserved acceptance of one's individuality. It may be that even today much of the power of scientism resides in its promise of such an easier route, in the hope that history need not be *aufgehoben* but can be circumvented. Ultimately,

Freud hoped, the analyst would come to know the psychic apparatus as the physician the body, the analytical cure would become as detachable from the patient's individuality as in surgery. (Compare here the emphases of Wollheim, 1971, Rieff, 1960, Habermas, 1969.) In spite of this, the Freudian apprehension of history, its insights into the nature of its sedimentation, its transmission, its unconscious and omnipresent compulsions which disguise themselves as historical necessities, raises a whole set of problems which the discipline of history – and of sociology – cannot afford to ignore.[8]

F Meaning and significance

According to Whorf, the Hopi language, which in many respects is much less sophisticated than European tongues, shows a refinement concerning the distinction between 'inner' and 'outer' reality quite beyond the scope of most civilized languages (1967, pp. 57–64). It has different nouns and prepositions for inner and outer space, while for us the same word 'space' denotes the two incommensurables. Hopi therefore cannot appreciate our distinctions concerning 'inner' and 'outer', nor the consequent ambivalences, because it has its distinct 'ins' and 'outs' for the spatial and the psychic world.

This difference seems to point at a basic ambiguity. On the one hand there is no doubt that the 'inner', the psychic world is totally different from the 'outer'. It is neither its image, nor mirror, nor camera. One has to strain one's definition of analogy substantially, before one dare call the one analogous to the other. What, for instance, is analogous between a sun-like star 'out there', of dimensions and temperature beyond physical imagining, and our experience – where and how? – of a tiny, twinkling speck of light dubbed the Polar Star? How many perceptual and conceptual grids are necessary to correlate the one with the other? Or again: what analogy is there between Juliet and Romeo's image of her, between her physical-psychic presence as experienced by herself and that experienced by Romeo's passion, or by us, the impartial observers? Or, one step further, and as counter-question to the behaviourists: What kind of analogy or relation subsists between Romeo's endocrinal secretions in face of Juliet – and anyway why not in face of another girl? – and his feelings for her?

On the other hand, the widespread linguistic neglect of the incommensurability of the internal and the external cannot be explained as a simple oversight. It expresses the equally incontestable other aspect of the same phenomenon or reality. First, I do not experience my 'inner' apprehension of the 'outer' space as inner, as separable from the outward phenomenon, at least not unreflectively. Second, all my 'inner' apprehensions, no matter whether I am star-gazing, feeling heart-broken, or in love, or have a headache, are in some way external to the experiencing self if not to my body; just as that self itself becomes external to itself, the moment it is focused as such by a self. This is one aspect of the paradox of immanence and transcendence, of real-ideal, mental-material, which constitutes the mystery of individual-social actuality.

Another aspect of this mystery can be illustrated by contrasting Greek and Hebrew metaphysics. The latter sees man as a whole. He is body-soul. He is not a body who has a soul or vice versa. As such an entity he is part of undivided nature, i.e. of a reality not split into natural and supernatural, which is God's creation. He lives in a time which, as God's time, as directed, meaningful time, is eternity 'at the same time'. Everything is immanent in such a universe, except God. Yet even he is not transcendent in any formulable way. Although not of the world, the Hebrew Yahweh is totally in it, acting in it, hence actual only in it. For Hebrew thought there is no 'outside' of the world. For that very reason it cannot separate, for example, religion from politics, ethics from aesthetics, could not have conceived or articulated a separation of science from value. (Was Einstein's psyche trying to recapture the universe for the Hebrew spirit?)

Greek thought separates body from soul, time from eternity, the natural from the supernatural, idea from reality. This peculiar conceptualization Europe has inherited and cannot now easily transcend. These divisions are basically a peculiar dichotomization of inner and outer. They also reflect the separation of mental from physical work. They create insoluble problems of immanence and transcendence, of subjectivity and objectivity, not only concerning questions of meaning, God, the good, but also in relation to Kantian, phenomenological or scientistic contributions to understanding, and to questions of value.

These problems intrude into arguments of and with positivists, contemporary linguistic philosophers, as concerning 'meaning', 'non-problems', 'non-questions', validity or truth. For the grand dichotomization of reality had another consequence: it had been from the beginning a reflection of the division of society into leaders and led, consumers and producers, *Geniesser* (gourmets) and labourers. Intellect, soul, spirit, was on one side; body, flesh, brawn on the other. The ideological function of the dichotomization was the justification of the leaders and the domestication of the led whose brawn the brains needed for the buttressing of their position. Good, noble, just, eternal, pertained to the intellect; base, brutish, low, ephemeral, pertained to the flesh, the labouring body (cf. Nietzsche, *Genealogy of Morals* with Hegel, *Phenomenology of the Spirit*, IV, A). In philosophical as well as in social terms, this means an evacuation of all values from the natural to the supernatural, from body to soul, from earth to heaven, from labour to profit. When modern man gradually lost his belief in the supernatural and the soul – possibly because of growing bureaucratization – he was left with a depleted nature, a soul-less body, an uneternal time, each of which proved infinitely divisible. He also was left with work without meaning, busyness without end, with work and business as the only meaning. So, having lost *was die Welt im Innersten zusammenhält* (what universes the world from its very core), he seems to have become intent on tearing everything into ever smaller pieces, as if he believed he could discover the lost cohesion behind the final atomization and the meaning of labour in such labouring. For it seems as if man cannot live without suspecting 'meaning' somewhere.

Within the Hebrew conceptual scheme all significance is immanent in the sense that all immanence is significant. Everything both *is* and signifies. As part of a created whole everything belongs and therefore, in its place, either represents or distorts the whole. All things work together for good in a God-directed movement. Hence every action and reaction furthers or hinders the progress of the whole, enhances or detracts from its life. 'Good and evil' are not privatized so that the soul in its privacy may accrue eternal merit or blame, or fulfil its private *karma*. One serves the whole or rebels against it, loves creation or hates it. A criminal is a curse on the whole community (Deuteronomy 21: 23).

Within the Greek conceptual frame meaning is both immanent and transcendent in such a way that the immanent meaning is vindicated by the transcendent one. Greek intellectualism excelled in defining and confining spheres, universes of discourse, within which each separate item, itself defined in relation to the whole, could be definitely and meaningfully correlated to each other. This had remained rather a game among the élite, to while away the labourless hours. It was forgotten while people showed little inclination to play in that fashion. Even Plato's philosophy remained a game, a self-enclosed system, until Christianity translated its originally social and political intentions into socio-religious terms, into a vindication of political structures which had their origin elsewhere. The Middle Ages created or elaborated further contexts of meaning which fitted, or were meant to fit, into each other like Russian dolls (cf. Huizinga, 1965, ch. 15). In this way everything related meaningfully to everything else in its own sphere and pointed beyond that into and through the next right up to the Holy Trinity.

By the time the Greek intellectual game was rediscovered, the feudal set-up had begun to crumble. Science with its strict immanence of meaning came into its own at a time when transcendent meaning had absolutized itself out of existence via Calvin's absolute and predestinating God. It gradually absorbed into itself the whole pathos and intensity of longing for transcendental meaning which man experiences in a dichotomized universe. Some philosophers, like Hegel, fought rearguard actions and at the same time demonstrated willy-nilly to what a degree the supernatural had always been an abstraction. For a time, while theistic, pantheistic, deistic, and finally humanistic and rationalistic assumptions still functioned indubitably, scientific investigations seemed to possess a transcendent meaning. Some of the older scientists certainly still thought of themselves as vindicators of God's order in the universe. Later still, technology came to function as science's transcendent significance – it was and is this as long as it helps staving off hunger and disease. Today it is easier to say that technology, in the service of man's liberation, could have such a significance, than to claim it has. Like economics, technology-science has become self-determining, automated, i.e. exclusively immanent in meaning and significance. Human need no longer impinges meaningfully on the mechanisms that accelerate their own and each other's processes. Science-technology has become a fully-fledged myth.

It is a totally immanent myth, like the Hebrew one. Unlike the latter, its immanence is that of a truncated, halved 'reality', of a depleted nature, body, time. Today scientific philosophy considers all questions of meaning as meaningless. In this connection too sociology wishes to be scientific. It aims to design systems of immanent meaning which would automatically obviate any questions concerning transcendent significance. It disdains hierarchies of value in which alone any other than immanent meaning can subsist. It is egalitarian and recognizes no subject matter of intrinsically greater significance than any other. In as far as it is dealing with man's actions, reactions and interactions, it has already pre-judged him as a being whose longing for significance is insignificant, or of significance only in as far as it can be treated statistically or as 'ideal type', i.e. as immanent. Yet sociology denies its *logos* when it confines itself to localized investigations of which the attempt to relate the part to the whole is not an integral concern. I cannot meaningfully investigate pervasive social problems without querying the whence and whither of society, its origins and aims. If I do I have merely accepted the *status quo* as an aim, an end. Such transcendent perspectives need not be religious or metaphysical. They could be of the kind suggested by dialectics, by Bloch's hope-principle, by Heidegger's understanding of *Sein* (see below, I), by Freud's totalizing view of the psyche which points towards the possible *Aufhebung* of societal dichotomies in individual actuality.

Even Durkheim's understanding of society as generating its own transcendence and significance is worth taking more seriously. Something of Hebrew holism speaks through it. All these views express attempts to see society as a living entity of which the individual *Dasein* is the indefinable transcendence-in-immanence, continually defining and redefining all rational definitions, because it is greater than reason.

Do we live in order to think or do we think in order to keep alive? The answer is rarely in doubt, except in academic arguments. Even arch-intellectuals like Hume and Freud agreed on the priority of life, of the passions. Yet it seems as if civilization *qua* civilization is a continuous rationalizing process. It engenders multitudes of immanent, bureaucratic meanings which gradually absorb most individual libido into themselves, until man comes to distrust all trans-bureaucratic significance and ends by dreading it. It may be that the tension between the individual and society has its roots in or is an expression of the tension between life and reason, between individual aspirations and the rationalization processes of civilization. One might say tentatively that this basic tension constitutes the phenomena and the problems of social consciousness.

Social consciousness is the introjection of the conflicts between the demands of 'life', of joy, pleasure, love; and the demands of rationality: security, certainty, stability, above all, productivity. Though reason when pressed may admit that security has no transcendent meaning, unless it secure joy and love which cannot be secured, its arguments, and possibly for this very reason, are all on security's side. So social, i.e. individual, consciousness and conscience, experience the demands of life as unreasonable and try to rationalize them, as, for example, recreation, relaxation, entertainment, leisure. Television is so far the ultimate in rationalization and containment of life: life is lived for us, outside us, in neat and manageable instalments, during measured periods of time, so as not to interfere with our rational, real pursuits. In its most total surrender to all possible passions it remains switch-offable at any moment. In this way what is left of life is perfectly integrated into the rationality of civilization – even in that entertainment can be justified as giving work to the entertainer. On the screen, in the privacy of the atomic family, life, meaning has become completely immanent. It entertains the living who watch it, i.e. holds them suspended between non-living and non-living by means of a pseudo-life (cf. Horkheimer-Adorno, 1969, '*Kulturindustrie*').

Footnote   It has often been pointed out that art began to function as a kind of religion, since the latter lost its hold over the Western imagination. We leave aside the fascinating question, whether religion, as understood by its founders and prophets, was ever anything but art lived, the art of living; whether art is ever less than religious, at least in its efforts to say what the artist cannot yet live. This much is fairly clear: something becomes a work of art when it has 'life in itself', speaks for itself, when, in other words, it expresses transcendence-in-immanence. To the extent to which it is satisfying in and by itself, it reaches and *is* beyond itself, it signifies. Yet it signifies what it is. A work of art is *ex-stasis*. It touches, moves, gives without losing. It has the character of individual life. It makes my life more meaningful to the extent to which I am able to respond to it as meaningful.

Now many contemporary artists, poets, composers, seem to have become chary, almost suspicious and ashamed of such transcendence. They often take great pains to make their work immanent, to make it contain or retain its meaning without yielding it. This to the point of built-in destruction. Sometimes they have gone to great lengths to explain why they do not wish their work to speak, move or touch (Gehlen, 1965, pp. 162–70, 185–7). Gertrude Stein said at the time of the first cultural revolution: 'A rose is a rose is a rose.' The contemporary artist's antiphon could be: 'A hose is a hose is a hose.' Yet such statements are either mere verbal equations: A–R–O–S–E = A–R–O–S–E, or they simply are not true. My rose is not your rose, nor is mine today the same as yesterday. No rose, neither the word nor the thing nor my *Erkenntnis* of either word or thing, is ever simply itself. Perhaps the artist really wanted to shout: I am I am I am I, which would not be much more meaningful but a little more comprehensible. So it is especially ironic that he should have tried to express his individuality as artist by a statement which merely reflects the immanence of total bureaucracy.

Perhaps the propaganda of the war years, the strident and ceaseless ideological assertions of the 'meaning of the struggle', had made the artist allergic to meaning and message altogether. Could it be one of the tasks of sociology to investigate not only the facts but the meaning of that aberration? Could it do the one without the other? Could it complement the artist, just here where he seems to be losing confidence in himself? Dilthey says (1914, vol. 7, p. 237):

> The coherence of experience in its concrete actuality lies in the category of meaning (*Bedeutung*). This is the unity which integrates the course of experiences and the living through it again in remembering. Yet the meaning does not reside in a centre of unity which lies outside the experience, but is contained within the experiences as that which constitutes their coherence.

To such labouring the Western mind condemned itself by accepting the Greek dichotomies.

G Subjective, objective

This is not the place to enter for the *n*th time into the problem of subjectivity, as it presented itself to Kant in his efforts to uphold the positing, positive rationalism of Descartes against the Humean doubts, as it presented itself to Husserl later on. Still less is there time to trace once more Hegel's gigantic attempt to establish subjectivism as objectivity, subjective *Vernunft* as universal spirit, by pointing out the inevitable and inherent contradictions in Kant's subjectivism and remaining silent on the fact that any and each intellectual position has inherent and inevitable contradictions. (Though it would be tempting to ask whether the claim to objectivity is ever more than a raising of the voice when the argument is getting weak.) Only this much is to be retained here – and who knows whether subjective idealism cannot be dissolved into just this – that there is no knowledge apart from the knowing of the knower, no *Erkenntnis* which is not somebody's act of response.

Could it be put like this: there is no such 'thing' as knowledge; only the communicating, receiving, holding, using, of this and that knowing? Only the knowers, the subjects, are substantival, and even their noun character needs qualifying. All the rest is sheer inter-communication, inter-subjectivity, a calling and reaching across, a gesturing, an infinitely intricate weaving of precarious mutuality. Nouns were invented for the sake of brevity and convenience, a mental shorthand, and possibly in order to hide from the subject both the precariousness of knowing and the fact of total inter-dependence. (Some Hindu teaching tries to stress this, and possibly Heraclitus, Socrates and Jesus; nominalism groped towards it, non-Cartesian idealism and, of course, dialectical materialism.) But if there are only subjects and their inter-communication, then objectivity is neither the opposite nor the complement of subjectivity. It simply does not belong in the same universe of discourse or, as Wittgenstein calls it, 'language game'.

The words 'subject', 'subjectivity', 'inter-subjectivity', are to imply here and in the following the full meaning of the personal and inter-personal – as against the connotation of mere subjectivity or mere inter-subjectivity implied by the usage of, for example, prag-matists, symbolic interactionists and even Popper. They are to denote movements between me and you, us and them. The word objective or objectivity denotes a convention, a conventional agree-ment concerning the status I and you and we wish to assign to a more or less clearly circumscribed aspect of our mutuality and inter-communication. Being a subject and as such involved in inter-subjective communications is the actuality of which we cannot help being aware directly and incontrovertibly; no matter how often we may mistake or mis-judge details or aspects of it, no matter that within its fluidity we can never hope to attain certainty. Certainty cannot belong in the realm of inter-subjective actuality constituted by mortals. It pertains to the distinct and separate universes of discourse which have been designed to produce certainty or at least an approximation to it. Objectivity *is* not, it has no necessary existence apart from inter-subjective conventions. It has only a limited reality among unlimited possibilities. It is constituted by and for a specific purpose or objective. Only specific objectives constitute objectivity. It is a convenience and can become a neurotic escape if taken for more.

This is not to say that inter-subjective communication subsists in a vacuum, but that outside it there is no 'thing' or object, no *res* or *chrema*, therefore no re(s)ality. For a thing as thing or object, from the first flint for making fire to the most complex industrial or conceptual machinery, is constituted by human needs and desires for human ends. It is raised into thinghood, into the re(s)ality of inter-subjective communication, becomes a *res publica*, through human intention and skill (cf. Heidegger, 1954, pp. 163–87). Man discovers and explores his humanity in the process of turning the earth which he cannot know into his world: into image, gesture, repetition, word, concept, tool, instrument, i.e. into social re(s)ality which is the possibility of communion, of the communication of personal desires and experiences (cf. Durkheim, 1968, 'Conclusion'). Whatever there be outside the reality defined and delimited by human inter-communication, cannot be re(s)ality. It cannot be conceptualized or conceived, for the moment it or an aspect of it has been conceptualized, it has been taken into man-made reality.

It may be that religious or mystic experience is an awareness of that which is beyond *Begriff* or *Zugriff* (concept or grasp), which could explain why any theology, the attempt to conceptualize this, is intrinsically self-defeating. It may be that the erotic encounter and, analogically, all undeniable love-experiences point beyond human reality. For that reason the religious and the erotic have often been felt to illuminate each other – no matter whether in love or hate. The fact that religion and love point beyond re(s)ality, that they are by definition such pointedness, does not mean that they are not a vital concern of sociology. Art has been perennially fascinated by religion and love. For in either man seems to be taken outside, beyond, beside himself, his ego and its reality, only to get all the more pathetically or comically or tragically or heroically enmeshed in 'reality'. Or to put it the other way round, to the lover and the mystic reality begins to appear as a man-made web of illusions that entangles him and prevents him from reaching his self or that of the other.

Can it now be said in turn that only experiences analogous to the mystic or erotic can be a touchstone or critique of reality, of things-as-they-are? What if it were true, not only poetically but socio-logically, that love is the lodestar of any human, i.e. individual-social endeavour, that indeed

> . . . it is an ever-fixed mark,
> That looks on tempests and is never shaken;
> It is the star to every wandering bark,
> Whose worth's unknown, although his height be taken.
>
> Shakespeare: Sonnet CXVI

As it undoubtedly is true that whatever I do, if I have not love, do not love doing it, it profits me nothing. Whether mystic or erotic experiences are illusions or delusions or intimations of the truth or of a truth, will inevitably remain beyond the possibility of proof, since proof and certainty only appertain to re(s)ality. Those experiences are transcendent and thus alone able to create a hierarchy of meaning and value. For there can be little doubt that our reality is torn out of as well as substantiated by that which cannot be conceived, by a meta-reality (cf. Habermas, 1967, pp. 179ff, 185ff, on Marx and Boehme). Mystic and erotic experiences are beyond argument. They are 'true' to the extent to which they are experienced as beyond argument. They are pointers and can be embodied only in a most personal, idiosyncratic, uncertain and easily contradictable communication. Integration into the social reality by argument and proof would, by definition, destroy them. However much I would love you to love, I do not wish my love to be your love.

Once again we find the individual, however fallible, infected, conditioned, distorted, as the carrier of social consciousness, in as far as he both constitutes and transcends reality. We may return to my contention. Whatever be the nature of that which lies beyond the inter-subjective reality of communication, it is not what is usually called 'objectivity'. This does not lie outside or beyond subjectivity. It is always constituted by the latter for a distinct purpose. Objectivity is a subjective or inter-subjective convention of great usefulness. It is, as the name would indicate, utilitarian in character, concerned with objects and objectives that can be handled and attained. Its degree of usefulness is in direct proportion to the strict limitation by and definition of its purpose, its objective. Precisely because the natural sciences, especially at the time of their inception, had distinct and definite purposes and ever since practised a ruthless method of abstraction and elimination, they proved to be so useful. Their usefulness became increasingly ambivalent, as the usefulness itself became their objective. Here again, as in any bureaucratization, the means became libidinized, usefulness was measured in terms of further usefulness, as capital by its own increase and no longer by its objective. This libidinization both produces the circle of interest and hides its circularity from the practitioner and researcher.

Today this circularity, possibly inherent from the beginning in civilization as we know it, has reached juggernaut proportions. In economics, political, military, scientific-technological, industrial thinking and non-thinking, automatism is almost total. The sorcerer's apprentice keeps on splitting the broomstick splinters, and each new splinter keeps on carrying and pouring out the bathwater with no master magician in sight to stem the flood. The consequent ecological problems created by our amateurism parading as expertise have therefore to be approached by a kind of thinking which has broken out of that objectifying circularity. The diverse limited spheres of objectivity which had been constituted by society for the production of *chremata* (objects) for use have proliferated and coagulated into an overwhelming re(s)ality. This is no longer the realm of things as things within the wider actuality of inter-subjective communion. It has become the total reality in which man himself is a thing among things, a function, in which communication and communion are subordinated to economic productivity, i.e. to the means and media of communication.

Was this the tendency since the dawn of civilization? Bureau-cratization = equalization = rationalization, whether of the more administrative kind as in Ancient Egypt or Mesopotamia, or of the more scientific-technological variety as in other civilizations, is a process that progressively reveals civilization itself as the universal leveller. (Weber appreciated this when he delineated as typical the descent from charismatic to bureaucratic power.) Now the levelling completes itself under a Pharaoh and his priesthood, now under a Tudor king, now under a bundle of unassailable assumptions in a democracy (cf. Simmel, 1922, pp. 147ff on the danger of the last). This process is so fundamentally identified with civilization that the possibility of its interruption seems to threaten chaos. It has been at work so universally, that the equally universal demands of individuality and desire have been universally distorted or repressed. So much so that we simply do not know yet what individuality, subjectivity and desire really are. Within civilization the subjective demands appear as eccentric and exorbitant and are channelled into religion and literature (Durkheim, 1968, p. 6, n1). Where they try to seek direct and open expression, they are immediately distorted into ostentation. History abounds in tragic and scurrilous caricatures of individuality with their infinite and repetitive variety of hierarchic fancy-dress, arrogance, brutality.

May one go as far as saying that history is the continual conflict between the levelling, objectifying processes of civilization, and the distorted, hence aggressive and assertive individual protests against them? These protests in turn, just because they expressed the aggressiveness of that which had been repressed, could always be made to subserve the civilized juggernauting. Hence the enormous drives towards political and social unification, empire building. Hence at the same time the vehement resistance to it, which has always proved futile, because it was always based on former, already perpetrated, violations and unifications.

It would obviously be more than naive to believe that the power which mankind has conceded to objectifying processes could easily be reversed. It does not merely tyrannize us from above or outside. Like the patriarchal family structure on which all other civilized power structures seem to be based and modelled, the power of objectification lies in its introjected authority. Here Durkheim is surely right when he claims that society has structured the very categories of our *Vernunft*. Any repudiation of societal pretensions has therefore to grow out of the still unplumbed depths of our social individuality (cf. Mitscherlich, 1969; Laing, 1965, 1970b). Yet though Durkheim understood certain societal functions very well, his work also reveals the sociologist's fascination with the civilizatory processes. He was actually longing for a rebirth of societal authority (Durkheim, 1969, pp. 1–33). Pareto believed firmly in an élite (1935, vol. 4). And what, in a post-Freudian perspective, was Weber's longing for the Messiah, if not the wish for a father figure who would absolve one from the awful responsibility of choosing and defending one's own values? Yet that responsibility appeared awful, because it was conceived in authoritarian terms, like Kant's.

In this connection Weber's thought is altogether instructive. He had argued that value-judgments, political, religious or ethical decisions, cannot be vindicated by science or by scientific evidence. In this he was perfectly right. Values are personal, emotive, born of love. They are of the self, although this, in the very depth of its selfhood, is in communion with all other selves. But Weber's passionate craving for objectivity, his implicit belief in its reality, left the realm of decision in terrifying Kantian or even Kafkaesque isolation, and ostracized value, as judgment, exclusively to that realm. According to Weber, a man was called upon to make decisions in face of an overwhelming reality which any continued objective study would, by its very nature, make appear ever more impregnable. Furthermore, the preoccupation with value-free science was also to have this odd effect: although one's values could not be defended by scientific arguments, one would feel compelled to defend them with arguments modelled on those employed by science and found useful in it. This is to say that a man was left with decisions based on groundless arguments. No wonder the sociologists and social philosophers succumbed to the powerful persuasion of things-as-they-are and called it objectivity – which indeed denotes the supremacy of the object. It is therefore important to remember that though things may have total power over us, they do not have it of necessity. It is still possible to believe that other possibilities exist and that these might become our humanity.

Every human action implicitly acknowledges this belief, even though it may fail to express it adequately. And as long as it does, the arguments about freedom and determinism will continue and will in themselves continue to express both freedom and determinism. The sociologist is neither the only nor the last man whose work, by the simple fact of its existence, perpetuates the paradox. If he genuinely believed in determinism, he could not carry on. It would be worse than a prisoner's filling and emptying of the same hole, for the latter would be dreaming of freedom while doing his work. So the sociologist is not free to behave as if the proof of determinism had been established. But whatever freedom he may have or take, may have to take, it is in the full sense of the word subjective, uncertain and insecure.

(Just as a kind of footnote: There is no doubt that many young people during the last decade or two entered sociology departments under the impression, more or less clear, that there they would find understanding, illumination and reforming or revolutionary zeal. They would be helped to understand society in order to improve it and themselves. It is hard to assess what the departments actually did to them and their capacity for understanding. It is at least possible that some of the most sensitive and gifted became disillusioned and cynical as a result of what is actually being taught, still more as a consequence of what is not. Perhaps they dropped out or they settled down in the accepted and acceptable routine. In either case the question remains: have we by our teaching confirmed, aided and abetted, or merely acknowledged determinism? Have we, by denying, if merely by implication, the relevance of the possible, made it a little less possible? Now even if the belief in the possible were an illusion, would it not have been better to strengthen it, than to resign oneself to the 'fact' that reality is totally disillusioning? There is the objection that human nature is what it is, that he who is not idealistic at twenty is a swine and he who is still an idealist at forty is an ass, and that most professors being near or over forty have no desire to be asses. But do we really know – *wissen* – what human nature is? And if it is what the just quoted tag implies, is it not preferable to be an ass? Has the society which the wisdom of the

F

disillusioned has built recommended itself without qualifications, and dare we assert for certain that other alternatives would have proved worse or that there were none? For sociology these may still be *fragwürdige* questions.)

We turn to a few possibly haphazard questions:

1 Information and its communication have become omnivorous, omniscient and omnipresent. Libraries can no longer hold the available books on any subject, hardly the bibliographies. We are getting used to speaking in terms of memory banks, computing systems which, unlike libraries, make any desired piece of information immediately accessible. Taken in conjunction with other kinds of computer work, this means that we have reached the stage where the knower can be by-passed to a large extent. Knowledge itself has become objectified and mechanized. It is becoming a well-nigh automated machine. It needs men merely as handymen and button pushers. Now in as far as this automation is applied in areas where the kind of thinking required by civilization had always been mechanized drudgery, such a development is to be welcomed. But today when all the important decisions themselves have become absorbed into the automation process, such a development could prove highly dangerous. All our most uncritical assumptions which therefore are most in need of scrutiny are built into our machines, are objectified. That is, they become what we think of as objectivity, they proliferate and become our reality beyond the possibility of contradiction. (Cybernetics is both a science and a problem which it cannot solve itself. Cf. Habermas, 1967, pp. 173ff.) To the extent to which we believe in objectivity as our reality such a development is logical.

How can we learn to draw the line between knowledge that can be computerized and wisdom that cannot? Does it help to recall that *Wissen* appertains to objectives, *Kennen* to the inter-subjectivity of which objectivity is merely an agreed aspect? And what is the sociologist's task here? He craves to be on the side of objectivity where all the power is, the assumption that power alone matters, and also measureless stores of manageable information. The price is total ineffectiveness except in terms of that power. Or is he ready to break a quixotic lance in defence of subjectivity which, according to Adorno, has become sheer ideological chatter? But if the subject has really disappeared before the almighty objectified forces, why does Adorno still write? Perhaps because his writings express his negative-dialectical belief that it is a man's task to undertake the impossible in full recognition of its impossibility and to think and act it through to its absurd limit, because it and only it might take him to the point where the impossible turns into its opposite, becomes possible.

2 Subjectivity is not anti-objective. Its problem is how much

room to give to the objective in relation to its subjective objectives. It circumscribes the objective to contain and direct its power. The individual knows or could know that objects are for his use, useful only in as far as they enable him to give himself more fully to useless or meta-useful pursuits. Only another subject is not exclusively there for use. Unlike objectivity – from theology and metaphysics to scientism – subjectivity is open to non-objectifiable 'meta-reality' and to the a-rational. It has no purpose. Like life itself, it has no definable objective. It is its own end.

3   That we experience the distinction between the objective and the subjective as contradiction is a symptom of social unease. Maybe it is another aspect of the discontent Freud thought to be endemic in civilization. Or it reflects once again the primeval class division that separated the thinker from the labourer, thought from its direct, practical, life-saving and life-enhancing application (Marx, ed Landshut, 1968, pp. 261–3). Would a classless society resolve this contradiction or merely perpetuate it in another form, and is a classless society a possibility? Does a Freud-Marxian synthesis point to a possible *Aufhebung* of civilization as yet beyond our imagination (cf. Simmel, 1911, pp. 278–317)? Such questions are not concerned with remote possibilities, although these must never be lost sight of either. Here they are envisaged as no more than lodestars for more immediate enquiries and necessary attempt at interpretation. For even our questions are determined by our aims, aspirations, objectives, as well as by our assumption concerning the *status quo*. The assumptions in turn are 'gestalted' by the objectives. For example, not to ask utopian questions is objective only in the sense that it expresses definite objectives.

So we ask again, what has happened and is happening to labour which has become the semi- or wholly-automatic execution of an alien purpose, planning, thinking, 'their' purpose? What has happened and is happening to thinking and thought processes divorced from both the difficulties, tedium, frustrations of direct application, and the sense of completion, of sensuous achievement? In how far does such a divorce inevitably stupefy the labourer and volatize the thinker? To what an extent does it inevitably express or breed contradictory purposes and desires which as inevitably lead to conflicts which establish antagonistic objectives? Of course separation of labour from planning is efficient. For 'nature' and 'life', whatever these be, efficiency seems to be a minor considera- tion. The most efficient are not necessarily the most lovable or loving persons. A too-efficient mother can damage her child badly. How to seduce a girl most efficiently is a possible question. How to fall in love or conduct an affair most efficiently is even today only an almost possible question.

Would the peculiar explosion of productivity have taken place, if thinking and labouring had not been divorced? Was it necessary, salutary? Perhaps it first created the destitution it later tried to cure. The ostentatious consumption which contributed so much to the development of capitalism might not have been possible except for the division of labour which left many with too many hours of leisure to labour through. How is belief in efficiency and its consequent productivity, affluence and stress on consumption, related to the growing depletion of those vital services in which thought and labour are not yet totally separated, because they are non-productive (Galbraith, 1963)? It seems, for instance, that an almost totally rationalized society cannot help losing just those members of the teaching profession who have the highest degree of just that kind of intelligence society values most. And it is possible that the increasing rationalization of human nature will increasingly fill hospitals with the casualties of its progress while rationalizing away the hospital staffs. As the refuse of the affluent society piles up, fewer and fewer will be found to be ready to collect it. Pollution which already has killed much life and may kill all in the foreseeable future is an adequate symbol of a society which believes in efficiency and rationalization and therefore can have no regard for life.

In our kind of society it can be said that the 'worker' is subjective, the administrator objective. The demands of the former for more leisure and more money are irrational, purely human, and within our rationalistic economic system actually self-defeating. The arguments of the former are impregnable within the economical universe of discourse. If everything were 'left to them', efficiency and productivity would doubtlessly increase, though not everyone would profit from it equally. Both workers and employers know this; the former vaguely and uneasily, the latter clearly and self-confidently. This fact alone engenders much friction and bitterness in endless negotiations which can merely shelve and never solve conflicts inherent in the situation and expressing themselves as those between the rational and irrational. The irrational, by the logic of the situation, is intent on proving its rationality. For as the dichotomy of objective-subjective reflects that of thinker-labourer, all the privilege and prestige is on the side of the objective, as is the police and the bigger guns. So even the protests of the subjective enhance the power of the objective. For the protestants wish to share the privileges and hence are driven willy-nilly into using 'objective' arguments which have prestige but are designed to preserve the privileges of others. In other words, all political, social and economic conflicts tend merely to stabilize and elaborate a social structure which is in danger of eliminating life on the planet earth.

Therefore the conflicts between the subjective and objective are another aspect of the life-and-death struggle of modern society, as possibly of any civilized society. It may never have been so urgent. The following questions therefore, or better ones, could be of urgent concern for sociology: In how far is it possible, socially, psychologically, philosophically possible, to define and circumscribe areas of objectivity? Where and how and how far is the subjective to be encouraged or at least not to be discouraged even in its more bizarre manifestations? To what extent and to what areas – of chores? and what are chores? – can and may the separation of labour and planning be confined? Where and how can and must it be undone? How can the purely rationalistic, hence unreasonable because inhuman, connection between production and profit be loosened? How much of essential labour, like sewage, rubbish collection, nursing, general labouring, can be taken out of the rationalistic framework and communalized? How and to what an extent can and must education be separated altogether from training? The former concerned with the preparation for life and the continuing enjoyment of life, with growth of the capacity for appreciation, the development of the senses and of sensuousness, of affection and special talents, with the better understanding of the psyche and its desires. The latter concerned with preparing everybody for the performance of one or the other of necessary chores for which he will get paid. Is such a separation feasible, desirable, avoidable?

4 The following illustration of objectivity is taken from Mitscherlich (1969, p. 4): 'We know that the living organism is *essentially* a *system* directed to the maintenance of its own *equilibrium* (a *homeostatic* system) with innumerable feedback mechanisms and reciprocal influencing of the organic functions, since Norbert Wiener's cybernetic systems.' (My emphases.) This particular abstraction is obviously useful for the elaboration of cybernetic systems and the construction of computers and robots. Rigorous abstraction from and exclusion of everything that actually constitutes life help towards the reproduction of certain life-like characteristics and activities in something which is not alive. As a definition of life itself or of a living organism the above abstraction is either totally tautologous or, taken as a mechanical analogy, nonsensical. Who decides what a living organism is *essentially*? That it is essentially a *system* and, moreover, one directed to the maintenance of its own *equilibrium*? This would be to say: A living organism is a homeostatic system whose essential function consists in maintaining itself as a homeostatic system whose essential function it is to maintain itself as. . . .

Now it can indeed be said that most living creatures most of the time have a tendency to maintain themselves. They do this by means of innumerable feedback mechanisms resulting in their actually feeding themselves. Whether life itself is *essentially* such a self-maintenance remains a wide open question. (Is a car essentially something that has to be refuelled periodically?) It is equally possible to say that the self-maintenance mechanism functions to enable the living organism to go on living its essential life which consists precisely in that which goes beyond the mechanistic feed-back systems. Therefore it remains arguable whether the quotation has actually said more than or as much as: life is life or, rather, keeping alive is keeping alive. If it wished to claim that life is *essentially* a *perpetuum mobile*, essentially a mechanism, it propounds a creed I can neither share nor refute. It has carried concepts of the automatism of scientific technology into life itself and, if only by implication, into individual-social existence.

But the quotation illustrates more. It not only shows how objectification is carried from one sphere into another, but how language itself has become objectified and mechanized. By this I mean that words seem to have become as transferable as all-purpose machines or the spare parts of standardized machinery. They seem to function more and more like mathematical symbols. But they are unlike mathematical symbols in that they once had, and now cannot shed altogether, age-old associations. In their apparent detachment they actually carry assumptions, prejudices, even sentiments, into fields where these do not apply or apply only most ambivalently. So it is in the quoted instance. And we must not underestimate the hypnotic effect of such a transference which now gives to words the peculiar power which magic had once ascribed to them, especially to names. For that reason a statement like the above is not so easily seen through. Thus it not merely expresses a peculiar objectification but accomplishes a further one. Beyond that it blurs old boundaries and its apparent precision and clarity con-fuses the issues. Because of this peculiar problematic, sociology cannot avoid becoming semantics, semantic sociology (cf. Whorf, Barthes, B. Bernstein, Lévi-Strauss, Benjamin, Adorno, Heidegger).

5 Another confusion clouds the issue of subjectivity. We let Meinecke's lovable and slightly pathetic autobiographical writing illustrate it. Here was a man whose life work had been the tracing of world-historical and power-political developments. In face of the actuality of the First World War and later on of Hitler and the Second World War, he proved naive, helpless, moralistic. He be-came nostalgically subjective. Had he been too subjective all through his scholarly life, capable merely of expressing the subjective interests of his class, its objective-directed subjectivity, without awareness of its ideological function? What would it have meant for him to be more objective? And who, as a matter of fact, had been

more objective? Who among those of his critics whom events proved right, i.e. objective, in their estimate of the situation, had gained such objectivity by anything but a lucky subjective twist? For example, the objectivity of the European Marxists had proved particularly subjective, precisely in the sense in which Meinecke, at the opposite end of the spectrum, had been accused by them of subjectivity.

What, anyway, are objective historical processes and who can ever prove that his interpretation is the right one until 'afterwards' and when it is too late for action? And how can it be demonstrated, even *post festum*, that anyone's correct prediction had been more than a lucky subjective hit? And what has been proved when things turn out, more or less, as someone had predicted? All kinds of dubious predictions do sometimes come true. Even soothsayers are right now and again. Who, except the predictor, would wish to insist that events had to take this course? The most passionate protagonists of an objective, non-ideological approach to history, the Marxists, who at the same time believe to have access to its underlying objective processes, have been as often mistaken as other groups of politicians and historians. And where they were right they had often proved as helpless as those that were wrong. And does this invalidate their approach and intentions altogether? If history is constituted by the intricate and never totally surveyable interplay of the individual intentions and intensions of individuals and groups, then the historians' intentions may make their contribution to the historical development, though the effect of each particular contribution may be too minute to be discernible. It is also possible that his understanding of the historical situation and his predictions based on it may affect the non-fulfilment of what he predicted, as was the case with Marx himself (cf. Habermas, 1967, pp. 164ff, 308ff).

Once again it may be that the confusion which prevails here, has filled libraries with esoteric polemics and keeps university departments busy all over the world, is due to a mistaken understanding of objectivity. It is at least possible that history, dealing with unique human actions and decisions, can only falsify its subject by objectifying it and by assuming it to be amenable to the scientific approach. Coming back to Meinecke, it is conceivable that his naive, earnest, moral investigation is neither more nor less mistaken than the most hard-headed and cold-blooded, empirical, cynical or dialectical estimate. According to Meinecke (1959, p. 420), Herder, like so many German *Dichter* and *Denker*, including Nietzsche, 'became disgusted with power and state'. These could not be fitted into the picture he and they had of nature, *physis*, the soul and the universe. And indeed astronomers for a long time, and now ethologists, following in some anthropologists' footsteps, seem to have discovered that power and power struggles are not nature's inevitable road. Religious teachers, Hindu, Buddhist, Jewish-Christian, have understood power, our understanding of it and its workings, as illusion, *maya*, the Fall. An attempt to understand history in the light of such an estimate of nature and human nature is not necessarily invalid, and no-one can say whether and what way it might affect history. It is unlikely to prove any less objective, i.e. objective-orientated, than, say, the Darwinian interpretation which reflected and justified Victorian, human economic reality. Between such objectives one ultimately has to choose, and choice is a matter of taste, of *Kennen* and not of *Wissen*.

Goethe's instinctive poetic answer to the world-shaking events of 1813–14 was the *West-östlicher Diwan*, a collection of love lyrics, drinking songs, gnomic wisdom, individualistic in form and content and only most idiosyncratically based on Eastern forms and intentions. In his introduction, and as man of the world totally misinterpreting his own poetic intentions and intuition, he wrote: 'It behoves us at this time to measure our small private conditions against the gigantic gauge of world history.' The poems, on the contrary, being personal, not private, measure the pretentious world events against the ′gauge of human, individual existence with its infinitely expandable scale of desires, emotions, sensibilities and appreciation. Goethe also wrote history. Was he more qualified to do so as man of the world or as poet? (Cf. Ortega y Gasset, 'In Search of Goethe from Within', *The New Partisan Reader 1945–1953*, Harcourt, Brace, New York, 1953.) It cannot be proved, either historically or philosophically or scientifically, that the Chinese poet who so deeply impressed Mahler was wrong when he wrote: 'A beaker full of wine at the right time is worth more' – and Mahler repeats, 'is worth more, is worth more' – 'than all the kingdoms of this earth'. And what would be the implication of such an admission for the sociologists?

6   Which takes us back again to the poet and artist, in the present context to his subjectivity. The artist, it has been said, achieves universality to the extent to which he succeeds in expressing and communicating his full individuality, its flavour, its incontrovertible thusness. This is true even when, as in the case of Goethe, the artist himself misinterprets his intention. The great neo-classicists thought they were approximating a classic, objective form of beauty. In actuality they expressed their often most peculiar interpretation of classical intentions. To our ears Racine resembles no-one as much as Racine. Goethe's *Iphigenie*, as he himself realized, could not have been written by Sophocles or Euripides. No Greek or Roman or Etruscan could have painted like Poussin, David or Ingres

whose paintings look totally French. What the artist mistakes for objectivity, he at best uses as a clothes hanger. For even the artist likes to have a fixed, if not an Archimedean, point. If he goes beyond that he becomes an imitator and, by definition, ceases to be an artist. (Even the merchants in art have to acknowledge that. When a painting has been proved to be a forgery, as in the case of the Vermeers, the drop in price, i.e. in value, is catastrophic.)

But the artist's subjectivity is not the opposite of objectivity. On the contrary, as artist he has preserved a more than ordinary trust in his subjective experience, its validity, significance and understanding. For that reason he is able to accommodate in it large areas of objectivity, of technical know-how and sheer *Wissen* about his subject. One thinks of painting from Giotto to Picasso, of Rembrandt's self-portraits, of Goya's etchings. One recalls Dante's concreteness which makes hell and purgatory more real than any historical place; Shakespeare's immense *Wissen* about the psyche and all its works. One cannot help being impressed by the objectivity of a Gogol, Tolstoy, Dostoevsky, Chekhov and Gorki, the independence they granted to their 'subjects', so that these at times would override their creators' most passionate intentions and convictions. Cervantes's detachment, his objectivity, permitted his Don to assert his true nature and stature against the mockings of his author. If objectivity is defined and circumscribed as at the beginning of this section, it is not a foregone conclusion that scientists, including historians, are more objective than painters, poets, composers. From Aeschylus's *Persians* to Tolstoy's *War and Peace*, from Homer to Shakespeare to Proust and Kafka, the poets' histories may be more objective than those of the historians. Who can be sure and on what grounds that Praxiteles and the Indian sculptors were less objective, within their objectives, concerning man and his bodiliness, than the anatomists, physiologists and biologists within theirs? Did Ricardo have a more objective understanding of human interest than Mozart, Beethoven, Lessing or Stendhal?

H Causality

Only a few words here on a subject to which we shall have to return later (chapter 4). Causality belongs strictly into the sphere of manipulative thought and intention. It is objective in that it is subordinated to clearly defined objectives: I flick the switch to cause the light to shine. But my switchflicking only has the desired effect, because it allows the electricity to flow over the wire in the bulb. The electricity is generated, caused, by a turbine which is driven by steam which is produced by the burning of coal which once stored the energy from the sun, which energy was and is caused by and the

F*

cause of nuclear fusion. . . . On the other hand, my desire to read did not, in a comparable fashion, cause me to turn on the light. Nor was that desire the result of a cause comparable to the chain of causation which took us back to the beginning of time. Here I am not primarily concerned to show how a chain of causation inevitably stretches back to a final cause or *Ur-Sache*, which in turn cannot be any more final than the tortoise of the Indian fable. One simply has to stop asking somewhere. (*Ursache* means cause in common usage. Yet the *Ur* prefixed to *Sache*, matter, matter of discourse, retains the association of primal, original, even primeval.) I wish to indicate how each cause is as much defined by its effect as it can be said to produce it.

Causality represents one of man's attempts to isolate certain aspects or processes for his use, his ulterior ends. In this sense, therefore, the – desired – effect is the cause of the cause. The arguments over the admissibility of final causes, not only in sociology but in the natural sciences, may well have been unnecessary, for each effect is the final cause of the cause which effected it, which was the effect's efficient cause. Crudely put: when I switch on the light, I not only cause an effect, I effect a cause. Language, even the philosophical term 'efficient cause', has preserved associations of the exchangeability.

Causality has proved startlingly successful in the natural sciences. It de-fines. This is its refining, insulating, abstracting and manipulative power. For a definition, like any concept, is a tool. It is also tautologous, like mathematics. The scientific, logical application of the concept of causality was a surprising culmination of Western theology and philosophy. Since Plato or Thales Western thought has been concerned with identity: of idea and replica, *Geist* and reality, knowing and object known, concept and percept, thought and its matter. These philosophical labours had been of little except literary avail, as concerning the ultimate question they had tried to tackle by means of their identifying, tautologous methods, designed to establish certainties and objectivity. The same methods, when applied to the swing of a pendulum, the movements of marbles down inclined planes and of planets round the sun, were soon to enable man to measure the motion and mass of everything between the stars and the electrons. The tautologous character of identifying thought had suddenly become a double-edged tool of great effectiveness. It trimmed both cause and effect into complete mutual congruence.

In metaphysics and in classical philosophy in general, the philosopher had always found himself up against some ultimate concreteness, particularity, irrationality, which resisted total integration into his scheme of things. In as far as he felt compelled – and he often did – to integrate it in spite of all, it had to be done by brute force. This always gave his successors legitimate grounds for attack. When being used in the natural sciences, causality was refined to the point where it became capable of radically eliminating all irrationality and concreteness from its clearly defined universe of discourse. Of course causality did not manage actually to eliminate irrational and individual aches. But it discovered how to exclude them hermetically from certain areas of investigation, how to constitute areas of investigation outside our mere humanity – as mercantilism and capitalism had already excluded the merely human from its intentions and considerations. In those areas the cause could be defined precisely, precisely to the extent to which the effect could be made to define the cause.

The achievements of the natural sciences are comparable to those of medieval theology. The latter had elaborated a particular, universal method of perfectly correlating cause and effect, for asking precisely and only those questions to which a precise and only answer could be given. Within its sphere, the question which proved unanswerable, no matter how burningly it clamoured to be asked, no matter by how many people, was no longer to be asked. It was anathematized. Science refined this intention. This may explain why mathematics has shown itself so perfectly suited to scientific research: it is the language of tautology *par excellence*, devoid of all non-tautological associations clinging to words. Mathematics also shows the complexity of the thought processes required to reduce all kinds of external relations to the relation of identity, to the two sides of an equation. Scientific refinement corresponds to the refinement of the tautologizing or identifying method. (Maybe that science and mathematics, together with the philosophies of identity, have common roots in a kind of pre-logical sympathetic and imitative magic, with its faith in correspondences, naming, identifying causes. Which magic in turn has its roots in language itself, in the primeval magic of its radically metaphorical character. It seems likely that deep-seated emotive beliefs and convictions lie behind the aesthetico-logical satisfaction of neat tautologization, of having proved, identified, named something.)

Thinking rigorously in terms of cause and effect is the culmination of the philosophy of identity which had shown itself less than convincing in its ability to cope with human problems arising directly out of the human situation. It has been almost exclusively an elaboration of their evasion. (Adorno, 1970, pp. 150, 185, 259, 292, 304, 313.) It attracted men, from Parmenides to Husserl, who were deeply suspicious of lived life. Plato constructed his immutable realm of ideas to remain untainted by life (cf. Popper, 1942, vol. 1, on the political intentions of that escapism). As to Husserl the following quotation may make the point (quoted Spiegelberg, 1964, p. 82; cf. Husserl, 1962, I, paras 5–6; also p. 275):

> I have passed through enough anguish from lack of clarity and from doubt that wavers back and forth. . . . Only one need absorbs me: I must win clarity or else I cannot live. I cannot bear life, unless I believe that I can achieve it.

One recalls Descartes's insistence on clarity and certainty.

It remains all the more problematical whether and in how far causal thinking is appropriate for the tackling of sociological – or psychological or socio-philosophical – problems, whether it is at all capable of focusing them. First, if not foremost, we have seen how cause-and-effect thinking is radically a matter of definition and delimitation. When man investigates man, i.e. in the last resort himself, he has no definition which can define the definer without infinite regression. In practice this means a cause can never be clearly isolated, because its effect, here a human situation, can never be trimmed to fit its requirements of clarity and definiteness without being violated and distorted. For no human situation is clear. It can be clarified 'up to a point'; at which point it has become a different situation, unclear in a new way. I can, 'up to a point', ignore this difficulty, as long as I have a fixed belief in the function of sociology or of this particular sociological enquiry in relation to a larger context. That is to say, I can be satisfied with a relative and temporary clarification in as far as this, however temporarily, achieves or moves towards a given or taken for granted purpose. Nowadays beliefs are frowned upon, except the belief in things-as-they-are-as-they-are. Which means in effect that sociology has become an instrument of bureaucratic intentions, a bureaucratic tool. The sociologist may point out that the same can be said about any science and that sociology can do no different. He may not debar others, including sociologists, from saying that even though every science were an instrument of bureaucracy, this does not prove that it had to be one, that sociology as science had to be one or that sociology had to be a science. Sociology may have an alternative.

I return to my conviction of the essential unclarity of any human situation. Any clarification, especially by means of causal considerations, can only be relative and provisional, 'successful' only within a strictly delimited field and a narrowly defined purpose. For example: in a factory relations between floor and office are not too good. Productivity is suffering or believed to be suffering because of this. What can and must be done? Now nobody is able to investigate satisfactorily, let alone conclusively, the shifting intricate web of human interrelations, interactions, interdependencies, in the hope of improving its general quality. Anyway, in which direction?

And what does it means to improve quality? Fortunately or unfortunately, this is not at all what is required. Improved productivity is the one and definite, because clearly measurable, aim. Difficulties in the relations between workers and staff are of interest exclusively in as far as they depress and can be shown to depress productivity.[9]

We see how the desired effect causes and effects as well as affects the search for and the nature of the looked-for cause, and how cause and effect are dovetailed into each other. When certain readjustments have led to increased productivity, the labours of the researchers have been justified and to that extent the causes they demonstrated to have been responsible for or guilty of the former deterioration. No effort would have appeared justified which had not raised productivity, no matter how deeply it might have altered the staff – worker relations. Such an alteration, not being measurable, could never justify the isolation of a cause. Two things are fairly clear. First, a different research party might have unearthed different causes and suggested different remedies – or their preconceived different remedies might have suggested different causes. They might have proved equally or more effective. This can no longer be tested, for the situation has been altered by the actual, merely the first, research group. Secondly, it is clear that what is called cause in such a context fulfils also an emotive function. It is something like a culprit or a scapegoat, something that can be blamed, condemned and exorcized, can be driven into the wilderness with the united curses of workers and staff on its back. It was to blame, not we; and now we, in fairly apportioning blame where it belongs, are united, at least for the time being. Causality then fulfils a powerful psychic need. But just because man's desire to blame something or someone is pretty powerful, especially when he is in trouble, any easy transposition of causality into social enquiries is fraught with dangers on this account. (A legal 'cause' is still trying to establish guilt. In Shakespeare 'cause' means accusation.)

We return to our factory. Suppose a quixotic social reformer really wished to discover the causes of the uneasy relations, not for the manipulative purpose of increased production, but in order to improve the *milieu humain*. Where could he start? What kind of cause could such a desired effect isolate? What kind of improvement does he aim at? A little more politeness, mutual consideration and co-operation? That would still be pretty close to the manipulative. Does he wish to establish a lively community spirit of mutual responsibility, a pristine Kibbutz mentality? A form of common ownership which would make of this factory a place to which all workers would like to come? He would soon discover that the causes which make such an improvement difficult to achieve are manifold, impossible to isolate. They are certainly not restricted to what goes on inside the factory. There is the different cultural, social, educational background of workers and staff. They speak different languages. Their respective life-experiences and hence their expectations differ considerably. Their ideas as to what industry is, is there for, could or should be, are, as yet, irreconcilable, though they may be vague beyond articulation. How could a reconciliation be effected? One would have to look at the educational system: what does it attempt to teach and why? To what extent are its methods and aims tied to the competitive society? What caused it to become what it is? To stay as it is? Could it be changed radically, as long as it is intended to prepare children for the kind of society in which it functions? What caused society to become, what causes it to stay, as it is?

Furthermore, suppose our reformer managed to turn our factory into a humane place, it is more than likely that it would soon be bankrupt. Unless, in its new shape, it would succumb to the old dehumanized pressures. So he would have to look into the economic forces which not only rule this factory but the globe. Do they cause the whole ideological and psychic set-up of which this factory and its organization is merely a symptom? Or can human *Geist*, spirit and determination, cause economic forces to change their direction? Does the psyche reflect economic drives, or economic trends psychic needs? The enquiry could not come to an end short of the *prima causa*, the *Ur-Sache*. It would still remain doubtful whether or not this proved anything, whether even a proof would inspire the still needful effort actually to effect the desired change. For after all, these questions are identical with: where and how can and must we start?

This seems to indicate that the approach to social change should or could be made along other paths than those of causality. For I have not even mentioned the polemics that would be possible and unavoidable at each step and steplet. Durkheim still believed that the uncovering of the underlying causes of social directedness was a possibility. Only by changing them – and he believed that having understood we could change them – real changes in society could be effected. Those passages in *Suicide*, *Division of Labor*, *Sociological Method*, even in *Religious Life*, where he expresses that belief sound sadly naive today. They give a peculiar pathos to all his work which was undertaken in that belief. Nevertheless it demonstrates how such a belief in certain desirable changes or effects enabled him to isolate the causes. Weber cannot be accused of such naivety. Yet his *Religionssoziologie* is a titanic endeavour to isolate one of many causes responsible for capitalist developments. Three big volumes crammed with information, with most concise inductions and deductions, witness to that intention. They are merely a fragment. Late Judaism, Parsism, Mohammedanism, early and medieval Christianity, were yet to be dealt with. Could he have proved his point? Would it have mattered if he had? And what would it have proved and to whom? And could it have proved that other causes might not have found equal confirmation?

For over and above the complexities of which Weber showed himself aware in his encyclopaedic labours, and underlying them, are further intricacies the surface of which he had not begun to scratch. He was not aware of them as of sociological significance. Yet, as we saw, the facts of projection and introjection make of the individual psyche *the* social phenomenon and problem. They lift family and other personal and intimate relationships into the very centre of sociological concern. For as the individual psyche is the only concrete manifestation of social consciousness, i.e. of social reality, it has to be studied as the field on which the actual social conflicts are fought out. What is cause here and what effect? Is motive a cause? And what causes a motive to have motive power? Is purpose a motive and what motivates purpose? Is my end my beginning? In which case, does the cause explain the result, has it any explanatory power? Is it not rather the result which at times can shed light on the cause – man on the amoeba rather than it on him?

Has such questioning anything to do with certain problems that are said to have come to life at the frontiers of the natural sciences? There too the distinction between cause and effect seems to have become fluid, as long ago the distinction between matter and energy had been found to be inadequate. Maybe the natural and not the social sciences have begun to think in terms of cause and effect interpreting each other, rather than of causes having effects. (As Goethe thought. Cf. Meinecke, 1959, p. 529.) Even such new thinking however does not seem applicable in sociology, except in strictly delimited areas. For if one took seriously Weber's search for causes, and his explication of the method for their isolation, even his work would have to proliferate a thousandfold. He explored at great length a path that proved a garden path. And across his work, as he already appreciated, may ultimately have to be written the inscription that graced the entry to Dante's Inferno. This does not detract from his merits which are beyond dispute. But it may encourage others to try new ways – not necessarily those of contemporary sociology which often feel like a Lilliputian retracing of Weber's Brobdignagian trail.

I Sein and Seiendes

Under this heading I wish to look at some of the complementary ideas and insights of Heidegger, Adorno, Marcuse, Habermas,

Mannheim, Bloch and Lukács, that have a direct bearing on our problem of understanding in the social sciences. I neither can nor would I wish to give a critical summing up of their arguments and counter-arguments. That would require many volumes. It also would lead me far from one of my purposes which is to suggest that argumentation is not necessarily the best method for exploring and communicating constitutive insights, least of all those concerning the individual in society. By constitutive insights I mean any new or rediscovered understanding which makes one 'see', i.e. which makes visible or comprehensible further connections, illuminates new contexts, opens new vistas – metaphors all! – makes one realize, sympathize, appreciate more fully. Much of this is not necessarily conveyable by logical argument or demonstration. Popper among others has confirmed that even in the natural sciences the discovery of new hypotheses and theories is not the result, certainly not solely the result of logical deductions and empirical inductions, but of intuitive processes to which we have not yet any access (1969, pp. 24, 26, 58). The logical arguments follow, like history, *post festum* to justify and consolidate the new discovery and to ease communication. This may be the most adequate method for the natural sciences. Yet scientists themselves have admitted that the scheme into which all arguments have to fit often conceals rather than reveals the actual thinking processes at work in scientific research, and thus tends to distort study and research methods.

In sociology and social philosophy, especially as understood by most of the German thinkers here under review, such a methodology is even more suspect. First of all, sociologists have not yet been able to agree on what it is that has to be proved, what constitutes a proof, within what area a proof can be constituted and can be said to have been constituted. It can therefore happen that two thinkers have chanced upon similar discoveries or insights; but having no generally-agreed terminology or procedure for demonstration, they expressed them in divergent terms or concepts, sometimes in conflicting ones, and tried to fit them into contradictory conceptual frameworks. As a result they may end up by arguing against each other with peculiar bitterness. Just because they see their own concern, the 'truth', vaguely reflected in the other's position, they experience apparent deviations as particularly painful and therefore dangerous distortions. Secondly, the philosophical arguments of at least the German sociologists, being part of a more than two-century-old discussion, are often especially complex and obscure. This raises the further question of whether and in how far such a complex discussion and its inherent structure preforms the insights, the very possibility of understanding and of communication.

I wish to illustrate these two points by an example taken from

Adorno's argument against Heidegger in *Jargon der Eigentlichkeit* (1969a, pp. 123ff). Heidegger is fundamentally a man of a few simple, if profound, insights. The complexity of his thinking arises from the fact that he wishes to accommodate within the philosophical heritage of the West ideas which do not yet belong into it. His post-metaphysical approach has to be fitted into a terminology and methodology which it radically criticizes – more radically than, for example, Kant criticized both metaphysics and empiricism. In space, time and temper he found himself, at least at the beginning of his career, as a phenomenologist (1969, *'Mein Weg in der Phäno-menologie'*). Now phenomenology had come into being as a protest against the sensational atomism of late nineteenth-century scientific-philosophical thought. (As *Gestalt* psychology had tried to supersede psychological impressionism.) Some of its inner contradictions were due to Husserl's endeavour to carry the scientific assumptions that had produced the atomistic tendencies into the new methodology. His aim was to establish phenomenology as an exact science. To vindicate itself before positivism and sensationalism of the Locke-Humean kind, phenomenology turned to Kantian and Cartesian arguments. Moreover it had to argue against Hegel in an effort to prove that his *Phänomenologie* was not to be mistaken for phenomenology. In its Cartesianism Husserl's phenomenology is static.

Adorno, on the contrary, like Horkheimer, Marcuse and Habermas, is Hegelian by temperament and training. His philosophy is dynamic, dialectical, historical. It is therefore anti-phenomenological as well as anti-positivistic. Has this to be so of necessity? Phenomenology could certainly remain open to the phenomena of dialectical thinking, to a possibly inherent dialectics in phenomena, or in the relations between *noesis* and *noemata*. Dialectics should be able to keep open a dialogue with phenomenology. I have chosen the following argument, one-sided in that to my knowledge Heidegger never answered, because of its glaring incomprehension due to divergent terminologies as well as temperaments.

Heidegger, in *Sein und Zeit* (1931, pp. 252–5), maintains that the full realization of my individual mortality is essentially different from the acknowledgment that 'one dies', sooner or later. Whatever *man* can say about death simply does not reach me, but may actually hide from me the actuality of my mortality which constitutes my individuality. Tolstoy had said just this in *The Death of Ivan Ilych*. 'All men are mortal. Socrates is a man. Therefore Socrates is mortal.' Ivan had known this syllogism since his school days. As his illness and pain grows he begins to realize that he himself is going to die, because he is dying. And this realization simply has nothing to do with the syllogism – for the logical connection between everyman's and my dying exists only on a high level of abstraction. It is likely that Adorno would not have wished to argue against this Tolstoyan story which Heidegger, as a matter of fact, quotes. But because Heidegger is Heidegger, because of his predecessors and successors, because of his peculiar argumentation and the inferences drawn by others later on, Adorno feels compelled to refute the obvious. More, he is really arguing against the central conviction of his own *Negative Dialektik:* That the particular cannot be conceptualized, not even his death. (Cf. not only Adorno, 1969a, but also 1970, pp. 67–134 for protracted polemics against Heidegger.) Heidegger had said (1931, p. 253):

> That '*man* dies' spreads the opinion that death, so to speak, befalls the *Man*. The public interpretation of existence says '*man* dies', because in this way everyone and oneself can persuade himself: 'not I, for this *Man* is no-one.'

Adorno, as pompous as Heidegger is supposed to be, replies (1969a, pp. 123–4):

> The interpretation that death, so to speak, befalls the *Man*, already presupposes Heidegger's hypostasis of the existentials of which the *Man* is the black side, and falsifyingly disregards that which is rightly expressed by the no matter how threadbare saying: that death is a universal destiny which embraces the *alter ego* as much as the own. If someone says: '*Man* dies', he includes himself, if euphemistically. The adjournment however which Heidegger objects to is a fact. The speaker is actually still permitted to live, else he could not speak.

Adorno adds immediately: 'Such arguments, initiated by Heidegger, move inevitably in a sphere of imbecility.' Yet he qualifies this, as immediately, by actual repetition of the above arguments, and ends his refutation with a lengthy quotation from Schopenhauer which confirms what Heidegger said.

Adorno is a most intelligent, perceptive and sensitive man. That he lets himself be dragged into imbecility and adds that it is the other man's fault may well demonstrate something of sociological interest concerning the nature of academic arguments at large. It would be easy to choose at one's pleasure examples to show how again and again two or more divergent points of view, each of which had been attained by any but strictly logical or empirical reasoning, are defended and attacked by logical arguments. Such arguments, of necessity, can neither reach the point to be attacked, nor are they grounded in the conviction they are defending. For those reasons I am trying to appreciate some of the insights of German scholars which I consider to have illuminative power outside their argumentative context. As I have tried before, I wish to detach them, a risky affair indeed, from their too long historico-philosophical involvement. I wish to take them out of the sphere of argument. Whether or not this does them a mortal injustice cannot be argued. It can only be tested, as one tests a light bulb. (See below, chapter 5, where I am trying to justify such a procedure at greater length.)

Heidegger

Sein und Zeit and his later essays of greater clarity and simplicity of style raise a few fundamental questions concerning *Sein* which are, so I believe, of constitutive importance for the *Geisteswissenschaften* and therefore for sociology. The difficulty of putting Heidegger's questions meaningfully lies in their utter simplicity. (Also in the fact that *Sein* can be translated as both 'to be' and 'being', while Heidegger's thinking is based on a radical distinction between these two terms which in German is denoted by that between *Sein* and *Seiendes*.) He asks: 'What *is*?' What does 'is' circumscribe, designate, signify? Does it define? Does it add anything to any statement, except, tautologically, its confirmation? Does it perpetuate a primitive linguistic habit with overtones of magic power over that which the 'is' affirms? Have not some languages been able virtually to dispense with it (1931, pp. 1ff)?

A definition is so difficult, because it cannot be framed without containing an 'is'. So let us listen instead: 'One is one and all alone and ever more shall be so.' The 'is' of identity, here placed in an emotive context which may actually teach us something about its nature and function. Could one as well say: 'one one'? Does the 'is' add anything? If it does, what? Does it signify, and what, that the 'is' as = , as 'equal to', is the fulcrum of the scales on which all mathematical and other equations hang? (Cf. A fact *is* a fact. Such and such *is* the case.)

This book is large, it is long. It is heavy, it is difficult. It is made of paper, it is full of wisdom. It is brown, it is excellent. We have the 'is' of identification: This! This is this (cf. Wittgenstein, 1967, pp. 13ff). The 'is' of affirmation: So! What is being affirmed and identified? Does 'the heavy book' say the same as 'the book is heavy'? Does the 'is' do more than shift the emphasis from subject to predicate? And what would such a shift signify? Shakespeare knew that 'degree is all' and degree means emphasis. Love flourishes on emphasis and wars are being waged over emphases. So emphasis or a shift in emphasis might be significant. Don Quixote's change into a knight-errant goes hand in hand with his insistence that the Lady Dulcinea *is* the most beautiful lady – as the whole book is centred in the question whether the Don is or is not what he thinks he is and whether the others who think they know that he is not what he thinks he is are what they think they are. The old Greek legend understood the Trojan War as a result of the conjunction of two emphases: Helen is the most beautiful woman. Helen is mine. This the 'is' of insistence, possession, possessiveness.

'The beloved miller girl is mi-ine i-i-i-is mine.' The 'is' of insistence and triumph, again of possessiveness. And the poor lad kills himself in the end, not because the girl no longer is, but because she no longer i-i-i-is his.

'This music is lovely, it is.' The 'is' of confirmation and appreciation. 'My beloved is all radiant and ruddy. . . . His head is the finest gold. . . . His body is ivory work. . . . His speech is most sweet, and he is altogether desirable. This is my beloved and this is my friend.' 'My love is like a red, red rose.' The opposite of 'a rose is a rose is a rose'. Yet in each we find the poetic 'is', 'is like', 'is what it is not', which continually strives towards its transcendence, *Aufhebung*, in that which it is not, not yet, not quite, and yet not quite not.

Could this poetic 'is' with its fluidity and openness possibly contribute to a better understanding and appreciation of the 'is' in more prosaic usage? 'God is.' 'God is light.' 'God is love.' 'Love is God.' 'God is not.' 'Life is good.' 'This is true.' Poetry? Affirmation? Pigheadedness? Nonsense? Boo or Aaah? Yet in each instance an 'is' a man might stake his life on, his *Dasein*, his individual, historical, his only actuality, his is.

Finally the odd case of the *cogito ergo sum*. It is fairly clear in the light of his whole philosophy that Descartes had intended to say: *cogito ergo ego*. For some reason he felt he had to prove that he *is*. (Perhaps because of his scholastic training which had insisted that all reality is real in as far as it is in the God who is.) Here Husserl took him to his logical conclusion: The miracle of miracles is the 'I' which can say 'I am', though all 'am' and 'is' may have to remain bracketed in eternity. For Heidegger on the other hand the miracle is that anything *is* – which is the mystic experience, rooted, perhaps, in childhood, in Freud's 'oceanic feeling', beautifully expressed by Traherne (*Centuries of Meditation*, III, 1–25).

I could go on and on. I must not. It is important to realize that nothing is being proved here. We are listening. We are wondering whether these various intentions of 'is' cast light upon each other. Is there a trace of magic power, of assertion, insistence, confirmation, triumph, possessiveness, poetry, faith, metaphor, as well as of identification and identity, in each 'is'? Can any 'is' ever be more or less? And this is the rub: Is there justification for such affirmation, triumph, or for mere identification? Is there any solid ground for such attitudinizing? Or is our use of 'is' sheer imposition? Is there any consolation or hint of an answer in the fact that the question itself is impossible without an 'is' in it?

Sum ergo dubito. Surely we all, including Descartes outside his study, know that this formulates our situation. Yet we must beware of sophistries here. There obviously is not something to which the 'is' really refers, the thing-in-itself, or a Platonic idea, an Aristotelian essence. It is precisely this kind of metaphysics Heidegger wishes to avoid as a cul-de-sac. He is not an ontologist and Adorno's onslaught on him as such totally misconceived (Adorno, 1970, pp. 67–134). For philosophy-metaphysics, from Thales to positivism and nihilism, used 'is' as if it did refer to something, usually something static, beyond the flux of experience and the experience of flux, as if it were strictly metaphorical. So ultimately we have always been left stranded with one thing-in-itself or another, or with an idea, as that which is. Ultimately man always seemed to know – *wissen* – what *is*. And most of the time he thought it was the *status quo* or the *status quo ante* projected into eternity. As a consequence, so Heidegger contends, a pervasive nihilism, of which positivism, idealism or naturalism can be specific expressions, by denying such metaphorical reality, came to believe, either optimistically or pessimistically, that all reality and all understanding of it are human impositions, the exercise of the will to will (1954, pp. 72–3).[10] In as far as nihilism is a reaction against and not an *Aufhebung* of metaphysics, it continues the metaphysical argumentation. Positivistic scientism is the demonstration. As against all the conflicting forms of metaphysics – realism and the diverse reactions against it – Heidegger seeks to justify the 'is' not in reference to something or other but to itself.

It is impossible to enter here into the intricacies of *Sein und Zeit*, of *Zunhandensein* and *Vorhandensein*, *Sein* and *Dasein*, between 'to be' and 'being(s)', and how the various connotations and associations of 'is' reflect the intricate relations between all those forms of being and between them and time. This much emerges for our present use: any 'is', just because it contains significations of power, belief, affirmation, poetic *Aufhebung*, cannot help remaining fluid. Its 'is-ness' therefore may consist in our refusal to let it settle firmly into any definite and fixed meaning. No 'is' used seriously has exclusively poetic or affirmative or identifying character, nor is it admissible to consider any 'is' no matter how scientifically, factually, or dogmatically used, as purely factual, expressing identity with facts. We cannot use 'is' in a way which does not inevitably retain an ever-varied proportion of all the varying connotation of 'is'. Every 'is' is in continuous motion along a sliding scale between 'God is love' or 'love is good' and 'one is one'. The 'is' of 'this is the case' or 'this is a fact' contains its *quanta* of poetry and faith, of magic evocation and incantation. The 'is' of the Hindu belief 'all reality is *maya*' – if Sanskrit permitted such a formulation – contains its

169

quanta of identifying, of factuality, of inductive empiricism and deductive logic. Each *erat* of any QED implies a *credo* which repetition has dulled into a creed, not into factuality and identity. For a proof as such cannot tell what it proves.

If this be true or possibly *is*, there would no longer be so much justification for our pigeon-holing and departmentalization of understanding, as is commonly assumed to be self-evident. Poet and positivist gambol on the same see-saw, and both might enjoy it more, if they dared admit it. (We remember Plato in whose mind they thus gambolled for a time and wonder what would have happened to European thinking, if he had not pushed off the poet.) There may be a little more of the prophet in some professors than Weber thought permissible.

The 'is' does not point to a fixed idea or thing-in-itself. Nor does it fix phenomena or facts, though it does represent a standing temptation to let itself be used for just such a purpose. In science and its philosophy the 'is' in 'so it is' and 'this is the case' has rather hypnotized the initiates and mechanized not only the matter under consideration but the expectations and reactions of the investigators. Today statements like: 'A man is only H_2O plus a few trace elements' or 'a table is really an electro-magnetic field' are beginning to look ludicrous again. Yet 'man is really a kind of animal' is still rather fashionable; and even more so statements like: 'Politics is the art of the possible', 'sociology is a science', 'the economic imperative is increased productivity', or 'increasing productivity is wealth'. If we accepted the full function of 'is', such statements would question as much as they affirm: Is sociology a science? Is wealth increased productivity? Is politics the art of the possible and man a kind of animal? Recognized in its questioning power the 'is' might even help to undo some of the damage its too positive use has caused.

For example: 'This happens to be called Bristol University' is a fairly unambiguous statement. As against this the assertion, 'this is a university' would imply the question: 'Is this a university?' I may say about something which happens to function like something we are accustomed to call a university: this is a university and not a factory. (Can I be sure of even that?) Well, it certainly is not a tube station. I can say: This is Bristol University and not Leeds University. I can say: This accumulation of faculties and departments – what *are* faculties and departments as against the tautological 'these' which was invented to evade the question? – and this collection of buildings and what 'goes on' in them are called a university. Which leaves open the question how I can know that something *is* what it is called. (We need only remember Goebbels and *1984*.)

We try again: This cluster of definitions circumscribes what we demand and desire of something we name a university. This parti-

170

cular structure embodies these definitions accurately enough for our liking, hence it is a university. Now precisely to the extent to which we take the 'is' seriously here, the statement turns into a question, it challenges us to the question: Is it? Does it embody the definitions? Do the definitions express adequately our intentions? Are the intentions impelled by our desires? Are the desires ours or do they already reflect power-intentions that may have impressed our desires without being necessarily congruent with them? And is a university whose structure and aims represent powers beyond our intentions and against our desires a university? i.e. is a university a university simply by virtue of happening to be about? May we call it a university even though it contradicts our intentions and definitions as to what is meant to constitute a university? (Cf. Adorno, 1969b, p. 88, and *passim*; Habermas, 1967, p. 239, and *passim*, and 1969, pp. 325–6 quoting Freud.)

Here the 'is' and the whole philosophy of identity has come home to roost. We are left with the statement: This is this – and in this context it becomes an affirmation and a creed. What we call a university is what we call a university is. . . . What *is* democracy? What *is* science? What *is* sociology? Questions no less *fragwürdig* for being awkward. And each points, not to a primal cause or *Ursache*, but to a primal question or *Urfrage*: What is man as against what he happens to have made himself? A question surely of some interest to the sociologist, even though no obvious and immediate answer seems in sight.

But then if the 'is' has the fluidity and ambiguity we impute to it, perhaps questions raised by it and concerning it do not call for answers but for responses, decisions, hopes, resolutions. They may call for *Erschliessen* and *Entschliessen*. *Erschliessen* means opening up, making something available for someone, as we *erschliessen* a newly discovered continent. *Entschliessen* means to resolve, decide, but not in the sense of de-termine, fixing an aim or end, but in the sense of becoming ready to unlock, unleash, let free, let grow, *let be*. Hence *Entschluss* means resolution, yet not as the will to impose, but as the willingness to let something come into its own, possibly something that is prevented from coming into its own by what-happens-to-be. (Compare here Freud's implicit contention that what we have made of ourselves often prevents us from discovering what or who we are.)

We are back at the simplest of all questions: Is whatever-happens-to-be the embodiment and expression, the realization of what it claims to be, what it is claimed to be? May one still say that the status quo *is*, that things-are-what-they-are-what-they-are, except by using the 'is' unambiguously, and therefore illegitimately, in its limited, tautological, identifying sense, as exclusively equivalent to = ? Can one even use it in that sense without affirming something, namely the *status quo*?

If any 'is' raises at least as many questions as it can possibly answer others, and if the questions it raises do not call for answers but for the response or responsiveness of responsibility, of *Erschliessen* and *Entschluss*, then nothing is necessarily what it happens to be or claims to be, then once again everything becomes *fragwürdig*. Then the aim of education or philosophy, for example, of sociology or psychology, can no longer be the traditional one of *Bildung* ('gestalted' understanding) as if we knew what is that which we have to hand on. Nor could theirs be the contemporary aim of training, i.e. preparation for the *status quo*, as if that were our only possibility (Heidegger, 1954, pp. 69–70). The knowledge or know-how we intend to pass on may not be what it is claimed to be. First and foremost our aim would be *Besinnung* (contemplation) as well as reorientation or even repentance. Is this knowledge knowledge and in how far and for how long? Is it the knowledge we require and desire? And what *is* it we require and desire?

Finally: the essence of 'is', the heart and centre of 'is-ness' – there are no appropriate terms yet for such probing – is possibility. And here again possibility is not to be restricted to what here and now and practically seems possible, to 'the art of the possible', as if possibility were one thing among others. Possibility *is*, it is our being. Our *Dasein*, in as far as it will not come to rest in what-happens-to-be, subsists in our possibilities. Yet it may well be that an understanding of this can only grow and finally grow into actuality out of a slow process of *Besinnung*. For while it is true that whatever-happens-to-be, of which the *Man* is the social and sociological aspect, shapes our thinking, and most radically our thinking what *is*, it may not be doing it totally and of necessity. So a new and growing apprehension and appreciation of that which *is*, once it becomes really more than an elaboration of the old or a reaction against it, may for all we know totally reshape what-happens-to-be (cf. Bloch, 1970, pp. 224–87).

Adorno

I realize how much he would hate to be compared to and coupled with Heidegger. Yet it seems to me that not only his concerns and conclusions were similar. Even his apparently so different route which he defended with such acrimony against any imputation of Heideggerianism – proves not to have been so divergent, once allowances have been made for diverse terminologies and different starting points.

Adorno's thinking is dialectical *par excellence*. He not merely takes Hegel and Marx a few steps further along the road of their avowed intentions. He continues what is best in the dual dialectics of Judaism. First, that everything has to be argued, dialogued again and again, until it becomes, temporarily, acceptable to the pupil or the antagonist, and second, every generalization has to be dialogued, until it fits a particular eventuality, individual or predicament. As in Marx, echoes of the Judaic tradition may have been responsible for Adorno's 'materialism'. For it is to be remembered that matter, since Aristotle, has been considered as the individuation principle; and that for Judaic thought matter had never been that left-over half of reality or being which it had been for Greek and, later on, Christian thought.

Hence Adorno's materialism expressed itself as a concern for the individual which Hegel would not have appreciated. His restless, total, therefore 'negative' dialectics, gives voice to the belief that neither conceptualization, abstraction, logic, nor any other of the intellective processes as such, can ever come to grips with, fully grasp or conceive the particular or the individual which alone exists or subsists, while everything else is merely through or about or by him (cf. Heidegger, 1931, pp. 38, 57, 118, 122 *inter alia*). Even his understanding of the individual still retains some of the ambiguities he had for Hegel and Marx, yet it is always anchored in the Judaic respect for the particular which is irreducible and has its own irreducible ambiguities. Nevertheless, as Heidegger's apprehension of the problem of 'is' – which Adorno mistook for ontology – made him a critic of all metaphysics, so Adorno's apprehension of the actuality of the subject, the particular, made him suspicious of all fixing thoughts.

His dialectics is negative also in the sense that it claims no knowledge or comprehension, as no perception, can be more than ephemeral, one-sided, conditioned as well as conditional. It cannot define the particular or the individual from whom all definitions are derived. Freud had called belief in psycho-synthesis a folly. All the analyst can do is to clarify or to clear out of the way misapprehensions and misinterpretations. If he succeeds the psyche may have a chance to grow, to develop according to its inner necessity which is beyond rational understanding and manipulation. (In this it is not unlike the body. Only about its malfunctioning can we be rational.) Adorno viewed the thinker's function or the functioning of thought in a similar fashion. It could merely and at its best preserve the individual from ossification, from the fossilization, i.e. idolization or fetishization, of any partial or ephemeral 'truth', concerning himself and/or society. The validity and adequacy of thought lies in its momentary *Aufhebung* of any former knowing, in as far as this is always in danger of becoming ideology or fetishism.

173

And each idea or concept points at its own *Aufhebung* in the face of the individual. This seems to come pretty close to Heidegger's understanding of *is* as possibility, as never fully actualizable possibility; yet in such a way that the two approaches are complementary, not repetitive.

Adorno, with Horkheimer, understood the rationalism of the Enlightenment as authoritarian and absolutistic. It reflected the absolutism of the mercantilistic prince, his rational and therefore absolute authority. That same absolutism also liberated society from the incubus of many decaying structures and customs and released new energies as well as controlled them. Similarly Enlightenment philosophy was both liberation and enslavement. Yet its roots were in the Yahweh of the Old Testament. There already liberation from superstition, idolatry, fossilization, involved obedience to the One and only One (Horkheimer-Adorno, 1969, pp. 20ff). Thus a fairly straight line runs from the reasonable demands of Yahweh to the enthronement of reason and to modern scientific positivism. (Though I believe that the prophets' understanding of Yahweh was actually close to Adorno's position, in that their Yahweh, as the one who 'makes true', was not to be conceptualized, forbids conceptualization and promises self-understanding to the man who does not try to conceptualize but to follow the movements of him who 'makes true'.) Again here is an undeniable resemblance between Adorno's view and Heidegger's critique of metaphysics as imposition.

Adorno maintains that we are all so involved in the intricate cannibalism of the politico-economico-social system constituting contemporary society that any action of ours can only add to its intricacy and impetus, its compulsiveness. In a situation in which, as he believes, schizophrenia is the human actuality, an understanding of schizophrenia, which cannot be an objective knowledge, and through it of the society which seems to make all other responses impossible or sub-human, appears to remain as the only human possibility (1970, p. 275). Not even traditional wisdom, *Kultur*, can substantially help in this situation which merely reveals *Kultur* as having always been at least schizoid (cf. above, chapter 2, Note on literature). How far is that from Heidegger's rejection of *Bildung* and his belief that today not action but *Besinnung* is the only human possibility (1954, pp. 13–70)?

Finally: apropos alienation Adorno says that it is a dangerous doctrine, for it seems to imply that we know the humanity from which we have strayed. Equally Heidegger's *Letter on Humanism* claims that so far all humanism has been metaphysical or ontological, in as far as it did not acknowledge that as yet our very *humanum* is in question (1967, p. 153; cf. the whole essay). Humanism interpreted it as from our *animalitas*, while it is possible that it can be interpreted only as towards or from our possibility, our *humanitas* as possibility. Are these sociologically relevant questions? Is sociology apart from such questioning relevant?

Various

Freud was a rationalist if ever there was one. This enabled him to bear his insights. It also made him take the sting out of them. His insights into the family structure and its universal conditioning processes opened up completely new possibilities of understanding, both of this individual, son of this mother and this father; and of what individuals share across all other divisions as children of mothers and fathers, as individuals. (A similar confluence of the most individual and intimate with that which is universally shared humanity, can be seen in literature since Proust, Joyce, Kafka and Virginia Woolf. Cf. Auerbach, 1957, ch. 20.) Freud's approach, because it compelled us to see the individual as the focus of all social conflicts, and social conflicts as expressing themselves as psychic repression and disorder, cannot be contained by Freud's rationalism, for the individual cannot be contained. (Here the confluence with Heidegger cf. 1931, pp. 57, 118, 122, 195, *inter alia*.)

Marcuse, not only a Freudian but also a Hegelian and Marxian, takes Freud further. He intimates how the new Freudian insights into the psyche, via a new way and method of remembering, may help towards the reconstitution of what we have been conditioned to think of as reality. They can do this, because they also reveal how much that reality is at odds with what the psyche could not help experiencing as its actuality before the social 'reality' was imposed upon it. (And we remember that in the psyche that which once was, always is.) These insights have also taught us how the generally accepted reality gains its feeling quality of being 'really real' through a psychic process of projection and introjection, in the course of which the libido, the psychic desire, becomes forcibly invested in externals in which the psyche cannot really believe (1969, chs 7 and 10). For the areas where it belongs and feels at home, where it can *wohnen*, are those of narcissistic, erotic, interpersonal flow. These in turn become increasingly eroded in favour of the externalities in which the aberrant libido is invested. Which is to say that reality may be no more than a particular and particularly oppressive phantasy. (Compare this with Heidegger's *Geschick* as against *Schicksal*.) Whether or not thoroughgoing libidinal reinvestment is possible or desirable remains an open question. Sociology is not free to treat it as if it had been closed or to behave as if it were a non-problem. For such a question may well be *the* question on which hangs the destiny – the *Schicksal*

175

rather than the *Geschick* – of sociology and of the *Geisteswissen-schaften*. Not to face it would be sociology's *Geschick* pure and simple.

It may be impossible to show whether Heidegger was influenced by Marx's transformation of Hegel's philosophy, beyond the indirect influence which the climate of opinion created by Marxism was bound to exert. There are marked resemblances between Marx's understanding of history as a process constituting reality and its *Aufhebung*, constituting our not yet accomplished humanity, and Heidegger's understanding of *Sein* and *Zeit*. Not only Sartre's writings bear witness to this, but also those of some Marxists who show nothing but scorn for Heidegger and his ilk. These may be right in their belief that his thinking can easily be put to reactionary use. This has happened. It also happened to founders of religion. It happened to Marx and Freud. I suggest that a fuller appreciation of Heidegger's thoughts would reveal them as anything but conservative. Lukács at his best, as in his literary criticism, is close to Heidegger. There he shows how the poet – *Dichter* and *Denker* – holds before man his possibility. The greatness of a writer, according to Lukács, consists in the comprehensiveness of his vision which embraces the possible and the real, sees and makes us see how the possible is rooted in the real, how the real distorts the possible and for that reason must not be acquiesced in. The great writer sees all this in such a way as to leave us with the hope that the possible is yet and in spite of all possible. As a literary critic Lukács knew that possibility pertains to the individual. To the extent to which the poet succeeds in making us re-experience how his characters realize their possibilities, are permitted or forbidden by society to realize them, how they tragically or comically, inevitably or by accident, fail to realize them, how they become conscious of them and of having failed, to that extent his work is significant. In as far as an author can show the conflicts of society as enacted by an individual and between individuals, he is a significant writer (1964, *passim*).

Finally Ernst Bloch and his *Prinzip Hoffnung* must be mentioned in this context, although it would be impertinent to attempt a summing up of that compendious and infinitely suggestive work which, like Mahler's symphonies, was to contain and yet not to 'contain' the world. Bloch set out to demonstrate that hope, active hope, hopeful action, hopeful openness to the future, openness in the face of death, is a constitutive aspect of our humanity, of human actuality. The Greek hope of Pandora's box which consoles over a miserable present and whose place has now been taken by entertainment is not the hope of his principle. This is the Old Testament hope of the prophets who saw the possible future judging the present and, as Yahweh's future, man's reality. It is the philosopher's hope which makes him think and write, the scientist's hope which makes him work, the revolutionary's hope which makes him rebel, the lover's hope which gives him the courage to woo. It is Bach's hope which enabled him to hold transcendentally beautiful sound into the darkest mystery of death. This hope is an integral part of our dynamic humanity. To attempt or do anything without hope is not to be unbiased but inhuman, anti-human.

This is to say once again, whatever happens to be can never be the full expression or embodiment of what *is*, for that includes the openness towards and readiness for change. The possible, that which hope sees as possible, always *is* part and parcel of any situation. And since hope, though it be hope for the whole of mankind, can be experienced and expressed only by the individual, can become actual only in and through him, it is the constitutive principle which intimately and intricately fuses the individual and society. Hope is the ever-changing and through all changes continuing element of social consciousness which constitutes our reality as human.

4 A particular instance of sociological understanding and the snares of causal thinking

I begin with a short summing up of the points raised under headings A–I in chapter 3, to clarify the connections and interrelations between the diverse questions and approaches.

A Positivism, as we have seen, is a peculiar, concentrated attention, a particular, temporary condensation and directedness of social consciousness. But it also expresses and consummates a definite intention which has been reflected throughout the civilized ages in the social structures as well as in philosophy and religion. In a way positivism finalizes the intention inherent in Western – and possibly also in Eastern – civilization. First, it absolutizes the belief in power or force, natural and political, and in the necessity of control which had been embedded in shifting class structures, by detaching it from those structures which this belief had shaped and by which it had been confirmed in turn. Today everyone is being controlled and nobody is in control. Economic-scientific-technological controls have become automated, perpetuum-mobilistic. Power itself has been absolutized (Weber, 1964, p. 900). Second, positivism absolutizes and pragmatizes the intention inherent in metaphysics in as far as this had reflected and tried to justify the aims of a power-structured society. In this way, by reducing the philosophical and political intentions to their common denominator, positivism accomplished a particular form of totalization: total externalization. Everything becomes external to the observing mind which exists *in vacuo*, even the observing mind itself. Everything is reduced to a democracy of things-to-be-looked-at-as-they-are. Such reductionism and externalization positivism posits as reality, explicitly or implicitly. To be realistic means to LATATA. The only exhortation that survives in an objectified and value-free approach to the universe is: LATATA! Questions as to what things really are, what it therefore could mean to LATATA, who it is that does the looking, and what is the nature of looking, are consigned to the large lumber room of non-questions, non-problems.

Thus LATATA reaffirms and fossilizes an attitude, a state of social consciousness, i.e. a social actuality, for which individual and society, I and you, reason and emotion, part and whole, knowledge and wisdom, remain external to each other, as Descartes's bodies, his bodies and souls, Leibniz's monads. It is true that civilization from the beginning was based on some kind of externalization which was designed to make each part of a mechanized whole replaceable. Yet this process was taken a marked step forward in post-medieval Europe. Now everything, including space, time, labour, profit, matter, bodies, was atomized into discrete units.

Positivism aims at complete intellectualization and preconceives the intellect as external to everything. Divorced from the emotion, the intellect knows no values beside that of its own rationality, no hierarchy of significance. Hence it moves towards the totalization of rationalization, control without a controller. Its tests are verifiability and manipulability, which are merely two aspects of the same intention of power and were discovered, used and developed in army and factory, plantation and mine, the civilized organizations in which the individual had to be discounted. Verifiability like manipulability 'proves the truth of . . .' as an army or a factory does, it makes true, it 'facts', to the limits of the intender's or the intention's capacity. Only what can be repeated, what can be made true again and again, what can be made to yield the intended answers, is true. Verifiability is objective in that it totally subsumes the contingent or individual to its objectives which are nobody's objectives, merely *the* objective: objectivity, reality, necessity.

B Sociology was one of the children of positivism. Some of its founding fathers were avowed and assertive positivists. In others positivism, though hedged about by qualifications, prevailed none the less. Ultimately they were united in the belief that the social, no matter how it was to be defined, could be detached, externalized, and studied *sui generis*. Where they disagreed, it was on method and particular aims, or on the degree of insulation either possible or desirable. Moreover the social sciences, especially economics and, later on, sociology, became academic disciplines in their own right just during that period of transition from a bourgeois to a neo- or post-bourgeois culture when class control became control pure and simple. The intentions of the economist as well as of the sociologist were scientific and objective, i.e. positivistic, in that they were to serve an objective which seemed or was no longer that of anyone in particular nor of everyone altogether.

One intention of objectivity might be explained by the appearance of the 'ordinary man' above the academic horizon. There were so many of him. He demanded to be noticed and thus constituted economics and sociology, and as sciences, for it seemed that he could be contained only by the old civilizatory methods of army and factory, even on the level of academic understanding and even though such methods were bound to lead to the objectification of everybody. To think in terms of non-containment or, at least, not exclusively in terms of containment, to think in terms of possibilities beyond the one stamped by civilization as necessity, was not possible then and hardly seems possible now. The social sciences demonstrate society's determination to objectify and manipulate at any price, because an alternative seems inconceivable.

Doubts however remained in the minds of at least the German sociologists concerning the competence of investigators who are part and parcel of that which they wish to investigate, as human beings and as citizens. Either everyone is totally manipulated or conditioned by impersonal economic-social-physiological-biological forces. In that case the sociologist's observations, be they ever so accurate, would have no more significance than a conditioned reflex. Or, in some meta-phenomenological fashion, in an at least partially autonomous sphere, man is the manipulator of his being manipulated. Then the sociologist would be investigating manipulators as their manipulator. For such a pursuit the methods of positivism and rationalism seemed to call for certain modifications. Hence there arose the problems of differentiation between the natural and social sciences, differentiation of approach and aim. These problems evaded the basic question: whether in the humane sciences manipulability can ever be the aim, whether in this area *understanding*, *Verstehen*, has not a totally different connotation. I showed how neglect of the dual meaning of knowledge as *Wissen* and *Kennen*, *Dichten* and *Denken* reflected the evasion and compounded the resulting confusion. The social sciences remained deeply involved in attempted imitations of the natural sciences, the voices of protest sound confused and confusing against the by now monolithic positivist back-drop.

Where and how could a possible movement towards a new understanding of and in the social sciences start? How could it begin to discern between mere pretensions, poetizings, and possible insights in what is by now a totally unchartered area? Is it not bound to look irrelevant, irrational, purely subjective against the unified rationalization processes? Nevertheless, the barely possible, i.e. the emancipation of the social sciences, seems to have become a necessity: the need to salvage the fuller implication of 'understanding' from the erosion of scientific pretensions.

C   From here the problems surrounding 'value' appear in a new light. We have seen why, for example, Weber in his particular historical situation saw a value-free approach to sociology as a supreme value. We understood his passionate insistence on objectivity as the expression of a subjective desire, a most personal objective (cf. Dahrendorf, 1962, ch. 2). For objectivity is constituted by and presupposes an objective. This may be a circumscribed one, as in any given discipline or pursuit. It may be uncircumscribed, totalitarian, as in Western civilization today. Now within such an objectivity, value, as a matter of fact, has not disappeared. It has merely become completely immanent. In economics it functions as price, in sociology, as elsewhere, as comparability, as exchange-value. Everything has its price, everything is comparable, has its precise position within a generally accepted system or mythology of co-ordinates. That position alone constitutes the value of everything, its reality. Just as our interest has become correspondingly measurable in terms of financial or academic increments or of status. Perhaps the following illustration may serve: In medieval economics a tension existed, or was thought to exist, between true value and price. For instance, in time of scarcity prices rise, but they should not. For the true value of anything is not dependent on contingencies. In modern economics with its habit of looking-at-things-as-they-are, price came to denote simply and solely market price. Price and value coalesced. The individual was valuable to the extent to which his labours could be priced. Whatever had once been denoted 'true value' was left homeless, outside reality. Whatever libido had been attached to it, now became attached to price. (Not even the neo-medieval Marxian *Mehrwert* or surplus-value could salvage the old concept.) But since value denotes the quality of my direct, individual, incommunicable and incommensurable experience and also the resulting directedness of my existence, I am left outside reality – or in that totally abstract Weberian-Kantian freedom where I have to defend my values as judgment. The separation of value-experience from the increasingly all-absorbing scientific pursuit obviously reflected a societal dichotomy which is experienced by the individual as schizophrenia and was experienced as such by Weber.

Such a separation ratified a peculiar paradox. It constitutes value-freedom, which spells automatism, as highest societal value, as highest value even within society's attempts at self-understanding. Apart from that it devaluates all value by privatizing it. The separation between value and science requires for its effective maintenance just the kind of aggressiveness which has been institutionalized in the 'sciences' of the university departments. In this way the fact that value-experience is personal – not private – instead of leading to mutual acknowledgment and openness, is utilized to feed the academic debate by means of the energy inhibited from finding

G

creative, personal expression. Similarly the method of scientific debate is then carried back into the discussion of value. Once upon a time the aims of political and military campaigning had been adopted by and adapted to scholastic and then scientific disputations. Here as there victory, domination, the humiliation of the adversary, his elimination, is the aim – of course always in the name of God or of truth. The methods developed and refined are then transferred back to ideological conflicts, to arguments over values that cannot be argued.

Is it possible that phenomenology as intuited by Husserl at his moment of illumination could bridge the gap between value and science (see below, chapter 5, on Husserl)? It tried to see both value and science, and other areas of desiring, willing, intending, as self-contained constellations of meaning, as *Gestalt* and as autonomous. It also tried to demonstrate and with some measure of success that something akin to valuing, to the kind of 'Gestalting' which life needs for its preservation as well as for its self-delight, is already implicit in those basic forms of perception on which in turn even scientific knowledge is based. It understood facts themselves as value-shaped, tailored for a purpose. It understood the experience of value as a fact. It also understood most, if not all, statements, whether of value or of fact, as intentional or intensional (Spiegelberg, 1964, pp. 548ff). (Alas, Husserl's attempt to establish phenomenology as an exact science soon turned it into a new scholasticism. What might have become a revolutionary *Aufhebung* of Marx and Hegel, Kant and Weber, became another debating area. Is there a possibility of return to Husserl's pristine apprehension?)

D Dialectics means to restore the dialogue between value and fact, theory and practice, to keep alive the tension between idea and reality. Or rather, to remain aware of this tension as one between two aspects of one reality which had been dichotomized since Plato's days. Dialectics tries to break the compulsion of rationalism and rationalizations, to find a synthesis, *Aufhebung*, of Hebrew and Greek thought. It tries to restore on a new level of consciousness or self-awareness the unitary Hebrew understanding of the universe by means of that very Greek dichotomizing thought which seems to have made such a unitary conception inconceivable. From here we may understand better and pardon the tortuousness of some dialectical thinking. For the Greek dichotomy does not merely represent one possible philosophical approach which might as well be discarded. It reflects the social reality. This is to say that Greek philosophy, in as far as it endeavoured to justify the social structure, was revealed as ideology. In as far as it expressed social facts, its *Aufhebung* was a socio-political not just a philosophical task.

It is interesting that Marx, the Hebrew German, saw more

clearly than Hegel, the Christian-Platonic German, that a reconciled society alone could produce a new unitary myth which was not just another ideology. (Cf. Durkheim's belief in the dynamic and regenerative powers of society.) Dialectics also wishes to reconstitute the dialogue between knower and knower as being different in kind from any communication and processes that constitute the intercourse between knower and known. In the dialogue between knowers, interests and values could be and would have to be openly acknowledged. They would not have to be concealed behind ideological assertions of objectivity, as has to be done as long as the knower, and for manipulative purposes, treats other subjects as simply known. Values would not have to be separated from the scientific discussions and would thus not be ostracized from an area of discourse which today is considered as the only rational one. Because the concern and committal of the participants would not be relegated to the private sphere, relativism and relativizers would be relativized. For relativism, even as understood by the sociologists of knowledge and by their denigrators, is a symptom of the dichotomy of the personal and the social. Full inter-subjectivity is restlessly relational, having its rest and its end in the dialoguing, communing, not in anything this produces.

Furthermore, dialogue between persons who do not divorce desire from reason, fact from value, 'what is' from 'what could be', is likely to reveal that interest, far from being the simple, rational thing the economists claim it to be, is something of infinite diversity and gradation. On the contrary, our true interests, because they are rooted in childhood experiences which know no economy, may reveal the economists' interest as irrational. It was the dichotomy of fact and value which aided the gradual reduction of interest to its narrow economic and sociological meaning, according to which 'I may be interested in many things', but 'my real interest is . . .'. That interest usually had to remain concealed and therefore most battles and debates have so far been 'interested', ideological, a waste of life and time, while the huge diplomatic and debating machinery was deployed to conceal the interest which had brought it into being.

E   Which brings us to history and the fact that all knowledge, like every human being, is historical. It is relative in the sense that it can never be final and can always be superseded. It is absolute in that, even as error, it contributes to further possibilities of understanding. (Until now and because we usually took for error what was simply the expression of a different interest, we felt we had to fight and eliminate it.) In dialogue error is as important as that which, temporarily, reveals it as error. The difficulty we meet here – it was experienced, if not to its full extent, by German historism – is this:

historiography has not yet reflected on its activities with sufficient seriousness and radicalness. We saw that German historism, partly because of the German situation, partly because it originated in the minds of men who were as much *Dichter* as *Denker*, had begun to wrestle with the problems of individuality and inter-individuality. Yet the historists failed. The individual as such was not permitted to raise his head. When Burckhardt (1963) devotes a chapter to 'The Individual and the Commonwealth', he as inevitably thinks of the world-historical individual as Hegel, i.e. he thinks of the individual in whom and by whom individuality is denied or ignored.

By means of various examples I tried to show that historians have not yet begun to listen, either to their subject and its subjects, or to questions, raised by their subjects, which altogether put in question their aims and methods, the contents and form of their work. In history more than in any other subject, it remains problematical whether the academic discipline or the intellectual pursuit since the days of Thucydides does not hide more, possibly much more, than it reveals. By this I do not mean the obvious: that historiography is bound to leave unmentioned very much, that it has to select, shape etc. I mean that its approach, methods, aims, principles of selection, obscure rather than clarify its putative subject matter. History, together with philosophy, mathematics and astronomy, is the oldest science. It remains an archetypal example of positivism, of positing and imposition. Heidegger, by his understanding of mortality and 'situation', of *Schicksal* as against *Geschick*, Freud, by his use of case-history, opened up new vistas of historical understanding. History was revealed as a most intricate web of individualities and individual interactions and inter-penetrations. Psycho-analysis and its further developments unravelled layer after layer of complex interdependencies: of personal relationships, events, their interpretations and rationalizations, of suppressions and distortions, of constant mirroring and counter-mirroring.

So historiography and, of course, sociology, could – should? – see its task in investigating these subtle and subtlest interdependencies of events and individuals and groups, of conscious and unconscious intentions, of conflicting interests. The further intricacies and interrelations between history and historiography, between historiography and the histories of historiography, between the changing academic and cultural pattern which reflect those intricacies, also demand consideration. The historiographer might find it profitable to find out whether or how his labours and those of his colleagues become part of history before they in turn become part of historiography; or how frequently they are by-passed by history, possibly because they by-passed history.

Also questions concerning the part(s) and the whole become

urgent here (cf. Dilthey on need and impossibility of universal history, 1914, vol. 1, pp. 26–39, 93–4). Can literature and art be of assistance here? Or phenomenology with its potential understanding of the infinitesimal gradations of reality? Questions concerning 'levels of abstraction' and the possibilities of re-earthing would have to be raised radically. One problem is certainly and immeasurably intensified once the contingent is given its proper weight on the scales of human mortality: the rationalist Enlightenment historian had an explicit measure against which to measure epochs and individuals. The historists, of whom Ranke is typical, had rejected such explicit grading procedure. Yet it remained their weakness, from Herder to Meinecke, that their implicit moralism or faith was as defintely the backbone of their labours and their measuring rod, as reason for the rationalist. What kind of measure are we left with, what possibilities of judgment and discrimination remain, once the individual, I, not *man* or reason, is made the measure of all things? Or, worse and more hopeful: What is the historian and sociologist left with when measuring has been recognized as inappropriate in this area?

F   Two thousand four hundred years of Platonic-Aristotelian philosophizing and the at least twice as old civilizatory tradition of which it was a reflection and vindication have created the ingrained conviction that significance or meaning is bound up with a hierarchic structure of reality, i.e. of society. 'Take but degree away' and all evils would be let loose. The supernatural gave meaning to the natural, as the faithful service that asked for no reward save that of knowing that it was doing the master's will gave significance to the serf's life – at least in the master's eyes. The masters themselves seem to have found it harder to discover significance in their own lives and only too often to have been afflicted by *ennui* (cf. *The Epic of Gilgamesh*, Penguin, Harmondsworth, 1968, ch. 1). Throughout history man had to create and apotheosize all manner of entities and wholes within which and as their insignificant part his existence would signify.

Since the structure of that which we experience as reality is a reflection of the structure of our society, it was inevitable that the gradual dissolution of social hierarchies made life appear increasingly insignificant. For a while the insulated intellectual individual posited a total rationality within which his reasoning would become meaningful. Later still even the old Goethe believed that resignation to technology, the ultimate externalized rationalization, was a meaningful attitude. Since then *anomie* has accelerated its encroachments. So we can appreciate Durkheim's desire to reinstitute professional hierarchies, and why a sceptic like Pareto took élitist structures for granted. We understand the compulsion of the positivist Comte to recreate religion or sociology as religion; also Weber's passionate conviction that power, imperial power, was the sole ultimate source and guarantor of order. All such individual attempts at integration in or identification with, Rieff defines as 'commitment therapy'. Personal neuroses and psychoses are contained by being geared to 'higher or communal purposes', i.e. to communal neuroses and psychoses (Rieff, 1966). Historiography as well as history presents the balance sheet of this method. Rieff maintains that for all kinds of reasons – including, for example, the hydrogen bomb – such therapies are no longer fruitfully available, except in crudely regressive forms, like fascism, racialism, doctrinaire communism, evangelism, or in the form of *Ersatz*, like status or the big corporation. Is he justified in his hope that man might learn to find meaning in his own individual life, in its slow growth and labours towards new possibilities of wholeness and an as yet not imaginable health? Is it possible that such learning might eventually lead to new possibilities of relating to others, of friendship?

What may be deduced from the fact that the artist has always been thought of as significant to the extent to which he succeeded in presenting the individual and the particular as significant, and to make his work appear meaningful in itself? Could Hebrew thought help, once it has been disentangled from the peculiar religiosity it produced, because it never dichotomized reality – possibly because it reflected an earlier, less civilized social structure or memory?

G The problems clustering round 'subjectivity' and 'objectivity' are related to those of meaning and whether for example friendship or an empire gives meaning to life. I tried to clarify the situation by showing that inter-subjectivity constitutes and again and again reconstitutes the social reality than-which-nothing-greater-can-be-conceived. For the moment that 'greater' has been conceived, it becomes part of the inter-subjective reality. Within that objectivity is constituted by more or less clear-cut definitions and circumscription, expressing more or less clear-cut desires, expectations or intentions: objectives. Only fairly definite objectives, freely or not so freely chosen, create enclaves of objectivity, spheres of relative certitude and precise meaning, because within them meaning is immanent. Subjectivity and objectivity are far from being contradictory by nature. A particular if fairly universal development brought them into conflict, turned that which is being constituted and to be reconstituted into the one and only constitution.

Civilization as we know it goes hand in hand with the emergence of certain objectives, with consequent depreciation of the personal to the private and its subsumption under some 'common-weal'. Civilization in one form or another substituted the imposition of the will and its rationalizations for the diverse possibilities of symbiosis.

186

It imposed wilful order not only on nature but on human nature. In this way it created enclosures of apparent safety and stability, of objectivity. Law courts, police and prisons are the symbols of objectivity. The citizen's unhinged libido became increasingly attached to the external safeguards and assurances, possibly to the degree to which it had evacuated the areas that were to be safe-guarded. Thus the citizen began to forget the precariousness of his individuality, his mortality, which is his actuality. The libidinization of the means was accomplished: that which was designed to protect me, has become that which I am ready to protect with my life which thus feels protected. That which was to have enabled me to find a meaningful life has become the meaning of my life. My life has been objectified. I can now be objective about it, except that it is no longer my life.

At first theological and philosophical, later on scientific and technological thinking, could not help reflecting the objectives of civilization. These overall objectives in turn usurped the place of that inter-communication and communion which had constituted them. Thus the areas of objectivity, now invested with all the glamour of civilized power, became the sanctuary of subjects no longer able or willing to bear the memory of their mortality. The entrance fee to that enchanted realm is the subordination of the individual life, *Dasein*, to external, common – not communal – objectives. The objective gains power and then, to the degree to which we lose living faith in this objective, the power becomes mechanical, inexorable, totally alienated from our living intentions. Yet as our libido has been squandered on it, the alien objective confronts us with the power of our alienated libido. Today, as a final irony, inter-sub-jectivity vegetates self-consciously and guiltily in the cracks and crevices of a monolithic objectivity (cf. Poole, 1972, 'Philosophical Space'; also chs 3 and 5).

H In the meantime objectivity remains apotheosized, for the sociologist as much as for the technocrat or bureaucrat. Within sociology this finds expression in the persistence of causal and statistical thinking. More will have to be said about this presently. Here we remind ourselves of the contention that causal thinking is tautologous. Like logic and mathematics it is designed to make certain implications explicit and to function within clearly defined universes of discourse. We saw that causal thinking is a form of definition, of letting two or more events define each other in terms of a manipulable relation. It is also a means of creating clarity and precision by rigorous exclusion. When the sociologist applies causal categories in analysing social, i.e. human, situations, he is abstracting from them. He is not dealing with them. His abstractions may prove useful in many intellectual contexts. As a sociologist he will have to continue asking himself whether such abstracting conceals or reveals his subject, obscures or illuminates it.

I   This finally brought us to the problem which Heidegger focused in the question 'what *is*?', Adorno in the insistence that dialectics must remain 'negative', Bloch in the contention that the hope-principle is a constitutive element of any human actuality. We have returned to the point where everything is once more wide open, any conceptualization radically questionable. Hence only a continuous effort of de-scaffolding, de-conceptualizing, intellectual negativing, can give substance to the hope of an eventual approach to understanding. For anything that happens-to-be may not merely hide, but actually inhibit and repress the coming into being of what could be, what we may hope to be. Freud showed how deeply that which we happen-to-be may be no more than an artificially constructed and imposed defence which represses what we actually could be by means of the very energy of that which is being repressed. Therefore our attitude towards what-happens-to-be is a constitutive element both of what-happens-to-be and of what-could-be. Our hope, despair or indifference – and the last is as biased as the other two – our *Stimmung*, mood, which determines the quality of reality as far as we are concerned and the quality of our thinking, feeling and acting which constitute reality for us, is both intimately personal and of profoundest social significance.

Once again we are driven back upon the individual, at least the searching and researching individual, as both the originator and victim, the beginning and end, the ends and means, of social consciousness. More precisely, we always find the individual as actually the victim of social consciousness. And yet there is no search, no attempt at understanding which is also self-understanding, in which the researcher does not experience himself in his researches as at least potentially an originator. For just as the act of becoming or making conscious and the events of perception and awareness defy definition in that every definition merely increases the conscious awareness, so the interplay between awareness and that which it is aware of – between *noesis* and *noemata* – will necessarily remain beyond the possibility of definition or explication (cf. Husserl, 1950, vol. 1, part 3, ch. 4). One might also say: The sphere of perception, consciousness, awareness, intellectuation, reflection, is the sphere of possibility. And possibility, outside its mathematical-statistical connotation, is essentially indefinable – also in the sense of uncircumscribable. Hence to treat the possible as negligible involves a definite value-judgment that cannot be justified in terms of the rationality it tries to defend: Moreover it is a judgment as nearly certainly wrong as anything can be. For it is itself an insistence on a particular possibility: that the possible is negligible. (In as far as possibility is the sphere of the artist, his importance in and for society will be proportionate to society's belief in its possibilities.)

We see the individual as actual embodiment of social consciousness. We simultaneously see him as the one who bodies forth and gives substance to social consciousness. Now if it were true that any possible bodying forth could be no more than a refraction of the actual embodiment, the expression never more than the impression, then all thinking and researching, at least in the *Geisteswissenschaften*, would be sheer masochism. However the problem here is not the hoary one of conditioning versus freedom, determinism versus free will. It cannot be, for we now see that neither of these terms can be defined. It can only be delimited by the other.

I can demonstrate the possibility of conditioning and determinedness in various directions and *ad infinitum*. At no stage could I prove the conditioning to have been total or necessary. That would mean demonstrating necessary causality, and causality is a concept, quite external to the chain of conditioning it is intended to define. Even causality is a possibility. So conditioning remains a possibility and as such undefinable. Freedom is experienced and understood altogether as possibility. It is even more immediately indefinable. To put it positively, freedom and conditioning, free will and determinism, are strictly dialectical, even dialogical terms. They define each other, delimit and circumscribe each other. They find their meaning over against each other. Either is meaningless apart from the other. I could not be aware of or understand the actualities of conditioning, apart from the apprehension of a possible freedom. I could not experience or understand the possibility of freedom, apart from the more or less painful actuality of conditionedness, for freedom remains a possibility. Freedom *is* possibility, the possibility which modifies fatality, *Schicksal* as against *Geschick*.

Arguments between determinists and free-willers are barren and interminable. They can be sustained only *as* arguments, as mutual explication mistaken for contradiction. As soon as the behaviourist propagates his doctrine, he has already relativized it. The idealist's defence of freedom is automatically relativized by his dependence on language whose structure reflects primeval assumption and preconceptions, by his philosophical academic tradition, by his desire to prove or defend the existence of freedom – which has no existence, because it is existence, my existence in as far as I can be free. Hence Descartes's attempt to make rationality omnipotent, to give to reason the freedom of sovereignty – the only kind of apparent freedom civilization recognizes – not only reflected the actual conditioning of his reason by economic, political processes external to itself, it also led directly to the impotence of reason as it capitulated before the factuality it felt powerless to change, because it could not yet realize that it had constituted the factuality (Borkenau, 1934, on Descartes, p. 297 *passim*).

Domination implies servitude, not only of the ruled but of the ruler. A power-structured understanding of freedom is self-contra-dictory, for here freedom and necessity do not define each other but are in conflict, and the conflict is the inevitable result of the desire of one part of society to 'get' or 'keep' the freedom by leaving the necessity to others. This was Kant's dilemma: he tried to salvage freedom as an actuality in its own right. Thus he literally turned it into an impossibility, namely into Prussian duty (about which much might be said, but not that it was a felicitous example of freedom). How immediately Kantian thinking reflected the political reality, *Geschick*, Frederician absolutism, can be gleaned from the fact that Kant quite naturally understood freedom as self-determination, *Selbstbeherrschung*. On the other hand, Kant's separation of reason into two or even three autonomous departments give positivism right up to Weber and beyond a better conscience in its pursuit of causality.

It was Hegel's merit to have restored the tension and inter-dependence between freedom and necessity. It was his failure not to have done it on the level of individual experience where alone the tension exists as meaningful and real. To put it pointedly: the scholastic, intellectual Hegel experienced a little of that tension in his own mind. He could so easily project it into an abstraction called the *Weltgeist* or world-history, because, and this was his conditioning, he already experienced the tension mainly as a philosophical problem. When Marx 'turned Hegel upside down', he not merely substituted economics for objective idealism, the 'means of production' for the *Weltgeist*, he dragged the Hegelian tension between freedom and necessity into the socio-economic actualities of the day. As passionate revolutionary he experienced the tension in his own life as well as in his thinking, and was thus able to help others to experience it more distinctly and more consciously. He therefore created new possibilities, of understanding as well as of action, by his insistence on necessity. This is not a simple paradox, but dialectics in action. (Just as the real tension of the first volume of *Das Kapital* is that between the abstract argument and the documentary chapters.)

Freud, the only other individual who changed social consciousness to a comparable degree, owes his success to a similar though more implicit and subconscious dialectics. Like Marx, he insisted on the power of necessity, of conditioning and determinedness, nor wasted any energy on arguments for or against freedom. By recognizing and acknowledging the force of conditioning even far beyond the then accepted and acceptable evidence, his efforts to understand its workings created quite new possibilities of freedom. More poignantly than Marx, Freud saw the tension between freedom and necessity, which is also that between the individual and society, the conflict of social consciousness, as taking place, via introjection and pro-jection, in the conditioned, historical, mortal individual with his possibilities, except for which there could be no conflict.

A change of social consciousness

Maybe something can be learned about the interplay of freedom and necessity, of *Schicksal* and *Geschick*, by looking more con-centratedly at an actual observable change in social consciousness, as well as at the way in which scholars who recognized it and its significance tried to interpret and explain it. Now from the days of Tönnies and Weber – and most likely as a consequence of Hegel's and Marx's interpretation of history and that of the historists – German scholars in particular understood the changes that took place in Europe since the Middle Ages as both unique and universally significant. They were aware of the enormous difficulties involved in focusing such an epochal change and in trying to establish a generally acceptable and scientifically respectable methodology for such an approach. They were painfully conscious of the inherent epistemological problems. But they tried, again and again. For bureaucratic capitalism, rationalism and progressive rationalization, were then and still are the most powerful forces at work in con-temporary society, by now all over the globe. The questions, there-fore, when, where, how and why they originated, where lay and lies the source of their power, ask to be asked. On the other hand, those 'forces' became questionable only as men began to experience them as problematical, as neither just 'natural' or inevitable, as not altogether desirable. Only as it became clear that capitalism did not express the fulness of human potential, was not natural to man, could one begin to ask: What change of mind, attitude, desire, or of underlying social processes, gave rise to capitalist developments? What change of *Stimmung*, mood, temper, spirit, made capitalism possible or accompanied its possibly inevitable rise? (For the following see especially: Weber, 1920; 1964, pp. 691–1102; Tönnies, 1955; Sombart, 1927; Scheler, 1960; Borkenau, 1934.)

1   After the gradual collapse of the Roman Empire in the West, towns began to grow again slowly, round ecclesiastical foundations, the *Fronhof* or manor, around the conspicuous consumers, ecclesias-tical and secular, who spend rather than accumulate the surplus produced by their dependants. Unlike the Greek city, the medieval city was generally part of a larger political and economic structure, however loose and ill-defined. Unlike the Oriental city, it managed

to gain an increasing measure of independence. That it had to fight for it and was able to do so, was partly inherent in the circumstances. In this fighting its peculiar structure became elaborated: it became a burghers' city. Its air became and remained free, i.e. freer than the feudal air outside its walls, to the extent to which the outsider was welcomed as ally within them. The persistent tension between the city and the feudal lords proved fertile, as it kept the burghers' spirit militant while the city needed each for its defence. When the tension slackened, as during the rise of mercantilism, the cities lost their independence.

2   It was the *Wehrgemeinschaft*, the fact that each master craftsman could and would man the wall and take part in the sorties, that gave power to the guilds and reality to a kind of democratization. For though the medieval city reflected the stratifications of the feudal surroundings, it also modified them. Urbanization was slow but thorough. The medieval city lasted and grew. For it was not endemically at war with its neighbours, nor was it dependent on a substructure of slavery or, exclusively, on the luck of merchant adventurers or princes. The city had time radically to alter the life rhythm of its citizens: their tenor of life, their religion and philosophy, their expectations and chances, in Weber's usage; their psychic structure, in Freud's. 'Burghers have different gods from peasants' (Weber, 1964, pp. 946ff).

3   Relatively independent of the seasons, not immediately at the mercy of a failed harvest, man could develop new patterns of living and thinking. Society, to use Durkheim's language, increasingly became man's nature. Money gained in importance and subtilized the possibilities of exchange. Appreciable finds of silver and gold, not inevitably flowing into imperial treasuries, stimulated trade. Money rationalizes values, as we saw, levels them and makes them comparable. Its increasing use gradually substituted the concept of exchange-value for the reality of use-value. Gradually money, on account of its pliability, the limitless diversity of its possible use, its storability, its promise of limitless gratification, all the more tempting for being deferred, became the substitute for heaven. It attached to itself the libidinal forces which before had found religious and communal expression. Correspondingly, city life became rationalized slowly and painfully. And no economist or sociologist has yet found it economically or sociologically relevant to ask whether such rationalization suits human nature which, whatever it be, is not rational. Freud was the first non-romantic to appreciate the depth of the discontent that balanced the apparent advantages of civilization, most of all capitalist civilization.

Theology as well as book-keeping is rationalized, though the former had initiated the process before the latter had been thought of.[1] Learning is systematized as well as trade and industry. As the hierarchic order of society, and thus of the universe, begins to crumble, the useful takes the place of the exorbitant and absorbs into itself all the former's libidinal cathexes. Man exorbitantly multiplies utilities. This change too is slow. For a long time a mainly ideological democratization uses utilitarian exhortations as an ideological veiling of the sheer exorbitance of extortion in the pursuit of luxury. But finally the change is accomplished. Everything becomes a commodity or utility, even thinking and learning. These in turn, as everything else, are institutionalized. Institutions depend on a growing number of people wishing to use them and then produce and reproduce men who increasingly desire to make rational, measurable use of their thinking and learning. This is the bourgeoisification of knowledge, its utilitarianization – as before knowledge had been feudalized. No wonder that such learning cannot help seeing the whole of civilization in terms of utility, if only to justify itself, and all interests in terms of *Zins*, interest.

4   Communal functions became ritualized to a degree quite unknown in antiquity. Athenian rationalizations, though brilliant, were haphazard and volatile, even those of imperial Rome fragmentary (Weber, 1968, pp. 1–26). Contractual ties take the place of familial bonds. This change, a consequence of economic expansion, eases further economic expansion. The family becomes or longs to become a company. The company usurps the dignity and claims of the family. Wealth is separated from its owner and becomes capital. Prices are abstracted from the actual processes of production and exchange, profit from the products and labour which yield it. As trade expands, there is a proliferation of trades. Needs expand and with them the accumulations necessary to satisfy them. Later on the accumulation will become so rapid that the needs will have to be produced as well by means of an advertizing industry.

All this calls for expanding areas of security. The reasonably well-policed mercantile nation state begins to answer this demand. It takes over from the church, its securities take the place of those previously offered by the church. Via the half-way houses of Lutheranism and Calvinism, nationalism becomes the new rationalized religion. It builds and destroys a rapid succession of empires on which the sun never sets. The political and social developments coincide with scientific and technological preoccupations, are aided and abetted by them and in turn aid and abet those preoccupations. These further the rationalization processes not only by astonishingly expanding the areas of manipulability, but also by absorbing into themselves the creative libidinal forces which before then had found expression in mainly non-rational activities, such as feasting. Thus the *ratio* which demythologized the world became the myth itself.

193

Here again we meet the libidinization of the means, literally the means of production.

5   Does the crucial change consist in the emergence of empirical science and technology or, rather, in the fact that these related pursuits are now taken up with unprecedented seriousness and persistence? It would be interesting to trace their mutual inter-dependence and the intricate fashion in which this reflects the growing economic rationalizations to whose demands they can then respond ever more rationally. In this way the whole of life was and is being rationalized. Rationalization becomes the end of life. Simply: rationalization results in invention, from double-entry to pumps to guns to *Gleichschritt*, or goose-step. This in turn leads to a marked change in attitude, in expectation, from that of the farmer knowing the circle of ploughing, sowing, reaping, and that as much has to be put back as is taken out of the ground; to that of the miner who merely takes out and slowly learns to wish to take out more more quickly. Here man enters a different kind of cycle: the growing mechanicalness of the means increases the yield. The increase is measurable in precise terms. This makes possible the continuous measurable improvement and sophistication of the mechanisms of production which in turn increase the yield, and so *ad infinitum* or, rather, until total exhaustion of material or spirit.

And this too must be noted: mechanism and mechanization reflect back on the rationalism which produced them. It narrows as well as refines the scope of rationalization by restricting it to the elaboration of ever more precise and constricted methods for the attainment of ever more precisely defined and constricted ends measurable solely in terms of profit. The resultant love of and exclusive preoccupation with profit, as Weber reminded us, is different in kind from the age-old love of filthy lucre. It is the extrapolation of a different social consciousness. Profit becomes the ultimate sedimentation and abstraction of all forms of exorbitance of which, according to Durkheim, religion as society's self-glorification had been the original expression (Durkheim, 1968, p. 6n; cf. Weber, 1920; cf. also N. O. Brown, *Life against Death*, ch. 'Filthy Lucre', Wesleyan University Press, 1959).

6   Furthermore, there seem to be the following more specific chains of events and of changing conditions responsible for the rise of economic man. (a) Through the reformers, from Wycliffe to Calvin, through mystics like Sebastian Frank and through humanists, the church's dogmas were questioned on a deep emotive level. The actual arguments sound so tedious today, because they were sheer rationalizations. But precisely because of that, they at that time aided the general progress of rationalization. The conduct of argument, of reasonable discourse, was separated from its emotional

roots more completely than ever before. And here we realize that the diverse meanings of rationalization are not really separable. For in the various areas of experience rationalization functions, in one way or another, as the solution or dissolution or sheer evasion of problems created by the a-rational claims of living and living together. In the meantime the church's monolithic authority was eroded and with it the hierarchic, allegorical structure of the universe. Religious and metaphysical certainties faded, and it remains an open question, whether the growing affluence weakened the need of spiritual consolation, or whether the failing religious convictions produced the craving for new and more tangible certainties. Perhaps such questions, burning since the days of Marx, are the result of man's most arbitrary division of himself into body and soul.

(b) There is the growing problem of the individual *vis-à-vis* the mass – which is not to be mistaken for our central problem of the individual in society, Mass is desocietized, ultimately rationalized society. And in a completely rationalized universe man finds himself rootless and homeless, like a child in totally sterilized surroundings. This statement is almost statistically verifiable. Durkheim already made it in *Suicide* where he conceptualized societal rationalization as *anomie* (1952). When communal bonds have been loosened, and quite apart from the emotional havoc wrought by such a development in itself, contractual bonds take their place. These by their very character, by definition, inevitably favour the economically and politically stronger. They favour the more rational, because more rationalized, members of the society (cf. Weber, 1964, pp. 536, 562). Survival of the fittest was a social reality long before it became a biological ideology. Or rather, social actuality was by now so constituted that those who happened to survive were for that sole reason thought of as the fittest. Fittest for what? Well, for survival in a society which had mistaken 'making a living' for life, where success was proof and a proof success. As communal and familial ties failed, the cultivation of the personality or the surrogates that were taken for such a cultivation was a possibility only for the few. Only they could afford to play the elaborate charade of polite society which could parade as culture, because they could feed on the genius of the even fewer whom they could ostensibly exploit for their histrionic games. (The artist was indeed a flunkey and treated as such, while a grand event at the Royal Opera or the Royal Theatre during the eighteenth and nineteenth centuries epitomized the character of such a charading society.) Inexorably it becomes the aim of the many to belong to the few. This is at once the contradiction of early and not so early capitalism and its driving force. Society, no longer structured, becomes divided in a way different from former divisions. These divisions too become rationalized

195

into measurable differences between 'haves' and 'have-nots', the cultured and the illiterate who do not know the detailed conventions of the charade, between the burgher and the proletarian. It may well be that this glaring dichotomy merely brought into the open the true nature of all former societal divisiveness, that radical rationalization was also the revelation of social truth. Here we are noting the new aspects and awareness of social divisions, and how the resultant class consciousness was bound to falsify the situation of the envying as well as that of the envied.

(c) Rationalism presses towards the creation of larger units, as 'larger' and 'more' become the criteria of progress and success. The nation state emerged out of very complex religious, political and economic struggles, and gradually managed to focus its citizens' religious, economic and communal fervour on its being and aims. Thus developed the highly rationalized totalitarianism of the seventeenth and eighteenth centuries. This attempted total rationalization, embodied in the whole social and cultural patterning of 'polite society', the peculiar tableau-like culture of Baroque and Rococo, was a supreme achievement of sublimation. As rarely before, artificiality became human nature. To what extent did such artifacting prepare Western man still further for the rapid deracination which the rapid rational industrial progress needed and made inevitable? Soon the *ratio* of the age revealed itself as progressively and exclusively economic. Nations fought as bloodily and fervently over gold, sugar or slaves, as before they had fought over dogmas *ad majorem dei gloriam*. At the same time the peculiar irrationality of this *ratio* showed itself: economy, also in its connotation of thrift, which became the overruling consideration and interest, was both stimulated by and at the service of an exorbitance of conspicuous consumption practised by the few. Armies and navies were expanded and expended, hundreds of thousands of soldiers and millions of slaves died to enable a few to live in a luxury which mistakenly and vainly tried to verify childhood and adolescent phantasies.

The heaven of the many was bought up by the few and 'no trespassing' notices affixed and enforced by ruthless game-keepers. Religion and morality, as army, industry and politics, were geared to the maintenance and protection of those enclaves of snobbery, of tableaux and charades, and the whole structure was glorified as Empire. What made such an impossible reality possible and even lasting, if not the belief of the many that their own childhood and adolescent phantasies of omnipotence were actually lived out by the few and were therefore a promise and possibility for all? The few knew that it was not so. They managed to conceal the knowledge under a defence system of politeness or mannerisms which could integrate into its purposeless purposes even the critiques of the artists which at times threatened to give away the secret. The division between heaven and hell had become a social reality, though hell was largely constituted by induced envy and heaven made no more than tolerable by the dread of falling out of it. (Cf. French, English and Russian literature on high society.)

In this way the irrational rationalism carried within itself the force that was to dominate the earth: the passionate pursuit of economic ends, of ever-accelerating profit. At first there had been the hope of finding, and finding available, El Dorado. Then, as this receded in the very process of being conquered and exploited, the pursuit of profit continued for its own sake. For whenever heaven proves unattainable, the means for attaining it take its place. Puritanism moreover, as Weber has shown, had made its distinct contribution to this process. By separating the economic pursuit *in toto* from the attainment of salvation, i.e. by finalizing the dichotomy of the natural and the supernatural, and by yet keeping the two in continuous tension and treating the one as the measure of the other, it hastened and intensified the libidinization of the means. This totalized economic driving force which dichotomized society right into its family structure, increasingly imbued the many with the phantasy desires of the few. All religious intensity has gone into envy born of destitution. Marx, especially the young Marx, belongs to the few who not only recognized the revolutionary potential of this envy, but its fundamental dangers. Precisely because the contemporary world has succumbed to these dangers, has simply managed to universalize the original mercantile phantasy and is now trying to do the same for the non-Western world, Marx's early insights are still of importance (as against Tucker, 1961, 'Marx and the Present Age'; cf. also pp. 123–61).

Today the danger is real that the West, via the totalitarian mechanism of the stock exchange and the in-fighting of giant companies, will complete the proletarianization of two-thirds of mankind and will thus finally accomplish its own. Here I wish to emphasize: gigantic social-economic-technical transformations were achieved in pursuit of either a receding phantasy, the mercantilistic dream of Baroque and Rococo; or of a puritan, ever more abstract goal, profit, measurable gain, as indication of salvation. Contemporary society epitomizes the confluence of the two: profit and phantasy, status and luxury, success and glamour, are one and the same. Suburbia and exurbia, as well as the vast industrial constellations all over the globe, and the universal threat of pollution and waste, make an ironic comment on the thoughts and hopes of Comte and Spencer, on pragmatic optimism, on scientism and positivism in general. The despair and protest of romantic poets and philosophers appear more realistic, more scientific, today. Likewise the uncertainties, heart-searchings and confusions of German social thinkers, from the young Marx to the old Adorno, seem closer to the social actuality than the certainties of more western sociologists, economists and politicians. (Yet even they have been integrated into the universal mechanization, rationalization, bureaucratization, as 'prophets of doom', spine chillers, entertainers and as academy fodder.)

To sum up the various trends just hinted at in the preceding paragraphs, we might find Sombart's formula helpful: they all express the change from *Nahrung* to *Erwerb*, from a subsistence to a profit economy – both terms to be understood as 'ideal types'.

Nahrung means, at least in intention, 'to each according to his needs within his station'. The economy is geared to the attainment and preservation of such a state of affairs. Sombart maintained that *Nahrung* mentality survived into late capitalist days. Weber still found it among Polish agricultural workers: when their Prussian employers introduced piece-work to improve performance, the workers were inclined to stop as soon as they had earned the equivalent of their former wages. As against this, profit means gain, abstracted from both the means of its procurement and the 'purely human needs' and expectations of the executants. It means the absolutization of gain. *Nahrung* implies a transcendent faith, religious, ethical or mythical. It also implies a hierarchic structure, a community with its ritualized possibilities of communion without which there can be no unambiguous communication. It implies a farming rather than a mining ethos, a more or less conscious metaphysical attitude. (What B. Bernstein calls 'positional attitudes'.) *Nahrung* implies respect for and, up to a point, bondage to tradition, to that which defines, shapes and directs a man's expectations (cf. Lévi-Strauss, 1966, pp. 1–16).

Profit economy creates its own hierarchies which gradually usurp the place of all others. This may be the most striking sociological confirmation of its religious or pseudo-religious character. As any other attitude, profit economy is based on metaphysical assumptions. Yet these remain implicit and are always ideologically displaced, *verschoben*. *Erwerb* therefore cannot afford to deny the attitudes of *Nahrung* openly. On the contrary, it might try to assume them. In practice it relegates those attitudes to the second and third place, together with their explicit assumptions. The paradox, however, remains: profit is easily defined, yet its aims remain undefinable, except in terms of profit. Profit is the end of profit, and the end of profit is profit. It seems exclusively concerned with the measurable and the apparently concrete. Yet its objectives remain totally abstract. Does this paradox dissolve once it is realized that measurability, quantity, is already an abstraction, *the* antithesis of the concrete, namely the personal? Profit produces increasing specialization in pursuits that remain unspecifiable, except in terms of specialization or of profitability – economic, scientific, academic, military. *Erwerb* implies and produces a profusion of expertise, illimitable objectives with their corresponding objectivities, namely specializations. Profit economy is the Calvinist God made immanent and yet remaining absolute. It is also a childhood phantasy, i.e. the displacement of a childhood experience of deprivation, made absolute. (As the phantasy of omnipotence is reactivated by actual impotence.) Profit economy has to be understood as a form of radical alienation, schizophrenia. It may also be understood, as by the young Marx, as a pointer towards just that limitless individual potential, towards the infinite variety and possibilities of human relationships, which are now curbed and frustrated by it, and which nevertheless have become possibilities, only because the libidinal investment in profit had goaded man out of his traditional communal conditioning.

Causes?

I have tried to indicate a certain change in social consciousness which certain German thinkers believed to be profound and constitutive, also unique. Were they right? Was it as fundamental, as singular, as total as they believed? On the other hand, were they doing more than repeating on a higher level of refinement, and with a pessimistic twist, the sweeping evolutionary generalizations of a Comte or Spencer, who in turn had continued and formalized the Enlightenment attempts at universal history, which had been a secularization of *Heilsgeschichte* which goes back to St Augustine and beyond him to 'J', the oldest Old Testament historian? Were the Germans merely writing *Unheilsgeschichte* which had not lacked representatives from Thucydides to Spengler (cf. Meinecke, 1959; Dilthey, 1914, vol. 2)? Had man really changed significantly? Pareto, for instance, fills his four volumes of general sociology with wide-ranging anecdotes to illustrate the unchangingness of man's basic attitudes, which had been noticed by the author of *Ecclesiastes* 2,300 years before. Is it possible that these invariables are of a kind which prevents all changes from penetrating far below the surface? Freud had reminded us of what is implicit in the fact that we are all born from a mother and into a family situation which has not changed radically during the last four to six millennia, certainly not in as far as the young child's constitutive experiences of the surrounding adults and siblings and their relationships are concerned. This de-fines man most radically and lastingly. I as much as the eponymous hero am victim and expression of the 'Oedipus complex' –

199

or of whatever Freud intended to denote by this term. Nor are matters made to look more hopeful by Freud's successors – e.g. M. Klein, A. Freud, D. W. Winnicott – who claim that what Freud himself had understood by the Oedipus complex takes shape even earlier, in the relationship between mother and child, which is even more unchanging. (Will it change now when for the first time women are free of repeated pregnancies or the continuous fear of them and may discover in themselves as yet unexpressed possibilities?)

(In this context, French rationalism presents a peculiar mixture of beliefs. From Montesquieu to Lévi-Strauss, French thinkers acknowledge change, even progress. Yet their rationalism makes them see the various stages of human evolution as comparable. So by implication they demonstrate their belief in the essentially unchanging nature of man. Durkheim, for instance, thought that the study of totemistic religion could directly illuminate contemporary social actuality. Lévi-Strauss is at great pains to show that the medicine man and the scientist are essentially alike. Which may be taken to mean that for French thinkers even the advent of civilization did not make an essential difference to human nature. As against this extreme position, but still at variance with that of most German scholars, it could be maintained that a change which may be called fundamental took place as civilization became established with all its patriarchal compulsions and the consequent libidinal displacements. Freud can be said to support this view, and among contemporaries Adorno, Marcuse, Heidegger, Mumford – to give an odd selection.)

We return to those who agree on assigning a special significance to the change here considered and notice immediately that they cannot agree as to its nature, origin, time of origin, cause, extent, depth. Was the capitalist spirit the outcome of a conjunction of multitudinous events, as Sombart argues? Or could those multitudinous events in turn be reduced to a more general tendency, as Scheler tried to show and, in great detail and most brilliantly, Borkenau? Had Weber demonstrated that the protestant ethic was the efficient cause of an attitude which found expression in that specific form of capitalism which conquered Europe and now dominates the earth? Is the controversy between Weberites and Marxists due to the fact that both sides claim to have isolated *the* cause? That both treat as cause what might be no more than an aspect of complex and ever shifting patterns of interdependencies? Finally, how can a change of social consciousness be investigated at all by those who are the product of that change, whose intellectual tools for grasping it have been forged by it? How can one beware of missing the point? Of not being totally tautologous in an effort to be objective? And what does the isolation of a cause or of causes contribute to an understanding of societal change?

The problem of causality has caused much perplexity since the days of Hume. According to Dilthey it had already perplexed the late scholastics (1914, vol. 1, pp. 319–23). To Duns Scotus and Occam, as against the Thomists, it presented itself in this form: Is the will or the reason of God the cause of creation, i.e. is causation-creation wilful and free or rational and determined? If the latter, effects can be predicted. If the former, causes can at best be deduced *post festum* as a possible additional source of illumination. In their insistence on God's wilfulness Scotus and Occam reflected the break-up of the old order which no longer appeared as inevitable and therefore as rational, but as something that raised doubts and also intimations of possibilities of change (Borkenau, 1934, pp. 29–33). As against Hume's radical doubts, Kant once more made causality philosophically respectable. He de-transcendentalized it and anchored it securely in the head and heart of man – as pure and practical causality. As against Descartes, and in a way very different from Leibniz, he acknowledged two separate causalities, of intellect and will, of Aquinas and Occam. And never the twain can meet, except in the philosopher's dissertation. This did not make things easier for subsequent German philosophers. Hegel and Marx made comparable if contradictory attempts to bridge the gap between the two causalities. The former posited the spirit, the latter the means of production, as transcendental and immanent, as the matrix of all causation. For Schopenhauer and Nietzsche the will was the *Ursache*, in the sense of both efficient and primal cause; for phenomenology it was the subjective intellect. Among social thinkers Dilthey and Weber stuck most faithfully to the Kantian duality.

In the meantime, and much to the envy of social philosophers, the physical scientists, restricting themselves to Kant's rationalizing causality, continued on their way untroubled by epistemological hesitations and with astonishing success. But then they were active in areas of observation and experimentation, where the observer, for better and for worse, is in control, where causality functions as definition, and where the 'it works' and according to the observers' intention is the only test of validity. Here causality is descriptive, de-fining, narrowly purposeful (cf. Popper, 1969, pp. 255–8). Where the observer is implicated in that which he is observing, where observation is simultaneously self-observation, where the observing self itself is questioned, the category of causality remains problematical. This was precisely what Kant had realized. Yet his treatment of the problem did not lessen the ambivalence. No person was to be used as a means to an end, he said. He did not see that within his understanding of science when applied to humans, the person was already being used as means and that this reflected the fact of European society where the person is being used for ulterior ends all the time. Kant more than any other made the *machtgeschützte* (police-protected) inwardness of Luther and the German pietists philosophically arguable, by creating a sphere of free-will causality, free self-determination, which at no point interfered with the scientific causality which mirrored the social structures and intentions, the social reality.

In human affairs we deal with motives as causes, and motives are complex, future-directed as well as past-conditioned, determined by phantasies as much as or more than by reality and its principles, shifting as well as shifty. Motives have to be understood rather than defined – as against the theory and practice of the natural scientist who need not understand what he defines. Whatever definition may have to be attempted, for the sake of convenience or of a limited objective, remains tied to *Verstehen*, i.e. it remains flexible and cannot function with tautological precision, cannot be used as a tool, except within a strictly circumscribed objective. If at all, the sociologist deals with causes mainly in the Hegel-Marxian sense of the term, as with those powers or tendencies which underlie and substantiate motives, and of which the motives are manifestations in personal consciousness. We might look at such causes from a strictly materialistic or idealistic point of view, as working mechanically or of necessity. In which case we could by-pass all epistemological questions. If we remain dialectical in our approach, we have to take into account that those causes owe their moving or motivating power to some kind of correspondence or interplay between themselves and both the motives they inspire and the confluence of motives which once constituted them and continues to constitute them *as* powers and tendencies. For neither the simplest tool nor the most complex machinery, the most self-evident idea or the most elaborate mythology or ideology, merely conditions us. It is given its power to condition us to the extent to which it is the 'vectorization' of intentions, of social-individual intensionality. The complexity here is beyond apprehension and would remain so, even if we could make clear distinctions between motive and motive, cause and cause, motive and cause, between what we can *wissen* and what we can *kennen*. The post-Freudian necessity to take notice of unconscious motivation as well compounds what is bound to remain confusion, as long as we opt for causal approaches to social problems.

Causality, as Hume argued, is a metaphysical concept or a pragmatic, i.e. pseudo-metaphysical one. It is a matrix of possible assumptions, of assumptions concerning possibilities, a system of co-ordinates. Causal thinking expresses, functionalizes, vectorizes, particular intentions of social consciousness. As these, in the last analysis, are rooted in individual intentions or intensions, individual consciousness as such cannot be grasped by means of its own intentions, for the tool as well as the hand and mind which handle it remain part of that which is meant to be grasped. Therefore, when man looks at himself, at another man, a group of men, when consciousness scrutinizes consciousness and wishes to communicate its findings in comprehensible terms, in terms acceptable to social consciousness, man is no longer the sovereign de-finer. He is part of the definition and each definition has to be incorporated into that which is being defined.

As physicist, chemist, biologist, I can isolate certain precise phenomena as data. I may forget that strictly speaking they are not given, that I give them their givenness (cf. Spiegelberg, 1964, pp. 536, 548). I may abstract certain qualities, for instance the quality called quantity, and restrict myself to the observation of arbitrarily chosen interactions within that abstraction at second remove. Arbitrary means wilful: I choose to observe what and how I will, because it serves my purpose which is my will. As Heidegger put it, science like metaphysics is the will to will. Can the sociologist or *Geisteswissenschaftler* profitably follow similar methods of abstraction? As we saw, in his sphere it is at least possible that dealing with abstractions simply means not dealing with his subject matter. Or is he aiming at similar possibilities of manipulation? Of whom by whom? Even then he will discover that it is not only harder to isolate a motive than a cause, but to isolate himself from motives that might distort the motive he is investigating. Moreover, motive, unlike cause, is always more than a definition. The movement from motive to motive or from cause via motive to cause does not only take place in the enquirer's mind, but also in that of mover and moved. At each step of that trebly circuitous route there are chances, almost certainties, of distortion, displacement, projection, repression. (Freud showed how these mechanisms not only make it difficult to 'get at' the real cause, but that they have their own causality and rationality.) The more the investigator concentrates on details in order to obviate the chances of misinterpretation or subjectivity, the more he is likely to reflect unreflectingly the prevailing distortions of the social consciousness which he shares with his subject. (Simmel's question, 'How is society possible?' consciously echoing Kant's, 'How is nature possible?' is different in kind.)

The German penchant for the historical approach makes the problem of causality particularly vexing for them. Historical events are unrepeatable and the multiplicity of their causes and causal interrelations is, in the strict sense of the word, illimitable. Hence Dilthey's efforts' to *verstehen* were attempts to get through the historical events at something beyond mere historicity, amenable to some form of generalization and *Wesenschau* (glimpse of the very essence) to some kind of causal interpretation; yet to achieve this in such a fashion that the historicalness and uniqueness of each event need not be jeopardized. He was aware that *Verstehen* in this area implied a kind of intuition which was bound to contain elements of something he could not help considering as irrationality compared with the strict rationality of science and economics he was aspiring to. So he could only hope that the multiplicity of such intuitions, the fact that they were permitted a voice only after painstaking discipline of research and were then to be exposed to full inter-subjective criticism, would reduce the irrational element. He was not yet sufficiently aware that it was the arbitrary narrowing of the concept of *ratio* by scientism which had reduced most forms of human *Verstehen* to the status of irrationality. Nor does he seem to have wondered enough whether the break-through of historism as then understood was to take the historian to generalizations rather than to the individual which historiography anyway – even that of the historist – had already abstracted away. Nevertheless his difficulties were big enough. For if it is true that scientism had become the metaphysics of the age, and even Dilthey was aware of this possibility as a danger, if its rigorous externalization and logical procedure had become the sole criterion for truth and fact, *Einfühlung* (empathy) and *Erinnern* (re-membering) seem to have neither validity nor solidity. It is a contradiction in terms to justify *Erinnern* in terms of *Entäussern*. Moreover, externalization is the method of mastery. *Erinnern* is not a method at all. It cannot be, for who could be sure here that method might not conceal or distort the essence of what is to be *erinnert*? Nor is it a mastering, though Hegel saw it as such. *Erinnern* is mental and spiritual, a *geistige* osmosis and symbiosis, a readiness for unreserved dialogue and intercourse.

Here dialectics and phenomenology could join hands. For the phenomenological intention can be spelled out like this: to purify the channels of perception, to learn to see, hear, smell, taste, feel, without prejudiced and prejudicial conceptualizations, until we really are seeing, hearing, smelling, tasting, feeling. But also to come to understand what we actually are understanding, how and why we are trying to understand. Without denying the total subjectivity of perception and understanding, their character of *Erinnern* (re-membering), phenomenology believes that understanding need not be an imposition, need not narrow itself to pre-determined and pre-judiced methods of verification. It may open itself without reserve to and remain in dialogue and intercourse with perception and what is being perceived, precisely because it is not asserting to be in touch with anything else or wishing to be in control.

Phenomenology does not see reason as precariously lording it over an alien world. It understands understanding as an intensional and intentional wholeness within which inner and outer have only relative significance, because understanding is as much a response to what is being perceived, as the percept already is a response to our intentional and understanding perceiving. Phenomenology may be said to renew the Hegelian intentions without their pretensions and in such a way that dialectics could become phenomenology or vice versa. Naturally such an approach has its own difficulties: a tendency either to proliferate limitlessly, to get lost in detail, shadings, in doubts concerning accuracy, adequacy, exhaustiveness; or to make an arbitrary stop and to come to inevitably premature conclusions on open or hidden ideological or utilitarian grounds or on account of personal predilections – and simply because one feels unjustified, if one does not arrive at conclusions. But dare the *Geisteswissenschaftler* hope to find an approach devoid of difficulties?[2]

Unfortunately and because of Hegel's usage, *Erinnern* – like *Verstehen* and *Dialektik* – cannot easily shake off certain cannibalistic connotations. It retains associations and is at least partially the expression of childhood phantasies and needs of omnipotence, of swallowing the earth, internalizing the whole of a troublesome reality. Dilthey's more mature understanding of *Erinnern* remains troubled by the powerful Hegelian echoes as well as by those of an equally cannibalistic positivism which cannot help identifying Hegel's *Geist* with causality, understanding with identifying of causes.

Tröltsch devoted a whole book (1922b) to the problems of historism which, in the last resort, dissolve themselves into two questions: What is the nature of historical causality? What is its use? i.e. what has been established, what has understanding gained, once causality has been established? His first question, especially after one has followed him through so many scholarly intellectualizations, leads anew to the Heideggerian doubt: does the historic discipline, like others, conceal and distort rather than reveal and clarify its *Sache* (subject matter)? And how can it be *sachlich* (objective) while it is not sure of its *Sache* or whether it is doing it justice? It is possible that the desire to establish, above all, historical causality is merely an expression of the historian's limitation, his dependence on definitions in an area where they do not apply, where they are merely the straw the drowning man grasps for fear of perishing in an ocean of facts – and perhaps because he has not yet learned to swim. The very insistence on causality may prevent the historian from actually seeing history; partly because he wishes not to see, partly because he cannot help wishing to subsume the whole of history to categories that express temporary and partial interests and intentions. We need cause, if only to be able to apportion guilt.

A deep-seated atavism seems to lurk in our predilection for causality: to find the cause is a moral, religious, magical undertaking. It is also a personal compulsion, as illustrated by that Oedipus who might well have given his name to a very different complex for that reason. To know the cause, to be able to name it, gives both power and righteousness. To establish a causal connection bestows significance on the whole and fulfils redemptive functions. (Eliade claims that an Indian philosopher would see the European preoccupation with history, cause and origins, as an effort on the part of those who have lost the experience of eternity to regain it by means of the exhaustiveness of their investigations into the time processes. 1960, ch. 9, esp. pp. 234–6.) The discovery of a cause absolves, cleanses, renews. Causal thinking seems to enable me to integrate reality as a whole, it is another expression of an infantile phantasy. This is not intended to invalidate causal thinking as such but its totalitarian claims. In science the causal formula has indeed proved to possess magic powers. This does not absolve us from the question whether it is applicable in the field of inter-subjective actuality – unless we wish to exercise magic power just here.

Weber's method for establishing historico-sociological causality, for isolating the cause or causal complex responsible for the specificity of an event or situation, is a *tour de force*. Only Weber could have conceived and tried actually to apply it (Weber, 1920, pp. 12–13; cf. Parsons, 1968, pp. 610–11). For Weber the cause is that something in the absence of which a certain event would not have occurred or would not have occurred thus. Yet even Weber could not prove, not in his three-volumed *Religionssoziologie*, that and how even the finest discrimination could ever demonstrate that another cause or another constellation of events or causes could not have produced the same effect, or the same cause(s) a different effect. History is unrepeatable except in the imagination, in *Erinnerung*. Only there can the necessary process of elimination be conducted. And this precisely is our problem: Whether our imagination, when it is deployed in causal categories and methodologies and in possibly self-defeating and self-contradictory processes of elimination, has not thereby so cluttered and shuttered itself that it is prevented from seeing what actually happened.

To understand the conditionedness of any prevailing intellectual constellation and climate and thus the social consciousness which expresses it or out of which it grew, one must be able to compare one constellation with another. Though the question whether this is possible, whether and how one can step into a partial neutrality where alone comparing becomes feasible, remains open. Here it becomes clear that subjectivity and inter-subjectivity is unavoidable.

Which once again poses the question of relativism. Now as long as relativism is seen as a bogey, as not only by Marxists but also by scientists, its problematics can be evaded only by an act of faith. However, it has not been demonstrated that relativism in the social sciences, as relativity in physics, may not prove the as yet most adequate approach to an understanding of our most relative human situations (cf. Mannheim, 1960, pp. 239–56). 'Truth', or whatever we may call that which is meant to function as 'truth' once did, may be fluid.[3] Then understanding would consist in the appreciation of all things and all reflections of them and on them as fluid, as Heraclitus already had thought and feared. In that case our methods of research would have to reflect this as well as reflect on it, and equally our methods of communication. For if communion is our basic actuality, it subsists in the flowing. There would be no longer the necessity or even possibility of holding one view against another, to prove in order to disprove, to strive for even provisional fixation. And what is proof if not a fixation, the procedure of fixing something by hammerblows. On the contrary, any concept, as inevitable, at least temporary fixation, would be under suspicion of falsification. The truth would reside in scholarly antiphons, in the dance of contradictory and complementary insights and apprehensions. Striving to understand would no longer be competitive but merely the effort to play one's part to the best of one's capacity. And this would be committal to the 'truth'.

Moreover, if it be true that truth subsists in the fluidity of all things, in the committal not to this or that but to the flowing – as psycho-analysis and phenomenology as well as some Eastern philosophies seem, at times, to see it – we may be permitted to suggest first, that there could be as much truth or validity in viewing economics and politics as the epiphenomena of slow changes in the underlying psychic structure or actuality as vice versa, and second, that the scientists' conviction which practically treats the psyche or spirit as non-existent is legitimate only as long as it is balanced by the understanding that what the scientists treat as reality is *maya*, illusion, for the individual psyche. If this suggestion is allowed, we should not be left with another either/or, but with possibilities of new dialogues: between Marx and Hegel, Freud and Lukács, Adorno and Heidegger, between psychology and sociology, economics and epistemology, between philosophy and poetry, the *Geisteswissenschaften* and religion or mysticism (cf. Dilthey, 1914, vol. 1, pp. 138, 319, 383–6; also vol. 5, pp. 273–303).*

* I understand one aspect of Hindu philoscphy in this way: history, politics, economics, the sciences, i.e. what we think of as the social actuality, is an unbreakable and inescapable net of *maya*, which is woven by the guilt and errors of the self which has lost itself or refuses to acknowledge its self. As

For instance, much can be gained by listening attentively if cautiously to the advocacy of men like W. James, C. S. Peirce, G. H. Mead, K. Popper. They represent a liberalizing as well as liberal approach which, though it may not prove adequate for appreciating the human experience in its totality, should nevertheless remain an element in any future effort to understand. All the more I wish to stress that the antiphonal approach here hinted at is essentially different from their republics of argument, of conjectures and refutations, of symbolic interactionism, of pragmata sorting themselves out for the greater good of the greater number. Their *geisteswissenschaftlicher* positivism, as that of Dilthey and Weber, still mirrors the externalizing methods of the natural sciences. They all believe in objectivity and truth as something existing outside the dialogue and fixed enough to encourage the hope of a steady approximation to them. Their attitude to the inter-subjectivity of academic or general intellectual procedure is merely permissive, genially condescending. The free exchange of subjective views is encouraged, because it is believed to result in the gradual sedimentation of objective truth. Here the metaphysical, ontological, realistic assumptions of liberalism shine through and reveal it as a merely more jovial version of patriarchal authoritarianism in a power-structured and divided society. It was inevitable that under liberal auspices aristocracy gave place to meritocracy, to the Platonic ideal of timocracy, which simply reaffirms the divisions and is in no sense their *Aufhebung*, merely another form of oligarchy. Inter-subjectivity remains subordinated to some intensional objective mistaken for objectivity *per se*, the dialogue to the result it is expected to yield, man to his conceptualizations.

It is interesting to note in this connection how causality functions in their understanding of the nature of argumentation. It not merely defines and redefines, delimits and circumscribes, universes of discourse, areas of investigation. Nor is its function exhausted in the increasingly more stringent exclusion of all areas of basic disagreement or of those in which questions of agreement or disagreement do not arise. In their understanding of argumentation they insist that the accretion of agreed sedimentation, the sedimentation of such stringently delimited agreements on causality, is our approximation to the truth, is our truth. Once more the onto-

the lost self sets out on the journey towards itself which is also *the* self, it comes to recognize reality as illusion. Nothing except the self's acceptance of the self, the subject's full acknowledgment of its unrelieved subjectivity, can dissolve the illusion, the belief in the fixity of reality. If I am right, the elaboration of such thinking could be as illuminating an interpretation of psycho-analytical insights, as these in turn could illuminate Eastern thinking for us. The implications for social philosophy and sociology could be revolutionary.

logical, even magical implications are revealed and show themselves to be inherent in the very character of academic, causal, logical argument.

This is not surprising when we recall that academic argumentation took shape in an age that believed in ontic truth. The debate or disputation circled round a real, objective, substantive thusness. Its strictly defined task was the uncovering of this thusness by means of be-cause. The rules were elaborated to aid disputants in this task. The adequacy of the final representation in the form of conclusion redefined the truth. So belief in causality and the continued use of a medieval form of argumentation perpetuate ontological assumptions which are at odds with other assumptions of contemporary scientific disputants. This produces a deep-seated emotional as well as intellectual confusion which cannot be diagnosed or cured by means of the argumentation which produces it.

As against these implications of conventional academic, scientific procedure, inter-subjectivity and its truth is consciously nominalistic. This truth subsists in the flux of the dialogue. It now is here, now there, is in the movement of thinking and communing. Or rather: it has the chance, the possibility, of coming to be in the movement, for not every movement as such is truth. To believe that would be relativism indeed. Therefore to accept fluidity as truth, truth as being fluid, implies the subordination of objectives to inter-subjectivity. The conversation or intercourse itself is the end, *telos*. The objectives and their objectivities are means. They come and go, leaving behind, as sedimentation, not truth but utilities and conveniences, *pragmata* and *chremata*, also food for further thought and conversation which remain fluid.

Dilthey and Meinecke were still historians of ideas. They investigated areas of abstraction where causality can be established with a fair amount of plausibility. They could not yet ask questions like: Did Machiavelli, Hobbes, Frederick the Great, influence or merely reflect the structures and actualities of their respective societies and of their tensions? Did they discover a science of politics, or did they merely manage to produce a justification in rationalistic terms of what politics had always been? While certainly enabling politicians to vindicate their policies more rationally and to act more rationally in Weber's sense of this term, it is not clear whether the work of the great political scientists helped politicians to act more rationally in Marx's or Freud's or even Pareto's sense. It supplied new 'derivations' for old 'residues', contemporary rationalizations for hoary intentions (cf. Pareto, 1935, vol. 1). What gave to European Machiavellianism that peculiar coherence and supremacy which, according to Weber, Indian Machiavellianism did not achieve?

According to Bloch – and Borkenau – Machiavelli proclaimed intellectual mastery, or the intellect as mastery, in politics, before Descartes did the same in philosophy and Galileo in science; but not before rationality had become rationalization in finance, trade and industry (Borkenau, 1934, p. 103; Bloch, 1970, pp. 1108–12). This suggests an underlying constellation of intensions to give cohesion to the diverse forms of mastering which in turn are the historic sedimentations of those intensions. Bloch suggests that in *Il Principe* Machiavelli managed to clarify, systematize and condense, a prevailing state of affairs, and that for this reason it caught on much better than the other parts of the *Discorsi* which may have more fully expressed the authors' heart and mind. So the question obtrudes, especially when one is thinking in causal categories, that if so-called influential, original intellectual works merely reflect and articulate the underlying actualities of a situation, unable essentially to modify them, what is their status? Can one believe in an even temporary adequacy of such clarifications, unless one assumes an underlying directedness of history, Hegelian, Marxian or Crocean? Apart from such assumptions those works would be *de trop*, historians' fodder, the epiphenomenal chatter accompanying reality as the splashing wavelets indicate the flow of the river. Unless we dare understand reflection as possibly creative, initiating activity, and as such outside causality, we cannot explain its existence. For an explanation is either creative-reflective or non-existent as explanation.

No creativity is *ex nihilo*, unmediated and unconditioned. We may no longer understand it naïvely as positivistic, as if it posited reality; nor as realistic, as if it simply mirrored reality. We may try to understand the creative aspect of thinking as dialectical or dialogical, as an integral part of that very inter-subjectivity which reflection constitutes, even as it is constituted by the inter-subjectivity; in as far as conversing, communing, inter-coursing, it the human actuality. One might also put it this way: the influential thinkers of the past may merely have been articulating things-as-they-are-or-happen-to-be. Their clarifications, to the extent to which they become and remain part and parcel of a continuing conversation, not argument, create their own historical corpus and reality, as utopian possibilities or hope-principle (Bloch, 1970, pp. 177, Marx quotation, 217–18).

Again we must distinguish between conversation and argument: for example, Sombart believed that a multiplicity of causes was responsible for capitalist developments. Weber emphatically rejects his contention that not only Protestants but all kinds of religious emigrants, including the Jews, played an essential part in the rise of capitalism. As always, Weber's argumentation has the intensity and compulsiveness of the neurotic which appears overwhelming, especially when, as in this case, it is backed by an extraordinary intellect and phenomenal erudition. Looking back at it now, one sees it was not only inconclusive but inconcludable, and much passion and intellectual acumen misspent. This argument, to be joined by many other scholars, not only illustrates the futility of arguments where laurels, as in war, go to the strongest and not necessarily to the one who is right; but also the futility of reproducing and continuing it by trying to argue the respective merits of each separate point.

Sombart's painstaking and comprehensive analysis of the genesis of modern capitalism (1927) raises a further question concerning the functioning of causality: given the constellation of the Carolingian age from where he starts, was the development towards capitalism and our peculiar kind of capitalism inevitable? Would a Carolingian Laplace, having been put in possession of all the relevant data, have been able to predict the actual development? Sombart himself would have doubted such Laplacean possibilities even in respect of much more limited changes, in that he could treat the technological revolution as something in the nature of a surprise. Of course such questioning of causality is proved nonsensical by the fact that one can never gain possession of all the facts and can never, until afterwards – if then – hope to be able to assess the relevance of those one had been led to choose at one time or another. Moreover, sociologists, economists, historians, have as yet been unable to predict anything accurately, except sometimes developments that had been accurately predicted without their help. But if social necessity cannot be demonstrated, if it is impossible precisely to isolate and dovetail social effect and cause, is this not one more reason for dropping the word and concept 'cause' from sociological usage and trying to modify one's thinking which has succumbed so totally to the habit and fascination of causality (cf. Popper, 1960, chs 1 and 2, esp. ch. 1, para. 6)?

Moreover, if causality could be established, the causal thinker would simply reason himself out of the market, out of his necessary existence. His thinking would become an aesthetic or, rather, anaesthetic exercise. Once more scientific insistence would lead to the point where the attempt at mastery is revealed as enslavement, especially in the social sciences where the attempted mastery is over man himself. Yet this paradoxical effort reflects the social reality of a divided society. Weber's labours culminated in the challenge to obey the summons of a positivistically-oriented day, which sounds remarkably like Nelson's call to his sailors at Trafalgar or Frederick's to his grenadiers at Leuthen – '*Kerls, wollt ihr denn ewig leben?*' – like the call of any general or admiral or managing director to his company. For the summons is to engage with open eyes in the endless and endlessly superseded struggle to understand that which understanding must not hope to affect. It may well be that Weber was driven to this point of tragic resignation, because he could conceive of scientific or rational thinking in terms of causal thinking only.

This, as we have seen, though not necessarily leading to truth, certainly not to *the* truth, proves useful when applied in areas where manipulation is the end, where the ends are means, namely utilities, and not 'ends in themselves'. When applied outside the areas of possible or necessary manipulation, causal thinking betrays its theological genesis. It is rooted in the need of some ultimate certainty or dependence, of something to depend on; it feeds on age-old magical connotations and associations of power. It is the modernized longing to find that which will finally vindicate the thought that found and thought it and thus will give power to that – namely the thinking – which is experienced as powerless in itself (cf. Heidegger, 1954, pp. 71–3, 87–8, 118, 121 *inter alia*; 1967, pp. 166, 174; also 8–18, 80ff). Causal thinking is one form of expressing the wish to find the thought's justification outside the thinking, the meaning of the dialogue outside the dialoguing, of human relationships outside the actual intercourse. It implies the belief of magic that to know, to know the name, to know-what-is-what and what-is-so, gives one power over or the power of that which one knows. And be-cause we do not yet know the possibilities of inter-subjectivity, have not yet explored the fulness of inter-coursing, we feel alone and impotent like a forsaken baby and, like the baby, desire power over that which we cannot or dare not relate to.

Theology rationalized magic and turned the belief in manipulation into belief in and dependence on a god who would do the manipulating for us. Science re-rationalizes theology and restores confidence in direct manipulation, leaving *Ursache*, cause, primal cause, to function as god. It is therefore no accident but inherent in the very intension of causal thinking, that it always finds itself compelled, wishes to be compelled, to acknowledge as ultimates: energy and power, the former in the natural, the latter in the social sciences.

I have already mentioned how passionately Weber believed that all social achievements are the products of power, that he would subordinate all other considerations to those of power, of power politics and national power. We can now appreciate why this had to be so for the most causal and rationalistic thinker among German sociologists. Weber believed in power as the old Puritan believed in God and his predestination. He threw himself into the investigation of causality as the Puritan had thrown himself into labouring: to confound the devil and all his works and to find in the adequacy of his labours a confirmation of his justification or salvation which the labours themselves could not effect. Like the Calvinists he understood so well, Weber did not believe he could change the nature of his God by such efforts, nor his attitude towards and plans for his servant. The efforts could at best prove that he had always been justified. The intensity of his polemics against any objections to his views was obviously not motivated by his rationalism, but by that Puritan passion of which the rationalism itself was merely one expression. His analysis of Protestantism and capitalism was an oblique self-analysis, a titanic detour to a never consciously looked for or found self-understanding. For, again like the Puritan, he would have considered the quest for self-knowledge futile and presumptuous. Only God knew and God could not be known. He may eventually send the Messiah who would know. In the meantime the professor was not to play the prophet. He was to turn his attention away from himself and all human concerns, even from God, towards the processes of a totally demythologized nature and society, a world fallen from grace and at the mercy of necessity. This research is to investigate, asking for no reward, and thus becoming, like life itself, a kind of purgatory for the shriving of the elect.

The problem of causality is alive in every work of Weber. In the early pages of *Wirtschaft und Gesellschaft* he is working out in rapidly proliferating details the basic general sociological categories and the conceptual framework; later on those more specific ones appertaining to economics, politics, law, religion, class. In whatever way he over and over again defines, circumscribes, describes, the various inter-penetrating areas of sociological research, he is always restlessly trying to disentangle one web of causality after another, one from another. It is as if he hoped to establish the utility, incontrovertibility and weightiness of causality by the accumulation of illustrations, demonstrations, definitions. His arguments also illustrate the near-identity of cause and definition (1964, pp. 3–41 and 41–155). In his *Religionssoziologie*, on the other hand, he proves himself almost demonically obsessed with the desire to establish one specific cause as one of the causes of the rise of capitalism. Even so there still remains the further question: What was the cause which constituted Puritanism as the cause of capitalist intensity, what gave Puritanism its motive power? Such questions crave for God, the *Ur-sache* and the *Verursacher*, and can take no less for an answer. In a godless universe or universe of discourse they crave for god-knows-what, for Godot.

Weber as well as Dilthey had been impressed by the rigorous neo-Kantianism of Rickert. The latter had argued that the proper understanding of history, the only possible historical knowledge – *Wissen* – we can gain, is as categorical as Kant's understanding of

H

any possible knowledge of nature. It is also categorical as in Kant's understanding of the working of the will (cf. Tröltsch, 1922b, pp. 227–39, 561–2; also 151ff). Thus Rickert's approach to history involved a twofold imposition: 1 Kant had understood the function of reason as inevitably imposing its categories on whatever it tried to grasp. He believed human reason to be so structured that it can manage to comprehend only what it has first processed into correspondence with its own structure. As against Goethe, '*Wär*' *nicht das Auge sonnenhaft, nie könnt's der Sonne Licht erblicken.*' Kant would have said, '*Wär*' *nicht die Sonne augenhaft, das Auge könnt*' *sie nie erblicken.*' 'Were not the eye sun-like, it never could perceive the light of the sun,' says Goethe. Kant says, 'Were not the sun eye-like. . . .' In as far as Kant's analysis of our knowledge of nature was based on an analysis of the natural sciences, it was possibly quite correct. His mistake, if it be one, consisted in universalizing, in extrapolating from part to whole, a peculiar mode of manipulative understanding and taking that for *Erkenntnis per se*. As Sombart, Scheler and Borkenau would put it, he mistook the Western scientific-technological, managerial-utilitarian categories for those of the human mind altogether. Which explains something about the total ambiguity of Weber's and Dilthey's use of *Verstehen*.

Rickert intended to impose those narrowly manipulative Western categories, which he also mistook for universally human ones, on history. Such a procedure not only begs all possible questions. It formalizes to the point where form is emptied of content, except that of sheer imposition, of power. Power becomes the sole content of history. Does Rickert merely give away an old secret of the historians? Since Thucydides, since the recordings on Assyrian tablets, they have been fascinated by power. Their accounts have been the story of its shifts and changes. 'Who's in, who's out.' It may be Rickert's merit to have made explicit what has always been practised, if less rigorously. Needless to add that the main category to be applied to history was that of causality.

2 Kant's understanding of the will as the agent of human morality and freedom was also categorical. (We recall the categorical imperative.) The difficulty was that one could arrive at a proper understanding of the will, i.e. of practical reason, only by totally detaching it from the realm of nature and necessity to which even I, the possessor of the will, belong totally. The will can be appreciated only in its complete transcendentality or, in Kantian imagery and to show how easily extremes meet, in its total immanence. It is the Platonic 'good' now implanted in my breast only to make me feel the dichotomy between nature and supernatural demands all the more painfully. But then pain, especially when experienced as duty, is good for me. I am free only in following my will, since inclination

and passion, pertaining to the realm of nature, enslave. I can will only what I do not desire, for what I desire I cannot will, and desire drags me back into the realm of necessity. I am free only when I am doing what I do not desire to do. I am good only when I act against my inclinations, when I obey the will, the summons of the day. This is indeed the apotheosis of both Lutheran and Calvinist Puritanism and also of capitalist-scientific-technological bureaucracy.

Kant's insights into the workings of the will are fruitful. They reveal the actual and total bondage of man as a willing being. (Has it any sociological significance that in England, the home of capitalism, 'willing' means both to will and to be at another's will?) By implication they reveal that the bondage is to his own categories of thinking, to his own, narrowed and manipulative intentions, to his obsession with power and energy. Kant's teachings are also confusing. They rationalized the prevailing situation, and so of necessity subordinated the precarious, threatened freedom of the will as a utopian intention to the *status quo*. They made the actual exercise of the will impossible and then made us understand the impossible demands of the will as our freedom and our duty (cf. Tucker, 1961, pp. 31–6; cf. 36–44). In order to arrive at a possible explanation of the will in his own terms, Kant had to purify it of all necessary, natural, earthy, individual ingredients. It functions in a vacuum of nouminality, of privacy understood as man's essence. And the nouminal was the solipsistic self, capable of knowing itself solely as a willing, free being. Kant's will was both megalo-maniacal and impotent. like the baby's will. The categorical im-perative already stated what Sartre was to explicate with Kantian conviction: that the exercise of freedom enslaves, and that therefore freedom must be exercised. (We see that no great gulf separates Kant's will from the wills of Schopenhauer and Nietzsche, nor from the peculiar area of the id Freud called the super-ego.)

Freedom is experienced as duty. It means total obedience to the categorical claims of the will which countermands the claims of desire, pleasure, affection, passion, i.e. of emotions which drag the self back into the realm of necessity and tragedy. Kant's will is the consummated introjection of patriarchal authority, as it is institu-tionalized and universalized in capitalist bureaucratic society. 'Its service is perfect freedom.' We are free when we unquestioningly obey its summons which, on Weber's own authority, calls into the treadmill of limitlessly accelerating productivity, whether in industry or academe (1968, pp. 334–9). Once again categorical thinking has led to sheer formalism, the formalities of power. This Weber applied faithfully in all his researches by concentrating on the causality of power and the power of causality.

To sum up, Rickert's dual categorical imposition of positivism reflects the social reality of late capitalism or possibly of civilization as a whole. More precisely: in his extreme formulation, which was taken over by Weber, it reflects the extremities of capitalism and civilization, as it articulates the assumption of all European historiography. It demonstrates the omnipotence and impotence of the will, its perpetual self-cancellation, the civilizing will's inherent contradictoriness embodied in and expressed by a power-divided society. It demonstrates that since Plato the intellect had been at the service of the will – not just since Schopenhauer. For this reason the intellect has not been able to overcome the dichotomies, social and personal, which the inherent contradiction of the will cannot help perpetuating and which the philosophical intellect is designed to justify. So it had to be content with rationalizing and universalizing the contradictions and call them 'human nature'. Positivism, the latest expression of the dual imposition, most urgently raises the question whether our wilful, purposeful, power-oriented, objectifying intellect, is our only or most appropriate possibility of understanding nature or human nature, the individual – i.e. the indivisible – and society.

We have shown that causality and objectivity can be explained only in terms of each other. When I have an objective I can decide which steps to take to achieve it. Such steps constitute a causal chain. I can have an objective, as against a dream or phantasy, only in as far as I can more or less consciously, more or less rationally, conceive an order of steps to attain it. Any kind of objectivity is constituted by the setting of an objective. An objective is the expression of intention, intension, desire, will. It cannot itself be objective or rationalistic – unless we accept the behaviourist circle in which everything is as insignificant, as social reality as a whole is unsignifying. (It is interesting that near-behaviourists, like G. H. Mead, tend to reduce all human behaviour and experience to its objective or objective-directed expressions, and having done this imply that this aspect constitutes the complete human actuality. Mead, 1967, pp. 268–9.)

An objective is always to some extent personal and present, even when its subject matter is the atom, the distant past or future. It is constituted by some direct or indirect present interest which in turn condenses various direct or indirect wishes. This means that until we come to understand what it is we *wish* to understand and why we wish it, our understanding will remain at the mercy of unacknowledged, arbitrary wishes. An unacknowledged wish is always in danger of becoming will, will to power. Unsure of its objective, its objective becomes power to enable it to gain any objective. An acknowledged wish, on the other hand, might discover less wilful means of fulfilment, might realize that fulfilment cannot

216

be willed. Also, unacknowledged wishes have a tendency to become displaced. We think we want what we do not want. A displaced satisfaction can rarely compensate the loss of the originally desired one. So wishing and willing become exorbitant, quantity is to make up for the loss of quality.

It is important for any scientist to know what, inside and outside his scientific field, he desires to prove and to understand. This is especially true for the *Geisteswissenschaftler*. One usually manages to prove what one wishes to prove. This does not invalidate a proof but limits its validity. The wish not only begets interest which begets an objective. It limits the objective, makes it subjective. It gives shape to it. Now the acknowledged wish enables me to arrive at a conclusion, a *telos*, beyond which I do not wish to go, at least not here and now and in this direction. It enables me to experience an inevitably fragmentary and temporary solution or resolution as consummation – as in sexual intercourse, in solving a puzzle or a mathematical equation. The unacknowledged wish remains shapeless and limitless. It drives on, feeding on phantasies equally unacknowledged, and imbues the undefined and unattainable with promises of fulfilment I cannot experience in the present. The unacknowledged wish cannot contemplate, for example, the sheer beauty of its object. It must analyse, take to pieces, hoping to find behind the given what it is looking for. It cannot find fulfilment in a present conversation or inter-coursing. It must argue in pursuit of an elusive truth and subordinate the intercourse to an ulterior objective or interest. On the physical or erotic level Don Juan is the analogue of the academic.

Again we arrive at the contradiction: objectivity cannot be an end in itself. It is absurd to treat it as such. The poetic Plato still realized this when he subordinated the useful to the useless. We do useful or necessary things to be able to do nothing or something useless like feasting, playing, talking and making love. We cook to eat. We do not eat in order to wash up. Did Plato realize what he was doing, as Popper claims he did (1942, vol. 1, ch. 6), when for reasons of political expediency or utility he began to treat the objective as if it were detachable from the useful and expedient and then absolutized it? The 'good' and the 'true' are objective in our sense of the word. They are always part of a larger subjectivity or inter-subjectivity, of personal or communal temporary desires. Who will ever gauge how much damage has been done by making the 'good' and the 'true' absolute, so that any power interest, as already in the case of Plato himself, could conveniently and easily hide behind the ideological smokescreen provided by those 'absolutes' of objectivity which merely absolutized a particular objective.

Objectivity, with all the attendant ceaseless efforts to attain and remain faithful to it, is another aspect of the libidinization of the means: of tools and machinery, of industry, commerce and finance, of all that which is intended to serve our ends. This in turn meant and means the libidinization of power. For when the means or tools which serve a particular drive towards mastery, quite apposite within a limited sphere, are divorced from the particular end in which that drive finds its consummation, when those means are then absolutized as ends-in-themselves, the power-drive is absolutized. Alexander, Caesar, Napoleon, Hitler, remain fairly adequate representatives of social consciousness as constituted by the civilized assumptions of which formal, positivistic, causal determination and determinism are aspects.

One brief glance at Tröltsch to spotlight, in passing, another facet of the problem. He is both theologian and sociologist. There is little doubt that he exemplifies the dangers of value-determined research. His ends obviously determine his means, the desired effect selects the causes. This, by the way, is as obviously the case with Durkheim, though both scholars tried most ardently and not unsuccessfully to emulate the required standards of scientific objectivity. In both, however, the discrepancy between ends and means, between the foregone conclusions and the facts and methods by means of which they were to be established, remained visible. Yet is greater objectivity the answer? Could this not rather lie in the appreciation of the subjectivity of any objective? What is disturbing about Tröltsch and Durkheim is not the fact that their ends are subjective and value-determined (they could not be anything else), but that both, the former explicitly, the latter implicitly, treat them as fixed, as objective. They are the victims of a scientific conditioning against which their emotive nature rebelled, but in vain. So instead of ends and means, value and method, interpenetrating each other, they pull apart, leaving the visible gap. If especially Tröltsch's vast tomes seem to add up to disappointingly little, is this due exclusively to a lack of personal genius? And was not the scientific method designed to by-pass such a contingency? Or do they illustrate how the value, i.e. the use, goodness, interest, beauty, of the intended conclusion may stand in inverse proportion to the attempted objectivity of the method? Christian dogma and practice throughout the ages embodied insights and distortions well worth studying and unravelling. Trying to trace and prove their causal, arguable connections and influences – what caused what? – reduces them and thus the arguments themselves to insignificance. Again the question: What gives power to a work of scholarship? Certainly not the amount of scholarship: Weber's passionate intelligence, not his depressing erudition; Durkheim's passionate moralism and Jewish faith in the possibilities of a redemptive community, not his peculiar documentation and argumentation.[4]

I am going to end this section with another leading, post-scientific question: What are we afraid might happen, if instead of our grooved, academic, logical, argumentative efforts to establish truth, instead of our endeavours to be causal and scientific, we would concentrate, if not exclusively, on savouring and sampling, on *Kennen*; on savouring as the lover of wine, not the competitor in a savouring contest, will have it? For instance, we could immerse ourselves in a period, a group, one person, one work, taste rather than define, appreciate rather than explain. We should neither have to prove anything, nor refute, nor fear being refuted. Bach's *Mass in B Minor* did not intend to prove anything neither did his *St Matthew Passion*. Yet those two works still tell us more about religion, about the specific religiosity of an age, they even prove more, than any number of theological or sociological treatises, be they ever so objective and erudite. So we would not have to discount but to go on accumulating objective evidence. We should **not** have to struggle to achieve ever greater objectivity, for we are **not** to establish the precise vintage but to enjoy the wine and possibly help others, through our appreciation, to enjoy it and themselves better. Yet in our new efforts we might discover that scientific method and precision has taught us much which need not be forgotten. Ultimately, however, we shall aspire to grow in sensitivity and sensibility, even in sensuousness, all of which, because they are ends in themselves, cannot be finalized or de-fined by the understanding, because the understanding is at their service, becomes meaningful and significant only in their service. So we hope that when we have been able to express what we have experienced, our communication will aid others to understand what we have experienced and enable them to experience for themselves. Such intention cannot be achieved without much discipline. But it will be of a kind that owes as much to the discipline of the artist as to that of the scientist (cf. Marx, 1968, pp. 242–6).

Are these altogether ridiculous questions and hopes? Dilthey comes to life whenever he savours rather than argues. So do Lukács and Bloch and Adorno and Simmel. So does Weber whenever the armour slips a little. So did Marx throughout the first volume of *Das Kapital*, be the savouring there of the actual conditions of the poor ever so bitter. That, one realizes, made him write and argue. Freud lives in his disciplined savouring, not in his theories which prevent his followers from living. Naturally such savouring might dissolve disciplinarian boundaries whose arbitrariness it might demonstrate beyond argument. It might also show up the incapacity for savouring of those who wish to preserve the separate disciplines. Thus the question will raise itself, whether our present form of academicism is not simply a form of *dépassé* asceticism, of sadomasochism?

5 Contemplation and manipulation

I have tried to look at the way in which a number of scholars attempted to understand and interpret a change of social consciousness which took place between the Middle Ages and the nineteenth century. Now, belief in the actuality and far-reaching consequences of that change had by then become a generally accepted part of European educated opinion. Almost everyone would have agreed that there was an essential difference between medieval and modern mentality, between the old awareness of the self and his world and the new, between the ontological and critical consciousness, 'faith' and 'reason'. The scholars under review were investigating a change that was taken for granted. They therefore found it easy to agree on its character and extent. Here and in a sentence or two I wish to hint at one aspect of its nature and in Huizinga's terms, if only for the sake of momentary convenience (Huizinga, 1965, ch. 15).

It was a change from an allegorical, hierarchically, ontologically and theologically grounded rationalism, to a quasi-empirical, quasi-critical, equalitarian rationalism based on belief in rationalization. (The *quasi* not meant as judgment but as question mark.) Medieval questioning came at least temporarily to rest when it had been proved to the disputants' reasonable satisfaction that the problem under discussion had been fitted harmoniously into the structured whole which had its origin, shape and *telos*, in the wisdom and will of God.

A modern question finds its temporary rest and answer when it has been proved to the disputants' reasonable satisfaction that this answer fits economically into a precisely circumscribed rational structure which has its origin, formulation and *telos* in the desire for a more complete rationalization, for a smoother, more economically rational functioning. These various structures are related to each other, if at all, in terms of strict functional, economic rationality, in terms of further possibilities of rationalization.

220

Furthermore we might say, if rather crudely, rationalization believes to have found its most adequate tool in causal thinking which in turn has become identified with rationality *per se*. It does indeed express the modern mentality. Causal thinking ineluctably 'gestalts' any research, including that into the change of mentality from one causal conceptualization to another. More than others, German social philosophers were conscious of this fact and that it created peculiar difficulties. They nevertheless continued the scientific quest and we saw how their own causal approach to an agreed subject matter immediately led to disagreements. If we had wished to, we could have witnessed the original disagreements spawn ever more detailed arguments concerning ever more detailed disagreements concerning ever more minor aspects of the change. Instead of leading to a deepening and growing appreciation of the significance and quality of the change in social consciousness which might have opened up new possibilities of comprehending our not yet fixed humanity and our situation with its possibilities as our reality, scholarship got shunted into scholastic specializations which by now totally blur any possible view of the whole. Today no respectable scholar would dare to start again where Weber had started or Freud or Marx, Comte or Spencer. Yet the power of the influence of any of these thinkers, to say it yet again, resided in the new possibilities of viewing man in his possible wholeness which their insights had made available, though they themselves were the first to forget this and obscured their own insights by the detailed argumentation which was intended to prove them.

Dilthey's insights into the change that took place between Aquinas and Descartes and was finally ratified by Kant was helpful, fruitful because it was interesting, i.e. his insight draws me into and involves me in the very change he sees, makes me experience it and realize that it concerns me and my understanding not only of it but of myself (cf. Poole, 1972, chs 5 and 6). The insight is true – recalling that truth is fluid – in that it makes me appreciate a certain movement of ideas as something that still moves me, motivates me. His repetitive and painstaking argumentation adds remarkably little to the originating insight and detracts from it quite a lot. What remains illuminating are those passages where the argument is reinterpreted by the resurgence of the insight; as when he writes about those he loves, because they made him see, or who made him see, because he loved them.

Weber's insights into the relationship between Puritanism and capitalism are almost as illuminating as and not so different from Freud's into the civilizatory functioning of repression. They are more helpful, fruitful, interesting, also much more frightening, than is admitted in either theory or practice by even those who acknowledge the importance of Weber's contribution. His exhaustive and exhausting documentation and argumentation remain immeasurably more readable than the interpretations of his successors, mainly because they are interspersed continually with illustrations and instances of the constitutive insights. But the arguments do not prove what they are meant to prove. On the contrary, they considerably subtract from the power of the original insights to prove themselves. They also sent off his followers on many a wild goose chase. The same can be said about Freud and even more about Husserl whose pristine insight, as against his arguments, reopened radical questions concerning the nature as well as the form of our knowing and the various autonomies of understanding – also concerning the way we are tempted to think we know what we (think we) know (see below, end of chapter).

Durkheim had already raised a similar question in a more rudimentary form but in a more directly sociological manner (1969, pp. 362–73, 404). In his defence of specialization against those who deplored it as fragmentation, he insists that specialization is not only inevitable but possesses its own virtues. All knowledge is fragmentary, and so is any attempt to unify the fragments. The gentlemanly ideal of a rounded education was an illusion and convention, an ideology. Roundedness was defined by what the ruling élite of the moment believed to be desirable and necessary for its continuance as an élite. It was that of which politeness, politicalness, doing what it was politic to do, was the complement and expression. Educated society was polite society and only within its charmed circle politeness prevailed or was meant to. (Courtesy, meaning courtly behaviour, was designed to keep and advance a man at court.) A rounded gentlemanly education was as arbitrarily defined and limiting as any specialization. It was, as a matter of fact, a most specific specialization. Why should it be considered of greater intrinsic merit than what we have since come to understand as specialization? Furthermore, Durkheim points out, there is an essential difference between the knowledge of the expert, gained by personal research, and that acquired by listening to the expert's report. There is a further difference between such second-hand knowledge acquired by concentrated study, if merely of secondary sources, and the appearance of knowledge resulting from popularized generalizations, the throwing together of all kinds of information, the artificial harmonization of all manners of discipline. This last is the nearest approximation to what was once called *Bildung* for which there is no English term beyond 'deportment'.

Durkheim was aware of the sociological significance of different kinds of knowing. Unfortunately he did not pursue this, but was content to integrate his temporary findings into his conceptual framework without wondering how far they applied to his own conceptualizations. Schutz on the other hand, one of the few direct disciples of Husserl who tried to activate the latter's insights in the service of sociology, set out to show that the difference between various kinds of knowing is radical. These cannot, without violation, be integrated into one conceptual system. All the conceiver can do is to try to remain aware of them. Schutz goes to a quite inordinate length to demonstrate that and how the observer's experience as well as his time – his *Sein* and *Zeit* – are qualitatively different from those of the observed. Therefore any conceptualization, at any of its many possible stages, must remain conscious of and make allowances for the discrepancy between itself and that which it is conceptualizing. Moreover, and for similar reasons, he tried to widen the understanding of causality to include what might be called final cause. Making Weber his starting point and trying to take him a step further along Weber's own intentions, he insists that no justice can be done to human phenomena, unless it becomes clear that here each cause contains both its 'be-cause' and its 'in order to' (1962, part I, ch. III, 1–6; also chs 1–6 *passim*; also 1967, chs 19–27; also chs 13–18).

Caesar crossed the Rubicon – my example – because he was Caesar and because the political situation was such and such, i.e. because of the peculiar confluence of his personal conditioning and character with the political conditions of Rome. He crossed in order to achieve certain projects, attain certain objectives, personal and political ambitions. The distinction can be concealed by the fact that one could also say: Caesar did this and that, because he was ambitious, because he wanted to achieve certain objectives. Now it is clear that the second 'because' is partly justified. Caesar, being himself, is ambitious. He has certain objectives because he is who he is, and because he is a member of a particular structured society at a particular moment of time. Here we are not concerned with problems of determinism and to what an extent any 'in order to' is reducible to a 'because'. We are trying to understand Schutz's intention: He is separating the 'because' from the 'in order to', to grant his subject a possibly arbitrary measure of freedom or self-determination, and thus to remind himself and us that his, the observer's, understanding of Caesar's action cannot be Caesar's. Only a measure of tension, uncertainty, liberality, in the observer's approach can hope to correspond to the experienced tensions and uncertainties of the 'observed'. Nothing less can make allowance for the indeterminable which can be eradicated only by and in the observer's determination, i.e. arbitrarily, by grace of the indeterminable (cf. Dilthey, 1914, vol. 7, pp. 86–7, 140; also pp. 72–3, 194).

I shall now take Schutz a little further along his own intentions by means of another example. I have chosen the following purposefully, because it poses the question as to what is the use of sociology anyway, or of philosophy or education or civilization for that matter (cf. Adorno, 1969d, '*Erziehung nach Auschwitz*'). A man has been compelled to witness how his wife and children were tortured and killed, before he is systematically worked, starved and tortured almost to death. The liberators arrive in the nick of time. They save him, if not a few million others. I am among the liberators. I interview him in depth and come to know him well. He tells me everything, he tells me all his heart, over and again. I also have time to 'take in' the place, look at the ovens, savour the stench. I am deeply sympathetic, for some of my family and almost I myself shared his fate. (What a world of difference in that 'almost'.) Yet even if I had shared his fate would our respective experiences have been comparable? I am waiving this point for the time being. As it is my experience is totally different from his. Therefore my knowledge, no matter how much detailed information I manage to accumulate, is and remains different in kind. My understanding of his experience is different from his experience, different from his memory of it, my interpretation essentially different from his. His experience, memory, interpretation, fit into a totally different space-time in my mind from that which they occupy in his even now. I know about that which he knows, *weiss* something about that which he *kennt*.

My knowledge of the socio-political conditions that victimized him may be much superior to his. In some ways I may know and understand much better what happened to him and why than he himself. (As a doctor may understand a patient's complaint better than the patient.) I cannot know what and as he knows. Twenty years later I remember him. I refresh my memory by looking up the notes I took at the time of our meetings. 'I remember it all, as if it only happened yesterday.' But what I know and understand now, the quality of my present knowing and understanding, is different in kind from what it had been then. It is in the mode of a present past, it belongs to another *ex-stasis* of time. And once again different in kind from the three foregoing modes of knowing, is the knowledge gained by the man who reads my account. Perhaps this would not be so, if I were a poet. A poet may have the ability to bridge the gap between the various modes of knowing. That may make him a poet. Which raises the question how far the sociologist may have to become a poet. However it still remains problematical whether the poet enables me to share another's experience and therefore his understanding of it, or whether he merely manages to create still another mode of understanding. Hence the further question: To what an extent should the poet become a sociologist?

224

I could continue my illustration of the differentiation processes between diverse kinds of knowledge, *Erkenntnis*. I could take it into the future when others might wish to compare my account with that of the victim or with that of another interviewer, or with those of my and/or his interpreters, in order to assess our comparative understanding of the historical situation in the light of their understanding, or to check our correctness in respect of factual and chronological details. Their understanding would again be different in kind. And so far I have been dealing merely with general modes of understanding. I have left out of account the fact that the modes of knowing and understanding of any two readers or interviewers or victims would be different, because they in turn depend on the individual's history and background. Often these would be discernibly different, when, for example, their social and cultural conditioning differs markedly. At other times the differences of understanding would be as imponderable as they are incontrovertible, unless we fall back on behaviourist assumptions. Any attempt to harmonize the different perspectives, and they would have a value of their own, create additional modes of knowing. Is this one more reason why sociology and psychology have fallen back on causal thinking, for that does not take notice of and cannot explain the quality of difference between modes of understanding? Thus it can by-pass all these modalities and the human being who experiences them; it can reduce the investigation to the level where that which constitutes the quality of life and gives it whatever significance it may have, can be ignored. Everything that matters is discarded, like secondary qualities in physics – which were discarded by physics long after profit had discounted all qualities. In compensation causal thinking grants the satisfaction produced by the magico-logical capacity of prestidigitating all sorts of things into and out of all sorts of patterns, as the power of magic resides in its simplifications and generalizations. *Causal thinking gives the experience of power where the power of experience has been lost.*

We have come back to the problems we have been trying to focus in the concept of social consciousness, problems relating to the tensions, contradictions, interactions, between the individual and society, the contingent and the universal, the necessary. Is there any form of thinking which can hold both the person and society, the unique and the universal, in balance; which can recognize and acknowledge all possible and incomparable modes of knowing and encompass them? This would understand understanding as just such a negative capability of holding the as yet irreconcilable together without wishing to enforce reconciliation. It would be a form of thinking which, from the start, refuses to consider the logically contradictory simply as contradiction, because it would

225

understand the logical itself as both dichotomizer and dichotomized, as an instrument of division, separation, reflecting societal division and its instruments of power (cf. Adorno, 1970, pp. 142, 146, 162; also Heidegger, 1954, parts 1 and 2).

The dichotomy of manipulative and 'contemplative' thinking is probably as old as civilization. What is new in modernity is merely the extent to which manipulative thinking has proved successful in so many areas that man has become persuaded he is most closely in touch with reality at the moment when he is in danger of losing all touch with himself as the constitutor of reality. In its success manipulative thinking seems to have absorbed into itself the satisfactions of contemplation. Now this dichotomy which has been weighted so one-sidedly had from the start reflected the separation of thinking from labouring. Only the few had the time and opportunity of developing their intellectual capacities in ways which they, the rulers, deemed acceptable. Naturally their thinking would be largely directed towards the preservation of their own opportunities. Only as a by-product of such sharpening of the capacities in the struggle for élitist survival, and as well-policed order and privilege left progressively more time for further thought, new forms of contemplation were discovered – or old rediscovered – and developed.

Some archaeological, anthropological and literary evidence seems to indicate that contemplation is older than manipulative thinking, that originally the latter grew out of the former. It may be important to find out. For just as it makes a difference to our thinking, if we believe that civilization is the mother rather than the child of need; so it could make a difference to our thinking, and therefore being, here and now, if we believe that thought originally was and is a luxuriance rather than a tool for survival. Be this as it may, it is fairly clear that the early civilizatory efforts to secure and extend administrative powers and elaborate all sorts of complex organizations gave increasing preponderance to 'practical' thinking. (Kant's 'pure' is really 'practical' *Vernunft*. His practical reason is pure impracticability.) It may well be that civilization turned practical-theoretical-manipulative reasoning into a tool of unnatural survival and selection. Only gradually contemplation seems to have re-emerged, in different guises and with different emphases, mainly as a special opportunity of the few and of the specifically institutionalized. In the meantime the residue of pristine contemplation may have lingered on in bureaucratic, ossified religious organizations, or among the poor pagans, the inheritors of the land. Early civilization seems to have gone hand in hand with a ritualized, externalized, formalized, hierarchic form of religion, a distorted survival of osmotic thinking, until the prophet or new founder appeared as reactivator of live contemplative thought. His fate and that of his insights may illustrate most clearly the *Geschick* of contemplation in civilized society.

In his *Soziologie der Herrschaft* (1964, pp. 691–1102), Weber presents his only too well-known analysis of the deterioration of charismatic leadership via patriarchal, patrimonial, traditional rule to impersonal bureaucratic domination. He traces the change of social consciousness from the moment of 'inspiration', when the individual and society are welded into an almost mystical union by a transcendental summons – not yet that of the day – via the long period during which communion turns into community and becomes structured into classes and castes or stations, to *Gesellschaft*, community's subsidence into bureaucracy. He sees the movement as inevitable. However the distortions and changes of the original inspiration Weber maps out – and possibly not without some ingredients of impermissible nostalgia – merely illustrate the changes society enforces in regard to ideas, aspirations, beliefs, which had been manipulative from the beginning. The distance from Alexander to the bureaucracy of the Ptolemies, from Caesar to Augustus and to the 'good Emperors', from Napoleon to Metternich, may not be as big as appears at first sight.

What happened to those rarer charismatic figures and their insights who challenged society more radically in that they did not sum up its aspirations as the hero did, but questioned them radically? Such men may be placed into two fairly distinct categories, though the boundary in any particular case may not be marked distinctly: There is the prophet or religious re-former, here the artist or visionary. For the moment we shall ignore the latter. Society easily manages to shrug him off. It relegates him to the periphery of practical real life. By prophets I here mean those few who manage to stir society enough to be remembered and at the same time defy its immediate efforts to treat them as poets, to domesticate them. It is not easy to clarify what happens to them and their insights, because it is hard to establish their *ipsissima verba* and to reconstruct their personalities.

The Buddha's speeches are largely a later, often quite late, interpretation of his teaching, in the light of changed conditions and filtered by minds which did not have his original experience that had shaped the insights and given substance to them. How quickly interpretation can take over from and contradict the original teaching can be seen in the Gospels. By the time the disciples began to record story and words, they already found they had to defend themselves, as followers of this leader, in a changed and precarious situation. They could not help using the words of him who had led them into this to defend their interests which they would naturally identify with his. At times their interpretations, which they usually claimed to have been his, are a direct contradiction of the original parable or saying they are intended to clarify. It is equally difficult to get at Socrates whom I am inclined to see as a prophet, an inspired or daemonic man. For while any disciple is prone to misinterpret his teacher, because the experience which produces the interpretation is different from that which produced the original insight, a disciple of supreme genius, and with such definite and conflicting interests, is most likely to distort his master's teachings to vindicate his own (cf. Popper, 1942, vol. 1, pp. 303–13 n56). There remain the Hebrew prophets. Many of their sayings were written down near the time of their delivery, sometimes by their disciples, sometimes by themselves. Yet even here little is clear. The chronological and intentional order of the oracles is confused, the direct historico-political implications are often irretrievable. Moreover the prophet is now in a book. He has become what he defied his age to make of him, a poet. His consciously and explicitly timed proclamations, timed like bombs, are defused, made timeless, put into a museum called the Bible.

So we have remarkably little to go on. Yet this much seems to be gleanable, especially if we start with the Hebrews: the prophets' insights – we might let ourselves be reminded tentatively of Marx and Freud – are the result of a kind of experiencing and thinking which *per se* questions the very foundations of civilized society and assumptions. Amos, for instance, the first of the writing prophets, sees private ownership as the root of all evils. Isaiah followed him closely in this. Hosea and Jeremiah harked back to the good old days in the wilderness. They symbolized the times when social structures, laws and political ambitions, above all property, had not yet corrupted that communion between man and man which depends on direct, spontaneous, libidinal communion with and in 'God'. By the time St Paul said that money was the root of all evil, it may have become a cliché. For him it was an echo of the prophetic, anti-civilizatory vision. He himself had experienced the reality of community and communion at prophetic depth. He knew that in such a community money and possessions have little reality, that where these seem to be most real there is no communion. (Cf. Marx's *1844 Manuscripts*, Weber on charisma, Durkheim on communal enthusiasm, Sartre's 'fused group'; also Tönnies's *Gemeinschaft*.)

Weber's analysis of the post-Davidic situation explains why prophecy was both possible and ineffective in the divided kingdoms of Israel and Judah. From his scientific, power-oriented point of view he can see why the prophets did not gain power and why, when for a moment they gained the appearance of it, they ceased to be prophets. He could not fully appreciate that their insights are anti-civilizatory in their very essence, that they question precisely all those assumptions on which the civilized belief in the necessity of force, coercion, control, is based. The prophets express attitudes, expectations and possibilities which civilization seems to have foreclosed and prejudged, and which could not be enforced or imposed, because they are the protest against impositions. It was not accidental that Jesus's message embodies an even more radical protest. At that time his people were governed by aliens and the Roman Empire had reached an apex of civilized intention and repression. Government was experienced directly and painfully as alien imposition. The contrast between Roman political assumptions, which merely epitomized the general political assumptions of all times, and those assumptions of communal possibilities in which Jesus's expectations and images are rooted, is total. (For example, cf. Mark 10 : 42, Matthew 5–7; John 18 : 36.) That is why the church which could not help perpetuating imperial policies had to relegate his teaching to the private sphere – which is not to be mistaken for that of the personal.

It is important to recognize that Jesus's teaching, as that of a Jewish rabbi-prophet, is inevitably this-worldly even where it employs supernatural imagery. It suggests a possibility of living, here and now and as if it were the most obvious and feasible thing, in which all considerations of power, prestige, ambition, are totally irrelevant. Here contemplation is the way of life, the end in itself. And contemplation is not understood in the Greek most class-conditioned sense of 'thinking rather than labouring'. It did not mean gazing upon external, eternal, ideal realities. For the Jew did not recognize the supernatural as separable from the natural. Contemplation meant the attuning – *Stimmen* – of the whole of life to the rhythm of the cosmos which was experienced as fundamentally and in spite of all the creation of a good God and as very good. 'Look at the ravens. They do not gather into barns, but they live. Look at the lilies in the field. They do not spin. Yet Solomon in all his glory was not arrayed as one of them. . . . God looks after the sparrows, two of which are sold for less than a penny. . . . Will he not look after you, oh you of little faith? Therefore, be not anxious about tomorrow. Seek first and foremost God's rule which is unlike anything we call rule here and now. Everything else will be given, added. . . . Others seek authority. Let it not be so among you.' (Matthew 6; 10.) Jesus acknowledges manipulative thinking in its sphere without reservation, but altogether subordinates it to *Besinnung* or communion as to the 'better part' (Luke 10 : 38–42). If his images have retained some power in spite of all distortions, *Geist*-power, moving power, it may be because they express irreducible nostalgic-utopian longings. These have their deepest roots in childhood experiences, in the child's psychic reality; while our social actuality is rooted in childhood repressions and phantasies.[1]

Freud believed that adults can find no more than superficial satisfaction in any activity or experience which does not connect with childhood fulfilments and longings. Money, wealth, cannot give happiness, for it has no meaning to the child. It is the supreme abstract of civilization, and Freud thought that civilization, except in the form of its partial evasion, namely of the arts, cannot make happy. He remained willing to pay the price of unhappiness to be protected from that which might prove worse (cf. *Civilization and its Discontent*, esp. ch. 8). Jesus, like Rousseau and Marx, did not have these fears. His teaching, viewed in the light of Freud's insights, amounts to an unreserved indictment of civilization and all its works, i.e. of civilization as we know it. In the Freud-Jesus view of childhood experience and phantasy as constitutive of both the possibilities of fulfilment and of their frustration, it becomes at least questionable, *fragwürdig*, whether civilization is attainable only at the price of deep discontent. It still remains possible that we have to resign ourselves to frustrations as to the inevitable. On the other hand, we can no longer simply rule out the possibility that if only we could learn more about the way in which reality is constituting itself in the infant's and child's feeling and understanding, other forms of social actuality and civilization become imaginable, possible, possibly practicable. Are such possibilities of sociological interest, or do we consign them, like Weber, to the repertoire of value-ethically directed enthusiasts (Weber, 1968, pp. 187–201; 263–310)?

About the Buddha I dare not say more than that his teaching also, though on a higher level of sophistication, is totally anti-civilizationary. It also grew out of a contemplative vision of life which, like that of some Hindu philosophers, would go as far as seeing all civilizatory efforts as a kind of delusion, at best an inevitable illusion. Buddhist understanding seems to accept the split between society and the individual as irreversible. Its salvation is strictly personal, almost in the sense of private. It does not know the Hebrew prophetic intimations of new possibilities of communion, community, society.

Whether or not Socrates belongs into this prophetic company I cannot argue here. I believe his primal, daemonic experience was mystical, his view of life contemplative, almost in the Hebrew sense, in that he saw the individual as ineffable, the philosopher's task, like that of the midwife, as helping the individual, the fully social person, to bring to life his own truth or understanding. (I think it was Plato who rationalized the individual into individualism and that into ideality.) Finally, it might be interesting to note that the one prophet who proved most immediately successful, Mohammed, was closer to the manipulative in his thinking than any other.

It was least anti-civilizationary, perhaps because it expressed the experience of one and spoke to those who had not yet known the full impact of civilization.

On the whole society coped fairly easily with the disturbing contemplatives. It utilized their insights for its own purposes of domestication, i.e. manipulation. The call of the prophet becomes liturgical reading. The radical individualism of the Buddha spawned sects, communities, multitudes of divinities. The profoundly anti-civilizatory message of Jesus was used to build up, preserve and justify the most Caesarian religious organization the world has yet known. This demonstrates that contemplative thinking when it is subordinated to manipulation is not merely suppressed. It becomes falsified and turned into its opposite. Its creative energies, analogous to those in the psyche, pre-eminently of the child, are put to work in the service of that which represses and falsifies them, until we are left with a monolithically manipulative society which handles contemplative insights for its ideological justification, as 'opium', as a drug that deadens the pain of reality. Eventually religion, like literature, is reduced to the level of entertainment and public opinion, is granted freedom, because it is completely harmless. Contemplation is depressed to such irrelevance and unreality that the experience of it as undeniable can lead only to impotent protests, to crankiness, to schizophrenia or other forms of mental disturbance (cf. Laing, 1965, 1969, 1970b).

Here we may have another reason why it was not accidental that the most significant break-through in modern thought resulted from the study of mental disease. It was the *Geist*, that which has its life in contemplation, which had become uneasy. By taking seriously the logic and rationality underlying psychic deviancy and by realizing how easily rational processes can be used to rationalize any irrationality, Freud helped us to get in touch again with other forms of thinking which rationalism can only distort or repress. For instance, a vital religious or mystical experience can today be expressed only in conventionalized, i.e. self-contradictory, terms, or in forms society considers as abnormal, sick, mad. Others rather than Freud himself took his insights further along the road towards that which Nietzsche had called the 'wisdom of the body' and Groddeck the *ratio* which makes and remakes our brain (1966). Yet this much must be acknowledged: Freud's patience of approach, his readiness to let his method be determined by his subjects, had a religious quality. So his thinking, apart from his self-conscious theorizing, as long as it remained observant without succumbing to the kind of positing which today goes by the name of observation, remained essentially contemplative. Unlike most social scientists, he remained willing to let not facts but his subjects speak for themselves.

231

If I believe that contemplation was and is the original and originating form of thinking, no matter by what accident or design it was brought about, and that the manipulative grew and grows out of it, continues to have its roots in contemplation, it is because even now practical and scientific thinking deteriorates into senseless chatter, as soon as it is totally cut off from its contemplative soil. However much a scientist may disdain value considerations, emotional judgments, ontic doubts, he cannot continue to work creatively in his subject, unless it holds some direct or indirect interest for him, unless it has one aspect or another or is related to such an aspect, which he can contemplate with pleasure or with some other significant, worthwhile, substantial emotion.

What I am trying to say here is so hard to say, because it is so simple and as self-evident as the kind of understanding embodied in language itself. All rationalism has its roots in something which, from its own point of view, is irrational, yet without which it could not be rational, because it just could not be. Contemplation is a kind of intellective-emotive compound of seeing-hearing-smelling-tasting-feeling. It is appreciation and savouring. It leaves things as and where they are. It neither proves nor disproves, though it may approve and disapprove. It is the psychic equivalent of eating, drinking, breathing. Cut off from it, manipulative thinking functions in a vacuum. It can do this for a while by means of what we called the libidinization of the means; just as bureaucracy can function for quite a while, before a new revolution or conquest starts a new evolution towards the old bureaucracy. In the meantime manipulative thinking has to make up for what it loses in sensuousness by ever increasing effectiveness and violence of assertion. For once sensuousness with its infinitesimal gradations of satisfaction has been lost or feels in need of outside justification, the self craves for violent shocks and tests to be assured of its continuing existence, to feel justified in being there at all.

One might also say that while contemplation diffuses love or libido, investing everything contemplated with at least a little of it, rationalism and rationalization condense and vectorize the disembodied libido into ambition, i.e. into craving for power or the form of power. For, and this may sound paradoxical, the acceptance of one's bodiliness and sensuousness, of one's self as embodied, is the result of much contemplation, at least for civilized men. For rationalism has reduced the body to tool function. This means it has conceptualized it. Sensuousness is reduced to sexuality, to reproductivity. Contemplation is the basis and the basic form of thinking-experiencing, just as my personal existence or the existence of the species or of anything at all is prior to any rationality of rationalization. It *is*. In connection with logic we saw that its function was exhausted in the smooth conveyance of something from here to there with least possible friction. Now we may add that the function of rationality in general is exhausted in certain definite, useful, functional transactions between person and person. (And only one kind of such transactions and only one aspect of this is the concern of economics.) In the last analysis only trans-actions can be rational, manipulative. Actions are their own *telos*, like the sexual 'act'. We contend that rationalism is circumscribed by contemplation and action – or simply by what the Hebrews thought of as contemplation – neither of which is rational in our contemporary understanding of rationality; analogous to the way in which any objectivity is circumscribed by inter-subjectivity (cf. Arendt, 1958, *passim*, on labour, work, action). *Sum ergo cogito!*

Though contemplative thinking is ineradicable, it can be badly neglected, distorted, repressed. I must eat, but can subsist for a long time on an inadequate diet with a dis-eased body. I must breathe, but may have to breathe badly polluted air. I cannot help being a totally erotic and sensuous being from the day of my birth – or before. But my sensuousness can be hampered and confined; my whole existence may become warped, because I was never permitted to experience and now cannot reach that flow of deep sensuous satisfaction which is the source and nourishment of all meaning and significance and therefore of all understanding and *Erkenntnis*. This can be said about contemplation: No-one can do without it and live. But one can get by for quite a while on remarkably little, if to one's own and others' greater or smaller distress. (Durkheim's anomic suicide might be better named a-contemplative. Yet the two are one: while social structures retain the libido invested in them by individuals, the latter are not aware of their uprootedness. As society relinquishes this libido, the individual finds himself cut off from all contemplative sources.)

Literature has always been an implicit, sometimes an explicit, protest against the purposeful or unconscious subordination of contemplative thinking and living, which is the correlate of the sensuous flow which gives meaning to life, to the arbitrary necessities created by the most diverse forms of manipulation. (Cf. Antigone with Effi Briest; Oedipus with Kafka's K.) It is interesting that the form which literature, from tragedy to farce, found most congenial, because symptomatic of the world of manipulation, whether in war or peace, love or business, was the intrigue. To the extent to which it becomes inevitable for us to think in terms of manipulation, practicalities, perhaps because we have forgotten how to contemplate, or never experienced the sensuous flow whose fulfilments lie beyond struggle or achievement – at least not since babyhood – to that extent we cannot help carrying the categories of machinations, appropriate to the power games, into even the most intimate spheres of our *Dasein*. (*Kabale und Liebe – Cabals and Love* – may be a bad play, but the title accurately sloganizes the civilized situation.) At all times and in the most varied manners, love and affection have been subordinated to family, tribal or national ambitions, to power and economics, concepts and safeguards. Love had to intrigue to be itself, if only for a moment. It was externalized and allegorized, as in knight-errantry; externalized, vulgarized, sexualized, as in Renaissance, Baroque and Rococo painting, literature, opera. It was romanticized and absolutized, as in *Tristan und Isolde*. Only the few very great artists managed to have and give glimpses of love's fuller possibilities which we have not yet begun to verify. (Perhaps could not before the 'pill'.) We do not know yet what love *is*. Today one marries 'for love'. Yet the categories of possession and manipulation cannot be shaken off so easily. Even Proust experienced love mainly as jealousy, as the terror of never being quite sure of exclusive possession. A limitless procession of mediocre novels and plays still understand the love-game more or less blatantly as intrigue, as uninteresting except as an intrigue. We have not yet reached that contemplative existence in communion – except at discrete moments of passion – where human actuality reveals itself as beyond possession and possessiveness and therefore beyond manipulation. (D. H. Lawrence was one of the first and few who tried to convey intimations of this in novels which for that reason defied the conventional novel form.)[2]

The sociologist, like the psychologist on his left and the philosopher at his right, suffers most from the dilemma created by this dichotomy of contemplative and manipulative thinking. His work becomes unilluminating and uninteresting to the extent to which it approximates scientific precision. (For example, Weber and Durkheim, it seems to me, are often so exciting, because they always want to and seem to, but never actually get near such precision.) To the extent to which he gives free play to his debilitated contemplative faculty, his work is considered useless by his colleagues who are not interested in interesting work. Or he suffers in the sense that he himself experiences the dichotomy imposed on his own thinking, as he tries to tackle manipulatively what can only be contemplated, tries to *wissen* where he may merely hope to *kennen*. In this case he is likely to crave for ever greater precision and clarity, like Weber and Husserl, partly to deaden the pain caused by the dilemma by repressing the awareness of its existence, partly because he cannot help hoping to find in clarity or logical conclusiveness a surrogate for the mystical illumination of the 'I see'.

It might be suggested that a kind of *karma* can be seen at work here – and we do not suggest that *karma* exists, but use it as a concept to aid understanding. The philosopher had been the first who self-consciously attempted to reduce actuality to manageable, conceptual proportions. From the beginning he reflected and furthered all civilizatory endeavours to mechanize, technicize, functionalize the citizens' surroundings, and conditions, rather than made any effort, as against the civilizatory intention, to humanize and anthropomorphize them. Logic took over completely from mimesis. To say it again: the philosopher was always on the side of the management. Since there has not yet been a society in which management was not class or caste control, a power function expressing power interests, he is on the side of the managers. Eventually the manufacturer, the bureaucratic administrator, the technological scientist, took over the tools the philosopher had forged. These they refined and modified to serve their respective purposes. The irony was that in each sphere the tools proved immensely more useful and successful than they had ever been in the hands of their inventors. Philosophy, and with it all the *Geisteswissenschaften*, was left stranded in an intellectual and academic no-man's-land somewhere between the 'arts' and the 'sciences', envious and with a violent desire to learn how to use the tools it had fashioned, with comparable and comparably measurable success in its own territory. Philosophers and social philosophers have not yet begun to ask themselves what was and is implied by their inability to handle their own tools in their own field.

'Philosophy begins', Adorno said, 'where the struggle for survival ends.' Perhaps we have not yet had a philosophy, because civilization has taught man to see the social reality as a struggle for survival, and because that belief had created conditions in which the individual had indeed to struggle in order to survive and which were then read back into 'nature'. Yet Marx already had suggested that an ossified social possibility, and the limited expectations and interests it engendered, might have been more directly responsible for man's seeing his life as a struggle for survival, than either nature or human nature. The education and humanization of the senses and of our sensuousness – which Marx saw as history's task – may well be in some kind of accord with nature's intentions, since nature produced the senses which may be understood, with greater justification, as the avenues of life and of 'life's self-delight', than as tools of survival, since there must be life before there can be survival.

We return to the social philosopher in his no-man's-land. Should he, and of course the sociologist, opt for science or, rather, persevere in his first choice, though it proved a problematical one? As scientist the social thinker posits, defines, manipulates. As scientific sociologist he cannot help doing this in an area where such methods must remain either unilluminating or counter-productive. Human material can be manipulated quite easily for a while and within limits. It retains a tendency to escape and to surprise the manipulators, even to manipulate them and their manipulations. This is inevitable, even logically, as the positing is done by those who are part of the human material. Here we have our old circle and it has often enough shown itself as quite vicious. For instance, the methods and concepts, the tools of sociology, psychology, philosophy, can be used indifferently by cops and robbers, by Roosevelt and Hitler, industrial researchers and advertisers. They can rationalize, i.e. make more forceful, the arguments of both employers and employed, of the right and of the left, of those that think they are right and of those who know they are wrong. It has been proved an error to believe that rationalization would facilitate agreement between conflicting interests.

Conceptual, tool-like reasoning not only lends itself to rationalizations in the Freudian connotation and to ideological distortions. It is inevitably ideological, since it is used by one person or group against another. Like any tool it is designed to achieve a purpose and to impose it on recalcitrant material, to satisfy an interest. Like a tool, it is easily turned into a weapon when used against another person. As a matter of fact, belief in rationalism is similar to belief in militarism. (War is merely an extension of diplomacy.) Arguments like armies are marshalled to protect causes and interests, possessions and territories, and to expand them. Both reflect the same social reality.

Are there no other possibilities of thinking, of exploration and discovery? Can the sociologist afford to ignore this question? This much at least he should acknowledge: in turning from 'poetic', contemplative, subjective thinking to other forms, he is making a choice and decision beyond rationality, he decides in favour of a form of rationalization which has no rational basis, at least not in his own understanding of rationality. Am I simply suggesting once again that the sociologist become a poet, moreover the kind of poet the poet himself has not yet been, except at rare moments? Perhaps. It could be of sociological significance that the original motive behind a young person's wish to become, among other things, a sociologist, might be the desire and hope to come to understand himself and others in the diverse forms of togetherness. At that time of life his understanding of understanding would be poetic, contemplative, at least as much as scientific, analytical. And the young person's understanding of and interest in science is also at least partly poetic. This can be and is shrugged off as immaturity, and universities might be thought of as the place where such bees are let out of bonnets. But could not our maturity be dubbed resignation with equal justification? Is it still so easy, since Freud, to think of maturity as inevitably the denial rather than possible fulfilment of youthful expectations? (Cf. Bloch, 1970, pp. 258–88.)

Marx had said in 1854 (quoted Klien, 1968, vol. 1, p. 535):

> The contemporary brilliant brotherhood of English novelists – whose plasticity and eloquence have conveyed to the world more political and social truths than all professional politicians, publicists and moralists together have expressed – has described every level of the bourgeoisie, from the most genteel *rentier* and possessor of guilt-edged securities who considers any form of business as vulgar, to the smallest shopkeeper and solicitor's clerk.

The realists and naturalists of the nineteenth century may not have been too conversant with the philosophical problems inherent in their approach. They may not have asked themselves searchingly enough what they meant by 'reality' and 'nature' – though many of them paid greater attention to such philosophical problems than philosophers are inclined to pay to the problems raised by literature. They certainly attempted an approach which enabled them to see the subject not only in his intersubjective, his social and personal reality, but embedded in and shaped by his social as well as natural conditions. In this way they were the first to look at the social background as something not to be taken for granted or to be mistaken for nature or necessity, but as something needing investigation and explanation, something to be protested against and to be changed. (The eighteenth century at large still accepted social structures as given.)

It is worth remembering that Balzac and Stendhal preceded Comte and Spencer. Were they precursors as well? The realists tried to be and often were as 'objective' as it is possible to be. As poets they did not have to pretend that their objectivity had no objective, that it had not been sparked off by most subjective and inter-subjective passions which in turn had been roused by the objective, most anti-subjective and anti-human conditions which they then described with such accuracy. Another circle here, but not necessarily a vicious one. The poet, here the novelist, is closer to human actuality, precisely because of his subjective passions; for these, if anything, and certainly not objective rational considerations move or halt historical development. I suggest that in some respects these writers were more objective than the sociologists who followed them. As poets they remained committed to a contemplative approach however qualified. Now it is a possibility which cannot be ruled out, except arbitrarily, that contemplation does more justice to object-subjects than manipulation. It lets them be and in that way sometimes lets them shout out for themselves that they are not yet what they would and could be. Contemplation does not wish to handle its subjects and need not therefore concentrate on looking for a handle. It is not exclusively interested in categorizing them according to function and utility within a conceptual framework designed by and for sectional societal interests. Science views objects as having their reality exclusively in their functionality, identifiability and manipulability. It does not and does not intend to do justice to them. It would not even admit that 'doing justice to an object-subject' has scientific meaning. Science enshrines the age-old assumption and presumptions of managers, oligarchs, bureaucrats, who never cared about doing justice to their subjects. For them subjects were objects to be manipulated for subjective objectives which were then ideologically justified as objective necessities.

In as far as science took over those managerial assumptions and applied them to the handling of matter, it made more profitable and less dangerous use of those socially evolved methods and tools. Yet we should by now be able to appreciate the perils and fatality of reintroducing those sharpened tools into the study of society, of the individual in society. They cannot avoid turning subjects into objects to be managed, impressed, used for subjective objectives. And because these are not the objectives of the 'impressed' subjects, the latter are being turned into objects, beings without subjective purposes. For that reason the historical, realistic and naturalistic novel or drama may well be more than a forerunner of sociology and social philosophy. It may be exemplary for them, for it mirrored as faithfully as possible the tensions between the impersonal objectives and the repressed or alienated subjective intentions.

And these tensions, rather than either the subjective or the objective intentions in themselves, constituted the reality of the age. It naturally would require much *Besinnung* as to what 'exemplary' could mean in this context. For literature as much as the *Geisteswissenschaften* suffered from the dichotomy of thought and actuality which we are discussing here. In some ways it may have proved more faithful to the possible as our reality and humanity, closer to the heart as well as to the mind of man. It has also, and often by its very success, aided and abetted the dichotomy by making it more tolerable, even entertaining, by permitting itself to be relegated to spare-time and leisure and by thus being used as ideological weapon. It could be the task of the *Geisteswissenschaften* as *Geisteskennerschaften* to explore the possibilities of translating the intentions of literature and art into social and psychic intentions. Which could mean, *pace* Weber, that the sociologist may have to become a bit of a prophet. (When Engels in 1893 disowned Marx's early writings as 'like poetry' he did not do justice to him, nor to himself. Cf. Tucker, 1961, p. 173.)

Realistic-naturalistic literature came to an end as a main artistic current, not because it had failed but because it had proved most successful. As realistic painting – even the Impressionists' realism of light – led to photography with all its attendant advantages and perils, realistic literature flowed into film and documentary. And the documentary, as film, television programme, book or article, may contain the most fruitful hints yet concerning a possible future for sociology and psychology, even for a casuistic philosophy. The documentary is undoubtedly the progeny of realistic literature and as such in danger of becoming entertainment. Any influence from the scientific side can probably be traced to psycho-analysis and its procedures and case-histories, i.e. its most unscientific and contemplative aspects. In turn the documentary is already increasingly influencing sociological work. Various projects begin to become assimilated not only to its forms but its intentions. They wish to entertain as well as to inform. They set out to be interesting. They do this, because they have objectives and intentions, wish to move and summon the reader, and know they can only hope to succeed in this by recreating him. They are beginning to realize, if not yet too consciously, that the only possibility and hope of constituting a new social awareness and intention is by way of recreation. For in this area alone, no matter how cribbed, crabbed and confined, has been kept alive the apprehension of the possible, here where fact and fiction are not yet or no longer easily separable. (I am thinking of works like those of Oscar Lewis, Ferdynant Zweig, Jan Myrdal, of many anthropologists.)

Now the power of a documentary, its possible personal and thereby social impact, is dependent for better and worse on the imaginative, pointed, interested and interesting manner of presentation. The facts or, rather, the meticulous accumulation of facts matters comparatively little. This can and does tempt producers and directors into abuse, dishonesty or sheer carelessness. It also reflects the fact that two or three facts judiciously chosen and imaginatively presented can yield more light and warmth than any multiplication of mere factualities. They may even yield more in-formation, if this is understood as forming one's inner, personal intention in the light of the outward, communal actuality. The fate of one man, one woman, one child, during a vast international upheaval or natural disaster, faithfully and sympathetically represented, can in-form us more thoroughly concerning the reality of that situation than any number of statistics or objective descriptions – whose objective it might well be to hide the human actuality. For if we come to think of it, an event is such, because it is experienced by this or that person. Multiplication here is not even addition. Dilthey may have been near some truth when he saw biography as the real stuff of historiography, as life is the real stuff of history, and Sartre has since taken up that thought. The documentary producer, as any film-maker, knows that personal interest, interest in a person or persons, has to be established, if interest in any problem of a social nature is to be raised and kept alive. Even science fiction has to rely on personal interest to carry its mechanisms.

As in a work of the imagination, the integrity of a documentary – as possibly of any sociological work – depends on the producer's faithfulness to and understanding of the essential passions that constituted the facts of a given situation and their significance.

Instances of contemplative insights

We shall now glance at some sociological thinkers and ask whether and how they were affected by that dichotomized thinking – and living – which has been the heritage of at least Western philosophy.

Marx, like most sensitive and educated men of his age, started by writing poetry, before he became attracted and fascinated by the philosophy least academic in intention if not in expression. Hegel himself had started as a poet, as a friend of Hölderlin, and one may still do best justice to his thought, if one understands it as a titanic attempt to embody an ultimately mystic vision which is obscured as much as elaborated by his detailed labours. Marx's *1844 Manuscripts* are the expression of a passionate conviction which his labours tried to but could not establish as rational – in the limited scientific connotation – but which gave power to them. He had 'seen' something, had experienced what can only be described as a prophetic vision. He had 'seen' the factuality of man's situation measured against his possibilities. And like the prophets he was convinced that these possibilities were his humanity, his human actuality, which the *status quo*, the appearance parading as reality, denied. For that reason he could say that until now philosophy had tried to understand, now it had to change the world, because it – or he – had understood. For the rest of his life he struggled incessantly to communicate his understanding of reality to enable men to change it.

Das Kapital is an example of how far a man can stray from his original intentions in his efforts not only to express but to justify them. While poets and prophets know that it is the intention which justifies the work. As I said before, the impact of this treatise stands in no proportionate relation to the density of its arguments or its accumulation of facts. It stands in direct proportion to the passion which produced the arguments and collated the facts only to be obscured by them. It *moves* wherever the passion breaks through the arguments and facts and the reader realizes for a moment why there is all this arguing and this particular amassing of facts. There is one exception: the multiplication of reports dealing with the workers' conditions. Here the accumulating moves, because it is the direct expression of the indignation which the facts themselves had caused; because the accumulation represents the only possible and partially contemplative view of a situation the horror of which lay in its meaningless multiplication and repetition of a meaningless, inhuman factuality. Just as here the unavoidable selective concentration of the poet on the 'human interest' has often obscured the inhuman factuality. It is as if Marx had wished to say: This is credible only because it is so, against all human credibility. It is actual, though thought could have barely conceived it as possible.

So already the work of Marx poses the question: What would have been the social and political impact of *Das Kapital*, what would have been its impact on sociology and its further development, if it had been presented in a form more immediately adequate to embody its intentions? And what might have been that form, if economical and scientific preconceptions had not prejudged the issue in Marx's own mind? Another *Comédie humaine* or Zola-like novels? A mightier *Confession* than Rousseau's? A vast collection of *Essays*, like Montaigne's? Or *Pensées*? A series of pamphlets similar to the *Communist Manifesto*? Whatever the form might have been, there is no necessity to believe that the influence of the intention would have been less, though most likely less measurable and ambivalent in terms of power politics. One need only recall the fragmentary and idiosyncratic nature of those works which, like Pascal's, Rousseau's, Herzen's, changed the social consciousness of their age and of the ages that followed. The importance of Marx's contribution does not lie in the form of its presentation. Though it must be admitted – as was already done in connection with Freud – that owing to the prejudices, of his age, owing to its presumptions and preoccupations, Marx might not have been taken seriously by either scholars or politicians, had he not employed and thereby perpetuated their conventionalized methods of obfuscation. (It is interesting to note that the passages in which Marx and Engels expatiate on art and literature add up to 1100 pages. See Klien, 1968.)

I called Dilthey a poet *manqué*. He was at his best when he tried to *verstehen* poets and their experience, or thinkers whose philosophy or theology was closest to poetry (1919, 1957). Yet again and again he feels driven to deploy a vast rationalist machinery which is totally inadequate for the apprehension of just that which he wishes to elucidate and secure by its help. In his collected works we find the account of a dream which sums up his character and his dilemma better than any facts (1914, vol. 8, pp. 219–22). After a philosophical discussion with a friend, Dilthey had gone to sleep under an engraving of Raphael's painting *The Disputation*. In the dream the picture comes to life, and into it streamed more and more of the later philosophers who 'had added lustre to man's greatest endeavour'. He describes some of them with loving, romantic idealism. As one might have suspected, the poetry, having lain dormant for so long, adds up to little more than a pastiche. This must not tempt us to mistake the seriousness of the underlying poetic intention. Gradually, we are told, the various newcomers group themselves round the original three clusters which had already formed round Plato, round Aristotle and round Pythagoras and Heraclitus. These groups now were beginning to draw apart. Smaller, intermediate figures flitted about between them in frantic efforts to effect a reconciliation before it was too late. 'The distance which separated the groups grew with each second – now even the ground between them disappeared. A dreadful, inimical alienation seemed to separate them. . . . I was overcome by a peculiar dread that philosophy itself seemed to be there three or even more times – the unity of my own being seemed to tear, as I felt myself longingly drawn now to this group, now to that, and I strove to confirm it.' It is not clear from the text what the 'it' is and, therefore, what is to be confirmed. Is it philosophy? Unity? Dilthey awakens and becomes aware of the stars and through them, like Kant and others before him, of the mysteriousness of the universe. (Or was it unlike Kant for whom the starry sky proclaimed Newton's laws?) Philosophy had always tried to unravel this mystery.

Now Dilthey had realized that all metaphysical attempts to arrive at a conclusion, at a fixed point, were mistaken. Yet he did not recognize that arguments evolved in the process of wishing to establish fixed truth may not be apposite for the exploration of a new kind of truth; nor had he begun to wonder whether a mystery was something to be unravelled. The dream reveals two interrelated things: the simple longing for unity, universalizing, for a totality of meaning; ultimately the child's longing to be gathered into the mother's arms and breast, into the mother altogether. Such longing is not to be despised or neglected. It may be close to our actuality. The dream also shows the infinitesimal gradation of volatilization and sophistication by means of which man has tried to recapture a satisfaction which may not be capturable in this fashion. It is worth noting the treble artificiality of the professor's dream: via the copy of a painting of an allegorized disputation between the world's master abstractors, Dilthey remembers and immediately forgets the passion of intension which had created all those layers of artifice.

Here we may be up against the central riddle of the *Geisteswissenschaftler* which cannot be explained simply by their longing

242

to imitate the natural sciences. For the riddle lies in why they have this longing and why it proved so irresistible. Let me put it like this: at least some of them were without doubt sensitive, poetic, at times mystically inclined souls. They had not only an extraordinarily fine intelligence, but a refined and responsive sensitivity and sensibility. For them the study of sociology or philosophy was obviously the inevitable expression of a vital, personal concern. Each of them had had one of those universalizing visions or glimpses which Sartre calls '*totalisation*', the Hebrew prophets 'thus says Yahweh', and which throughout the ages philosophers had learned to domesticate by turning them into universes of discourse. Why did the late-comers follow their precursors? Why did they, each and all and without demur, impose upon themselves disciplines of rationalization which their sensitivity must have experienced as arbitrary, tyrannical and painful, and against which they all rebelled at moments though always with a bad conscience? (How one wishes they had been a little more like Huckleberry Finn, that simpler but greater philosopher and moralist, who decided to go against his conscience rather than against his sensitivity. Ch. 31.) They accepted an age-old imposition and thus authorized it all over again. As social philosophers they submitted to it without serious questioning, while at the same time submitting most other impositions to the most rigorous critique. They continued to believe in that which frustrated their best virtues.

(Had their belief in objectivity its roots in this peculiar masochism, the joy to submit to that which one wishes to manipulate, the relief of abdicating all responsibility in face of that which causes one such exorbitant troubles? Maybe sado-masochism is the inevitable result where the emphasis is on manipulating and doing. Maybe the craving to manipulate and to be busy is the consequence of an eradicable infantile sado-masochism. Yet it could be that this is aroused in the infant, because society does not leave parents the time or teach them the wisdom to give to their children the depth of unhurried attention they need to grow up without intolerable disappointments which manifest themselves as sado-masochistic tendencies. Now the manipulator, though possibly no longer conscious of the violation he inflicts, may crave to be violated in turn or to violate himself in order to prove justified in continuing his violations.)

Meinecke records in his biographical sketches (1970) how sometimes on his return past midnight from some friendly gathering or festivity, he would notice a light still shining in a colleague's study and know he was burning his midnight oil. Meinecke would feel guilty, because he could not work so hard and patiently. Mommsen had said that a scholar must learn to manage on four hours' sleep a night to be able to fulfil his tasks. Meinecke would remember that when he saw the light. Why this asceticism? Today it is reflected in 'arts' departments wishing to be seen to work as hard and as long as any science lab., mastering as many facts. Is it possible that the power politics of academe and its intrigues, the virulence of much scholarly argument, the aridity of so many scholarly publications, are symptoms of a deep discontent which reflects the dichotomy of intention and formulation, and which communicates itself to the new students who soon begin, and as a matter of course, to look for their pleasures outside the curriculum?

Now in the *Geisteswissenschaften* in particular the question of why this should be so remains pressing. It should be absorbing and most satisfying to be given time and space for exploring, and together with others of one's own age, man and society in all the complexities of their interrelations and interdependence. If anywhere, here where everything is still in much darkness and confusion, research could be full of the joys of discovery. And here, by its very nature and the multi-facetedness of each possible approach, no discovery could possibly be exclusive. It would not have to be defended, only retested by increasingly sharpened sensitivities; for even a contradictory discovery could merely complement the first, not eliminate it. That is why sociological and all social studies should be and could be a communal quest, beyond the competitiveness which some sociologists recognize for the limited and limiting conceptual attitude it is (cf. Sombart, 1927, vol. 2, p. 410). In the social sciences, including psychology, philosophy, history, an organic connection could subsist between the communal life and the studying, for the studies are of men in community, of man as a social being, of society as man's personal actuality. Such studies cannot be pursued apart from communal commitments, else they would be an abstraction from the start, a dealing with what is not. And the community of students, some of them very eager, is there! Are the social sciences going to make use of what is at hand, or will they continue their barren imitation of art and science departments?

Once again the question cannot be avoided whether the social sciences as yet *are*, whether what-happens-to-be is anything but a confusion which suppresses what could *be*. One thing is clear: Man has not yet learned the one and most vitally important skill of all, namely how to live together with others of his kind creatively, amicably and joyfully. He does not yet know how to educate himself and his children for this, how to set about discovering and exploring and exploiting the possibilities of community. He has not even begun to wish to learn. Anything rather than a direct confrontation with this question concerning the possibilities of community and communion. That is left to cranks – Weber already left it to sectarian fanatics (1968, pp. 173, 193) – to groups of badly confused teenagers. Their inevitable failure can be used as proof against the aspirations themselves. It is left to religious communities whose disciplines, foreshadowing those of industry and science, have until now been an evasion rather than a facing of the question. Surely such a situation is *fragwürdig* for sociology.

The *Geisteswissenschaftler* cannot simply try to turn into a poet or prophet. We have not yet discovered what a poet really is, how a prophet can communicate his vision without immediately distorting it. As far as sociology is concerned, I believe that, as essentially a communal endeavour, it needs to develop methods and objectives with their own inherent logic. It has to discover and explore quite new possibilities of inter-subjectivity as group-work and group-listening and group-life. It will have to experiment with means of communication, more direct modes of formulation, so that the method need not necessarily conceal the intention. It may have to learn how to accept as testing of its discoveries not scientific, logical argumentation, but the kind of test which works of art and human relationships have to undergo. One of the first tasks of a new sociology might well be to enquire why the artist and prophet have failed until now, though everyone knows they are right. It is in the light of such a possible and necessary sociology – psychology, philosophy, economics, history – that I ask whether the existing methodology of the *Geisteswissenschaften* is at all adequate, apposite, feasible.

We continue to look at the works of the greater ones among social philosophers to suggest that this is not an arbitrary or perverse question, that it is a question implicit in all their works, a question which only a sustained effort on everybody's part prevents from asking itself.

Kant's separation of 'pure' from 'practical' reason – really of practical, manipulative, universal, from impracticable, private reason – of phenomena from noumena, was not the result of failing intelligence or sincerity or of fading sensibility. It was the consequence of the Prussian ardour with which the philosopher subordinated his searching insights to a totalitarian and totally alien discipline – admittedly a discipline hammered into European children's heads since at least the Middle Ages. Let me illustrate my point by an example from outside this area. It requires an almost Pauline genius to retrieve the insights of St Paul from his arguments and illustrations. (As against the poetic Jesus whose images embody his insights.) His understanding of freedom as hope, faith, passion, directedness, as possibility over against the whole weight and clamour of reality and its powers; his insistence that no law, no institution, no external or introjected authority, not the authority of God himself, can save a man or make him free, all this has the stature of Jesus's and Freud's, even of Marx's, insights. His peculiar intellectual discipline which is a little more discernible to us than our own because it is not our own, his mixture of Pharisaism and Hellenistic, syncretistic philosophy, has effectively hidden his insights for almost 1900 years. St Augustine and Luther had intimations of their intentions and in turn covered these over by means of Paul's own arguments. Similarly it requires an almost Kantian genius, possibly of an alien culture, to retrieve Kant's truly illuminating insights and apprehensions from his ratiocinations. These have been and still are the bushel that hides his light. We today do not seem to find it much easier to break through his arguments and penetrate to his insights than those who lived in between. (Which, by the way, is another reason why quotations, however copiously used, are rarely illuminating and often confusing. However, cf. Kant, 1966, an eye-opening anthology and condensation.)

Hegel seems to have appreciated Kant's insight and intention well enough to wish to restore the intolerable tension inherent in them and reflecting the tensions of society. So he placed that Kantian tension at the centre of his thought and system, as dialectics, only to succumb to the same alien imposition, and this to the extent to which he desired his own insights to be wrought into a philosophical system. If I had a dream like Dilthey, it might be of Hegel, Schelling and Hölderlin having remained bosom friends and close together all their lives. Joined by their equally sensitive wives and, gradually, their marvellous children, they would have communed, conversed, contemplated and, of course, lived, would have shared their experiences and understanding, until their complementary insights condensed, like the *Tao Te Ching*, into a slim, utterly translucent volume of. . . .

Marx recognized the overbearing Hegelian spirit as tyrant, certainly as the justifier of tyranny, only to fall for another. And it was not the tyranny of economics he succumbed to, but the tyranny of arbitrary economical conceptualization. His method made him a serf in a system which his insights might have helped to weaken. Economics as communal householding is a given actuality which needs contemplative and manipulative investigation. There is no reason to assume that the specific conceptualization Marx took for granted was the only possible or even an adequate one (cf. Sombart, 1927, pp. 920ff). In the final analysis, Marx's, Hegel's, Kant's insights or visions of the human condition are messianic, utopian. They may be illusory or even delusive. We can never know, for anti-utopian, realistic assumptions also could be delusive. Their respective methods could not make the insights any less illusory or ambiguous, but did turn them into megalomania or monomania.

Weber's messianism is patent, no matter how pessimistic a twist he gave to it. He denounces professorial messianic pretensions with messianic authority. But more than that: the original inspiration behind his work, certainly behind the *Religionssoziologie*, is religious-poetic. Nothing else can explain the Herculean labours he undertook to prove the power of *Geist*, even though it was a *Geist* who had in the meantime by-passed us. But why did he feel compelled to prove his inspiration, to establish *Geist* as causal agent in competition to the Marxian *Geist* of economics? Once again Weber shows himself as an autobiographer when at his most impersonal. He deploys the world religions to establish at that level the effectiveness of an inspiration which corresponds to the one he had experienced and which made him embark on his proof. Weber's method may not have concealed his intentions as totally as happened in the case of others. It nevertheless proved of greater fascination to his followers than his intentions. Hence their work proliferated into increasingly detailed studies of narrowing areas. The intention is being buried under the evidence it discovered and accumulated. Passion dug its own grave: its method.

Durkheim is an apparently unlikely yet striking example. In three of his main works (1952, 1968, 1969), and one could add his *Method* (1966), his conclusions have only the most tenuous connections with his evidence and statistics, which could have proved many other conclusions, even with the interpretations based on evidence and statistics. His logic, which he handles with skill and cunning, does what it is often made to do: it hides the disconnections instead of revealing them. Durkheim was as passionately prophetic as Weber. His utopianism, instinct with the eternal Mosaic nostalgia, with Enlightenment messianism and the enthusiasm of the French Revolution, expressed his vision of true community (1969, pp. 210–18). His conclusions preceded his arguments. His evidence was collected to prove them. This always happens but usually in the service of smaller, less noticeable objectives. The objective determines both the evidence and the rationalization, i.e. the induction and the deduction. What is surprising is that the passion of his rationalism was able to obscure the discrepancy between evidence and con-clusions even to his own mind. Surely more persuasive evidence could have been unearthed. It is as if Durkheim had wished to establish his convictions by means of the most ambivalent examples, so to speak, in the very teeth of the evidence. Rationalism sits more lightly on French than on German shoulders. Durkheim, as, for example, Comte before and Lévi-Strauss after him, could deduce much and with a good conscience from few and haphazardly chosen examples (cf. Lévi-Strauss, 1966, pp. 16–36). Weber had to ransack the earth and amass mountains of evidence to satisfy his conscience that he was justified in deducing from all this the little he dared. This divergence of methods is a further incitement to question the adequacy of either.

Pareto presents us with a most peculiar case: he had set out to construct a purely logical-scientific framework of general sociology. He emphatically insisted that he made no extraneous claims for his work. It might not prove useful. There was no reason to assume that it could accomplish anything in or for society as a whole or for an élite in particular. He knew that men were moved by emotions and rationalization, by 'residues and derivations', not by logic. At best they were moved by interest, economic interest of course which he thought of as almost rational. He knew men preferred the semblance of logic to the real thing. His work, he reiterated, was purely logical and scientific, that is, empirical. If he believed that many might wish to read it he would not have published it (1935, paras 86; also 46, 47, 50, 64, 70, 75). It was for the few who would understand and would also know that understanding is useless, i.e. because of the unacknowledged dichotomization of Western thinking, Pareto is driven into the paradoxical claim that his purely manipulative thinking is not intended to manipulate anything, its end is contemplation of itself.

The picture of himself Pareto is at pains to present is of a man who believes in nothing, believes that belief is irrelevant, and who is moved by nothing, who certainly will not let any belief interfere with his work. He does not even believe in rationality, except that it alone is rational. He is not sure whether eventually there will be a few more rational men about, nor whether it is desirable there should be, though he permits a slim hopefulness to creep into his argument here (ibid. 44, 72, 144, 2002, 2342). He is writing his logico-empirical treatise simply because he happens to be a totally reasonable man, at least in his scientific thinking, happens to have seen through all the tricks of deception and self-deception, though admitting that deception sometimes works where truth does not.

The result is a teasing and readable book, shot through with ironic insights and hindsights and *aperçus*, brimful of anecdotes and universal gossip. Yet if one looks at it today, the impression is not one of overpowering rationality, but of arbitrariness, special pleading, at best playfulness. It does not hang together as it was designed to. Although it tries to disprove so much, it does not prove anything. Its definitions are imprecise. One never quite knows what 'residues' are or 'derivations' and why there are just so many and not more or less. At times they seem to approximate Freud's understanding of complexes, aspects of the id, and of rationalizations. But while Freud emphasized the dynamics of the connections between id and ego, repression and rationalization, Pareto was content to fix them

CONTEMPLATION AND MANIPULATION

all in a static scheme. His deductions are anything but clear and necessary, except where they are tautological. No inevitable progression of argument or observation leads from the investigation of human illogicality, of residues and derivations, to the analysis of society as necessarily élitist. One feels tempted to say that the whole work embodies and is meant to embody a lack of vision and conviction.

Yet can one imagine that frail aristocrat of most refined sensibility to have gone to all those labours merely to demonstrate that they were valueless? Would that have been reasonable by his own standards? But if in spite of all protests to the contrary, he had his vision and the resultant convictions, what were they and it? Perhaps the vision was after all the old Platonic one of a truly aristocratic society, of a static, deeply conservative one openly acknowledging its élite; where aristocrats could hold their heads high and be tolerant of lesser breeds, especially in respect of their sexual behaviour. It may not have been accidental that thinkers of fascist tendencies were most impressed by his work. This may explain his disavowal. An open confession of such intentions would have flouted contemporary susceptibilities too blatantly, while their surreptitious presentation might allow them to do their subversive work. Those who had ears to hear would hear. And nothing is more likely to attract the many with intellectual pretensions than an assertion that a book is meant for the few. Is it possible that the great rationalist was not aware of his own intentions (ibid. 2252)? We need not go into this. What matters is to see once again how message and medium, intention and method, are at odds with each other. The method blurred the intention. And here, in as far as Pareto's belief in logic and scientific method was genuine, the method blurred itself. Rationality itself, when it is not geared to an extraneous objective but to itself as its own objective, becomes irrational, a dog biting its own tail. Pareto proved that Weber was right in defining rationality as the most economic means for the attainment of an objective. This cannot be rationality.

Meinecke presents another aspect of the dichotomy of contemplative and manipulative thinking. In his book on *Staatsräson* (1963) he glorifies, at least justifies the culmination of manipulative thinking and its stringent application to imperial power politics. He treats Machiavelli as if he were not merely the reluctant, diplomatic discoverer and exponent of the actual mechanisms of politics but a benefactor of mankind. As if the acknowledgment of the necessities of *raison d'état*, requiring the subordination of even the prince's interests in as far as they are still human, represented the final liberation of mankind. One has to read the book to savour its unconscious paradox (ibid. pp. 198-9 for example). In his *Historismus*

249

on the other hand (1959) and without any apparent awareness of its contradictoriness, he delineates with obvious sympathy and approval the growth of a kind of historical understanding which at least intends to see the individual as *ineffabile*, as sick of national power pretensions, wishes to contemplate history in its uniqueness and irreducibility rather than manipulate it into historiography to the greater glory of the *status quo* or of *Staatsräson* (ibid. 30ff, 50ff, 298ff, 313, 328, 390ff, 395ff, 439, 468, 497).

What are we to make of his paradox: a pacific, gentle German professor glorifies power politics just before the outbreak of the First World War – and we recall that Weber, Sombart, Scheler, Durkheim and Pareto, among others, had been doing likewise. Then he begins to move towards a non-manipulative understanding at the very time when the whole of Germany is being most crudely manipulated. May one suggest the following explanation: *Staatsräson* epitomizes the glowing, militant, unselfconscious patriotism and jingoism that drove millions mad with enthusiasm when war was declared in 1914. The book sums up a probably badly mistaken but comprehensible emotion. The scholarly method did not make the emotion rational. It produced rationalizations to present it as rational. Painstaking scholarship, copious documentation, thus tried to make the irrational appear rational. It prevented at least Meinecke himself from recognizing his motives and his possible error. Had he been permitted by academic conventions to give poetic, i.e. appropriate, expression to his enthusiasm, it most likely would have looked rather stale in 1919. The solid respectability of his scholarship not only masked the emotional and parochial character of his intention. It enabled it to survive under changed circumstances, in which it had become irrelevant or pernicious.

Yet such a survival is symptomatic of many other rationalizations on left and right which, on account of their appearance of general rationality, perpetuate emotive attitudes far beyond the time of their partial plausibility or usefulness, until they constitute a constant if potential danger. Furthermore the very method which enabled Meinecke to enshrine his out-of-date patriotism, later on prevented him from reaching a fuller appreciation of the possibilities of historism and individuality. Instead it twisted his intimations into a form which, surely against the author's wishes, could easily be given a little further twist to justify tendencies he intended it to counter. May I add here that to the extent to which English, American and even French social thinkers have not fallen into Meinecke's – and Weber's and Dilthey's – dilemma, they have not seen the promised land of possibility even from his distance.

Simmel is the *causeur* among German social philosophers (cf. Meinecke, 1970, p. 200). He abounds in *aperçus*. The progression of his ideas is rather like that of an avalanche. He seems to be the least committed; until one begins to realize that his very cleverness is a defence, as much as, for example, Weber's sacrificial rationalistic rigour. Yet while the latter's Prussian puritanism made him elaborate a chinkless armour and try his sword and pike ceaselessly on any challenger, Simmel hides behind arguments as behind a smoke-screen, following the hoary tradition of the Yeshiva disciple who has learned to give at least ten arguments for and against any proposition. Simmel's *Soziologie* (1922), although obviously the result of a powerful if unacknowledged longing for totalization, exudes an air of total unreality. No premonitions of disasters soon to come ruffle the equable, often fine and perceptive analyses of struggle and competition, of political, social, economic constellations. A peculiar ivory-tower arrogance pervades the work, as if to say that 'we in academe' have long since seen through everything, though it may take some time yet, before they outside will learn. He actually begins his book with the suggestion that *Erkenntnis* was no longer geared to survival, i.e. to interest, that it had become a pursuit in its own right (ibid. p. 1). Thus he can produce an interesting, often suggestive *Philosophie des Geldes* (1907) in which he treats the monetary evolution as if it had already created an almost perfectly rational society. He pays disproportionately little attention to the ways in which money always has been and still is functioning as instrument of power, of often totally irrational power, of subtlest or crudest manipulation, as the reservoir of infantile projections of omnipotence phantasies. Although he knows Marx reasonably well, he seems to have forgotten or discarded what the 'poet of commodities' had to say about the power of money as the commodity above all others to distort the human apprehension of reality altogether.

However there are indications throughout his work that he too had had his vision and the consequent experience of loss which made him turn to philosophy and then to social philosophy in order, perhaps, to recapture and to be able to communicate something which, one cannot help feeling, he hoped would become clearer in the searching and telling. (This may still be the best reason for writing.) He reveals his vital concerns most clearly, if still obliquely, in *Philosophische Kultur* (1911), a collection of essays. On the problems of the contemporary religious situation he writes (ibid. p. 29):

The uncanny seriousness of the present situation is that the need which used to be satisfied by the transcendent as such, is now paralyzed by the disappearance of the contents of faith. And so it is as if that need, however much a psychic reality itself, were cut off from the way to its own life. . . . Not the

251

religious person is endangered by the loss of a transcendent God, but the irreligious who need him as an inspiration. Can they too be given the capacity to find in their soul what the soul had projected into the sky? Or is religiosity a special category possessed by the 'religious person'?

Simmel himself is one of the endangered, a rationalist in quest of a faith, a descendant of both Leibniz and Voltaire. His temper predisposes him to long for the Enlightenment faith in reasonableness, for a reasonableness that rests securely in a reasonable faith. So one may understand his main works as essays in that kind of reasonableness in which men may be gradually persuaded to put their faith. And once again the disciplined elaboration conceals the intention.

Up to a point Simmel himself realized this and understood his difficulty as one of the inevitable dilemmas of civilization. In '*Der Begriff und die Tragödie der Kultur*' (1911) he deals with the inherent tendency of all creativity to become alienated from its original intention in its formal expression. This is the tragedy of *Kultur* as of *Zivilisation* that works of art, like those of scholarship, or the communal endeavours that find expression in religious and secular institutions, intervene between the intention of the creator and the sensibility of the recipient as much as they communicate the intention. The accelerating accumulation of such expressions of creative intentions or inspirations leads to further alienation symptomatized, for example, by the museum. Simmel, unlike Marx, does not see in feudalism or capitalism but in civilization as such the source of continuing and increasing alienation of man from his works, from his fellow men, from himself. The fetishist character of all productions is not only typical of commodities in capitalist society, but of all cultural works. Once again capitalist rationalization merely seems to reveal an older actuality (ibid. p. 270). This is the tragedy 'that the destructive forces directed against his essential being have their source in that being itself, that a fate fulfils itself in man's destruction which is grounded in himself' (ibid. p. 272). For from the beginning civilization has that 'form which is inevitably and inherently fated to divert, harden, confuse and make schizoid those intentions which subsist in the soul's attempt to travel from its imperfection to its fulfilment' (ibid. p. 277). No matter whether or not one accepts this estimate and terminology, Simmel reveals himself in them as a poetic and mystic soul. His intellectual and formal approach hides, and is partly meant to hide, the religious intentions which would measure society against a pristine vision lost, so Simmel fears, beyond retrieving. (One would need a sociology of the emancipated Jew in search of a substitute for the lost faith which had been his people's only home for 2000 years.)

Because of his poetic predilections, Simmel is at his best in his excursions and digressions, when he can give free rein to his fine discrimination, to his capacity for savouring the infinitesimal gradations and complexities of things (cf. 1922, ch. 5, pp. 287–8, 278–81; also 1911, chs 3 and 7a). It is not accidental that he approximates the phenomenological practice here, for phenomenology was born of a similar mystic vision and longing for totalization, and in the mind of another emancipated German Jew, together with a similar susceptibility for the infinitesimal gradations and shadings of reality.

Husserl was undoubtedly a most passionate and total philosopher, like Descartes and Kant. To be a philosopher was his life. In his late *Krisis* (1962, p. 15) he proclaims:

In our philosophizing we are truly the functionaries of humanity. The quite personal responsibility for our own truthful being as philosophers in our inner personal vocation holds within itself at the same time the responsibility for the true being of humanity, which is the being towards a *telos* and can be actualized, if at all, solely through philosophy – through *us*, *if* we are philosophers in earnest.

Therefore philosophy today can be no less than a historical and critical *Rückbesinning* (reorientation) in view of the past (ibid. pp. 15–16),

to care and provide, prior to any decisions, for a radical self-understanding: through enquiring once again what was originally and in each case intended as philosophy and what was the continuing intention throughout the historical inter-communication of *all* philosophers and philosophies; but this as critical consideration of that which in aim and method demonstrates the ultimate *Ursprungsechtheit* (pristine genuineness) which, having been recognized, compels the will apodeictically.

In other words, Husserl himself wishes to penetrate through his predecessors' disciplined expressions to their intentions. This, so he believes, would point to *the* intention of philosophy: to arrive at a total, unified, necessary, apodeictic, i.e. self-evident, understanding of man and his actuality, nothing less. Philosophy is intended to guide man to the point where he realizes his 'self-understanding as [having its] being in his vocation to a life in apodeicity' (ibid. p. 275).

Husserl's religious intention and intensity are apodeictic. We should not be put off by the apparent jargon. Mystics through the ages have felt impelled to clothe their most burning and precious insights in atrocious terminologies. In the literally one-large-page-long sentence of impenetrable density which concludes this work,

Husserl affirms a utopian and ultimate vision of philosophy: it is moving towards the point where self-understanding and self-evidence become one, where therefore all distinctions between theory and practice and enjoyment, between pure reason, practical reason and judgment, between *Wissen* and *Kennen*, science and art, truth and goodness, have been *aufgehoben*; where, in other words, we shall know even as we are – or long to be – known, where all shall see God and live. Yet Husserl continued to believe, more passionately than anyone else, that the final clarification, the consummation of the new innocence, where self-understanding is self-evident, could only be reached via the two-thousand-five-hundred-year-old philosophizing tradition which had intended that culmination, though it had always forgotten its intention in the efforts to express and prove it.

There seems little doubt that Husserl's measurable influence would have been more negligible, if he had not veiled his experience of the mystical union or his longing for it, even from himself, in the most austere academic jargon. (Just as most Christian mystics would probably have been burned on the stake, had they not robed their naked experiences in the conventional theological draperies.) Yet his influence, as on Scheler, Sartre, Merleau-Ponty, is as indubitably due to the underlying mystic-poetic intention rather than to the scholastic academic argumentation. Husserl, like Marx and Isaiah, experienced the full unmitigated impact of a pristine philosophico-mystico-religio-poetic illumination. Like them he had seen the glory of the Lord and the whole world judged and found wanting in the light of that glory. He also answered the cosmic 'whom shall we send and who will go for us' with the 'send me'. Both Husserl and Marx felt they had experienced the end of philosophy, its *finis* and its *telos*. Both understood their own labours as the beginning of the fulfilment of philosophy's intention. (So the Buddha and Jesus had experienced their illumination as a consummation of the intentions of their respective traditions.) Both wished to repristinate the intentions. Both felt impelled to express their convictions and intentions in forms and terminologies which they knew to be inadequate, simply because an adequate medium of communication did not yet exist. Husserl turned to the philosophical discipline, although he had his suspicions as to how thickly that had overlaid the original intentions, as Marx turned to economics, although he knew, or had known when he was writing his *1844 Manuscripts*, it was adequate in its own sphere only in as far as it was the immoral explication of an immoral society (cf. Marx, 1968, pp. 257–60). In them, more even than in Freud, the discrepancy between intention and expression reaches its climax. Yet this discrepancy, just because it accurately mirrors that between intention and actuality in society at large and in each individual within that society, is our truth: schizophrenia.

In the foregoing it was certainly not my intention to denigrate the sincerity, intelligence or the peculiar genius of those I reviewed. On the contrary, I chose them because of my respect for them; because I wished to show that the discrepancy between intention and expression is not due to any lack in those who fell victim to it. It is the inevitable result of the constitution of the *Geisteswissenschaften* since the Renaissance and of philosophy since Plato. What I am pleading for is nothing more nor less than their reconstitution as *Geisteskennerschaft*, a *Rückbesinnung* not only concerning the intentions but the methods of the social sciences – possibly of the 'humanities' in general and in the light of Heidegger's wonder as to whether we as yet know what our humanity is. The medium may not be but merely pretend to be the message. Yet the two cannot be detached from each other either. Form and content, as in art and literature, are not separable, barely distinguishable. They either illuminate each other, or they darken the artistic intention altogether. *We have yet to discover a method which illuminates our intentions and is illuminated, made transparent, by them.*

One final consideration and exploration in this context. I have already referred to the indeterminable variety of what might be called 'levels of abstraction'. I am using this loose phrase to denote an obvious state of affairs: any verbalization or conceptualization is an abstracting from that which it is trying to grasp or merely to point at. The possibilities of such abstracts or of their use cannot be delimited. For the sake of convenience some of these possibilities can be placed in an ever shifting similitude of hierarchical order. The various stations or positions within that order I call levels of abstraction.

Let me illustrate: James Joyce described the experiences of a few people during twenty-four hours in well over 500 pages. In *Finnegans Wake* he fills more than 400 with the dreams of one man during one night. Those dreams, as we know, may actually have taken no more than a few seconds or minutes of that night. Joyce knew that even in those instances judgment was needed, selection and exclusion, not merely to make the material amenable to artistic presentation, but simply to make it manageable. Not even his minutely detailed treatment could comprehend the totality of experience or of the impressions which constitute one waking day or one dream hour. There is not only the stream of consciousness – or of phenomena, as Husserl will have it – with its possibly distinguishable atomic units which defies enumeration. There is the indefinable interplay between each of them and one or two or more or all of the others; and each interplay has its own trails of associations. And each association in turn may be placed anywhere along a sliding scale of emotive connotation ranging from ecstatic illumination to barest perceptibility. This densest of materials which can no longer be atomized, because each atom is constituted by its positioning among the others, constitutes the individual actuality on the level of consciousness. It constitutes the quality, i.e. the reality of personal existence, of *Dasein*, and the whole is bathed in ever changing emotional light which, of course, contributes to the changes. So already *Finnegans Wake* represents a level of abstraction. Like any work of the imagination, it is true, artistically true, to the extent to which the artist succeeds in letting the inevitable positing he practises be balanced and redetermined again and again by that on which he is imposing; so that in this tension the reader is enabled not only to rethink but to re-experience what the writer has embodied as well as volatilized in his words.

One step closer to sociology and we find the works of Oscar Lewis: the lives of one man, one family, one small group of people, as reconstituted by themselves in their own words (see Appendix). It is astonishing how complex a single, simple life appears even to those whose limited articulateness and whose limiting background may have seriously impaired their capacity for experiencing, certainly their ability to interpret their experiences. Yet the story of Pedro Martinez or of Consuelo Sánchez, as recorded by Lewis, could be expanded over and again.[3] The only limit is that of the interrogator's time and patience. And even within Lewis's books we can discern various levels of abstraction: chapters dealing with years in the life of a family, others, like the first long chapter of *La Vida*, encompassing half a day in the life of a Puerto Rican negress. The undisciplined chatter of uneducated men and women mediated, admittedly, by a listener of genius, reveals a complexity of personal, social, political relationships far beyond conceptualizations. On the one side it shades into almost psycho-analytical individualism and the borderland between the conscious and unconscious intentions and intensions, on the other it reveals global implications.

On a comparable level, more educated, intellectual, sophisticated, we find the biography and autobiography. They look at one individual life now from this angle, now from that. None can ever be final. Next there are the studies of quite small and self-contained groups: a family, a tribe, a village, a particular community. Much work has been done in this area by anthropologists, also by the occasional sociologist like F. Zweig. It could be seminal if it were permitted to fall on good sociological and psychological ground. Yet all such studies of necessity have to exclude almost everything that would have been of relevance to the biographer, although he already has to exclude so much. In any study of institutions, countries, movements, epochs, i.e. in historiography and sociology, even villages and town have to be severely disregarded. Here the investigator is moving on a level where hardly anything human still prevails – except the foibles and predispositions of those in apparent command of the situation. He is in the position of an observer of ants.

In their turn the practice of what is commonly called history or sociology affects and possibly distorts the understanding and writing of biography and the living of the lives of biographers and of their subjects. It has already affected both the groups the anthropologist is studying and his possibilities of comprehending them. For my conception of history, as of society, economics, religion, morals, de-fines and only too often seriously confines my *Dasein*, hides from me its possibilities which are my actuality over and beyond the conceptions of historiography.

One can think with nothing but awe, and perhaps therefore prefers not to think at all, of the limitless variety of possible and actual interplay, in individual understanding and experience, between all those levels of abstraction. And we have barely taken into account the extra dimension Freud has added to our possible understanding of personal and communal actuality (cf. Erikson, 1965, 1972). Yet this dimension is vital. For it is the unconscious or subconscious – and we need not understand it precisely like Freud or Jung – which determines the feeling-tone, the *Stimmung*, of individual and communal life, which creates values, grants or withholds that which makes life worth living. It is also, as we have seen, the level or dimension where the individual and society are inter-penetrating each other. As we learn to take it into account our approach to all the other levels will be subtly but radically transformed.

Precisely because of the infinite complexity of interaction between each and all, it surely seems questionable to wish for a method here which would hope to establish certainties, simple propositions, clearly defined factualities, definitive theories, and to do so by means of argumentation, i.e. of refutation and exclusion. What certainties, anyway, are we looking for and what makes them certain in a world where everything that matters to us as mortals is uncertain? Here where by the very nature of our situation and by the very constitution of our mind everything and nothing can be proved and disproved, from global statistics to the interpretation of a dream, where dreams and global statistics may well be inter-penetrating, it seems a waste of time to argue. Where everything is in continuous flux and at ever varying speed in relation to everything else, it seems odd to wish to make sure. For this flux is our human actuality, our situation. In as far as we, as *Geisteswissenschaftler* or sociologists,

257

wish to understand it and ourselves a little better, rather than to manipulate it and ourselves in accordance with untestable and possibly panicky preconceptions, it demands a radically different approach from any we have as yet attempted.

Appendix

A comment on the work of Oscar Lewis, no matter how inadequate because too brief, seems desirable, since it exemplifies certain new possibilities of understanding as well as anything I can think of.

His books occupy an area between art and sociology. They represent a compound of biography and autobiography. In them Lewis obviously exploited procedures pioneered by and used in psycho-analysis, social case work, anthropological studies, the documentary approach of film, newspapers, television. His training as a sociologist enabled him to put his investigations into a particular frame of reference. He was studying the sub-culture of poor Mexican peasants and the changes it underwent as they moved from village to city slum. It is equally true that, because he let his subjects speak for themselves, refused to frame them, the result burst the frame. His work required a discipline different from that of the artist, but also from that which the scientist is used to impose upon himself before imposing it on his subjects. It was a discipline of committal, of openness and expectation, the actual discipline of inter-subjectivity. Nothing could be more misleading than the belief that anyone merely has to take along a tape recorder, ask people to talk, and the result will be another Lewis-type record. More than a reporter, editor or producer of documentaries, Lewis had to get involved in the lives of his subjects. His involvement not only had to be comprehensive, it had to be felt to be so by them, so that their subjectivity and subjecthood could be kept inviolate all along. Unlike the psycho-analyst, the observer was in no position to preserve Olympian detachment. For the analytical situation, no matter how deeply it involves the analyst, is designed to enable the analysand to pass through the various stages of transference into a new independence. The analyst knows some of the signposts on the way. Lewis did not. He, and this is his peculiar genius, could get his results only by entering the as yet largely unexplored territory of mutuality, of Buber's 'between', where the sympathy and empathy of the observer enables the subjects to understand themselves better in their talking to him and to reveal in their telling, as the poet does, more than they or he could understand at the time. He made it possible for them to communicate by establishing communion between them and himself. He gave to them the space-time which permitted them to grow in articulation and to grow as they articulated. They grew rapidly and demonstrated how much creative potential there is in what we think of as the most unlikely places.

Let us for a moment compare his work with Young and Willmott's *Family and Kinship in East London* (1962). Like Lewis's book, it grew out of reasonably clearly defined intentions. The authors wished to investigate family patterns of the comparatively poor in a well established community, before they were moved to new housing estates where these patterns were likely to change radically. The approach of *Family and Kinship* is also sympathetic. A feeling of nostalgia and benevolence permeates the study. Yet it never gets beyond its intentions. Where it threatens to do this, it is rigorously drawn back into tabulation and statistics. The result is unilluminating. It confirms 'scientifically' what was known all along, certainly by the researchers. The subjects which momentarily sprang to life were soon swallowed up again by the investigators' objectives and objectivity. They ceased to be what they were. Information concerning them becomes irrelevant, because it does not concern *them*.

Because the subjects of Lewis's enquiries are allowed not only to remain but to become themselves, they transcend the intentions of the investigation. They reveal quite unintended and unexpected aspects of reality as possibility. For instance, (a) the articulateness of those illiterate or semi-literate peasants and slum dwellers is startling. We may make allowances for the editing which will not always have been able to avoid the temptation of making a point or making it more dramatically. We are still left with a pungency, appropriateness and poignancy of expression, a capacity for shaping and penetrating experience, which at times goes beyond that we would expect of ourselves. A sorry sociologist he who is not appalled at the waste of human potential thus revealed by Mexican peasants and Puerto Rican negroes. In Lewis's book the age-old conviction of the general stupidity of the majority of mankind is shown up as an ideological myth (Horkheimer-Adorno, 1969, pp. 274–5). That the human potential which showed itself in unexpected articulateness was neither illusory nor ephemeral is demonstrated by the fact that Lewis was able later on to use two of his Mexican 'subjects' as research assistants in Puerto Rico. He adds: 'These assistants gave me a Mexican view of Puerto Rican slum culture and helped point up the similarities and differences between Mexican and Puerto Rican subcultures' (1968, p. 22). (Corroborative evidence of the genuineness of Lewis's records can be found in the fact that his style deteriorates as soon as he does not report and translate.)

(b) Quite unintentionally, so I believe, but in a multitude of ways, the books confirm psycho-analytical insights and modify them. Each subject in turn bears witness to the density and intensity of childhood experiences, to the child's as yet barely imaginable vulnerability, and to the intricate way in which the growing child and adolescent organizes his life attitudes as defences round intolerable memories of childhood sufferings and the phantasy fears of their recurrence. Over and over again as one listens to those uneducated voices, one appreciates how the fine sensibility of each child is hurt beyond endurance and blunted by the continual onslaughts of the adults who unconsciously take their revenge for having had their sensitivities blunted in like fashion. One understands and feels how the inexhaustible energy of the child condenses into armoury, into violent reactions – for attack is the best form of defence – into ambition and self-assertion in the pursuit of civilization's phantasy aims. Gradually the fate of, for example, the Sánchez family begins to assume cosmic proportions, a pattern which is instantly recognizable as that of society at large and thus illumines the latter. Social, political, military structures, functions, ambitions, the whole of the societal paraphernalia with its infinitely refined ritual charades, its periodic outbursts of violence and apathy, is the elaborate defence system organized by badly hurt infants to protect them against the excesses of the violence it, the system, engenders.

(c) Lewis's books reveal the texture and quality of social actuality, of social consciousness and conscience. They uncover the interwoven patterns of familial and social patriarchy and authority. They show how the processes of projection and introjection work among those who have never heard the words; how social reality is generated, regenerated, perpetuated in the family which is the product of a repressive, divisive, alienated social order. They make us appreciate how the social order creates and recreates the painfulness of the family situation which in turn, via psychic defence systems, makes the order appear necessary, even desirable, so that it is able to enlist the repressed energies in its own defence.

(d) Lewis's books, just because they are not what we are pleased to call fiction, have made another thing quite clear: the writing of social, political, military history, the whole machinery of historical research, is a narrowly specialized, conceptualized, intellectual business which has little more immediate application to life than metaphysics or mathematics. When it is mistaken for more, it becomes phoney or sheer ideology. The historical writing capable of recreating the qualitative 'feel' of historic, social-individual existence has not yet been discovered. Lewis was a sociologist whose sociological labours compelled him to give up sociology as heretofore practised. His works are an explicit critique of sociology and history, all the more searching for not consciously being intended as such.

Notes

1 The problem poses itself

1 Cf. Dilthey, 1914, vol. 8, p. 20. Contrast vol. 7, pp. 3–13, 49, 86–7, 140, 148 *inter alia*; vol. 8, pp. 12–13; vol. 5, pp. 90–138, 232ff; vol. 1, pp. 375ff; with vol. 8, pp. 175–7; vol. 2, pp. 167, 318–19; vol. 5, pp. 273–303; vol. 7, pp. 197–202. Cf. Dilthey-Yorck, 1923, p. 71: '. . . *nicht ist . . . sondern lebt. . . .*'
2 Cf., for example, *Civilization and its Discontent* with Marcuse's *Eros and Civilization*, with Mitscherlich's *Society without the Father*, with Laing's *Politics of Experience*, with Reich's *Function of Orgasm*; also with Adorno and others on the totalitarian personality.
3 For example, in *The Future of an Illusion*. Cf. also his hope that analysis would eventually give way to biochemistry.
4 One of the points where psycho-analysis and phenomenology impinge upon each other. Yet our contentions lie beyond those of subjectivity versus objectivity.

2 Philosophical background

1 Cf., for example, Habermas, 1967, pp. 176–8, 232, 242; Scheler, 1960, pp. 1–50; Mannheim, 1960, pp. 14–18, 252–63. Also, in respect of history and sociology, Scheler, 1960, pp. 149ff; Mannheim, 1960, pp. 190ff; Bloch, 1970, pp. 163, 217–38. See Dilthey, 1914, vol. 1, on Plato and Aristotle, vol. 2, on the influence of Stoicism on the whole intellectual development in the West; Simmel on Kant, Schopenhauer; Adorno on Husserl and Heidegger, and his *Negative Dialektik*, a continuous controversy with the whole of Western philosophy. Lukács on young Hegel, 1967, in Dilthey's footsteps here, cf. pp. 71ff, 169, 183, 211, 598, 672.
2 Dilthey, 1914, vol. 1, pp. 26–39; vol. 7, cf. pp. 3–69 with 197, 206–7, 218. Cf. Lukács, 1960, pp. 335–45; Habermas, 1965, pp. 60ff; Fromm, 1969, pp. 108–9, also 270–1.

3 'Beyond doubt, all the great thinkers of the seventeenth century have compromised with the existing order in one way or another. But the possibility of such compromise lies for all of them – the faithful Catholic Descartes, the unbelieving Spinoza – in the firm conviction that the alteration of the world cannot consist in anything else than in an alteration of one's thoughts about it; that the altered interpretation of the world already *is* the alteration of the world itself' (Borkenau, 1934, pp. 297–9; cf. also 33ff, 42ff, 266ff, 372, 380ff).

4 Cf. Ryle's translation of G. H. Mead's symbolic inter-actionism into linguistic philosophy. Cf. that in turn with sociological field studies designed to avoid any possible category mistake (Ryle, 1950, chs 2, 6, 8).

5 Cf. Durkheim, 1968, pp. 9, 19, 76, 144–7, 188–9. Also Sombart,1927; Scheler, 1960; Borkenau, 1934, *passim*; see *The Epic of Gilgamesh*, Penguin, Harmondsworth, 1966, chs 1 and 2.

6 Lukács and Bloch as much as Dilthey and Meinecke are at their best when engaged in literary-sociological appreciation. See also Horkheimer-Adorno, 1969, on de Sade and the *Odyssey*; Adorno, 1958; W. Benjamin on Proust and Baudelaire; Kracauer, 1966, on the film in *entre deux guerres* Germany. Also Heidegger, esp. 1950, 1959.

7 Horkheimer-Adorno, 1969, ch. '*Kulturindustrie*'; Simmel, 1911, ch. '*Der Begriff und die Tragödie der Kultur*'; Heidegger, 1931, pp. 167–80.

8 Schopenhauer saw music as the most direct expression of the Will, which is our reality, in our Imagination (1902, book 3, par. 52).

3 Diverse approaches to the problem of understanding

1 On the tyranny of identifying thought, the compulsiveness of this particular Enlightenment conviction turned into myth, see Adorno, 1970, pp. 15ff, 144–7, 149–50, 172, 185, 259, 292, 304, 313; also Horkheimer-Adorno, 1969, ch. 1.

2 From Kant to Dilthey and then to Adorno, German thinkers realized that *Wissen* was 'categorical', theorizing, relational. They nevertheless too often equated it with all forms of knowing, including *Kennen*, which is not categorical. Cf. Scheler, 1960, pp. 202–28. This is also the theme of Adorno, 1970, and of Heidegger, 1954, esp. '*Was heisst Denken?*'. It is also the core of Dilthey's attack on metaphysics. Compare however Scheler's defence of metaphysics, for example, 1960, pp. 72–3, 85, 112; 1955, pp. 358, 377–8. Cf. Husserl, 1950, vol. 1, pp. 86, 100–1, 134.

3 This is the reverse and therefore complementary of Husserl's position. Cf. 1950, vol. 1, pp. 52, 86, 134, 163, 194, 290.

4 No *Iphigenie, Tasso, Tell, Bruderzwist im Hause Hapsburg, Prinz von Homburg, Joseph und seine Brüder*, were possible, post-Shakespeare and Milton, as an integral part of the central literary tradition of Britain, nor in the France of the eighteenth and nineteenth centuries. Cf. the comparative stature of Scott and Jane Austen, of *Salammbô* and *Madame Bovary*. Again Italy is the exception with its *I Promessi Sposi*. And it was in Italy that Croce could revive a historism closer to Hegel than to Vico.

5 Schiller's *Räuber*, *Kabale und Liebe*, even his *Fiesko*, convey the stuffiness of German politics more powerfully than the genuine and noble rebellious passions. Cf. Goethe, *Die natürliche Tochter*; Lessing, *Emilia Galotti*.

6 Here the theologian Karl Barth comes closer to Marx than any Marxist in his *Kirchliche Dogmatik*, part 4, vol. 3, which deals at length and most sensitively with the relationship between man and woman. Otherwise only poets and novelists, painters and musicians, have found in the man-woman relations the measure of human and social reality. Cf., for example, Lukács, 1964, pp. 489–91 on Fontane, and see *Effi Briest* and all the late Fontane novels.

7 Compare and contrast Bergson, Husserl, Schutz, already Dilthey, in their understanding of time lived and time observed. See also Kracauer, 1963.

8 Both *Psycho-Pathology in Everyday Life* and *The Interpretation of Dreams* are suggestive source books for showing the sedimentation at work.

9 It is interesting to note how much *Wissen* Weber still believed to be an essential prerequisite for undertaking even such a piece of industrial research. See '*Zur Psychophysik der industriellen Arbeit*', 1924, esp. the introductory remarks.

10 Kant's will points towards Hegel's spirit, and both towards Schopenhauer and Nietzsche's will, and all point towards scientific positing. Cf. Habermas, 1969, pp. 346–63.

4 A particular instance of sociological understanding and the snares of causal thinking

1 Compare '*extra ecclesiam . . .*' with '*quod non est in libris non est in mundo.*' Sombart, 1927, vol. 2, pp. 118–19.

2 Here Heidegger is Husserl's executor, as in 1967, pp. 80ff, 184–8, *inter alia*. See Spiegelberg, 1964, vol. 2, pp. 550, 556, on Merleau-Ponty. Scheler is the best example of one who arrives at premature conclusions on account of personal predilections. Also see Schutz, 1967, chs 7–12, 19–27.

3 See preface. Work is in progress on the 'truth-function' in society.

4 Scheler's *Wissensformen*, 1960, are instructive on two counts. First, as a cautionary tale. He gets himself into futile entanglements over attempts to explain or define a causal relationship between *Geist* and matter. Though at better moments he is aware that *Geist*, if taken notice of at all, can only be explicated in its own terms. Once matter and mind have been separated in social actuality as well as in philosophical thinking, they cannot be glued together again by a bit of causality. Second, Scheler is suggestive, if not convincing, in what he has to say about metaphysics as totalization attempts, undertaken by individuals, in the pursuit of which the individual has a chance to mature rather than to find completion in a system, and about the autonomy of religious, metaphysical and practical-scientific thought-forms and the possibilities of 'inner technology' as exploited in Eastern thought and practice.

5 Contemplation and manipulation

1 Cf. Erikson, 1965, 'The Legend of Hitler's Childhood', and 'The Legend of Maxim Gorki's Youth'. Cf. the work of Anna Freud, Melanie Klein, H. Marcuse, D. W. Winnicott.

2 Could this explain why today's entertainment – except for moments of tragedy achieved mainly in films – has to appeal rather directly to infantile, pre-civilizatory satisfactions; and also why, in its very clichés, it is so often more 'true' than the more sophisticated literature or theatre. One remembers Kafka's liking for 'trash'.

3 Growing self-understanding is a proliferating process. Cf. Liebrucks, 1963; Freud's case-histories; Winnicott's work with children; Milner, 1969, where she records a twenty-year-long analysis in which the analyst learns at least as much as the analysand. Compare great literature in general – for that is what it is about – and in particular the German *Bildungsroman: Wilhelm Meister, Maler Nolten, Der grüne Heinrich, The Magic Mountain, The Man without Qualities.*

Bibliography

For English translations of German books, see additional Bibliography, pp. 273–4.

ADORNO, T. W. (1958) *Noten zur Literatur*, Suhrkamp, Frankfurt a. M.
—— (1962) *Minima Moralia*, Suhrkamp, Frankfurt a. M.
—— (1969a) *Jargon der Eigentlichkeit*, Suhrkamp, Frankfurt a. M.
—— (1969b) in *Der Positivistenstreit*, Luchterhand, Neuwied and Berlin.
—— (1969c) *Prismen*, Suhrkamp, Frankfurt a. M.
—— (1969d) *Stichworte*, Suhrkamp, Frankfurt a. M.
—— (1970) *Negative Dialektik*, Suhrkamp, Frankfurt a. M.
ANTONI, C. (1962) *From History to Sociology*, Merlin Press, London.
ARENDT, H. (1958) *The Human Condition*, University of Chicago Press.
AUERBACH, E. (1957) *Mimesis*, Doubleday, New York.
BENJAMIN, W. (1966) *Briefe*, Suhrkamp, Frankfurt a. M.
BERGER, P. (1968) *Invitation to Sociology*, Penguin, Harmondsworth.
BERGER, P. and LUCKMANN, T. (1972) *The Social Construction of Reality*, Penguin, Harmondsworth.
BLOCH, E. (1969a) *Spuren*, Suhrkamp, Frankfurt a. M.
—— (1969b) *Thomas Münzer als Theologe der Revolution*, Suhrkamp, Frankfurt a. M.
—— (1970) *Das Prinzip Hoffnung*, Suhrkamp, Frankfurt a. M.
BORKENAU, F. (1934) *Der Übergang vom feudalen zum bürgerlichen Weltbild*, F. Alcan, Paris.
BURCKHARDT, J. (1963) *Weltgeschichtliche Betrachtungen*, Ullstein, Berlin
CASSIRER, E. (1923) *Philosophie der symbolischen Formen*, Cassirer, Berlin
CROCE, B. (1966) *Philosophy, Poetry, History*, Oxford University Press, London.
DAHRENDORF, R. (1962) *Gesellschaft und Freiheit*, R. Piper, Munich.
—— (1964) *Homo sociologicus*, Westdeutscher Verlag, Opladen.
—— (1966) *Gesellschaft und Demokratie in Deutschland*, R. Piper, Munich.
DILTHEY, W. (1914) *Gesammelte Schriften*, ed B. Gröthuysen, G. Misch, H. Nohl, vols. 1, 2, 4, 5, 7, 8, B. G. Teubner, Stuttgart.

——(1919) *Das Erlebnis und die Dichtung*, B. G. Teubner, Stuttgart.

—— (1957) *Von deutscher Dichtung und Musik*, B. G. Teubner, Stuttgart.

DILTHEY, W. and YORCK, P. (1923) *Briefwechsel*, B. G. Teubner, Stuttgart.

DURKHEIM, E. (1952) *Suicide. A Study in Sociology*, ed G. Simpson, Routledge & Kegan Paul, London.

—— (1966) *The Rules of Sociological Method*, Free Press, New York.

—— (1968) *The Elementary Forms of the Religious Life*, Allen & Unwin, London.

—— (1969) *The Division of Labor in Society*, Free Press, New York.

DURKHEIM, E. and MAUSS, M. (1970) *Primitive Classifications*, ed R. Needham, Routledge & Kegan Paul, London.

ELIADE, M. (1954) *The Myth of the Eternal Return*, Routledge & Kegan Paul, London.

—— (1958) *Yoga: Immortality and Freedom*, Routledge & Kegan Paul, London.

—— (1959) *The Sacred and the Profane*, Harcourt, New York.

—— (1960) *Myths, Dreams and Mysteries*, Fontana, London.

—— (1964) *Myth and Reality*, Allen & Unwin, London.

—— (1965) *The Two and the One*, Havill Press, London.

ERIKSON, E. H. (1965) *Childhood and Society*, Penguin, Harmondsworth.

—— (1972) *Young Man Luther*, Faber, London.

FREUD, S. (1951) *Collected Papers*, trans. J. Riviere *et al.*, Hogarth Press, London.

FROMM, E. (1969) *Escape from Freedom*, Holt, New York.

GALBRAITH, J. K. (1963) *The Affluent Society*, Penguin, Harmondsworth.

GEHLEN, A. (1965) *Zeitbilder*, Athenäum, Munich.

—— (1970a) *Anthropologische Forschung*, Rowohlt, Munich.

—— (1970b) *Die Seele im technischen Zeitalter*, Rowohlt, Munich.

GRODDECK, G. (1966) *Psycho-analytische Schriften zur Psycho-Somatik*, Limes, Wiesbaden.

GUNTRIP, H. (1961) *Personality Structure and Human Interaction*, Hogarth Press, London.

HABERMAS, J. (1965) *Strukturwandel der Öffentlichkeit*, Luchterhand, Neuwied and Berlin.

—— (1967) *Theorie und Praxis*, Luchterhand, Neuwied and Berlin.

—— (1969) *Erkenntnis und Interesse*, Suhrkamp, Frankfurt a. M.

HEGEL, G. W. F. (1952) *Die Phänomenologie des Geistes*, ed J. Hoffmeister, Felix Meiner, Hamburg.

HEIDEGGER. M. (1931) *Sein und Zeit*, M. Niemeyer, Halle.

—— (1950) *Holzwege*, Klostermann, Frankfurt a. M.

—— (1954) *Vorträge und Aufsätze*, G. Neske, Pfullingen.

—— (1959) *Unterwegs zur Sprache*, G. Neske, Pfullingen.

—— (1967) *Wegmarken*, Klostermann, Frankfurt a. M.

—— (1969) *Zur Sache des Denkens*, M. Niemeyer, Halle.

HORKHEIMER, M. ed. (1963), *Zeugnisse*, Europäische Verlagsanstalt, Frankfurt a. M.

HORKHEIMER, M. and ADORNO, T. W. (1969) *Dialektik der Aufklärung*, S. Fischer, Frankfurt a. M.

HUGHES, E. S. (1959) *Consciousness and Society*, Macgibbon & Kee, London.

HUIZINGA, J. (1965) *The Waning of the Middle Ages*, Penguin, Harmondsworth.

—— (1970) *Homo Ludens*, M. T. Smith, London.

HUMBOLDT, W. VON (1963) *Über die Verschiedenheit des menschlichen Sprachbaus und ihrem Einfluss auf die geistige Entwicklung des Menschengeschlechts*, Cotta, Stuttgart.

HUSSERL, E. (1960) *Ideen zu einer reinen Phänomenologie und phänomenologischen Philosophie*, 1–3, M. Nijhoff, The Hague.

—— (1962) *Die Krisis der europäischen Wissenschaften und die transzendentale Phänomenologie*, M. Nijhoff, The Hague.

JONES, E. (1964) *The Life and Work of Sigmund Freud*, Penguin, Harmondsworth.

JUNG, C. (1933) *Modern Man in Search of a Soul*, trans. W. S. Dell and C. F. Baynes, Routledge & Kegan Paul, London.

—— (1938) *Psychology and Religion*, ed G. Adler *et al.*, Yale University Press.

—— (1963) *Memories, Dreams, Reflections*, trans. R. and C. Winston, Routledge & Kegan Paul *and* Collins, London.

KANT, I. (1933) *Die drei Kritiken*, ed Schmidt, Kröner, Leipzig.

—— (1966) *Kant-Brevier*, ed J. Pfeiffer, W. Goldmann, Munich.

KEYNES, J. M. (1964) *The General Theory of Employment, Interest and Money*, Macmillan, London.

KLEIN, M. (1949) *The Psycho-analysis of Children*, Hogarth Press, London.

KLIEN, M. (1968) *Marx-Engels, über Kunst und Literatur*, Europa, Verlag, Vienna.

KRACAUER, S. (1963) 'Time and History', in *Zeugnisse*, ed M. Horkheimer, Europäische Verlagsanstalt, Frankfurt a. M.

—— (1966) *From Caligari to Hitler*, Princeton University Press.

LAING, R. D. (1964a) *Reason and Violence*, Tavistock Publications, London.

—— (1964b) *Sanity, Madness and the Family*, Tavistock Publications, London.

—— (1965) *The Divided Self*, Penguin, Harmondsworth.

—— (1968) *Dialectics of Liberation*, Penguin, Harmondsworth.

—— (1969) *The Self and Others*, Tavistock Publications, London.

—— (1970a) *Knots*, Tavistock Publications, London.

—— (1970b) *Politics of Experience*, Penguin, Harmondsworth.

LEACH, E. (1970) *Lévi-Strauss*, Fontana, London.

LE BON, G. (1932) *Psychologie der Massen*, Kröner, Leipzig.

LESSING, G. E. (1962) *Dramen*, Fischer Bücherei, E.C.53, Frankfurt a. M.

LÉVI-STRAUSS, C. (1964) *Totemism*, Merlin Press, London.

—— (1966) *The Savage Mind*, Weidenfeld & Nicolson, London.

—— (1967) *The Scope of Anthropology*, Jonathan Cape, London.

—— (1968) *Structural Anthropology*, Allen Lane, The Penguin Press, London.

LEWIS, O. (1964) *Pedro Martinez*, Secker & Warburg, London.

—— (1968) *La Vida*, Panther Books, London.

—— (1970) *The Children of Sánchez*, Penguin, Harmondsworth.

LICHTHEIM, G. (1971) *From Marx to Hegel*, Herder & Herder, New York.
LIEBRUCKS, B. (1963) *Reflexionen über den Satz Hegels: 'Das Wahre ist das Ganze'*, in *Zeugnisse*, Europäische Verlagsanstalt, Frankfurt a. M.
LORENZ, K. (1966) *On Aggression*, Methuen, London.
LUKÁCS, G. (1960–8) *Gesammelte Schriften*, Luchterhand, Neuwied and Berlin. Vol. 2 (1968) *Geschichte und Klassbewusstsein*, vols 4 & 5 (1963) *Probleme der Realismus 1 & 2*, vol. 7 (1964) *Deutsche Literatur aus zwei Jahrhunderten*, vol. 8 (1967) *Der junge Hegel*, vol. 9 (1960) *Die Zerstörung der Vernunft*.
MADGE, J. (1963) *The Origins of Scientific Sociology*, Tavistock Publications, London.
MALINOWSKI, B. (1922) *The Argonauts of the South-West Pacific*, Routledge & Kegan Paul, London.
—— (1926) *Crime and Custom in Savage Society*, Routledge & Kegan Paul, London.
—— (1927) *Sex and Repression in Primitive Society*, Routledge & Kegan Paul, London.
—— (1960) *A Scientific Theory of Culture*, University of North Carolina Press, Chapel Hill.
MANNHEIM, K. (1960) *Ideology and Utopia*, Routledge & Kegan Paul, London.
MARCUSE, H. (1954) *Reason and Revolution*, Routledge & Kegan Paul, London.
—— (1964) *One-Dimensional Man*, Routledge & Kegan Paul, London.
—— (1969) *Eros and Civilization*, Sphere Books, London.
MARX, K. (1942) *Selected Works*, ed V. Adoratsky, vol. 2, Lawrence & Wishart, London.
—— (1968) *Die Frühschriften*, ed S. Landshut, Kröner, Stuttgart.
MEAD, G. H. (1967) *Mind, Self and Society*, Phoenix Books, University of Chicago Press.
MEINECKE, F. (1959–70) *Werke*, R. Oldenbourg, Munich. Vol. 1 (1963) *Die Idee der Staatsräson in der neueren Geschichte*, ed W. Hofer, vol. 3 (1959) *Die Entstehung des Historismus*, ed C. Hinrichs, vol. 5 (1962) *Weltbürgertum und Nationalstaat*, ed H. Herzfeld, vol. 8 (1970) *Autobiographische Schriften*, ed E. Kessel.
MERLEAU-PONTY, M. (1964) *Signs*, Northwestern University Press, Chicago.
MERTON, R. K. (1968) *Social Theory and Social Structure*, enlarged edition, Free Press, New York.
MILLS, C. W. (1956) *The Power Élite*, Oxford University Press, New York.
—— (1963) *Power, Politics and People*, Oxford University Press, New York.
—— (1970) *The Sociological Imagination*, Penguin, Harmondsworth.
MILNER, M. (1969) *The Hands of the Living God*, Hogarth Press, London.
MITSCHERLICH, A. (1969) *Society without the Father*, Tavistock Publications, London,
MITZMAN, ARTHUR (1970) *The Iron-Cage: An Historical Interpretation of Max Weber*, Knopf, New York.
MUMFORD, L. (1934) *Technics and Civilisation*, Routledge & Kegan Paul, London.

—— (1940) *The Culture of Cities*, Secker & Warburg, London.
—— (1944) *The Condition of Man*, Secker & Warburg, London.
—— (1952a) *Art and Technics*, Columbia University Press, New York.
—— (1952b) *The Conduct of Life*, Secker & Warburg, London.
—— (1957) *The Transformations of Man*, Allen & Unwin, London.
—— (1967) *The Myth of the Machine*, Secker & Warburg, London.
MURDOCH, I. (1967) *Sartre*, Fontana Books, London.
NIEBUHR, R. (1932) *Moral Man and Immoral Society*, Scribner's, New York.
—— (1941) *The Nature and Destiny of Man*, Nisbet, London.
NIETZSCHE, F. (1924) *Jenseits von Gut und Böse* and *Genealogie der Moral*, (1 vol.) ed A. Bäumler, Kröner, Leipzig.
—— (1970) *Geburt der Tragödie*, ed A. Bäumler, Kröner, Stuttgart.
PARETO, V. (1935) *The Mind and Society*, vols. 1–4, trans. A. Livingston and A. Bongiorno, Harcourt Brace Jovanovitch, New York.
PARSONS, T. (1962) *Certain Primary Sources and Patterns of Aggression in the Social Structure of the Western World*, from *Man in Contemporary Society*, Columbia, New York.
—— (1964) *Social Structure and Personality*, Free Press, New York.
—— (1968) *The Structure of Social Action*, Free Press, New York.
POOLE, R. (1972) *Towards Deep Subjectivity*, Allen Lane, The Penguin Press, London.
POPPER, K. (1942) *The Open Society and its Enemies*, Gollancz, London.
—— (1960) *The Poverty of Historicism*, Routledge & Kegan Paul, London.
—— (1969) *Conjectures and Refutations, the Growth of Scientific Knowledge*, Routledge & Kegan Paul, London.
REICH, W. (1946) *The Mass Psychology of Fascism*, Orgone Institute Press, New York.
—— (1968) *The Function of Orgasm*, Panther Books, London.
RIEFF, P. (1960) *Freud, the Mind of the Moralist*, Gollancz, London.
—— (1966) *The Triumph of the Therapeutic*, Chatto & Windus, London.
RIESMAN, D. (1955) *The Lonely Crowd*, Doubleday, New York.
ROHRMOSER, G. (1970) *Das Elend der kritischen Theorie*, Rombach, Freiburg.
RYCROFT, C. (1966) *Psychoanalysis Observed*, Constable, London.
RYLE, G. (1950) *The Concept of Mind*, Hutchinson, London.
SARTRE, J.-P. (1948) *Existentialism and Humanism*, Methuen, London.
—— (1964) *The Problem of Method*, Methuen, London.
—— (1969a) *Being and Nothingness*, Methuen, London.
—— (1969b) *Words*, Penguin, Harmondsworth.
SCHELER, M. (1955–63) *Gesammelte Werke*, ed Maria Scheler, Franke, Berne. Vol. 3 (1955) *Vom Umsturz der Werte*, vol. 6 (1963) *Schriften zur Soziologie und Weltanschauungslehre*, vol. 8 (1960) *Die Wissensformen und die Gesellschaft*.
SCHOPENHAUER, A. (1902) *Die Welt als Wille und Vorstellung*, A. Weichert, Berlin.
SCHUMPETER, J. P. (1951) *Imperialism and Social Classes*, Blackwell, Oxford.
SCHUTZ, A. (1962–6) *Collected Papers*, vol. 1 (1962), vol. 2 (1964), vol 3 (1966), ed M. Natanson, M. Nijhoff, The Hague.

271

—— (1967) *The Phenomenology of the Social World*, trans. G. Walsh and F. Lehnert, Northwestern University Press, Chicago.

SIMMEL, G. (1907) *Philosophie des Geldes*, Dunker & Humblot, Leipzig.

—— (1911) *Philosophische Kultur*, Klinkhardt, Leipzig.

—— (1922) *Soziologie*, Dunker & Humblot, Leipzig.

SINGER, C. (1959) *A Short History of Scientific Ideas*, Oxford University Press, London.

SOMBART, W. (1927) *Der moderne Kapitalismus*, vols 1–4, Dunker & Humblot, Munich and Leipzig.

SPIEGELBERG, H. (1964) *The Phenomenological Movement, an Historical Introduction*, M. Nijhoff, The Hague.

STIRNER, M. (1892) *Der Einzige und sein Eigentum*, Reclam, Leipzig.

TÖNNIES, F. (1955) *Community and Association*, Routledge & Kegan Paul, London.

TRÖLTSCH, E. (1922a) *Die Soziallehren der christlichen Kirchen*, J. C. B. Mohr, Tübingen.

—— (1922b) *Der Historismus und seine Probleme, 1. Buch: Das logische Problem der Geschichtsphilosophie*, J. C. B. Mohr, Tübingen.

TUCKER, R. (1961) *Philosophy and Myth in Karl Marx*, Cambridge University Press.

WEBER, M. (1920) *Religionssoziologie*, vol. 1, *Die protestantische Ethik und der Geist des Kapitalismus. – Die protestantischen Sekten und der Geist des Kapitalismus. – Die Wirtschaftsethik der Weltreligionen. – Konfuzianismus und Taoismus*, J. C. B. Mohr, Tübingen.

—— (1921) *Religionssoziologie*, vol. 2, *Hinduismus und Buddhismus*, J. C. B. Mohr, Tübingen.

—— (1922) *Religionssoziologie*, vol. 3, *Judentum. – Die Pharisäer*, J. C. B. Mohr, Tübingen.

—— (1924) *Gesammelte Aufsätze zur Soziologie und Sozialpolitik*, ed Marianne Weber, J. C. B. Mohr, Tübingen.

—— (1951) *Gesammelte Aufsätze zur Wissenschaftslehre*, ed Marianne WEBER, L. J. C. B. Mohr, Tübingen.

—— (1964) *Wirtschaft und Gessellschaft*, ed J. Winckelmann, Kiepenheuer und Witsch, Cologne and Berlin.

—— (1968) *Soziologie, weltgeschichtliche Analysen, Politik*, ed J. Winckelmann, Kröner, Stuttgart.

WHORF, B. J. (1967) *Language, Thought and Reality*, MIT Press, Massachusetts.

WILLIAMS, R. (1961) *Culture and Society 1780–1950*, Penguin, Harmondsworth.

WILSON, E. (1960) *To the Finland Station*, Fontana, London.

WINCH, P. (1958) *The Idea of a Social Science and its Relation to Philosophy*, Routledge & Kegan Paul, London.

WINNICOTT, D. W. (1958) *Collected Papers*, Tavistock Publications, London.

—— (1965a) *The Maturational Processes and the Facilitating Environment*, Hogarth Press, London.

—— (1965b) *Therapeutic Consultations in Child Psychiatry*, Hogarth Press, London.

—— (1969) *The Child, the Family and the Outside World*, Penguin, Harmondsworth.

WITTGENSTEIN, L. (1967) *Philosophische Untersuchungen*, eds G. E. M. Anscombe and R. Rhees, Suhrkamp, Frankfurt a. M.

WOLLHEIM, R. (1971) *Freud*, Fontana, London.

YOUNG, M. and WILLMOTT, P. (1962) *Family and Kinship in East London*, Penguin, Harmondsworth.

English translations of some of the German source books

ADORNO, T. W. (1967E) *Prisms*, trans. S. S. Weber, Spearman, London.

BUBER, M. (1968E, 1969E) *Tales of the Hasidim*, vols 1 & 2, Schocken, New York.

BURCKHARDT, J. (1943E) *Reflections on History*, trans. M. D. H., Allen & Unwin, London.

HABERMAS, J. (1972E) *Knowledge and Human Interest*, trans. J. Schapiro, Heinemann, London.

HEGEL, G. F. W. (1931E) *The Phenomenology of Mind*, trans. Baillie, Allen & Unwin, London.

HEIDEGGER, M. (1967E) *Being and Time*, trans. J. Macquarrie and E. Robinson, Blackwell, Oxford.

—— (1971E) *On the Way to Language*, trans. P. D. Hertz, Harper & Row, New York.

HUSSERL, E. (1970E) *The Crisis of the European Sciences and Transcendental Phenomenology*, trans. D. Carr, Northwestern University Press, Evanston.

LUKÁCS, G. (1971E) *History and Class Consciousness*, trans. R. Livingstone, Merlin Press, London.

—— (1972E) *Studies in European Realism*, trans. E. Bone, Merlin Press, London.

MARX, K. (1961E) *Economic and Philosophic Manuscripts of 1844*, trans. M. Milligan, Foreign Languages Publishing House, Moscow.

MEINECKE, F. (1970E) *Cosmopolitanism and the National State*, trans. R. B. Kimber, Princeton University Press.

—— (1972E) *Historism. The Rise of a New Historical Outlook*, Routledge & Kegan Paul, London.

NIETZSCHE, F. (1971E) *The Portable Nietzsche*, ed W. Kaufmann, Chatto & Windus, London.

SCHOPENHAUER, A. (1967E) *The World as Will and Representation*, trans. R. B. Haldane and J. Kemp, Dover Publications, New York.

STIRNER, M. (1971E) *The Ego and his Own*, ed J. Carroll, Jonathan Cape, London.

WEBER, M. (1958E) *From Max Weber*, ed and trans. H. H. Gerth and C. Wright Mills, Oxford University Press, New York.

—— (1967aE) *The Protestant Ethics and the Spirit of Capitalism*, trans. T. Parsons, Allen & Unwin, London.

—— (1967bE) *The Religions of India*, ed and trans. H. H. Gerth and D. Martindale, Collier-Macmillan, New York.

—— (1967cE) *Ancient Judaism*, ed and trans. H. H. Gerth and D. Martindale, Collier-Macmillan, New York.

—— (1968aE) *The Religions of China*, ed and trans. H. H. Gerth, Collier-Macmillan, New York.

—— (1968bE) *Economics and Society*, trans E. Fischoff, ed G. Roth and C. Wittich, 2 vols., Bedminster Press, New York.

WITTGENSTEIN, L. (1953E) *Philosophical Investigations*, trans. G. E. M. Anscombe, Blackwell, Oxford.

—— (1961E) *Tractatus Logico-Philosophicus*, trans. D. F. Pears and B. F. McGuinness, Routledge & Kegan Paul, London.

Index

For Product Safety Concerns and Information please contact our EU
representative GPSR@taylorandfrancis.com
Taylor & Francis Verlag GmbH, Kaufingerstraße 24, 80331 München, Germany

www.ingramcontent.com/pod-product-compliance
Lightning Source LLC
Chambersburg PA
CBHW050704280326
41926CB00088B/2447

9 781138 998087